TARBELL'S

KJV & NRSV
Lesson
Commentary

BASED ON THE INTERNATIONAL SUNDAY SCHOOL LESSONS

DR. WILLIAM P. BARKER

DAVID C. COOK CHURCH MINISTRIES CURRICULUM
COLORADO SPRINGS, COLORADO/PARIS, ONTARIO

TARBELL'S TEACHER'S GUIDE © 2000 Cook Communications Ministries, 4050 Lee Vance View, Colorado Springs, CO 80918, U.S.A. All rights reserved. Printed in U.S.A. May not be reproduced without permission. Lessons based on International Sunday School Lessons: the International Bible Lessons for Christian Teaching, © 2000 by the Committee on the Uniform Series.

Edited by Dan Lioy

Cover photography © 1998 by Dan Stultz

Cover design by Jeffrey P. Barnes

ISBN: 0-7814-5559-6

CONTENTS

■

September, October, November 2000
RULERS OF ISRAEL

■

December 2000; January, February 2001
GOOD NEWS OF JESUS (THE GOSPEL OF LUKE)

CONTENTS

■

A group of teachers in a small church worried because the congregation's budget could not include the purchase of a large television with a VCR and a computer for accessing the Internet. "How can we teach if we don't have the latest equipment?" one woman wailed.

A sense of gloom began to pervade the meeting. Then someone related how he had been awakened to the meaning of Christ while attending a large, affluent congregation years ago. The believer said, "We had film strips and tape recorders and all the fancy gadgetry that was in vogue back then. But do you know what really made a difference for me? It was Mr. Hanson, not the slide projectors and all the pricey stuff our church had bought. It was old Henry Hanson! Old Henry was told to use the expensive new set of slides, but he seemed to get them in upside down or out of focus the first few times he tried, then finally quit on all the new technology. Now I realize we don't have to worry about VCRs and computers for our classes, as much as they might help. What's most important is being like Henry Hanson. Do you know why? Mr. Hanson had *enthusiasm* for us and for the Lord!"

What a superb way of describing the ideal teacher! We need to have *enthusiasm*! The word comes from a Greek verb that means "to be inspired." When a teacher like Mr. Hanson is filled with a genuine zeal for Christ and the members of a class, faith is nurtured!

As you teach a class of adults this year, you initially may feel inadequate because of a self-perceived lack of skills, tools, or learning. But if you have enthusiasm for the Gospel of Christ, you will have the essential ingredient you need for successful teaching. And you will find that your study of Scripture and the lesson material in this publication can help you communicate God's truth in a relevant way. As you faithfully do your part in teaching the Word, your students will grow spiritually. They may even find your enthusiasm for the Lord contagious!

Your fellow learner at the feet of the Master Teacher,

William P. Barker

A Note of Appreciation

A special note of thanks to Dr. John Barker and Ellen Meier for their assistance in preparing this edition of Tarbell's Teacher's Guide.

Sunday school materials from the following denominations and publishers follow the International Sunday School Lesson outlines (sometimes known as the Uniform Series). Because *Tarbell's Teacher's Guide* follows the same ISSL outlines, you can use *Tarbell's* as an excellent teacher resource to supplement the materials from these publishing houses.

Denominational:
> Advent Christian General Conference—*Adult*
> American Baptist (Judson Press)—*Adult*
> Church of God in Christ (Church of God in Christ Publishing House)—*Adult*
> Church of Christ Holiness—*Adult*
> Church of God (Warner Press)—*Adult*
> Church of God by Faith—*Adult*
> National Baptist Convention of America (Boyd)—*All ages*
> National Primitive Baptist Convention—*Adult*
> Progressive National Baptist Convention—*Adult*
> Presbyterian Church (U.S.A.) (Bible Discovery Series—Presbyterian Publishing House or P.R.E.M.)—*Adult*
> Southern Baptist (Baptist Sunday School Board)—*All ages*
> Union Gospel Press—*All ages*
> United Holy Church of America—*Adult*
> United Methodist Church (Cokesbury)—*All ages*

Nondenominational:
> David C. Cook Church Ministries—*Adult*
> Echoes Sunday School Literature—*Adult*
> Standard Publishing—*Adult*
> Urban Ministries—*All ages*

Rulers of Israel

DEBORAH

BACKGROUND SCRIPTURE: Judges 4—5
DEVOTIONAL READING: Psalm 68:1-6

KEY VERSE: Deborah said to Barak, "Up! For this is the day on which the LORD has given Sisera into your hand. The LORD is indeed going out before you." Judges 4:14.

KING JAMES VERSION

JUDGES 4:2 And the LORD sold them into the hand of Jabin king of Canaan, that reigned in Hazor; the captain of whose host was Sisera, which dwelt in Harosheth of the Gentiles.

3 And the children of Israel cried unto the LORD: for he had nine hundred chariots of iron; and twenty years he mightily oppressed the children of Israel.

4 And Deborah, a prophetess, the wife of Lapidoth, she judged Israel at that time.

5 And she dwelt under the palm tree of Deborah between Ramah and Beth-el in mount Ephraim: and the children of Israel came up to her for judgment.

6 And she sent and called Barak the son of Abinoam out of Kedesh-naphtali, and said unto him, Hath not the LORD God of Israel commanded, saying, Go and draw toward mount Tabor, and take with thee ten thousand men of the children of Naphtali and of the children of Zebulun?

7 And I will draw unto thee to the river Kishon Sisera, the captain of Jabin's army, with his chariots and his multitude; and I will deliver him into thine hand.

8 And Barak said unto her, If thou wilt go with me, then I will go: but if thou wilt not go with me, then I will not go.

9 And she said, I will surely go with thee: notwithstanding the journey that thou takest shall not be for thine honour; for the LORD shall sell Sisera into the hand of a woman. And Deborah arose, and went with Barak to Kedesh. . . .

14 And Deborah said unto Barak, Up; for this is the day in which the LORD hath delivered Sisera into thine hand: is not the LORD gone out before thee? So Barak went down from mount Tabor, and ten thousand men after him.

15 And the LORD discomfited Sisera, and all his chariots, and all his host, with the edge of the sword before Barak; so that Sisera lighted down off his chariot, and fled away on his feet. . . .

22 And, behold, as Barak pursued Sisera, Jael came out to meet him, and said unto him, Come, and I will shew thee the man whom thou seekest. And when he came into her tent, behold, Sisera lay dead, and the nail was in his temples.

NEW REVISED STANDARD VERSION

JUDGES 4:2 So the LORD sold them into the hand of King Jabin of Canaan, who reigned in Hazor; the commander of his army was Sisera, who lived in Harosheth-ha-goiim. 3 Then the Israelites cried out to the LORD for help; for he had nine hundred chariots of iron, and had oppressed the Israelites cruelly twenty years.

4 At that time Deborah, a prophetess, wife of Lappidoth, was judging Israel. 5 She used to sit under the palm of Deborah between Ramah and Bethel in the hill country of Ephraim; and the Israelites came up to her for judgment. 6 She sent and summoned Barak son of Abinoam from Kedesh in Naphtali, and said to him, "The LORD, the God of Israel, commands you, 'Go, take position at Mount Tabor, bringing ten thousand from the tribe of Naphtali and the tribe of Zebulun. 7 I will draw out Sisera, the general of Jabin's army, to meet you by the Wadi Kishon with his chariots and his troops; and I will give him into your hand.' " 8 Barak said to her, "If you will go with me, I will go; but if you will not go with me, I will not go." 9 And she said, "I will surely go with you; nevertheless, the road on which you are going will not lead to your glory, for the LORD will sell Sisera into the hand of a woman." Then Deborah got up and went with Barak to Kedesh. . . .

14 Then Deborah said to Barak, "Up! For this is the day on which the Lord has given Sisera into your hand. The LORD is indeed going out before you." So Barak went down from Mount Tabor with ten thousand warriors following him. 15 And the LORD threw Sisera and all his chariots and all his army into a panic before Barak; Sisera got down from his chariot and fled away on foot . . .

22 Then, as Barak came in pursuit of Sisera, Jael went out to meet him, and said to him, "Come, and I will show you the man whom you are seeking." So he went into her tent; and there was Sisera lying dead, with the tent peg in his temple.

Monday, August 28	Judges 4:1-3	*Canaanites Oppress the Israelites*
Tuesday, August 29	Judges 4:4-10	*The Leadership of Deborah*
Wednesday, August 30	Judges 4:11-16	*Defeat of the Canaanites*
Thursday, August 31	Judges 4:17-24	*Death of Sisera*
Friday, September 1	Judges 5:1-9	*The Song of Deborah*
Saturday, September 2	Judges 5:10-23	*Praise for the Tribes*
Sunday, September 3	Judges 5:24-31	*God's Enemies Will Perish*

BACKGROUND

God's great act of deliverance, known as the Exodus, freed the suffering Israelites from captivity in Egypt. Tragically, the first generation rebelled against God, and because of it, He refused to allow them to enter the land of promise (Num. 13—14; Deut. 1:35; 2:14). It would be the next generation of Israelites whom Moses would lead to Canaan. Before dying, Moses passed on the mantle of leadership to Joshua, who in turn became the new authority figure over God's people (Num. 27:15-23; Deut. 1:38).

Joshua succeeded in establishing the Israelites in Canaan (Josh. 21:43-45). But taking full control of the land was another matter. The Book of Judges reveals that the Israelites began to disobey God not long after the death of Joshua, and that this infidelity grew more debased over time.

The Mosaic covenant forms the theological center of Judges. According to the law, God pledged to discipline His people when they rebelled against Him. As Judges makes known, the people were guilty of not completely driving out the Canaanites from the land, of becoming idolatrous, of intermarrying with the wicked inhabitants, of not heeding the judges, and of turning away from God after the death of the judges. A four-part sequence repeatedly occurred in this phase of Israel's history: the nation's departure from God; the Lord's chastisement in the form of military defeat and subjugation; the nation's cry for deliverance; and God's raising up of liberators who led the Israelites in victory over their oppressors.

The events narrated in Judges span about 350 years, from the conquest of Canaan until just before Samuel, who anointed the first king of Israel. The first of the judges in the book—Othniel—appears during the generation following Joshua. The last of the judges—Samson—was a contemporary of Samuel. During this period, Israel was oppressed from within by Canaanites and from without by the Arameans, Moabites, Midianites, Ammonites, Amalekites, Amorites, and Philistines.

This week's lesson concerns Deborah, whom Judges 4:4 identifies as a prophetess, judge, and the wife of Lappidoth. We will learn that she demonstrated special abilities as a mediator, adviser, and counselor. And when called on to lead, she was able to make plans, direct others, and delegate authority. She is a powerful testimony of what a person can accomplish under God's control.

NOTES ON THE PRINTED TEXT

The popularity of the film *GI Jane* and the huge success of television's *Xena Warrior Princess* have presented people in the West with the idea that women can fight and lead others in combat. In this week's lesson we will focus on another female leader named Deborah. Her valor and achievements were enormous.

Judges 4:1 states that when Ehud (one of Israel's early judges) died, the people again did what was evil in the Lord's sight. For this reason, the Lord *sold them into the hand of King Jabin of Canaan* (4:2). He reigned in Hazor, which was an ancient Canaanite fortress city in northern Palestine about 10 miles northwest of the Sea of Galilee. He oppressed Israel for 20 years, and his army was led by Sisera. The commander lived in *Harosheth-ha-goiim,* a town of Galilee on the north bank of the Kishon River about 16 miles northwest of Megiddo.

God's people had failed to drive out all the Canaanites, who in turn were regrouping and attempting to restore their lost power. Sisera experienced considerable success in doing so, being aided by 900 *chariots of iron* (4:3). These formidable weapons were made of iron and pulled by one or two horses. The lightly armed Israelites proved no match for them, and this explains why God's people *cried out to the Lord for help.*

In response, God commissioned Deborah to lead His people to victory (4:4). At that time, she held court *under the palm of Deborah* (4:5), which was a noteworthy tree that stood between Ramah and Bethel in the hill country of Ephraim. One day she sent for a man named Barak, who lived in Kedesh in the land of Naphtali (4:6). Deborah announced that God wanted Barak to assemble 10,000 warriors from the tribes of Naphtali and Zebulun. He was to *go, take position at Mount Tabor*. This was a limestone mountain in the northeastern part of the Valley of Jezreel.

The Lord planned to lure Sisera, along with his chariots and warriors, to the Kishon River and there enable the Israelites to defeat them in battle (4:7). However, Barak would only obey if Deborah agreed to go with him (4:8). The contrast could not be greater between Barak's timidity and Deborah's valor. Because Barak had made this request, he would receive no honor for the Lord's victory over Sisera. Instead, a woman named Jael would be remembered for this feat (4:9, 21-22).

When Sisera heard about Barak's preparations for war, he assembled his forces. He marched his troops to the Kishon River and prepared to trounce the Israelites in battle (4:10-13). But God had other plans.

Deborah told Barak and his warriors to get ready, for the Lord was about to give them victory over Sisera. In fact, she said that God was *"going out before you"* (4:14). Barak responded by leading the Israelites down the slopes of Mount Tabor into battle. God, in turn, *threw Sisera and all his chariots and all his army into a panic* (4:15).

Apparently the enemy's swift, maneuverable weapons of war became hopelessly mired and bogged down in mud (5:19-22). This enabled the Israelites to route Sisera's forces (4:16). But Sisera was able to abandon his chariot and escape on foot (4:15).

Sisera ran to the tent of Jael, who was the wife of a man named Heber the Kenite. Sisera went there because Heber's family was on friendly terms with King Jabin. Jael invited Sisera into her tent, covered him with a rug, and gave him some milk to drink. When he fell asleep from exhaustion, Jael quietly crept up to him with a hammer and tent peg. Then she drove the tent peg through his temple and into the ground, which brought about his swift death (4:17-21).

When Barak came looking for Sisera, Jael went out to meet him. She invited him to look inside her tent. *And there was Sisera lying dead, with the tent peg in his temple* (4:22). God used this chain of events to subdue Jabin and enable His people to overcome their foe (4:23).

SUGGESTIONS TO TEACHERS

The late great classical scholar, Frank Bourne, taught Roman history at Princeton University. He was fond of saying, "In the age of *Pax Americana*, there's no more important lesson we can teach young Americans than the rise and decline of *Pax Romana*." He always began and ended his course with the Latin words *De Nobis fabula narratur,* which means, "Their story is our story."

The same may be said about the accounts recorded in the Old Testament (1 Cor. 10:6). For instance, the narrative concerning Deborah and Barak is relevant and applicable to us. The struggles the Israelites faced and the way God intervened in their lives reminds us of how important it is for us to trust and obey the Lord. We also see that He is the source of our victory over sin and evil.

1. SCENE OF DESPAIR. The tribes of Israel had endured 20 years of harassment and oppression at the hands of the Canaanites. A sense of hopelessness pervaded God's people. Where would they find a person of courage and faith to lead them in victory over their enemies?

2. SAGE IN DELIBERATION. In stepped Deborah. She was respected for her wisdom, which undoubtedly came from her trust in and knowledge of the Lord. While others languished in despair, this great woman relied on God to liberate His people. Deborah's single-minded devotion must have been inspiring!

3. STRATEGY FOR DELIVERANCE. Deborah realized that God was the key to the Israelites' deliverance over Sisera. Point out that God chooses leaders by His standards, not ours. They are effective in their work because of their unwavering trust in the Lord.

4. SUPPORT FOR THE DISHEARTENED. Barak's demoralization possibly reflected the feelings of the rest of the Israelites. It took a person of faith and valor such as Deborah to instill hope and courage in Barak and his troops. God empowers those who trust in Him to stand up to the most negative and disbelieving doubter.

5. SUCCESS FROM DECISIVENESS. Because of Deborah's God-inspired confidence, the tribes of Israel were able to overthrow their oppressors in a battle. Because of the resurrection of Christ, believers have confidence in God's ultimate victory over the forces of evil. Regardless of the circumstances, Christians live in hope because of the Gospel.

6. SINGLE-MINDED IN DEDICATION. Have the class members read through the Song of Deborah, which is recorded in Judges 5. Then state that Christians are able to sing with joy when they have Deborah's kind of commitment to God's work.

■ **TOPIC:** Be an Encourager

■ **QUESTIONS:** 1. Why did the Lord allow the Canaanites to oppress the Israelites? 2. What are some noteworthy things that Deborah did as a judge of Israel? 3. What were some of Barak's strengths and weaknesses? 4. Who are some people who have encouraged you when you needed support? 5. How can you be an encourager to others in their times of distress and discouragement?

■ **ILLUSTRATIONS:**

Light-Bearer in a Time of Darkness. Deborah was married to a man named Lappidoth, whose name in Hebrew means "flames" or "torches" (Judg. 4:4). Some have rendered the text "woman of flames," which would imply that Deborah was a fiery, spirited woman. Deborah inspired the Israelites to depend on the Lord to throw off their oppressors. In a way, Deborah beamed brightly as a source of hope and courage in a time of despair. Her bright light of faith encouraged Israel's timid and reluctant warriors to act bravely. In this way Deborah proved to be without equal in her generation.

Encourager Despite Discouragement. Few today recognize the name of Carrie Chapman Catt. Probably more than any other, this individual worked to make possible the right for women in the United States to vote. But Catt had to endure much ridicule and hostility.

Early in Catt's career, when she was a young school teacher in Mason City, Iowa, she initiated a movement to permit women to vote in local elections. Her efforts won the praise of the illustrious Susan B. Anthony, who by then was growing old. However, Catt's efforts to work for women's suffrage seemed to be thwarted. The sudden death of her husband forced her to accept the low-paying jobs that were the only work open for widows in the late 19th century. As a result of experiencing first-hand the kinds of problems other women were encountering,

Catt dedicated the rest of her life to ensure that women had the right to participate as full-fledged citizens in the nation.

Catt devoted the following years to speaking throughout the United States and organizing peaceful protests. Despite her noble endeavors, the criticism she received was harsh and cruel. Nevertheless, Catt was determined to have ratified by 1920 a constitutional amendment that granted women the right to vote. That year was the one hundredth anniversary of the birth of her heroine, Susan B. Anthony.

Catt gradually began to overcome the opponents to women having the right to vote. When the House of Representatives approved a constitutional amendment in 1918, Carrie joyfully stood in the House gallery and sang a doxology. A year later, the Senate approved the amendment. Catt then traveled throughout the nation, encouraging citizens in the states to ratify the Nineteenth Amendment. On August 26, 1920, the necessary number of states approved the amendment, and women in the United States were finally granted the right to vote. The credit goes to the continuing encouragement of Catt, who was a deeply committed Christian woman.

Leader in Prison Reform. Elizabeth Fry is another forgotten encourager who lived in England in the last century when the conditions of that nation's prisons were terrible. She was the wife of a wealthy Quaker merchant and the mother of 11 children. She had done a variety of work among the poor of London, and she was serving as a minister of the Religious Society of Friends.

Though Elizabeth had a busy life, she added Newgate Prison for women to her burden of concerns. When she visited the correctional facility, she was appalled at what she saw. There was one male attendant and his son taking care of about 300 women and as many children, all of whom were crowded into four small rooms without beds, bedding, or extra clothing. There was no employment in the town, and the only recreation for the townspeople was to buy liquor at a taproom. Here the imprisoned women and children begged money from passersby.

With the help of a London clergyman's wife and 10 Quaker women, Elizabeth Fry formed the Association for the Improvement of the Female Prisoners in Newgate. Their first task was to convince these coarse, hardened, and foul-spoken women that they had come not to condemn, but to bring comfort and relief. Elizabeth and her associates provided clothing, bedding, instruction in orderliness and cleanliness, and lessons from the Bible.

The results were so successful that leaders from other countries came to visit Newgate and to consult with Fry. She was also asked to travel abroad to study conditions in other prisons and make suggestions for improvements.

Elizabeth Fry is known today as a pioneer in prison reform, but this concern led her to ever-widening activities for the homeless, the unemployed, and under-privileged children. As a follower of Christ, Fry willingly took upon herself tasks that seemed far too heavy for one person to carry and thereby glorified God.

■ **TOPIC:** Chosen to Lead

■ **QUESTIONS:** 1. Why did God sell the Israelites into the hand of Jabin? 2. Who was Deborah, and what did she say God wanted Barak to do? 3. Upon what condition would Barak do what God commanded? 4. What did God do for His people at Mount Tabor? 5. How did the death of Sisera take place?

■ **ILLUSTRATIONS:**

Good Role Model. The death of Florence Griffith Joyner on September 21, 1998 removed one of the most positive female role models for young girls. FloJo (as she was affectionately nicknamed) had been an Olympic gold medalist in the 1988 Seoul games in the 100 and 200 meters races and on a relay team. Known for her dazzling fingernails and speed, FloJo devoted large amounts of time and resources to helping children (especially those in devastated neighborhoods) find and use their own talents.

FloJo never shrank from taking big responsibilities such as her youth work. The commitment in time was huge. However, she willingly sacrificed her resources and energy. Like FloJo, Deborah did not hesitate to take on a big responsibility. She, too, was willing to serve others in a sacrificial and unselfish manner for their betterment.

Poor Role Model. At the peak of their popularity in 1997 and early 1998, the Spice Girls unleashed "Girl Power." This was a message that girls were able to lead others and achieve great things. Many applauded that message for young women.

Tragically, the Spice Girls did not prove to be good leaders and role models. For instance, Melanie "Scary Spice" Brown and Victoria "Posh Spice" Adams announced that they were pregnant. Though neither was married, both claimed to be in loving and caring relationships.

In Great Britain, where teenage pregnancies were already the highest in Europe, officials of a national school teachers association worried about copycat pregnancies. Bill Donohue, the President of the Catholic League in the United States, also sounded a similar warning. He said that the Spice Girls' message was harmful to adolescent females.

Here is a group of women that could have made a positive impact on young women. Instead, the Spice Girls chose to live only for themselves. What a far cry they are from the heroines of the Old Testament like Deborah.

Wants to Lead. At the age of 67, Jerrie Cobb landed her open cockpit plane in Bartlesville, Oklahoma. As she prepared to be honored at the Pioneer Women's

Museum in Ponca City, she became a media darling who was interviewed by CNN, Dateline NBC, *People* Magazine, CBS News, and a host of other news groups.

The Oklahoma native had been flying since she was 12, and had spent 35 years as a missionary bush pilot serving the Indians in Central and South America. She delivered medical supplies, seeds, and other needed items. But few people knew that Jerrie was also the lead woman of the Mercury 13. This group of women had endured all the grueling physical and psychological testing in the early days of the U.S. space program.

Cobb was invited in 1960 to become part of the program. However, in 1961, NASA declared that the United States only wanted astronauts who had been military test pilots. Since women were not allowed to fly military aircraft, they also were not allowed to become astronauts. Although the former Soviet Union had women in its space program in the early 1960s, the United States denied its women an opportunity for similar involvement and leadership.

History records that John Glenn traveled into space. Meanwhile, Cobb journeyed to South America. Decades later Glenn agreed to participate in tests concerned with the effects of weightless conditions on the elderly. Cobb decided to return, desiring the opportunity that was denied her in 1961. Her hope was bolstered by the input of health experts concerning the way in which women age. To date it remains uncertain whether Cobb will get her opportunity.

Thankfully, a person's gender and age are never criteria for serving God. The account of Deborah reminds us that God can use all sorts of people—whether young or old—to do His will.

2

GIDEON

BACKGROUND SCRIPTURE: Judges 6—8
DEVOTIONAL READING: Joshua 1:1-9

KEY VERSE: Go in this might of yours and deliver Israel from the hand of Midian; I hereby commission you. Judges 6:14.

KING JAMES VERSION

JUDGES 6:11 And there came an angel of the LORD, and sat under an oak which was in Ophrah, that pertained unto Joash the Abi-ezrite: and his son Gideon threshed wheat by the winepress, to hide it from the Midianites.

12 And the angel of the LORD appeared unto him, and said unto him, The LORD is with thee, thou mighty man of valour.

13 And Gideon said unto him, Oh my Lord, if the LORD be with us, why then is all this befallen us? and where be all his miracles which our fathers told us of, saying, Did not the LORD bring us up from Egypt? but now the LORD hath forsaken us, and delivered us into the hands of the Midianites.

14 And the LORD looked upon him, and said, Go in this thy might, and thou shalt save Israel from the hand of the Midianites: have not I sent thee? . . .

7:1 Then Jerubbaal, who is Gideon, and all the people that were with him, rose up early, and pitched beside the well of Harod: so that the host of the Midianites were on the north side of them, by the hill of Moreh, in the valley.

2 And the LORD said unto Gideon, The people that are with thee are too many for me to give the Midianites into their hands, lest Israel vaunt themselves against me, saying, Mine own hand hath saved me.

3 Now therefore go to, proclaim in the ears of the people, saying, Whosoever is fearful and afraid, let him return and depart early from mount Gilead. And there returned of the people twenty and two thousand; and there remained ten thousand. . . .

20 And the three companies blew the trumpets, and brake the pitchers, and held the lamps in their left hands, and the trumpets in their right hands to blow withal: and they cried, The sword of the LORD, and of Gideon.

21 And they stood every man in his place round about the camp: and all the host ran, and cried, and fled.

NEW REVISED STANDARD VERSION

JUDGES 6:11 Now the angel of the LORD came and sat under the oak at Ophrah, which belonged to Joash the Abiezrite, as his son Gideon was beating out wheat in the wine press, to hide it from the Midianites.

12 The angel of the LORD appeared to him and said to him, "The LORD is with you, you mighty warrior."

13 Gideon answered him, "But sir, if the LORD is with us, why then has all this happened to us? And where are all his wonderful deeds that our ancestors recounted to us, saying, 'Did not the LORD bring us up from Egypt?' But now the LORD has cast us off, and given us into the hand of Midian." 14 Then the LORD turned to him and said, "Go in this might of yours and deliver Israel from the hand of Midian; I hereby commission you." . . .

7:1 Then Jerubbaal (that is, Gideon) and all the troops that were with him rose early and encamped beside the spring of Harod; and the camp of Midian was north of them, below the hill of Moreh, in the valley.

2 The LORD said to Gideon, "The troops with you are too many for me to give the Midianites into their hand. Israel would only take the credit away from me, saying, 'My own hand has delivered me.' 3 Now therefore proclaim this in the hearing of the troops, 'Whoever is fearful and trembling, let him return home.' " Thus Gideon sifted them out; twenty-two thousand returned, and ten thousand remained. . . .

20 So the three companies blew the trumpets and broke the jars, holding in their left hands the torches, and in their right hands the trumpets to blow; and they cried, "A sword for the LORD and for Gideon!"

21 Every man stood in his place all around the camp, and all the men in camp ran; they cried out and fled.

BACKGROUND

Philosopher George Santayana once said, "Those who forget the mistakes of the past are condemned to repeat them in the future." This proved to be true of the Israelites living during the time of the judges. They repeatedly forgot the lessons of the past, and their disobedience led to the same disastrous mistakes being made again and again in the future.

For instance, when the people of Deborah's generation turned away from God and worshiped idols, they suffered dire consequences before finally returning to the Lord in faith. Sadly, the following generation failed to remember this painful lesson. Their infidelity is bluntly put in Judges 6:1. The people again did *what was evil in the sight of the LORD.*

What was so irresistible about the pagan religions of Canaan? Those who worshiped Canaan's idols were promised good weather for bountiful harvests and healthy offspring from their sheep and goats. The religious rituals were debased, for they involved lewd sexual acts and the sacrifice of infants. It's no wonder that God became displeased with His people and *gave them into the hand of Midian seven years.*

Genesis 25:12 indicates that the Midianites were descendants of Abraham through Keturah. During the time of the judges, the Midianites periodically harassed certain tribes of Israel. These fierce desert nomads swooped in on camels from the Transjordan region into the Jezreel Valley. The marauders not only drove the Israelites into the hill country but also raided their territory, plundered their crops, and stole their livestock (Judg. 6:1-6).

In their desperate situation, God's people cried to Him for help. He answered their prayers by raising up Gideon. The Lord would use Gideon to route the Midianites in the eastern Jezreel Valley and pursue them across the Jordan.

NOTES ON THE PRINTED TEXT

Gideon (also known as Jerubbaal) was the son of Joash of the tribe of Manasseh. Gideon was the fifth major judge of Israel, and served in that capacity for 40 years (Judg. 6:11, 32; 8:28). Hebrews 11:32 records Gideon as being a hero of faith. But as we will learn in this week's lesson, he initially was not a willing volunteer in delivering the Israelites from their oppressors.

Judges 6:11 says that Gideon was threshing wheat at the bottom of a *wine press* to hide the grain from the Midianites. A winepress was a square or circular pit carved into rock in which grapes were crushed. Wheat was usually separated on open threshing floors so the wind could carry away the chaff in the winnowing process. The fact that Gideon was forced to thresh wheat hidden inside a winepress shows how desperate the situation was for the Israelites.

An angel of the Lord appeared to Gideon and said to him, *"The LORD is with you, you mighty warrior"* (6:12). Despite this reassuring word, Gideon questioned the heavenly emissary. If God was present, why were the Midianites oppressing the Israelites? Where were all the saving acts of God that Gideon's ancestors had described? *"But sir, if the LORD is with us, why then has all this happened to us? And where are all his wonderful deeds that our ancestors recounted to us, saying, 'Did not the LORD bring us up from Egypt?' But now the LORD has cast us off, and given us into the hand of Midian"* (6:13).

The angel offered no explanation. Instead, Gideon heard only the staggering announcement that God had chosen him to rescue His people from their oppressors. Gideon was to do so in the strength of the Lord. *Then the LORD turned to him and said, "Go in this might of yours and deliver Israel from the hand of Midian; I hereby commission you"* (6:14).

In the verses that follow, we learn that Gideon twice laid out a fleece in what seems an effort to avoid the will of God by imposing impossible conditions. But the Lord met Gideon's conditions both times and then set out the strategy that would guarantee victory for Israel (6:15-40).

As the oppression of the Midianites intensified, Gideon sent out messengers to all Manasseh and the surrounding tribes to rally volunteers to Israel's cause (6:35). When these volunteers assembled, about 32,000 citizen soldiers stood in the ranks (7:1). Though there were 135,000 Midianites camped in a nearby valley, God directed Gideon to thin out Israel's ranks. *The LORD said to Gideon, "The troops with you are too many for me to give the Midianites into their hand. Israel would only take the credit away from me, saying 'My own hand has delivered me'"* (7:2).

After Gideon dismissed the fearful and the afraid, only 10,000 remained (7:3). Gideon's regiment was now outnumbered 13 to 1. But God told Gideon that he still had too many troops. Through an ingenious process, the Lord further reduced the army to 300 soldiers (7:4-7).

The Midianites now outnumbered Gideon's army 450 to 1. But God had a plan that would ensure victory for His people. Gideon was to divide his army into three groups. He then would give each soldier a trumpet, a jar, and a torch. At the appointed time, 300 trumpets would blast the air, 300 hands would raise their jars and smash them to bits, 300 burning torches would pierce the darkness, and 300 warriors would cry a victory shout (7:16-18).

It was just after midnight (after the changing of the guard) when Gideon and the 100 men with him reached the outer edge of the Midianite camp. They suddenly blew their horns and smashed their jars (7:19). Then all three groups blew their horns and broke their jars. They held the torches in their left hands and the horns in their right hands and shouted, *"A sword for the LORD and for Gideon!"* (7:20).

The Midianites were thrown into a panic (7:21). In the confusion, some committed suicide or killed their comrades. The remaining soldiers fled. The enemies of Israel were completely routed, and Israel's homeland was secure (7:22; 8:10). It was a marvelous victory for the Lord, and it made Gideon an instant hero (8:22).

SUGGESTIONS TO TEACHERS

One group of scholars insists that an understanding of a nation's history comes when its citizen's study its leaders' lives, for these people help to shape events. This week's lesson centers on Gideon, who shaped events in ancient Israel. The key to his success was his obedience to God. As you teach this lesson, be sure to encourage your students to become more yielded to God.

1. DESPAIR FROM DISOBEDIENCE. The rampaging Midianites and their allies had plundered the land of the Israelites so frequently and for so long that most of God's people felt a sense of hopelessness. The reason for the despair was their lack of trust in the Lord. But God had not given up on His people. For some of your class members, life may also seem hopeless. Remind them that there is hope in the Lord. His abiding presence enables us to do His will regardless of the circumstances we encounter.

2. DECLARATION BY THE DIVINE. God often raises up leaders to carry out His plans. In this week's lesson, we learn that God called Gideon to rescue the Israelites. The task appeared overwhelming to Gideon. But God promised, *"I will be with you"* (Judg. 6:16). Because God is always present in our lives, we can move forward with confidence in doing His will (Heb. 13:5).

3. DISBELIEF BY A DOUBTER. Gideon was skeptical of God's call and power. It took some special signs from the Lord to convince Gideon. Here is an opportunity for you to talk about the doubts your students have. Stress that the resurrection of Christ from the dead is the greatest demonstration of God's love and power (Eph. 1:20-21). The encouraging news is that Jesus lives!

4. DISPOSAL OF DOUBTS. Gideon was finally convinced to serve God with total confidence. He would not fail, for the Lord had given him a battle plan for victory. God has also told us in His Word how we can be victorious over the forces of darkness (Eph. 6:10-17). The key is for us to heed what He has revealed in Scripture.

5. DEMONSTRATION OF DECISION. The Lord told Gideon to reduce his fighting force to a mere 300 warriors. God would show His power by using this elite unit to defeat a numerically superior foe. The battle plan defied conventional wisdom. Nevertheless, Gideon obeyed God and victory resulted.

6. DEFEAT AND DESTRUCTION. Gideon's troops followed his orders completely and thereby routed the opposing army in a nighttime surprise attack. We may not always know how things will turn out when we decide to obey the Lord. But we have this reassuring promise in Scripture: *But thanks be to God, who gives us the victory through our Lord Jesus Christ* (1 Cor. 15:57).

FOR ADULTS

■ TOPIC: Be Obedient

■ QUESTIONS: 1. What was the situation like in Israel when the angel of the Lord visited Gideon? 2. How did Gideon respond to the angel's message? 3. What are some challenging ministries that God has called you to undertake? 4. How can your faith in Christ help you deal with feelings of inadequacy? 5. How can you encourage other believers in the difficult tasks God has called them to do?

■ ILLUSTRATIONS:

Lesson from the Math Class. Can you imagine a high school teacher in a mathematics class saying to some students, "Oh, you don't have to concern yourself with learning to add and subtract numbers. The most important issue in solving calculus problems is whether you're really tall!" Being a tall person has nothing to do with solving calculus problems. But knowing the fundamental rules of addition and subtraction is imperative to this and other areas of mathematics.

The same principle is true in terms of being godly. Whether we're tall or short doesn't matter. But knowing and heeding the fundamental rules of the Christian life is crucial, especially if we want to grow in our faith and mature in our relationship with God.

New Profession. Recently a new profession has appeared. There are people who insist on being known as "life coaches." Over 1,500 them make a decent income in the United States by advising clients on how to reorient their lives to reach what one coach calls "fulfillment" or "a happy ending."

These life coaches tell people how to organize their time, how they should deal with business matters, and whether to take a trip or host a party. One coach believes, "It's like painting a canvas for a 'life assignment.'" These coaches guarantee results for those who are willing to heed their directives.

In the spiritual realm, Jesus is the only perfect life coach for Christians. He alone has the authority to command our unwavering commitment and absolute obedience. If we refuse to obey Him, we will reap anguish and loss. But if we follow Him wholeheartedly, we will experience profound spiritual joy.

Gap between Profession and Performance. Almost all adults—whether young or old—state that it's important to be a person with "good character." Yet a recent poll by the nonprofit Josephson Institute for Ethics disclosed that most adults in college admit to lying and cheating and that nearly half say they've stolen something.

The survey, which had a margin of error of three percentage points, was conducted at randomly selected colleges and universities across the United States by the California-based Institute. Over 47% of the students admitted to stealing from a store in the past year, while 70 percent admitted to cheating on an exam. Ninety-two percent confessed to lying to others.

The survey shows that many adults in the United States are lying, stealing, and cheating at a greater rate than ever before. Since 1992, for example, there has been a 21% leap in thefts from stores. At the same time, 97% of the adults insist that it is important to have good character, and 98% of them are happy with the morals of their peers. These findings about the ethics of adults in the West are disturbing news for the future.

Ancient Israel seemed to show such a gap between profession and performance. People may have valued "good character," but many lived in ungodly ways. When such deplorable behavior persisted, the nation suffered.

FOR YOUTH

■ **TOPIC:** Chosen to Win

■ **QUESTIONS:** 1. Who were the Midianites? 2. Why did Gideon feel that God had abandoned Israel? 3. What was Gideon's initial response to God's call? 4. Why did God reduce Gideon's fighting force to just 300 soldiers? 5. How did the Israelites defeat the Midianites?

■ **ILLUSTRATIONS:**

Wanted—A Winner. Jim Leyland left the Pittsburgh Pirates to manage the Florida Marlins after he was promised a team with the potential to be a World Series contender. His team won the 1997 World Series. However, in 1998 his team was stripped of its talented players in preparation for its sale. The Marlins won only 54 games. Leyland left the team in early October, 1998, to go to the Colorado Rockies. This took place after the ownership of the Rockies promised to spend the money necessary to make their team a first-rate contender. Once again, Leyland wanted to manage a team with a possibility of winning.

Youth, like Leyland, want to be on the winning side. Gideon was no different. All his discussions with God were efforts to make sure that he and his troops would be a winner! However, God's methods upstaged Gideon's.

The Best Detergent. Charity Bantko set out to discover which dish detergent best cut grease. The 10-year-old fifth grader from Pittsburgh did tests on several major brands. She completed so many tests that she won third place at her school's science fair.

After concluding that a certain brand worked best, Charity wrote a letter to the company to tell them what she had found. The scientists who developed the dish soap responded by inviting Charity to share her findings with them at their headquarters in New Jersey.

Charity found a creative way of attaining her goal of recognition in science. Gideon did something similar. Even when the odds seemed against him, he continued to follow the unique mission God had given him. You, too, can experience God's approval by patiently and persistently following His will. You may not win recognition on earth, but you will be applauded in heaven.

Serving Higher Laws. Joseph D'Andrea, a 13 year old, and his mother took a couple and their young daughter into their home. Joseph and his mother were Christians who lived in the tiny Italian village of Molise. The young couple and their child were Jewish and fleeing the death camps of the Holocaust. For two months in 1943, the three lived in Joseph's bedroom as German S.S. patrols armed with machine guns searched the village each morning for Jewish runaways. They searched the D'Andrea home several times. The three finally escaped to freedom through the Allied lines.

Even though Joseph and his mother could have been put to death for harboring Jews, Joseph said that he was taught to love all people. Anti-Semitism was never taught. He and his village served God and His higher law.

SAMSON

BACKGROUND SCRIPTURE: Judges 13—16
DEVOTIONAL READING: Psalm 145:14-20

KEY VERSE: Lord GOD, remember me and strengthen me only this once. Judges 16:28b.

KING JAMES VERSION

JUDGES 16:4 And it came to pass afterward, that he loved a woman in the valley of Sorek, whose name was Delilah.

5 And the lords of the Philistines came up unto her, and said unto her, Entice him, and see wherein his great strength lieth, and by what means we may prevail against him, that we may bind him to afflict him: and we will give thee every one of us eleven hundred pieces of silver. . . .

17 That he told her all his heart, and said unto her. There hath not come a razor upon mine head; for I have been a Nazarite unto God from my mother's womb: if I be shaven, then my strength will go from me, and I shall become weak, and be like any other man. . . .

19 And she made him sleep upon her knees; and she called for a man, and she caused him to shave off the seven locks of his head; and she began to afflict him, and his strength went from him.

20 And she said, The Philistines be upon thee, Samson. And he awoke out of his sleep, and said, I will go out as at other times before, and shake myself. And he wist not that the LORD was departed from him.

21 But the Philistines took him, and put out his eyes, and brought him down to Gaza, and bound him with fetters of brass; and he did grind in the prison house.

22 Howbeit the hair of his head began to grow again after he was shaven. . . .

28 And Samson called unto the LORD, and said, O Lord GOD, remember me, I pray thee, and strengthen me, I pray thee, only this once, O God, that I may be at once avenged of the Philistines for my two eyes.

29 And Samson took hold of the two middle pillars upon which the house stood, and on which it was borne up, of the one with his right hand, and of the other with his left.

30 And Samson said, Let me die with the Philistines. And he bowed himself with all his might; and the house fell upon the lords, and upon all the people that were therein. So the dead which he slew at his death were more than they which he slew in his life.

NEW REVISED STANDARD VERSION

JUDGES 16:4 After this he fell in love with a woman in the valley of Sorek, whose name was Delilah. 5 The lords of the Philistines came to her and said to her, "Coax him, and find out what makes his strength so great, and how we may overpower him, so that we may bind him in order to subdue him; and we will each give you eleven hundred pieces of silver." . . .

17 So he told her his whole secret, and said to her, "A razor has never come upon my head; for I have been a nazirite to God from my mother's womb. If my head were shaved, then my strength would leave me; I would become weak, and be like anyone else." . . .

19 She let him fall asleep on her lap; and she called a man, and had him shave off the seven locks of his head. He began to weaken, and his strength left him. 20 Then she said, "The Philistines are upon you, Samson!" When he awoke from his sleep, he thought, "I will go out as at other times, and shake myself free." But he did not know that the LORD had left him. 21 So the Philistines seized him and gouged out his eyes. They brought him down to Gaza and bound him with bronze shackles; and he ground at the mill in the prison. 22 But the hair of his head began to grow again after it had been shaved. . . .

28 Then Samson called to the LORD and said, "Lord GOD, remember me and strengthen me only this once, O God, so that with this one act of revenge I may pay back the Philistines for my two eyes." 29 And Samson grasped the two middle pillars on which the house rested, and he leaned his weight against them, his right hand on the one and his left hand on the other. 30 Then Samson said, "Let me die with the Philistines." He strained with all his might; and the house fell on the lords and all the people who were in it. So those he killed at his death were more than those he had killed during his life.

HOME BIBLE READINGS

Monday, September 11	Judges 13:1-14	*Manoah Seeks Guidance*
Tuesday, September 12	Judges 13:15-25	*Manoah Offers a Sacrifice*
Wednesday, September 13	Judges 14:5-20	*Wedding Feast and Riddle*
Thursday, September 14	Judges 15:9—16:3	*Samson Defeats the Philistines*
Friday, September 15	Judges 16:4-17	*Samson and Delilah*
Saturday, September 16	Judges 16:18-22	*Samson's Capture*
Sunday, September 17	Judges 16:23-31	*Samson's Death*

BACKGROUND

In the early 12th century B.C., invasions in the Aegean area caused a massive upheaval of populations. During this unsettled period, displaced groups known as the Sea People migrated south to the coasts of the eastern Mediterranean. These invaders came to be known as the Phoenicians and the Philistines.

The Philistines were a powerful, warlike ethnic group who settled in southwest Palestine. (The name "Philistine" came to be the basis for the word "Palestine," which reminds us of the power exerted by these energetic settlers.) They established a highly organized city-state system comprised of five towns: Ashdod, Gaza, Ashkelon, Gath, and Ekron (1 Sam. 6:17). The Philistines dominated the Israelites for over a century, encroaching on the lands settled by the tribes of Israel and imposing their pagan culture on those who fell under their sway.

One reason for the success of the Philistines' incursion into that part of the ancient Near East was their monopoly on iron. Their artisans had learned the secrets of smelting and forging iron, and they carefully guarded the knowledge of the process for generations. Iron is much stronger than the bronze that was the ingredient for metal tools and weapons in use by the Israelites. With the Philistines' control of iron, they had an edge militarily and economically on God's people.

The Philistine domination of the Israelites eventually led them to demand a king. However, before this occurred, various leaders led the Israelites in war against the Philistines, often with mixed results for God's people. One such leader remembered in Israel's history was a flawed hero named Samson. His exploits won him admiration, but regrettably his weaknesses brought about his demise.

NOTES ON THE PRINTED TEXT

The first biblical geography map ever published was *A Pisgah-Sight of Palestine.* It was printed in London in 1610 by Thomas Fuller and contains 21 skillfully engraved maps filled with charming and delightful texts characterized by wit and wisdom.

One of the maps concerns Samson and the Shephelah. The latter was the intermediate zone separating the Judean hill country from the Philistine plain. Both the

Israelites and Philistines claimed this rich and verdant region, and whoever was stronger at the time ruled the area.

Incidents in Samson's life are depicted. In one scene, Samson is shown as an Israelite and a Nazirite from the womb. This agrees with Scripture, for an angel of the Lord told Samson's mother that her son would practice certain forms of abstinence, including not cutting his hair and refraining from the consumption of alcohol (Judg. 13:5, 7; 16:17). These practices were to be an expression of Samson's commitment to God. Though he became one of the most illustrious of Israel's judges, Samson proved to be a tragic character.

Perhaps most telling on the map are depictions of Samson's attraction to the Philistines, especially their coastal cities, their markets, and their beautiful women. In the northeast quadrant, Samson is shown pursuing the Philistines with the jawbone of an ass. In the southwest quadrant, the mighty Israelite is seen carrying off the city gate of Gaza. In addition, there are the depictions of Delilah's betrayal of Samson, which is the initial focus of this week's lesson.

For 20 years, Samson successfully harassed the Philistines (15:20). But then they learned that he was in love with a woman named Delilah. *The lords of the Philistines came to her and said to her, "Coax him, and find out what makes his strength so great, and how we may overpower him, so that we may bind him in order to subdue him; and we will each give you eleven hundred pieces of silver"* (16:5).

Three times the crafty seductress tried to coax Samson into revealing the secret of his strength. And each time Samson gave a misleading answer. Delilah pouted, complaining that Samson did not love her and was mocking her. She pestered and nagged him until she wore down his resistance. He finally stated that if his head were shaved, his strength would leave him and he would *"be like anyone else"* (16:17). This time, Delilah sensed that Samson had told her the truth.

Samson wrongly attributed his strength to himself (that is, his hair). His hair was merely a symbol of his dedication to God—a symbol that was about to be destroyed. As long as Samson's hair (and what it symbolized) remained intact, God gave him superhuman strength. When Samson lost his strength, the Lord taught him a painful lesson. Without God's enabling, he was powerless.

That evening, after Delilah had sent word to her Philistine lords, she spent time with Samson. She lulled him to sleep, with his head resting in her lap. Perhaps at a prearranged signal, a man entered the room and shaved Samson's head. *He began to weaken, and his strength left him* (16:19).

Then Delilah awakened Samson by shouting, *"The Philistines are upon you, Samson!"* (16:20). Samson jumped to his feet and prepared to fight. But he didn't realize that *the LORD had left him.* Samson's enemies easily subdued him. The Philistines gouged out his eyes, chained him with bronze shackles, and forced him to grind grain with a millstone in prison (16:21).

Israel's hero had been humiliated and wounded. *But the hair of his head began to grow again after it had been shaved* (16:22). The regrowth of his hair brought the renewed hope that the Lord might use him one more time to deal a mighty blow to the Philistines.

The Philistine leaders held a great festival at which they offered sacrifices and praised Dagon, a grain god. The guests also consumed large amounts of alcohol (16:23-24). The most commonly excavated Philistine item is the beer mug. Large or small, it is equipped with side spouts and strainers. Used to filter barley beer (the most popular beverage of the day), these steins show that there was considerable drinking at Philistine festivals.

The guests, now drunk, demanded that Samson be brought out so that he could perform for them. He was escorted out and made to stand at the center of the temple, between the two pillars supporting the roof (16:25).

Excavations at Tell Qasile and Ekron have shown that Philistine shrines were built around a large central hall (often about 18 by 24 feet) bisected by a row of wooden pillars about 6 to 7 feet apart on stone bases that supported the upper story and the roof. Plastered benches lined the walls, and a raised platform at the end mounted by two steps allowed ample seating. In this instance, over 3000 people were crowded into the building and on the roof (16:27).

At Samson's request, a servant placed his hands against the two pillars of the temple (16:26). Then he prayed, *"Lord GOD, remember me and strengthen me only this once, O God, so that with this one act of revenge I may pay back the Philistines for my two eyes"* (16:28). After this, Samson pushed against the center pillars of the temple (16:29). He prayed, *"Let me die with the Philistines"* (16:30).

The Lord answered Samson's request by destroying the pagan temple and its worshipers. Despite Samson's flaws, he began the process of delivering the Israelites from being dominated and absorbed by the Philistines (13:5). Samson thus proved to be a hero of faith (Heb. 11:32).

SUGGESTIONS TO TEACHERS

Oliver Cromwell (an English general and statesman) told the artist making his portrait, "Paint me warts and all!" The personalities of Scripture are also presented "warts and all," that is, with all their flaws. This week's lesson concerning Samson is a good example. His account reminds us that God calls and uses flawed people—people like us!

1. DEDICATION FROM BIRTH. Samson was the answer to his parents' prayers for a child. In gratitude, they dedicated their son to the Lord. As *the spirit of the LORD began to stir him* (13:25), it became clear that God was preparing Samson for special service. This example of godly parenting can be an opportunity for the class members to reflect on the importance of praying for those who are rearing children.

2. DISSIPATION OF ABILITIES. Samson had immense promise, for God had endowed him with amazing abilities. But Samson squandered these on self-centered living. Though Israel looked to him as leader for 20 years, Samson used his great strength for trivial pursuits as well as noble achievements. As you talk with the students about the unique abilities God has given them, be sure to encourage them to reflect on how these may be best used for serving Him.

3. DISGRACE FROM WEAKNESS. Samson's downfall came by allowing the crafty Delilah to take advantage of him. After being shaved and blinded, the once powerful hero of Israel was forced to perform degrading tasks by his enemies. His weakness was succumbing to the temptations of his sinful nature. Stress to the members of the class that everyone has weaknesses that can be destructive unless they are faced and conquered with God's help.

4. DEATH AS A TESTIMONY. Samson's final hour was a clear affirmation of his faith in the Lord. But suppose Samson had lived throughout his days with that kind of commitment! What would those in your class write if each of them were to pen his or her obituary? Would people remember them as those who used their lives to testify to God's goodness and grace?

■ **TOPIC:** Be Faithful

■ **QUESTIONS:** 1. Who were the Philistines? 2. What did Samson say was the secret of his strength? 3. How did Samson's moral lapses lead to problems for him and the nation of Israel? 4. What are some of the painful results of morally irresponsible behavior? 5. Why is it sometimes hard for believers to remain faithful to the Lord?

■ **ILLUSTRATIONS:**

Always Faithful. The suicide bombing attack on the American Embassy in Beirut, Lebanon, several years ago took the lives of 250 Americans and severely injured dozens of people. Shortly after the explosion, General Paul Kelley visited the wounded at the hospital where they were being treated. He came to the bedside of a young U.S. marine who had been critically hurt in the attack. Bandages covered the eyes of the soldier, and a tracheotomy had been placed in his throat.

General Kelley gently spoke to the marine and leaned over to allow the young man—who could not see or speak—to touch the four stars pinned on the officer's collar. (These indicated Kelley's rank.) Not long afterward, the General learned that the marine was going to have a birthday. Kelley visited again, gave the four stars as a present to the soldier, and told him how proud he and the nation were of him. Unable to say anything and still swathed in bandages, the marine reached for a pad and pencil. On the pad, the young man scrawled in crude letters SEMPER FI. This is the abbreviated form of the motto of the U.S. Marine Corps—*Semper Fidelis,* which means "always faithful."

The Lord wanted Samson to always be faithful to Him. Similarly, God wants us to be unwavering in our devotion to Him.

Involved and Responsible. Some Maine fishers tell the story of a landlubber tourist who insisted on accompanying a crew in a boat heading out to the Georges Bank. A severe storm suddenly arose, and the boat developed engine troubles. Then the vessel began to take on water.

Meanwhile, the visitor lounged in the galley idly drinking a cup of coffee. The skipper struggled with the wheel to try to keep the boat headed into the wind while the crewmen frantically worked below trying to operate a pump and restart the engine. Noticing the tourist not doing anything, one of the crew shouted, "Hey! Give us a hand here with the pump! We're in trouble and you're not doing anything!" Shrugging, the visitor took another sip of coffee and replied, "I don't care. It's not my boat!"

The moral of the story is that all Christians are to be mutually responsible as fellow crew members on the voyage of life (Gal. 6:1-2; Jude 23).

What Happened to Delilah? John Milton, in *Samson Agonistes,* suggests that Delilah repented, came to Samson in prison, and asked for forgiveness for her betrayal of him. Others have postulated that she was in the crowd that mocked Samson and that she perished along with the other Philistines.

The Bible, of course, doesn't tell us what happened to Delilah. But we do know what happened to Samson. His moral compromise led to his tragic downfall. Thankfully, he came to his senses before it was too late and thus is remembered as a hero of faith (Heb. 11:32). May his life example encourage us to avoid giving in to the temptation of sin and to remain wholly committed to Christ.

FOR YOUTH

■ TOPIC: Chosen to Be Faithful
■ QUESTIONS: 1. What did the Philistine leaders want Delilah to do with Samson? 2. How was Samson captured by the Philistines? 3. What were some of Samson's strengths and weaknesses? 4. How did Samson die? 5. What are some lessons you have learned from studying the life of Samson?

■ **ILLUSTRATIONS:**

Missing Ingredient. In August, 1998, Dr. Elihu Sussman, an Associated Press special features writer, lamented the poor physical shape of America's children. Citing a study by the National Center for Health Statistics, he claimed that children are in the worst physical shape ever!

The study, which was done between 1988 to 1994, noted that 14.7 percent of boys and 12.6 percent of girls between the ages of 12 to 17 are overweight. The causes were many: too much sitting and watching television, poor eating habits (particularly with fast food), and too many sedimentary activities with no outdoor play. Finally, poor role models were to blame. Children saw their parents flopped in front of a television eating chips and doing little, if any, physical activity.

For all of Samson's shortcomings, he was a model of activity. However, the missing ingredient in his life was not physical health, but rather spiritual devotion to the Lord. He was a spiritually flabby person who sought to gratify himself rather than serve God in a virtuous way. There is nothing wrong with us taking care of our body. But even more important from an eternal perspective is giving attention to our spiritual health (1 Tim. 4:8).

No Satisfaction. Each year, children are subjected to over 10,000 advertisements for fast food. In addition, every day seven percent of Americans eat at a fast-food outlet. Nutritionists note that this practice is unhealthy. Junk food simply does not satisfy our nutritional needs.

One might say that Samson was a spiritual junk food addict. His earthly diet of self-centered and loose living was ruining his spiritual health. Tragically, many youth are living in a similar way. They need to know that Jesus is the bread of life (John 6:35). Only those who trust in Him will be eternally satisfied.

Consequences of Trickery. Do you remember the story about the little gingerbread man? He first ran away from his home. Then he used all sorts of tricks to get his way and elude being captured. Ironically, however, he was eventually tricked by a sly fox, who ate him.

Like the gingerbread man, Samson used trickery throughout much of his life. And ultimately, he too was tricked by Delilah. Similarly, some youth try to use trickery to get what they want. However, the end is usually the same as that of Samson and the gingerbread man. They find themselves tricked by others, and this causes them great emotional pain. That's why it is always best to do what is true, honorable, and just (Phil. 4:8-9).

SAMUEL

BACKGROUND SCRIPTURE: 1 Samuel 3; 7:3-14
DEVOTIONAL READING: Luke 12:35-40

KEY VERSE: Speak, for your servant is listening. 1 Samuel 3:10b.

4

KING JAMES VERSION

1 SAMUEL 3:2 And it came to pass at that time, when Eli was laid down in his place, and his eyes began to wax dim, that he could not see;

3 And ere the lamp of God went out in the temple of the LORD, where the ark of God was, and Samuel was laid down to sleep;

4 That the LORD called Samuel: and he answered, Here am I.

5 And he ran unto Eli, and said, Here am I; for thou calledst me. And he said, I called not; lie down again. And he went and lay down.

6 And the LORD called yet again, Samuel. And Samuel arose and went to Eli, and said, Here am I; for thou didst call me. And he answered, I called not, my son; lie down again.

7 Now Samuel did not yet know the LORD, neither was the word of the LORD yet revealed unto him.

8 And the LORD called Samuel again the third time. And he arose and went to Eli, and said, Here am I; for thou didst call me. And Eli perceived that the LORD had called the child.

9 Therefore Eli said unto Samuel, Go, lie down: and it shall be, if he call thee, that thou shalt say, Speak, LORD; for thy servant heareth. So Samuel went and lay down in his place. . . .

19 And Samuel grew, and the LORD was with him, and did let none of his words fall to the ground.

20 And all Israel from Dan even to Beer-sheba knew that Samuel was established to be a prophet of the LORD. . . .

7:3 And Samuel spake unto all the house of Israel, saying, If ye do return unto the LORD with all your hearts, then put away the strange gods and Ashtaroth from among you, and prepare your hearts unto the LORD, and serve him only: and he will deliver you out of the hand of the Philistines.

4 Then the children of Israel did put away Baalim and Ashtaroth, and served the LORD only.

5 And Samuel said, Gather all Israel to Mizpeh, and I will pray for you unto the LORD. . . .

12 Then Samuel took a stone, and set it between Mizpeh and Shen, and called the name of it Eben-ezer, saying, Hitherto hath the LORD helped us.

NEW REVISED STANDARD VERSION

1 SAMUEL 3:2 At that time Eli, whose eyesight had begun to grow dim so that he could not see, was lying down in his room; 3 the lamp of God had not yet gone out, and Samuel was lying down in the temple of the LORD, where the ark of God was. 4 Then the LORD called, "Samuel! Samuel!" and he said, "Here I am!" 5 and ran to Eli, and said, "Here I am, for you called me." But he said, "I did not call; lie down again." So he went and lay down. 6 The LORD called again, "Samuel!" Samuel got up and went to Eli, and said, "Here I am, for you called me." But he said, "I did not call, my son; lie down again." 7 Now Samuel did not yet know the LORD, and the word of the LORD had not yet been revealed to him. 8 The LORD called Samuel again, a third time. And he got up and went to Eli, and said, "Here I am, for you called me." Then Eli perceived that the LORD was calling the boy. 9 Therefore Eli said to Samuel, "Go, lie down; and if he calls you, you shall say, 'Speak, LORD, for your servant is listening.'" So Samuel went and lay down in his place. . . .

7:3 Then Samuel said to all the house of Israel, "If you are returning to the LORD with all your heart, then put away the foreign gods and the Astartes from among you. Direct your heart to the LORD, and serve him only, and he will deliver you out of the hand of the Philistines." 4 So Israel put away the Baals and the Astartes, and they served the LORD only.

5 Then Samuel said, "Gather all Israel at Mizpah, and I will pray to the LORD for you." . . .

12 Then Samuel took a stone and set it up between Mizpah and Jeshanah, and named it Ebenezer; for he said, "Thus far the LORD has helped us."

HOME BIBLE READINGS

BACKGROUND

God had used Joshua to help the Israelites settle in Canaan. But despite their common heritage and faith, they had no cohesive, organized way of working together as a nation. Often, when a common enemy threatened their survival, some of them joined forces. Yet during the time of the judges, they mostly existed as independent clans without any centralized government.

God's people not only had external threats, such as oppression from the Philistines, but also internal struggles with idolatry, immorality, and injustice. For instance, the sons of Eli (the priest of Shiloh) were wicked men who had no respect for the Lord. They treated God's offerings with contempt, seduced the young women who assisted at the entrance of the tabernacle, and refused to listen to Eli's mild rebukes (1 Sam. 2:12-25).

It's within this context that God raised up Samuel. He was primarily a prophet, though he also served as a judge and military commander. This outstanding personality is recognized as the human link between the time of the judges and the beginning of the monarchy.

Samuel was born in answer to barren Hannah's tearful prayer, and she dedicated him to the Lord before his birth (1:10-11). Eli then raised Samuel at the Shiloh sanctuary (2:11). In fact, the priest became the human agent largely responsible for Samuel's religious and spiritual training.

Samuel was a young lad when he met God and received his first prophetic mission (3:1, 11-14). The Lord's initial word to Samuel concerned the divine rejection of Eli's family from service as priests as punishment for the sins of Eli's sons. Throughout the rest of Samuel's adolescent years, he grew *both in stature and in favor with the LORD and with the people* (2:26).

Following the deaths of Eli and his sons, Israel as a nation was plunged into turmoil. Samuel reemerged in the role of a judge. He called Israel to repentance and delivered them from foreign domination. Samuel also administered justice at Bethel, Gilgal, Mizpah, and Ramah (7:2-17).

In Samuel's old age, he reluctantly bowed to the wishes of the people for a king. But he warned them that kings demanded royal trappings and imposed burdens on their subjects. As God's agent, Samuel privately anointed a tall and handsome young man named Saul as the nation's first ruler, and then Samuel headed the public ceremony in which the people selected Saul as king by casting lots. Samuel sternly warned the Israelites that God was meant to be held in greater allegiance than any other. When Saul failed to obey the Lord wholeheartedly, Samuel censured Saul and foretold that God would replace him with another king. (8:1—13:15).

NOTES ON THE PRINTED TEXT

Samuel had the extraordinary opportunity to serve the Lord by assisting Eli (3:1). The lad wore a linen ephod (a long, sleeveless vest; 2:18). As Eli's helper, Samuel would have opened the tabernacle doors each morning, cleaned the furniture, and swept the floors (3:15). And as he grew older, he would have helped Eli in offering sacrifices.

One night *Eli, whose eyesight had begun to grow dim so that he could not see, was lying down in his room* (3:2). Most likely the priest was in the court of the tabernacle. The gold lampstand, which was located in the Holy Place, *had not yet gone out* (3:3). Samuel was sleeping nearby when the Lord called out, *"Samuel! Samuel!"* (3:4).

Samuel mistakenly thought that Eli was calling him. The lad thus jumped up, ran to the priest, and said, *"Here I am, for you called for me"* (3:5). Perhaps surprised and annoyed at Samuel for awakening him, Eli responded, *"I did not call; lie down again."* The same episode was repeated a second time (3:6).

What was going on? Verse 7 says that Samuel did not yet know the Lord, for the lad had never before received a message from God. This helps us to understand why, when the Lord called to Samuel a third time, he responded as he did previously. Thankfully, Eli realized what was taking place (3:8). Thus the priest told the lad, *"Go, lie down; and if he calls you, you shall say, 'Speak, LORD, for your servant is listening!'"* (3:9).

Samuel did as he was told and received God's message. This incident made it clear that God had chosen the lad to be a prophet in Israel. The Lord's hand of blessing remained on Samuel throughout his childhood (3:19). *And all Israel from Dan to Beer-sheeba knew that Samuel was a trustworthy prophet of the LORD* (3:20).

The next 20 years were an especially dark period for the Israelites. They experienced repeated attacks and defeats at the hands of the Philistines (4:1—7:2). Perhaps God's people thought He had abandoned them.

Samuel, now a grown man, roused the Israelites to action by saying that if they were really serious about wanting to return to the Lord, they had to *"put away the foreign gods and the Astartes from among you"* (7:3). These were Canaanite idols that the Israelites worshiped. Only when they destroyed these pagan objects would the Lord rescue them *"out of the hand of the Philistines."* Thankfully, the people responded as God had commanded through Samuel (7:4).

Samuel next told the people to gather at Mizpah. (This town was seven miles north of Jerusalem and eight miles northeast of Kirjath-jearim.). The prophet announced that he would pray on behalf of the Israelites before the Lord (7:5).

Meanwhile the Philistines advanced to attack. But God threw them into a state confusion, which enabled the Israelites to defeat them (7:11). After this stunning victory, Samuel set up a memorial stone and called it *Ebenezer* (7:12), which means "stone of help." In other words, God fought Israel's battles and blessed His people with victory. During the rest of Samuel's lifetime, the nation enjoyed God's protection from the Philistines (7:13).

SUGGESTIONS TO TEACHERS

During the past few years, there have been many examples of foolish leaders. Perhaps this is why some people are filled with cynicism. This week's lesson offers a ray of hope. It focuses on a leader whom we can respect for his faith and accomplishments as a servant of the Lord.

1. VALIDITY OF FAITH. God's call of young Samuel can serve as a reminder to the students that the Lord has chosen them to serve Him. Perhaps God has not summoned them as dramatically as He did Samuel. Nevertheless, God's claim on each class member is just as real and personal. The Lord knows each student by name just as He knew Samuel personally. Furthermore, God's choice of us should prompt us to respond in obedience. Samuel's reply of *"Here I am!"* (1 Sam. 3:4) is another way of saying "Reporting for duty!" Be sure to encourage every class member to respond to God's call with promptness and joy.

2. VALIDITY OF GOD'S CALL. The validity of the divine summons is seen in the fact that Samuel chose to serve the Lord wholeheartedly. Though the tasks he had to perform were sometimes difficult, Samuel nevertheless did them. There may be times when God wants us to do unpleasant tasks or experience difficult circumstances. Like Samuel, the validity of God's summons in our life is seen in our willingness to submit completely to His will, regardless of what it might involve.

3. VINDICATION OF TRUST. When Samuel was an adult, he urged the Israelites to repent and return to living as the people of the covenant. The great public service of rededication in which he officiated helped God's people to renew their commitment to Him. Samuel's devotion motivated God's people to live again as a responsible community. Clearly, Samuel's example was important! Encourage the students to live as examples of godliness during the coming week.

4. COMMEMORATION AT EBENEZER. Have the class look at 7:12, which concerns the Ebenezer stone that Samuel set up as a memorial. The stone was a means of remembering what God had done for His people. During tough times, we may need to remember the crucial turning points in our past to help us through the present. When we recall the the way God has worked in our lives, it bolsters our faith. We not only gain confidence and strength for today but also hope for the future.

■ TOPIC: Be an Example

■ QUESTIONS: 1. When and how did the Lord call Samuel? 2. What did the Israelites realize about Samuel? 3. What did Samuel urge the Israelites to do with their idols? 4. Why did Samuel name the memorial stone "Ebenezer"? 5. What may be some tasks that God is leading you to undertake?

■ ILLUSTRATIONS:

Sensitive to God's Leading. Samuel was sensitive to the leading of God in his life. Sadly, not many believers today are as open and responsive to God's leading. They allow a host of things to prevent them from discerning His will.

This is not hard to understand. After all, we are saturated with noise and bombarded with messages. Some are relatively easy to tune out. But there are others we readily welcome perhaps without even thinking.

For example, many people switch on the radio or television the first thing each morning. And throughout the day they follow talk shows. (A good number of these are nothing more than noise sessions in which different people shout slogans back and forth without conscientiously listening to what others have said.) Even when they sit down for a few minutes to eat, they might thumb through a magazine or skim a newspaper filled with advertisements.

These practices are ironic, given the fundamental premise of all good communication. It means far more than just speaking effectively or writing skillfully. It also includes attentive listening.

Franklin D. Roosevelt surmised that most people in his day were poor listeners. Reportedly one evening while at a reception, he decided to test his hunch that few truly listened. As people went through the receiving line to greet him, the president flashed his famous smile and then said genially, "I murdered my grandmother this morning!"

Persons in the line shook Roosevelt's hand and invariably smiled back. They were not really listening, but rather composing their replies. They said such things as "How lovely!" or "Yes, and just continue with your great work!" Only one diplomat—who was skilled in the art of listening carefully—heard the President's remark and bellowed, "I'm sure she had it coming to her!"

Paying attention to others is both hard work and important to do. This is especially true when it comes to our relationship with God. He is eager to lead us, but are we willing to follow? Are we as sensitive to His promptings as we ought to be?

Perhaps the difficulty that many believers have in knowing God's will and following His leading is that they really don't want to obey Him. They'd rather do things their way. How tragic this is! We will enjoy our walk with God much more when we are as open and responsive to His leading as was Samuel.

Example through a Diary. He was only 29 when he died of tuberculosis, but David Brainerd has influenced countless Christians since his death in 1747. He was left an orphan when he was 14, but became a devoted Christian at 21 and committed his life to sharing his faith among native Americans. Brainerd diligently mastered Indian languages, and traveled tirelessly among the tribes in New York, Pennsylvania, and New Jersey.

While experiencing loneliness, sickness, and criticism, Brainerd wrote that he wanted to "burn on in one continual flame for God." Though his health declined due to the ravages of tuberculosis, he helped acquire land for native Americans near Trenton. He also built a church, a school, an infirmary, and a carpentry shop.

The illustrious Jonathan Edwards brought the dying missionary-evangelist to his home and arranged for his care during the few months Brainerd had to live. Edwards found the young man's diary and published it as an example of a Christian life "most worthy of imitation."

Brainerd's diary was read widely, and it deeply affected future heroes of the faith. For instance, it impacted the English shoemaker William Carey (who became a pioneer missionary to India), Henry Martyn (who evangelized in India and Persia), and Billy Graham (the famous evangelist who has led many people to faith in Christ). Brainerd's example of unwavering Christian commitment lives on through his diary!

Presidential Example. John Quincy Adams served as the sixth president of the United States from 1825–1829. But unlike modern politicians who seem to strive for increasing power and prestige, Adams thought in terms of how he could best serve God and his fellow citizens. This leader became the only former president to get himself elected to Congress after leaving the White House.

Incredulous inquirers asked how Adams could possibly step down and run for a lesser office, especially after experiencing the glory of the highest office in the land. The former president gave evidence of his faith by indicating that he cared nothing about honors and acclaim, but only service and justice.

In 1837, as a member of congress, Adams continued to set an example by vigorously opposing Andrew Jackson's policy of relocating native Americans living in the eastern part of the United States to the western part of the nation. In 1844, while still in congress, Adams stated, "We have done more harm to the Indians since our Revolution than had been done to them by the French and English nations before. These are crying sins for which we are answerable before a higher Jurisdiction." (This statement brought him harsh criticism from his colleagues.) Adams also declared that slavery was "an outrage upon the goodness of God."

Where are current examples like Adams for us and our children? Admittedly, they are hard to find. Perhaps God is calling us to be as humble as Adams was in his attitude. The Lord may also be encouraging us to be as sacrificial in our service to others as Adams was in his day.

■ **TOPIC:** Chosen to Serve

■ **QUESTIONS:** 1. How did Samuel initially respond to God's summons? 2. As Samuel grew up, what kind of relationship did he have with God? 3. How did the Israelites know that Samuel was a true prophet? 4. Why did Samuel urge the Israelites to give up their idols? 5. What did Samuel pledge to do at Mizpah?

■ **ILLUSTRATIONS:**

False Gods. Every evening young people stand outside the "Propaganda"—a dance club in Moscow—to escape the heat of the crowded dance floor. The harried bouncers work to keep those pushing and shoving to get in from mixing with those cooling off. The partying youth, who are dressed in the latest fashions and pay enormous amounts of money to enter and enjoy a night, seem oblivious to the economic crisis facing their nation. This is due largely to their worship of the gods of position, money, cars, and pleasure.

The attitude of these youth is similar to the way people thought in ancient Israel. They continued to venerate powerless and lifeless idols. They also tended to be oblivious to the crises that resulted from God's judgment on the nation. Samuel urged his fellow Israelites to abandon their false gods and worship only the one true God. This principle is still valid today. As 1 John 5:21 says, *Little children, keep yourselves from idols.*

Poor Role Models. The tiny-mite football game was tied 6–6 in the first quarter. The Repton Bulldogs and the Lyeffion Yellow Jackets (part of the South-Central Alabama Football League) were playing in Repton, Alabama, on September 26, 1998, when the game was halted. It was not an accident or even a hurricane that brought the cancellation. The reason was that the parents were fighting!

National Guard members intervened, and police eventually arrested a woman and charged her with assault. As children, grandparents, parents, cousins, and friends all departed the athletic field, an adolescent from Repton said, "I'm disappointed and didn't like what the adults had done because it forced the cancellation of the game!"

Youth look to older people for guidance. Like the adolescent from Repton, they are disappointed when they see things taking place that are morally wrong. Samuel, having been called by God, saw abuses that were unethical. Perhaps he was disappointed that Eli did not try to correct the problems. This may be why Samuel dedicated his life in service to God and followed His guidance. Shouldn't we?

A Clear Sense of Purpose. On September 30, 1998, Dan Quisenberry, the star relief pitcher for the Kansas City Royals, died of a brain tumor. "Quiz" (his nickname) had a 12-year career, and he led the American League in saves five different years. His 45 saves in 1983 was a major-league record for a time.

The shy, pale, skinny, and physically unimposing kid from Laverne College was ignored by every major league team in the draft. Sensing that he was destined to play baseball, he drove to the home of John Schuerholz—who was the head of the Royal's scouting department—and pleaded for a tryout.

Samuel had a similar sense of purpose. He knew that God had called him to do a great work and he never seemed to regret it. The Lord has also called you to live for Him and serve Him. Like Samuel, accept God's will for your life and pursue it with a clear sense of purpose.

SAUL BECOMES KING

BACKGROUND SCRIPTURE: 1 Samuel 9:1—10:27

DEVOTIONAL READING: Psalm 119:1-8

KEY VERSE: Samuel said to all the people, "Do you see the one whom the LORD has chosen? There is no one like him among all the people." 1 Samuel 10:24.

KING JAMES VERSION

1 SAMUEL 9:1 Now there was a man of Benjamin, whose name was Kish, the son of Abiel, the son of Zeror, the son of Bechorath, the son of Aphiah, a Benjamite, a mighty man of power.

2 And he had a son, whose name was Saul, a choice young man, and a goodly: and there was not among the children of Israel a goodlier person than he: from his shoulders and upward he was higher than any of the people. . . .

10:17 And Samuel called the people together unto the LORD to Mizpeh;

18 And said unto the children of Israel, Thus saith the LORD God of Israel, I brought up Israel out of Egypt, and delivered you out of the hand of the Egyptians, and out of the hand of all kingdoms, and of them that oppressed you:

19 And ye have this day rejected your God, who himself saved you out of all your adversities and your tribulations; and ye have said unto him, Nay, but set a king over us. Now therefore present yourselves before the LORD by your tribes, and by your thousands.

20 And when Samuel had caused all the tribes of Israel to come near, the tribe of Benjamin was taken.

21 When he had caused the tribe of Benjamin to come near by their families, the family of Matri was taken, and Saul the son of Kish was taken: and when they sought him, he could not be found.

22 Therefore they inquired of the LORD further, if the man should yet come thither. And the LORD answered, Behold, he hath hid himself among the stuff.

23 And they ran and fetched him thence: and when he stood among the people, he was higher than any of the people from his shoulders and upward.

24 And Samuel said to all the people, See ye him whom the LORD hath chosen, that there is none like him among all the people? And all the people shouted, and said, God save the king.

25 Then Samuel told the people the manner of the kingdom, and wrote it in a book, and laid it up before the LORD. And Samuel sent all the people away, every man to his house.

26 And Saul also went home to Gibeah; and there went with him a band of men, whose hearts God had touched.

NEW REVISED STANDARD VERSION

1 SAMUEL 9:1 There was a man of Benjamin whose name was Kish son of Abiel son of Zeror son of Becorath son of Aphiah, a Benjaminite, a man of wealth. 2 He had a son whose name was Saul, a handsome young man. There was not a man among the people of Israel more handsome than he; he stood head and shoulders above everyone else. . . .

10:17 Samuel summoned the people to the LORD at Mizpah 18 and said to them, "Thus says the LORD, the God of Israel, 'I brought up Israel out of Egypt, and I rescued you from the hand of the Egyptians and from the hand of all the kingdoms that were oppressing you.' 19 But today you have rejected your God, who saves you from all your calamities and your distresses; and you have said, 'No! but set a king over us.' Now therefore present yourselves before the LORD by your tribes and by your clans." 20 Then Samuel brought all the tribes of Israel near, and the tribe of Benjamin was taken by lot. 21 He brought the tribe of Benjamin near by its families, and the family of the Matrites was taken by lot. Finally he brought the family of the Matrites near man by man, and Saul the son of Kish was taken by lot. But when they sought him, he could not be found. 22 So they inquired again of the LORD, "Did the man come here?" and the LORD said, "See, he has hidden himself among the baggage." 23 Then they ran and brought him from there. When he took his stand among the people, he was head and shoulders taller than any of them. 24 Samuel said to all the people, "Do you see the one whom the LORD has chosen? There is no one like him among all the people." And all the people shouted, "Long live the king!"

25 Samuel told the people the rights and duties of the kingship; and he wrote them in a book and laid it up before the LORD. Then Samuel sent all the people back to their homes. 26 Saul also went to his home at Gibeah, and with him went warriors whose hearts God had touched.

Monday, September 25	1 Samuel 9:1-10	*Saul Searches for a Prophet of God*
Tuesday, September 26	1 Samuel 9:11-17	*Samuel Recognizes Saul*
Wednesday, September 27	1 Samuel 9:18-21	*Saul Meets Samuel*
Thursday, September 28	1 Samuel 9:22—10:1	*Saul Anointed King*
Friday, September 29	1 Samuel 10:2-8	*Samuel Directs Saul*
Saturday, September 30	1 Samuel 10:9-16	*Saul Prophesies*
Sunday, October 1	1 Samuel 10:17-26	*Saul Proclaimed King*

BACKGROUND

In Samuel's old age, he appointed his sons to be judges over Israel. But unlike their father, who was a great prophet and leader, these men proved to be greedy. They not only accepted bribes but also perverted justice. In response, the leaders of Israel met at Ramah to discuss the matter with Samuel. They demanded that he give them a king like all the other nations had (1 Sam. 8:1-5).

Samuel was upset by the request of the people, and so he prayed to the Lord about the matter. God revealed that the Israelites' demand for a king was a rejection of His rule over them. Ever since He had rescued them from Egypt, they had continually forsaken Him and followed pagan deities. God told Samuel to fulfill the people's request and also to warn them about how a king would treat them (8:6-9).

Samuel told the Israelites that a king would draft the nation's young men into his army and conscript slave laborers for his building projects. Such a king would take the best of the Israelites' fields and vineyards and use their property for his personal gain. And the king would demand a tenth of their harvest and flocks (8:10-18).

Tragically, the people refused to listen to Samuel's warning. They still wanted a king so that they could be like the nations surrounding them. Their goal was to have a human ruler who would govern them and lead them into battle. When Samuel told the Lord what the people had said, He in turn told His servant to comply with their request (9:19-22).

Saul was God's answer to the demand of His people for a king. Saul's impressive height and good looks would make him appear to be a suitable candidate. But as Scripture reveals, Saul was a tragic figure, one who eventually failed both God and the Israelites in his duties as the nation's first king.

NOTES ON THE PRINTED TEXT

Saul was the son of a man named Kish. Saul's father was from the tribe of Benjamin and was known as a *man of wealth* (9:1). This suggests that Kish was similar to a feudal lord, that is, a rich land owner and a leader in time of war.

Saul was *a handsome young man* (9:2). In fact, he was so striking in his appearance that *not a man among the people of Israel [was] more handsome than he.* Saul was blessed with what seemed to be great potential for leadership and service. He had what it took to be a powerful earthly king.

One day Kish's donkeys had strayed, and so he told Saul to look for them. Saul eventually made his way to Ramah, Samuel's hometown, and this is where the two met. It is also where Samuel took a flask of olive oil and poured it over Saul's head to anoint him as Israel's first king (9:3—10:1).

Sometime later Samuel called all the people of Israel to meet before the Lord at Mizpah (10:17). This was a city in the northern part of the territory of Benjamin. It was here that Samuel delivered God's message to His people.

The Lord announced, *"I brought up Israel out of Egypt"* (10:18). The departure of the Israelites from Egypt was a pivotal event in the nation's history, for God had *"rescued [them] from the hand of the Egyptians and from the hand of all the kingdoms that were oppressing [them]."* God was saying to His people that all along He had been their king, ensuring their peace and stability. No human ruler could do a better job in leading and protecting His people.

In light of this, it is ironic that the Israelites would reject God. They were short-sighted in their desire to replace Him with a weak human ruler who could not save them *"from all [their] calamities and [their] distresses"* (10:19). Nevertheless, God granted their request and directed them to present themselves before Him by tribes and clans.

When Samuel *brought all the tribes of Israel near* (10:20), the tribe of Benjamin was taken by lot. These were objects that the people used to determine God's will. Despite the many references in the Old Testament to casting lots, nothing is known about the actual objects themselves. They could have been sticks of various lengths, flat stones like coins, or some kind of dice.

Once the tribe of Benjamin had been selected, Samuel brought each family of the tribe before the Lord, and *the family of the Matrites was taken by lot* (10:21). From them Saul the son of Kish was chosen. By this time the suspense among the people must have been great. And the tension undoubtedly increased when Saul could not be found!

Despite all the efforts of the people, it's as if the young man had disappeared. Thus the leaders *inquired again of the Lord* (10:22). They learned that Saul had *"hidden himself among the baggage."* Some say this was a reflection of Saul's modesty. Another possibility is that he was filled with self-doubt over assuming the position of national leader.

When the people found Saul, they brought him out from hiding so that the crowd could see him. And what a sight he presented! *When he took his stand among the people, he was head and shoulders taller than any of them* (10:23). Samuel announced that Saul, whom the Lord had chosen as Israel's first king, was without equal. The people responded by shouting, *"Long live the king!"* (10:24).

This was both a joyous and serious occasion. Israel's king operated under God's authority and was His ruling representative. Thus, Samuel *told the people the rights and duties of the kingship* (10:25). He may have reviewed his previous instruction (8:11-18), or he may have discussed God's laws for kingship (Deut. 17:14-20). The regulations were recorded on a scroll and kept in the sanctuary.

At the conclusion of the ceremony, Samuel *sent all the people back to their homes* (1 Sam. 10:25). Saul also returned to his hometown. He was accompanied by *warriors whose hearts God had touched* (10:26). Clearly, Saul got off to a good start and had much promise to be a great king.

SUGGESTIONS TO TEACHERS

Life is not static, and change brings challenge. The Israelites discovered this when they decided to become a monarchy instead of a loose confederation of tribes. This week's lesson, which concerns the selection of Saul as the first king of Israel, describes how this man and his nation tried to deal with the challenge of change.

1. INQUIRY BY A SEEKER. When Saul approached Samuel for personal reasons, the young man discovered that God had different plans for him. Sometimes we discover that God's plans supersede our own. As Saul was surprised by the changes in his life due to the working of God, so too we must be prepared for unexpected changes in our lives brought about by the hand of God.

2. INFLUENCE OF THE LORD. Samuel was reluctant to grant the people's demand for a king. But the Lord told His servant to do so, and Samuel submitted to the will of God. In obedience to the Lord, he anointed Saul as Israel's first king.

3. INTERRUPTION OF SAUL'S PLANS. After being anointed, Saul permitted the Lord to change his plans. We read that as Saul turned to leave Samuel, *God gave him another heart* (1 Sam. 10:9). And as Saul went on his way to Gibeah, *a band of prophets met him; and the spirit of God possessed him* (10:10). There may be times when God interrupts our plans, and we must be willing to submit to His will, whatever it may be.

4. INFORMATION TO THE ISRAELITES. On one occasion Samuel told God's people that their king served under divine authorization. Though Israel's ruler would exercise considerable power, he was still responsible to God and His people for his actions (10:25). Perhaps God has given some of us the privilege of serving as leaders among His people. If so, we should see it as a high calling and high privilege, one that must be exercised with great reverence.

5. INCLINATION TOWARD HESITATION. Saul seemed to be fearful of accepting his new responsibilities as king, and so he hid among the baggage. His timidity may have reflected his hesitancy to obey God. Undoubtedly, Saul was awed by the responsibilities he would have to accept. We, like Saul, may have misgivings about accepting the challenges God gives us. But we can rely on His strength and guidance to handle anything in our lives.

■ **TOPIC:** The Challenge of Change

■ **QUESTIONS:** 1. What was strikingly different about Saul's appearance? 2. What had God done for His people in the past? 3. What attitude toward the rule of God did Israel's demand for a king signify? 4. What process did Samuel follow in choosing Saul as Israel's first king? 5. Why do you think Saul hid himself among the baggage?

■ **ILLUSTRATIONS:**

Challenge of Change. There was a major disturbance in a church in Lexington, Kentucky, over using modern music in worship. Most in the congregation wanted it, but the minister was opposed. The squabble became disruptive. The minister, being unable to accept change in the music for Sunday services, was finally asked to resign.

This incident took place in 1792. The minister had objected to using Isaac Watts's hymn, "O God, Our Help in Ages Past" (despite the fact that the piece was based on Psalm 90). The minister insisted that singing only *literal* translations of the Psalms should be used in worship, and he defended his position by referring to church tradition. He was unable to accept the challenge of change in using paraphrases of Scripture (such as in Watts's hymns). Sadly, he continued to denounce what he considered to be a morally compromising act.

A Time of Fellowship. Many churches will observe World Communion Sunday today (October 1). This event is a reminder that God has called us as believers to fellowship and work together for His glory. But regrettably, loneliness and isolation seem to be the norm both in the church and community of the West.

This observation is illustrated by a report about a young man living a hectic life in Washington, D.C. The man was holding a half-eaten fajita as he zipped his truck through the local traffic. He then placed his food on the dashboard, and it didn't fall apart. This method of eating has been called "dashboard dining," and it's a practice so common that fast food chains are designing fare that is not only quick to make but also easy to eat while driving. The food can't be messy, and it must also be crumble-proof, lest clean shirts and dresses become stained. Moreover, the food is designed to fit easily into one's mouth.

Other industries are also becoming involved. For instance, mini microwaves are now being marketed for cars. And trash compactors and coolers are on the horizon. Some automobiles now have fold down trays on the steering wheel to enable motorists to drive and dine at the same time.

The young man mentioned above often eats alone in his truck. He is just following the mindset of his culture. In fact, many adults in the West eat alone and on the go.

World Communion Sunday is an excellent opportunity for us as a community of believers to break with our culture. We can take time to sit down and eat together as a Christian family. As we do so, we can enjoy one another's company and be enriched by the unique encounters we experience. It's a time when we can unite in fellowship and praise God for what Jesus did at Calvary.

Transition as an Opportunity. A little over 30 years ago, Swiss watchmakers refused to see a transition in their industry as an opportunity for enlarging their business. In 1968, Switzerland had 65% of the world watch market. Around that time a Swiss research group developed the quartz movement watch. However, the country's watchmakers didn't take seriously the new development because it was so different from the traditional watches that they had long excelled at making. Ten years later the Swiss controlled less than 10% of the world watch market.

One might say that the Swiss "got stuck in history" and history left them behind. We, too, can get stuck in history, especially if we fail to see transition times as opportunities to learn and grow in our walk with the Lord.

FOR YOUTH

■ **TOPIC:** What Am I Worth?
■ **QUESTIONS:** 1. Why did Israel want a king? 2. Why was Samuel reluctant to grant the people's request? 3. Whom did God choose to be Israel's first king? 4. What about Saul made it look as if he had the potential to be a great ruler? 5. Why do you think Samuel reminded the Israelites of the rights and duties of their king?

■ **ILLUSTRATIONS:**

Mentored. An adolescent went to high school in Pojoaque, New Mexico, merely to check out the girls and cause trouble. However, he also heard about a robotics class that excited students so much that it not only met after school but also on weekends. The class the student joined was a mentoring program developed by a Pojoaque High School teacher, a roboticist from nearby Los Alamos National Laboratories, and other professionals from the arts, engineering, and business communities. The program allows teenagers to design and construct original projects while instilling confidence in themselves.

The student mentioned above was on the verge of dropping out of high school when he found new confidence and pride in himself. While in the robotics class, he designed and built an automated hydraulic system that moved a Chevy "lowrider" up and down. (The student later won an award in international robotics competition for his invention.) The adolescent is now planning to attend college.

This student is only one individual who grew in self-confidence as a result of being affirmed by teachers and peers. King Saul was also someone who benefitted from the affirmation of others, especially Samuel. The Lord used the aging prophet to give Saul greater responsibility and challenges, and to encourage the young man to do noble things for God.

Hope for the Future. Prince William, the future king of England, may be "just one of the guys" at Eton, but he is also learning the ways of a future monarch. That's one reason why he regularly visits his grandmother, Queen Elizabeth, at Windsor Castle across the Thames from Eton. The queen and the royal family are determined that there will be no mistakes in his upbringing or his career development. The queen believes that William is the hope for the future of the British monarchy.

Despite his initial objections to a king, perhaps Samuel saw young Saul as the hope for Israel's future. If so, this explains why the prophet urged Saul to serve God's people with integrity and fairness.

Signs of Encouragement. He was the first hiker to walk the Appalachian Trail from end to end 50 years earlier, but 79-year-old Earl Schaffer wanted to do it again for a third time. His trip began on May 2, 1998, at Springer Mountain, Georgia. It took Schaffer 173 days—in which he hiked 12 hours per day—to make the 2150 mile trek to Mount Katahdin, Maine. Far from being discouraged about the long hike, each day brought Schaffer signs that he was nearing his goal.

Youth sometimes look for similar signs of encouragement. In some instances they are easily visible, and on other occasions they are difficult to spot. Young Saul likewise must have looked for signs of encouragement as he began his reign as Israel's king. It's true that he had no road map for ruling the nation. But he did have the help and guidance of God. What more did Saul really need?

SAUL REJECTED AND DAVID ANOINTED

BACKGROUND SCRIPTURE: 1 Samuel 15:10—16:13
DEVOTIONAL READING: Isaiah 55:6-11

KEY VERSE: The Lord does not see as mortals see; they look on the outward appearance, but the LORD looks on the heart. 1 Samuel 16:7b.

KING JAMES VERSION

1 SAMUEL 16:1 And the LORD said unto Samuel, How long wilt thou mourn for Saul, seeing I have rejected him from reigning over Israel? fill thine horn with oil, and go, I will send thee to Jesse the Beth-lehemite: for I have provided me a king among his sons.

2 And Samuel said, How can I go? if Saul hear it, he will kill me. And the LORD said, Take an heifer with thee, and say, I am come to sacrifice to the LORD.

3 And call Jesse to the sacrifice, and I will shew thee what thou shalt do: and thou shalt anoint unto me him whom I name unto thee.

4 And Samuel did that which the LORD spake, and came to Beth-lehem. And the elders of the town trembled at his coming, and said, Comest thou peaceably?

5 And he said, Peaceably: I am come to sacrifice unto the LORD: sanctify yourselves, and come with me to the sacrifice. And he sanctified Jesse and his sons, and called them to the sacrifice.

6 And it came to pass, when they were come, that he looked on Eliab, and said, Surely the LORD's anointed is before him.

7 But the LORD said unto Samuel, Look not on his countenance, or on the height of his stature; because I have refused him: for the LORD seeth not as man seeth; for man looketh on the outward appearance, but the LORD looketh on the heart. . . .

11 And Samuel said unto Jesse, Are here all thy children? And he said, There remaineth yet the youngest, and, behold, he keepeth the sheep. And Samuel said unto Jesse, Send and fetch him: for we will not sit down till he come hither.

12 And he sent, and brought him in. Now he was ruddy, and withal of a beautiful countenance, and goodly to look to. And the LORD said, Arise, anoint him: for this is he.

13 Then Samuel took the horn of oil, and anointed him in the midst of his brethren: and the Spirit of the LORD came upon David from that day forward. So Samuel rose up, and went to Ramah.

NEW REVISED STANDARD VERSION

1 SAMUEL 16:1 The LORD said to Samuel, "How long will you grieve over Saul? I have rejected him from being king over Israel. Fill your horn with oil and set out; I will send you to Jesse the Bethlehemite, for I have provided for myself a king among his sons."
2 Samuel said, "How can I go? If Saul hears of it, he will kill me." And the LORD said, "Take a heifer with you, and say, 'I have come to sacrifice to the LORD.'
3 Invite Jesse to the sacrifice, and I will show you what you shall do; and you shall anoint for me the one whom I name to you." 4 Samuel did what the LORD commanded, and came to Bethlehem. The elders of the city came to meet him trembling, and said, "Do you come peaceably?" 5 He said, "Peaceably; I have come to sacrifice to the LORD; sanctify yourselves and come with me to the sacrifice." And he sanctified Jesse and his sons and invited them to the sacrifice.

6 When they came, he looked on Eliab and thought, "Surely the LORD's anointed is now before the LORD."
7 But the LORD said to Samuel, "Do not look on his appearance or on the height of his stature, because I have rejected him; for the LORD does not see as mortals see; they look on the outward appearance, but the LORD looks on the heart." . . .

11 Samuel said to Jesse, "Are all your sons here?" And he said, "There remains yet the youngest, but he is keeping the sheep." And Samuel said to Jesse, "Send and bring him; for we will not sit down until he comes here." 12 He sent and brought him in. Now he was ruddy, and had beautiful eyes, and was handsome. The LORD said, "Rise and anoint him; for this is the one."
13 Then Samuel took the horn of oil, and anointed him in the presence of his brothers; and the spirit of the LORD came mightily upon David from that day forward. Samuel then set out and went to Ramah.

6

45

Monday, October 2	1 Samuel 15:1-9	*Attack against the Amalekites*
Tuesday, October 3	1 Samuel 15:10-16	*A New Word*
Wednesday, October 4	1 Samuel 15:17-23	*The Confrontation*
Thursday, October 5	1 Samuel 15:24-29	*God Rejects Saul as King*
Friday, October 6	1 Samuel 15:30-35	*Saul's Confession and Samuel's Departure*
Saturday, October 7	1 Samuel 16:1-5	*Samuel Is Sent to Bethlehem*
Sunday, October 8	1 Samuel 16:6-13	*David Is Anointed as King*

BACKGROUND

Ever since the monarchy had been inaugurated at Mizpah, there were those who questioned Saul's ability to command an army in battle (1 Sam. 10:17-27). But then the king led the Israelites in victory over the Ammonites, who had attacked Jabesh-gilead (11:1-13). This prompted Samuel to assemble the Israelites at Gilgal to reaffirm Saul's kingship. There the Israelites enthusiastically endorsed him as their ruler (11:14-15).

At Saul's coronation ceremony, Samuel addressed the people. In his message he urged the king and the Israelites to revere the Lord, serve Him wholeheartedly, and heed His commands. If the people and their monarch obeyed God, it would go well for them. But if they rebelled against the Lord by refusing to heed His decrees, then they would experience calamity (12:14-15).

Saul's unwillingness to do exactly as God had commanded was a prime reason for his downfall as king. For instance, in the continuing war with Philistia, Saul disobeyed what Samuel had specifically told him to do. (As a prophet, Samuel spoke for God in such matters.) As a result of this transgression, Saul learned that his dynasty would not last but rather be given to someone else (13:7-14).

Later in the heat of battle against the Philistines, Saul made a rash and foolish oath that displeased the Lord (14:24-46). Then, in a battle against the Amalekites, Saul failed to completely destroy the enemy. Instead, Saul spared the life of Agag (the Amalekite king) and kept the best the livestock that appealed to him and his soldiers. Because Saul refused to obey God's decrees, the Lord rejected him from being king. And because Saul had decided not to execute Agag, Samuel had to do the grisly act himself on behalf of the Lord (15:1-33).

Samuel then returned to his hometown of Ramah. He never again went to meet with Saul, but he constantly mourned for the king (15:34-35).

NOTES ON THE PRINTED TEXT

We can understand why Samuel was grieved over the state of affairs in Israel. Though the nation's first king had experienced some military success in battle, he failed to win the battle of sin raging in his own life. He allowed his wayward desires, rather than the Lord, to rule his heart.

Apparently Samuel had mourned a long time for Saul. At some point the Lord said to Samuel, *"How long will you grieve over Saul?"* (16:1). The idea is that the grieving period had lasted long enough and now it was time to move on.

God, for His part, had *"rejected [Saul] from being king over Israel"* (16:1). That's why He directed Samuel to fill his ram's horn with olive oil and go to Bethlehem (a town that was about five miles southwest of Jerusalem). There the prophet would find a man named Jesse. The Lord had selected one of his sons to be the new king of Israel.

Samuel, however, was concerned about how Saul would react when he learned about the matter. The Lord responded with an ingenious plan. Samuel was to take a heifer with him and say that he had come to make a sacrifice to the Lord (16:2). Samuel was also to *"invite Jesse to the sacrifice"* (16:3). At that time God would show the prophet which of Jesse's sons to anoint as king.

Though Samuel feared for his life, he did not hedge on obeying God. Rather, Samuel *did what the LORD commanded* (16:4). When the prophet arrived at Bethlehem, the leaders of the town became afraid. Perhaps the unexpected nature of the visit caused them to wonder if Samuel had come to bring judgment on them (7:15-16). When questioned about the nature of his visit, Samuel announced, *"Peaceably; I have come to sacrifice to the LORD"* (16:5).

The prophet then instructed the people to ceremonially purify themselves in preparation for the sacrifice to be made. Apparently Samuel personally supervised the purification of Jesse and his sons.

When Jesse's sons arrived, Samuel took one look at Eliab (the oldest son) and thought, *"Surely the LORD's anointed is now before the LORD"* (16:6). Evidently the appearance and stature of Eliab commended him to leadership. But these were also the same things that had commended Saul (9:2).

Unlike people, who tended to look at one's outward appearance, God looked the heart. He thus told Samuel, *"Do not look on his appearance or on the height of his stature, because I have rejected him; for the LORD does not see as mortals see; they look on the outward appearance, but the LORD looks on the heart"* (16:7).

Then Jesse paraded each of his sons before Samuel. But the prophet announced that the Lord had not chosen any of them (16:8-10). Samuel next asked Jesse, *"Are all your sons here?"* (16:11). The father indicated that his youngest son was still out in the fields watching the sheep. Samuel directed Jesse to send for him immediately. In fact, the prophet declared, *"we will not sit down until he comes here."*

Jesse thereupon had his youngest son brought to the ceremony. Samuel saw that the youth was *ruddy, and had beautiful eyes, and was handsome* (16:12). The Lord revealed that this lad was the person whom Samuel should anoint. In obedience, the prophet *took the horn of oil, and anointed him in the presence of his brothers* (16:13).

David was Jesse's youngest son. When Samuel anointed the youth, *the spirit of the LORD came mightily upon David from that day forward* (16:13). Many challenges lay ahead for the young man, and he would surely need God's power and guidance to face them.

SUGGESTIONS TO TEACHERS

Saul made many wrong choices, and these eventually cost him his kingship. Basically, his choices showed that he refused to follow God's directives. When charged by Samuel to obey God, and when challenged to choose God's ways, Saul repeatedly failed the Lord, the Israelites, and himself. This week's lesson points out the challenge of choosing to follow God throughout our lives.

1. DISOBEDIENCE. Saul tried to excuse his disobedience to God by claiming that he had spared the captured livestock in order to make a special sacrifice (1 Sam. 15:9, 14-15). Samuel, of course, saw through the king's lame explanation. No matter how clever we may be in trying to evade God's will, He recognizes our efforts for what they really are, namely, disobedience.

2. INSINCERITY. When questioned further, Saul continued to insist that his decision to disobey God was acceptable. But, as Samuel declared, obedience is far more important to God than sacrifice (15:17-23). We are foolish if we try to cover up our disobedience to God by insincere acts of piety.

3. REJECTION. Saul's continued acts of disobedience deeply saddened and upset Samuel. The Lord told His trusted servant, *"I regret that I made Saul king, for he has turned back from following me, and has not carried out my commands"* (15:10). And Samuel later declared to Saul, *"The LORD has torn the kingdom of Israel from you this very day, and has given it to a neighbor of yours"* (15:28). Here is a reminder to us as God's chosen people to obey Him in all that we do.

4. SELECTION. Samuel, knowing that God had rejected Saul as king, anointed young David as Israel's next ruler. Samuel knew that he was placing himself in danger by selecting David while Saul was still the nation's king. Nevertheless, Samuel accepted the risk out of his loyalty to God. This reminds us that some of our choices are difficult because of the risks involved in being a Christian. We can accept the risks, for our eyes are on the heavenly reward (Heb. 11:24-28).

FOR ADULTS

■ TOPIC: The Challenge of Choosing

■ QUESTIONS: 1. Why was Samuel grieving over Saul? 2. What did God tell Samuel to do with his horn filled with oil? 3. What concern did Samuel have about going to Bethlehem? 4. Why did Samuel initially think that Eliab (Jesse's oldest son) was the one whom God had chosen to be Israel's next king? 5. What happened to David immediately after Samuel anointed him?

■ **ILLUSTRATIONS:**

Morning-Glory Fizzle. A "fizzle" often happens in many realms of life. For example, in professional baseball coaches talk about the "morning-glory" syndrome. That name is given to young recruits who perform marvelously in spring practice in Florida or Arizona. But then as they travel north and experience the lengthy season, they begin to wilt like a morning-glory flower. By June their batting average drops to an unacceptable level. And by July they are released from their team.

The reign of Saul was like a "morning-glory" plant. At first, he seemed to have everything going for him as Israel's new king. After all, he was tall, handsome, and seemingly humble. But the promise of being a great leader was not fulfilled. He lacked the patience, fortitude, and willingness to remain obedient to God. Consequently, he fizzled out in his service. It's important for us to consider how we can prevent this from happening in our life of service to the Lord.

Silly Choice. The last time a full eclipse of the moon occurred, a survey revealed that more people in Washington, D.C., chose to view the dramatic event on their television screens than go outside their homes and see the phenomenon firsthand. The opportunity to personally witness such a rare event was available to them. But instead they chose the convenience of a picture tube.

There seems to be a spiritual lesson here. We often choose to experience life indirectly through radio and television broadcasts and the movies, rather than directly in one-to-one encounters with others. And tragically we prevent ourselves from being influential servants of God in a variety of daily events and activities.

Challenge, Choice, and Change. The Methodist movement began when John Wesley overcame his high church prejudices and brought himself to proclaim the Gospel in the open air before the common people. Wesley began preaching the message of Christ to a group of people who had assembled on Haddam Mount, which is outside Bristol, England.

Wesley later wrote in his *Journal* for March 31, 1739: "I have been all my life (till very lately) so tenacious of every point relating to decency and order, that I should have thought the saving of souls almost a sin, if it had not been done in a church." When Wesley went out to preach on the afternoon of April 2, 1739, he later noted in his *Journal:* "At four in the afternoon, I submitted to be more vile, and proclaimed in the highways the glad tidings of salvation, speaking from a little eminence in a ground adjoining to the city, to about three thousand people."

Such was Wesley's initial feeling about preaching in the open air. Nevertheless, despite his misgivings, he saw it as an opportunity for ministry and decided to change his ways. He made the right choice, for he saw many people trust in Christ for salvation. Wesley was willing to submit himself to the will of God, and the Lord greatly blessed him in his ministry.

■ TOPIC: What Really Counts?

■ QUESTIONS: 1. Why had God rejected Saul from being Israel's king? 2. Why was God sending Samuel to Bethlehem? 3. What did God say Samuel should do to prevent Saul from getting suspicious about his trip to Bethlehem? 4. What did God mean when He told Samuel that He looked on a person's heart (1 Sam. 15:7)? 5. Whom did Samuel anoint among Jesse's sons, and what did the youth look like?

■ ILLUSTRATIONS:

Minor Flaws Tests on iron rivets retrieved from the sunken liner Titanic have indicated that all of them had an unusually high slag content. William Garzke, the chief scientist of the Titanic investigation, announced this startling information while at the national meeting of the American Chemical Society.

Slag is an impurity that can contaminate forged iron. Normally, high quality rivets contain about three percent slag. But the Titanic's 3,000,000 rivets showed a level of nine percent. This made them especially weak and more likely to snap after the liner hit an iceberg. While stronger rivets would not have prevented the liner from sinking, the theory is that the vessel would have floated longer, allowing enough time for all the passengers on board to be rescued.

From this we see that even a minor flaw can cause devastating effects. For example, Saul's moral blemishes eventually caught up with him, and led the Lord to reject him as king and select another person to lead Israel.

Fame's Fifteen Minutes. The late artist of junk culture, Andy Warhol, once bellowed, "In the future, everybody will be famous for at least fifteen minutes!" In other words, fame is shortlived. It suddenly elevates people before the public. And then as quickly, they fade away. Consider Saul. For the moment he commanded power and prestige as Israel's king. But then he rebelled against God. As a result, the Lord rejected him, and he faded off the scene of history. What a tragic end!

Dry Rot. When the *U.S.S. Constitution* ("Old Ironsides") was restored in 1997, one suspicion was confirmed—dry rot existed in the vessel. While saltwater prevents decay, fresh water rots wood. The salt water had prevented decay below the waterline of the ship, but rain water had brought in wood-hungry organisms like marine borers. Rain also collected in the dark, warm crannies and compartments, which allowed airborne fungi to attack the wood and produce dry rot.

Sometimes people go through spiritual "dry rot." Events weaken them, sap their strength, and speed up the moral decay within them. Saul is an outstanding example of this phenomenon. Only the grace of God can spare us from experiencing something similar in our lives.

David Mourns Saul and Jonathan

BACKGROUND SCRIPTURE: 1 Samuel 31:1; 2 Samuel 1:27; 1 Chronicles 10
DEVOTIONAL READING: Psalm 77:1-9

KEY VERSE: Your glory, O Israel, lies slain upon your high places! How the mighty have fallen! 2 Samuel 1:19.

KING JAMES VERSION

2 SAMUEL 1:17 And David lamented with this lamentation over Saul and over Jonathan his son:

18 (Also he bade them teach the children of Judah the use of the bow: behold, it is written in the book of Jasher.)

19 The beauty of Israel is slain upon thy high places: how are the mighty fallen!

20 Tell it not in Gath, publish it not in the streets of Askelon; lest the daughters of the Philistines rejoice, lest the daughters of the uncircumcised triumph. . . .

22 From the blood of the slain, from the fat of the mighty, the bow of Jonathan turned not back, and the sword of Saul returned not empty.

23 Saul and Jonathan were lovely and pleasant in their lives, and in their death they were not divided: they were swifter than eagles, they were stronger than lions.

24 Ye daughters of Israel, weep over Saul, who clothed you in scarlet, with other delights, who put on ornaments of gold upon your apparel.

25 How are the mighty fallen in the midst of the battle! O Jonathan, thou was slain in thine high places.

26 I am distressed for thee, my brother Jonathan: very pleasant hast thou been unto me: thy love to me was wonderful, passing the love of women.

27 How are the mighty fallen, and the weapons of war perished!

NEW REVISED STANDARD VERSION

2 SAMUEL 1:17 David intoned this lamentation over Saul and his son Jonathan. 1:18 (He ordered that The Song of the Bow be taught to the people of Judah; it is written in the Book of Jashar.) He said:

19 Your glory, O Israel, lies slain upon
    your high places!
How the mighty have fallen!

20 Tell it not in Gath,
    proclaim it not in the streets of
        Ashkelon;
or the daughters of the Philistines will
    rejoice,
the daughters of the uncircumcised
    will exult. . . .

22 From the blood of the slain,
    from the fat of the mighty,
the bow of Jonathan did not turn back,
    nor the sword of Saul return
        empty.

23 Saul and Jonathan, beloved and
        lovely!
    In life and in death they were not
        divided;
they were swifter than eagles,
    they were stronger than lions.

24 O daughters of Israel, weep over
        Saul,
    who clothed you with crimson,
        in luxury,
    who put ornaments of gold on
        your apparel.

25 How the mighty have fallen
    in the midst of the battle!
Jonathan lies slain upon your
        high places.

26 I am distressed for you, my brother
        Jonathan;
    greatly beloved were you to me;
        your love to me was wonderful,
        passing the love of women.

27 How the mighty have fallen,
    and the weapons of war perished!

Monday, October 9	1 Samuel 31:1-7	*The Battle of Mount Gilboa*
Tuesday, October 10	1 Samuel 31:8-13	*The Rescue of Saul's Body*
Wednesday, October 11	2 Samuel 1:1-16	*The Amalekite Messenger*
Thursday, October 12	2 Samuel 1:17-27	*David's Lament*
Friday, October 13	Psalm 77:1-9	*Comfort in Times of Distress*
Saturday, October 14	1 Chronicles 10:1-7	*Death of Saul and His Sons*
Sunday, October 15	1 Chronicles 10:8-14	*Burials and a Judgment against Saul*

BACKGROUND

Just as the Spirit of the Lord came upon David, so too it left Saul, and an evil spirit began tormenting him (1 Sam. 16:13-14). Meanwhile, David's winsome personality and bold exploits won him increasing popularity (18:7). This caused Saul to resent David, and the king tried to have him murdered (18:8-9).

David quickly became an outlaw. But despite his plight, he proved resourceful. He formed a private army in the Judean wilderness (22:1-2). And as a local warlord, he defended his fellow Israelites against their enemies (23:1-5; 30:1-20). The nobility of David's character is seen in the fact that he spared Saul even when he had the opportunity to murder the king (24:1-22; 26:1-25).

As David continued to rise in power and popularity, Saul seemed to experience a corresponding decline. For instance, Saul's son Jonathan went against his father's wishes by becoming loyal to David (20:1-16). Also, in one episode, as Saul was pursing David and his followers, the king ordered the execution of many priests of the Lord (22:1-19). Furthermore, Saul violated Scripture by using a medium to communicate with the spirit of Samuel, who had died (28:1-19).

The tragic end came for Saul and Jonathan in a battle against the Philistines on the slopes of Mount Gilboa. As the enemy closed in on Saul, they killed three of his sons—Jonathan, Abinadab, and Malchishua. Saul then ended his own life by impaling himself with his own weapon (31:1-6).

Instead of gloating over the death of his former persecutor, David composed a moving song that lamented Saul's demise. David's sorrow in learning about the death of his dear friend, Jonathan, is also expressed in the song.

NOTES ON THE PRINTED TEXT

David and his men had just defeated the Amalekites in battle and returned to Ziklag when the news of Saul's death reached them. (Ziklag was a Philistine city.) Because Saul had driven David out of Israel, he had to pretend to be loyal to Achish, a Philistine ruler (1 Sam. 27). At Ziklag David was safe from Saul.

The report of the demise of Saul and Jonathan filled David with sorrow. He expressed his grief by composing a *lamentation over Saul and his son Jonathan* (2 Sam. 1:17). David then ordered that the Song of the Bow be taught to the people of Judah (1:18). (According to 1 Samuel 18:4, the bow had been one of Jonathan's prized weapons.) The people of Judah were to share in David's sorrow.

This funeral song was recorded in the now lost Book of Jashar. This document may have been a collection of heroic deeds of various Israelites, or a collection of war songs, or a poetic epic detailing various Hebrew conquests. Whatever the exact nature of the book, it was an important literary work.

David began his lament by declaring that Israel's glory *lies slain upon your high places!* (2 Sam. 1:19). This is a reference to Mount Gilboa, where the warriors had died in battle. It was a sad time, for the nation's *mighty [had] fallen!*

David wished that the news of the victory could be kept from the Philistine populace, though knowing the Philistines as well as he did, he undoubtedly suspected that the enemy would already have been rejoicing. David mentioned Ashkelon and Gath as representatives of all the Philistine cities (1:20).

David called the enemy *uncircumcised* (1:20). This was a term of contempt that not only underscored Israel's covenant relationship with God but also the illegitimacy of the Philistine presence in the land. David hoped that calamity, not prosperity, would be visited upon the enemy of Israel (1:21).

David next praised the military prowess of Saul and Jonathan. David mentioned *the bow of Jonathan* and *the sword of Saul* (1:22) to underscore that these two warriors of Israel used their weapons with great power, accuracy, and effectiveness. Thus, though the two had died in battle, their deaths were not in vain.

David then spotlighted the bond of love that had existed between Saul and Jonathan, his son. To their dying day they remained loyal to one another. *Saul and Jonathan, beloved and lovely! In life and in death they were not divided; they were swifter than eagles, they were stronger than lions* (1:23).

David especially appealed to the women of Israel to mourn the demise of their king. The nobility of David's character is evident as he recounted how Saul—despite all his flaws—greatly enriched the lives of those under his rule. *O daughters of Israel, weep over Saul, who clothed you with crimson, in luxury, who put ornaments of gold on your apparel* (1:24).

With the repetition of the lament's refrain, *How the mighty have fallen* (1:25), David shifted his attention to Jonathan. Indeed, these two had enjoyed a close friendship that began not long after David's victory over a Philistine named Goliath. Scripture says that *the soul of Jonathan was bound to the soul of David, and Jonathan loved him as his own soul* (1 Sam. 18:1). We also learn that *Jonathan made a covenant with David, because he loved him as his own soul* (18:3).

We thus can understand why David was distressed over the death of Jonathan. David declared, *greatly beloved were you to me; your love to me was wonderful, passing the love of women* (2 Sam. 1:26). It would be incorrect to read into David's remarks any sexual connotations. The idea is that their friendship was a noble, loyal, and selfless devotion, perhaps unlike anything either of them had experienced with a woman.

SUGGESTIONS TO TEACHERS

This week's lesson addresses the loss of loved ones. Some in your class may find this a difficult subject to talk about. But we all must deal with the deaths of people who are dear to us. Losing a spouse, child, parent, close family member, or friend tests our faith. The account of David mourning the deaths of Saul and Jonathan should bring insights into ways we may grieve.

1. TRAUMA OF LOSS. David did not make light of his feelings of loss, and he did not gloss over the finality of death. God's people are able to look death in the face and recognize its reality. Of course, Jesus is our best role model. He empathized with those who mourned the loss of their loved ones. We also remember that because of Jesus' resurrection, believers will overcome death.

2. TRAGEDY. No person except Jesus ever completed everything that he or she wanted to accomplish during his or her lifetime. Death always leaves a person with unfinished business, with unfulfilled plans. Perhaps part of the tragedy of the deaths of Saul and Jonathan was their inability to carry out all that they may have wanted to accomplish. Undoubtedly, David realized this and was sad because of it.

3. TRIBUTES TO THE BELOVED. David paid tribute to his departed friends. This was a healthy way of handling the challenge of loss. We too can tell others what our departed loved ones meant to us. We can also pray to God about our loss. Genuine prayer involves speaking openly to the Lord about our innermost feelings. We can also offer thanks to Him for the privilege of sharing in the lives of those who have subsequently died.

4. TEARS OVER LOSING LOVED ONES. David wept over his loss, and so did Jesus. Tears of bereavement are acceptable to God. Sometimes in our detached way of handling our feelings of loss, we try to be something other than human. Discuss with the class how they can properly express their grief.

5. TRANSITIONS AFTER ACCEPTING LOSS. David knew that his life was forever changed now that Saul and Jonathan had died. David faced the challenge of change with courage, and so must we when a loved one dies. Thankfully, the Holy Spirit—the Comforter—enables us to make such a difficult transition.

6. TEACHINGS. Have the students take a few moments to seriously consider 1 Chronicles 10:13. What does this say about the lasting legacy of Saul?

FOR ADULTS

■ TOPIC: The Challenge of Loss

■ QUESTIONS: 1. Why do you think David wrote a lamentation over the deaths of Saul and Jonathan? 2. What attitude toward Saul did David convey in his funeral song? 3. How had Saul benefited the people of Israel during his reign? 4. What is the kind of response Christians should have when confronted with the death of a loved one? 5. What is the promise through Christ that believers have when facing the death of loved ones in the faith?

■ ILLUSTRATIONS:

Faith Walk. In an article that Gregg Hartung wrote for the newsletter of the Pittsburgh Presbytery, he noted that Ruth Rylander's daughter, Lynn, was 15 years old when she was diagnosed as having the deadliest form of leukemia. (Ruth received the Peaceseeker of the Year award at the General Assembly.) Ruth described the ensuing months as follows:

> It was a grueling experience. There were lots of blood transfusions, and lots of reactions following high fevers and chills. I was at the hospital as much as I possibly could be. My husband would come in after work and stay with Lynn until bedtime.
>
> Lynn went into remission for one year. I found myself to be completely out of step with the rest of the family. I was irritable and argumentative. I considered it my job to make everything normal again. Yet I could not make things be the way they were before we found out about Lynn's illness. I realized that I was trying to control life itself, and that this is God's role, not mine. When you try to control everything, you are playing God. I couldn't be God!
>
> The doctor told Lynn that she was slipping and needed more chemotherapy. But Lynn said to me on the way home in the car that she didn't want any more chemo. I replied, "Lynn, you had a good year. If it hadn't been for the chemo, you wouldn't be here."
>
> When Lynn died, I told my pastor that I wished I wasn't a Christian because I wouldn't feel so guilty for being so angry with God. He said to me, "If you didn't have God, what would you do with your anger? God can handle your anger. Give it to Him." I finally felt free from the bondage of hatred and anger.

When her daughter was suffering, Ruth thought about others who had suffered throughout the ages (for instance, in death camps). Ruth noted the following:

> The difference between my daughter's situation and theirs was that there were caring people around Lynn. There weren't caring people in the death camps, and there aren't any when you're starving out in the middle of a poor country. We are the ones who make the difference. We are the ones who carry God's message. That's why I'm working in peacemaking and justice.

This realization, and the desire to alleviate the suffering of others, is what led Ruth further into peacemaking. This is her way of doing something constructive in the aftermath of her daughter's death. Ruth says that peacemaking "has to do with reconciliation and wholeness."

Answer to the Agnostic. The beloved Boston Episcopal Bishop Phillips Brooks was going through what he knew was his final illness. In his pain and weakness, he preferred not to receive visitors and politely declined offers of those wishing to call on him.

One day the famous agnostic, Robert Ingersoll, appeared at the bishop's home to offer his best wishes. Phillips Brooks and Ingersoll had known each other for years and had often had friendly clashes over the Bible and faith. Despite their profound disagreement, the bishop won Ingersoll's respect. When Bishop Brooks heard that Ingersoll had come to call, he sent word to have him sent up to his room immediately.

"I appreciate this very much," Ingersoll said to the ill bishop, "but why do you see me, an agnostic, when you refuse to see all your Christian friends?" Brooks quietly replied, "I feel confident of seeing my friends in the next world, but this is my last opportunity to see you!"

The Strong Foundation. Green Bay Packer legend Bart Starr and his wife, Cherry, were good parents. This is evidenced by the fact that their son, Bart Jr., was a loving son, a good student, and an outstanding athlete.

During Bart Jr.'s freshman year at college, he became addicted to cocaine. The parents arranged for treatment at a private facility, and they continued to surround their son with their warmth and concern. The young man, with his parents' help, became the owner of a pet shop in the Tampa area. He began to talk about returning to school. He kept in close touch with his folks, phoning every day, and telling them how much he appreciated their love and prayers.

Three weeks after sending Bart Starr a beautifully written Father's Day letter of appreciation for all his dad had meant, Bart Jr. failed to call his parents. That's when his father decided to fly to Tampa. He found the shades drawn at his son's place. And inside, Bart Starr found the young man's body on the floor. The death was attributed officially to cardiac arrhythmia. Bart and Cherry wept, and in their grief insisted on telling the truth in the hope of helping others. A trace of cocaine had been found. Though it was not an overdose, it was sufficient enough to kill.

The tragedy of their beloved son's death has prompted the Starrs to help others. In their grief, they also have grown in their faith. Bart testified, "If we put God first in our lives and really build from there, there's no guarantee that these things won't happen. But at least you have a very strong foundation that doesn't crumble under you" (*Parade Magazine,* July 30, 1989).

 FOR YOUTH

■ TOPIC: When You Lose a Friend
■ QUESTIONS: 1. What impresses you most about David's lament? Why? 2. Why do you think David honored Saul, especially after the miserable way the king had treated him? 3. What purposes did David's mourn-

ing serve for the nation of Israel? 4. How can we honor those who have fallen in battle? 5. Why are weeping and grieving appropriate for God's people to do?

■ ILLUSTRATIONS:

Unending Separation. Zvi Kamionka was eight years old when he escaped from Kalushin, Poland, in 1940. Months later, 2000 Jews, including 70 of Kamionka's relatives, were murdered by Nazi death squads. Today they lie buried in a mass unmarked grave under a green field dotted with daisies.

Kamionka cannot rest. Like many of his fellow Polish Jews, he wants to bring the bones of his relatives to Israel for burial. He fears that nothing will be remembered of them.

In a surprise move, a humanitarian Polish pathologist agreed to help the Israelis identify the victims' remains using DNA testing. This occurred in August, 1998. Forensic specialists in Israel, though, cautioned that finding relatives would be next to an impossible task. They considered it a noble but unrealistic dream, given the hundreds of thousands of Jews buried in Poland. Undaunted, Kamionka still wants the bodies of his deceased relatives brought to Israel, along with all the bones of Holocaust victims from other mass graves, regardless of whether they can be identified.

Many, like Kamionka, experience the death and separation of loved ones. David was no different. Saul and Jonathan had been close to him, and that's why David wanted them remembered.

Need for Grieving and Mourning. Steve was 15 when his mother died from breast cancer. Over the next three years his grades dropped. He also seemed to lose interest in sports and academics. His concerned father took him to a counselor. Steve confessed, "The day my mom died, I thought my heart had broken. I wanted to cry but everyone said, 'Be tough. Be a man. You can take it. Face up to it and get on with your life.' "

Looking back on the funeral, Steve remembered that he did not cry. The youth related, "I was so sad. The grief just built up inside me. I thought about my mother so much, but no one ever talked about her. I feel as if I can't take it, and I don't know what to do."

Steve is not alone. He is one of thousands of teenagers who experience the death of someone they love. (One in 20 children in the United States experience the death of a parent before the age of 12.) Some adolescents do grieve. However, many others never mourn.

For sound mental health, both grieving and mourning should be encouraged among people of all ages. Consider David. He grieved and mourned over the death of Saul and Jonathan, and urged others to do the same. We see that David was not afraid to tell God about his struggles and fears and to depend on Him to overcome them.

Mourning Customs. An Orthodox Jew named Joshua was well versed in mourning customs when his father died. Joshua knew that he was obligated to observe the ritual of mourning to help him realize that his loved one was gone and to fill the void in his life in a constructive way.

Centuries of tradition dictated the religious rites Joshua was to perform. He cut a black ribbon as a reminder of all the dark moments in the history of his people. Joshua performed this ritual while standing up to remind him that he should meet his sorrow standing upright. The tear was made on the left side of the heart as a reminder that the deceased person was his parent.

Immediately after the funeral, Joshua began seven days of Shiva, or intensive mourning. While he was exempt from many of the mourning rites, he did not miss the family gatherings, which gave him an opportunity to mingle with his loved ones. A lighted candle burned for seven days to remind those present that the Lord was their light and salvation. After the seven days of intensive mourning came 30 more days of Schloshim, or ritual mourning. Normal activity was resumed but places of entertainment were avoided.

Joshua also attended a Minyan. This is a service where he pledged or dedicated his life to God in remembrance of his father. In addition, each time Joshua recited the Kaddish (a Jewish prayer), he not only recalled his father but also affirmed his trust in God's presence. Finally, on the anniversary of his father's death, Joshua recited the Kaddish as he lit a commemorative candle.

This young Jew later described how all these practices helped him handle his grief in a positive way. He said that he performed all these rites with others as part of the community's way of mourning their loss. He furthermore noted that it was their way of reflecting their continued trust in God.

David urged the people of Judah to mourn. He wanted them as a community of God's people to grieve over the loss of Saul and Jonathan and thereby express their continued trust in God.

DAVID BECOMES KING OF ALL ISRAEL

BACKGROUND SCRIPTURE: 2 Samuel 2—5; 1 Chronicles 11:1-3
DEVOTIONAL READING: Psalm 78:67-72

KEY VERSE: The Lord said to [David]: "It is you who shall be shepherd of my people Israel, you who shall be ruler over Israel." 2 Samuel 5:2.

KING JAMES VERSION

2 SAMUEL 2:1 And it came to pass after this, that David enquired of the LORD, saying, Shall I go up into any of the cities of Judah? And the LORD said unto him, Go up. And David said, Whither shall I go up? And he said, Unto Hebron.

2 So David went up thither, and his two wives also, Ahinoam the Jezreelitess, and Abigail Nabal's wife the Carmelite.

3 And his men that were with him did David bring up, every man with his household: and they dwelt in the cities of Hebron.

4 And the men of Judah came, and there they anointed David king over the house of Judah. And they told David, saying, That the men of Jabesh-gilead were they that buried Saul.

5 And David sent messengers unto the men of Jabesh-gilead, and said unto them, Blessed be ye of the LORD, that ye have shewed this kindness unto your lord, even unto Saul, and have buried him.

6 And now the LORD shew kindness and truth unto you: and I also will requite you this kindness, because ye have done this thing.

7 Therefore now let your hands be strengthened, and be ye valiant: for your master Saul is dead, and also the house of Judah have anointed me king over them. . . .

5:1 Then came all the tribes of Israel to David unto Hebron, and spake, saying, Behold, we are thy bone and thy flesh.

2 Also in time past, when Saul was king over us, thou wast he that leddest out and broughtest in Israel: and the LORD said to thee, Thou shalt feed my people Israel, and thou shalt be a captain over Israel.

3 So all the elders of Israel came to the king to Hebron; and king David made a league with them in Hebron before the LORD: and they anointed David king over Israel.

4 David was thirty years old when he began to reign, and he reigned forty years.

5 In Hebron he reigned over Judah seven years and six months: and in Jerusalem he reigned thirty and three years over all Israel and Judah.

NEW REVISED STANDARD VERSION

2 SAMUEL 2:1 After this David inquired of the LORD, "Shall I go up into any of the cities of Judah?" The LORD said to him, "Go up." David said, "To which shall I go up?" He said, "To Hebron." 2 So David went up there, along with his two wives, Ahinoam of Jezreel, and Abigail the widow of Nabal of Carmel. 3 David brought up the men who were with him, every one with his household; and they settled in the towns of Hebron. 4 Then the people of Judah came, and there they anointed David king over the house of Judah. When they told David, "It was the people of Jabesh-gilead who buried Saul," 5 David sent messengers to the people of Jabesh-gilead, and said to them, "May you be blessed by the LORD, because you showed this loyalty to Saul your lord, and buried him! 6 Now may the LORD show steadfast love and faithfulness to you! And I too will reward you because you have done this thing. 7 Therefore let your hands be strong, and be valiant; for Saul your lord is dead, and the house of Judah has anointed me king over them." . . .

5:1 Then all the tribes of Israel came to David at Hebron, and said, "Look, we are your bone and flesh. 2 For some time, while Saul was king over us, it was you who led out Israel and brought it in. The LORD said to you: It is you who shall be shepherd of my people Israel, you who shall be ruler over Israel." 3 So all the elders of Israel came to the king at Hebron; and King David made a covenant with them at Hebron before the LORD, and they anointed David king over Israel. 4 David was thirty years old when he began to reign, and he reigned forty years. 5 At Hebron he reigned over Judah seven years and six months; and at Jerusalem he reigned over all Israel and Judah thirty-three years.

Monday, October 16	2 Samuel 2:1-11	*The Rival Kings*
Tuesday, October 17	2 Samuel 3:6-21	*Abner Defects to David*
Wednesday, October 18	2 Samuel 3:22-27	*The Plot against Abner*
Thursday, October 19	2 Samuel 3:27-39	*Joab Murders Abner*
Friday, October 20	2 Samuel 4:1-12	*The Death of Ishbaal*
Saturday, October 21	2 Samuel 5:1-12	*David, King of Israel, Captures Jerusalem*
Sunday, October 22	1 Chronicles 11:1-9	*David Rules Israel from Jerusalem*

BACKGROUND

David was publicly consecrated king at the city of Hebron, which at that time became the capital of the southern kingdom of Judah (2 Sam. 2:1-5). The northern tribes continued to claim allegiance to the house of Saul, which was headed by Saul's surviving son, Ishbaal. However, the real power in the northern tribes lay with a wily general named Abner (2:8-11).

Ishbaal carried on a war against David for seven years until Abner, the strong man of the state, finally realized the futility of the fight against David, and brokered a pact with him. Ishbaal was murdered by two from his inner circle. Israel's elders and warrior leaders then came to Hebron and joined the people of Judah in an anointing ceremony for David (2:12—5:5).

Though relatively young, David had proven to be an astute politician. He had shown the right combination of leniency and sensitivity in winning the trust of the northern kingdom by respecting Saul and Jonathan. Later, David refused to honor Ishbaal's murderers, and gave a proper burial to Abner, whom Joab (David's general) had treacherously assassinated.

Realizing that the united kingdom of Israel and Judah needed a new and neutral city for its capital, David shrewdly selected Jerusalem, which had been controlled by the Jebusites. David's commandos overtook this strategic fortress, and he renamed it the "City of David." For the next 33 years, David reigned as king over all Israel from Jerusalem (5:6-7).

Early in his reign, David turned his attention to the Philistines and decisively defeated them (5:17-25). He also quelled inhabitants to the east of Canaan who had menaced the Israelites for generations. Eventually, David became the undisputed leader of the area stretching south into the Sinai and north to the mountains of Lebanon, east from the lands across the Jordan (perhaps as far as the Euphrates) and west to the Mediterranean (8:1-14).

NOTES ON THE PRINTED TEXT

With Saul dead, Israel needed a new leader. Through the years of his exile, David had carefully and deliberately ingratiated himself with the elders of Judah. Now the time had come for him to act. *After this David inquired of the LORD, "Shall I go up into any of the cities of Judah?"* (2:1)

The Lord told David, *"Go up"* (2:1). David, wanting specifics, asked, *"To which shall I go up?"* (2:1). God said, *"To Hebron."* Hebron is located 19 miles southwest of Jerusalem and 15 miles west of the Dead Sea on the road leading to Beersheba. Though Hebron rests in a valley between two ridges, it is still over 3,000 feet above sea level. This makes it the highest town in Palestine. Hebron overlooks a fertile region containing an abundance of wells and springs.

David, his family, his 600 man fighting force, and their families occupied Hebron, a move that greatly swelled the population of the city (2:2-3). At Hebron, the representatives of Judah arrived, prepared to recognize David as their new monarch. *Then the people of Judah came, and there they anointed David king over the house of Judah* (2:4).

With his control over the south firmly established, David immediately began to court the rest of the tribes of Israel. For instance, when he learned that the people of Jabesh-gilead had risked their lives to take Saul's body from Beth-shan and bury it, he commended them (1 Sam. 31:8-13). David also praised them in the name of the Lord for their commitment to Saul. *When they told David, "It was the people of Jabesh-gilead who buried Saul," David sent messengers to the people of Jabesh-gilead, and said to them, "May you be blessed by the LORD, because you showed this loyalty to Saul your lord, and buried him!"* (2:4-5).

David next offered his friendship to the people of Jabesh-gilead. *"And I too will reward you because you have done this thing"* (2:6). He did not offer material reward, but rather favor and goodwill. While encouraging them to be brave and strong, David also subtly reminded the people of Jabesh-gilead that their political future lay with him. After all, Saul was dead, and David had been anointed king. *"Therefore let your hands be strong, and be valiant; for Saul your lord is dead, and the house of Judah has anointed me king over them"* (2:7).

Despite David's efforts, the rest of Israel crowned Ishbaal, Saul's son, as king. And Abner—Saul's cousin and military commander—supported the kingship of Ishbaal and vigorously fought David's army in battle. Seven years of treachery, betrayal and power-plays followed. But David prevailed, and eventually *all the tribes of Israel came to David at Hebron* (5:1).

These leaders declared, *"Look, we are your bone and flesh"* (5:1). This was their way of affirming that a common ancestry united them. The people also acknowledged the key role David had served during Saul's reign as his military leader. *"For some time, while Saul was king over us, it was you who led out Israel and brought it in"* (5:2).

In a sense, David had led the nation by directing the Israelite troops into battle. The tribal leaders affirmed that it was the Lord's will for David to be their king. They thus invited him to shepherd them. *"The LORD said to you: It is you who shall be shepherd of my people Israel, you who shall be ruler over Israel"* (5:2).

David agreed to this request and thus made a covenant with the leaders of Israel before the Lord. This sacred pact was the basis for the leaders anointing David as their king. *So all the elders of Israel came to the king at Hebron; and King David made a covenant with them at Hebron before the LORD, and they anointed David king over Israel* (5:3). Thus began David's long and noteworthy reign over God's people (5:4-5).

SUGGESTIONS TO TEACHERS

Regardless of whether your class members realize it, they are looked upon by God as leaders in our society. The Lord has graciously chosen them to show the world how He wants everyone to live. Such spiritual leadership brings with it many challenges. This week's lesson, which is based on David's acceptance of the leadership of God's people, can serve as a guide for us as we assume our responsibilities as the Redeemer's servant-leaders.

1. RELYING ON GOD. David recognized that the Lord was his leader and guide. And David did not presume to think that he, rather than God, was supreme. Tragically, many leaders today are not so enlightened in their thinking.

2. RECONCILING FOES. David deliberately brought harmony between former enemies. For instance, he took steps to reconcile those in the northern tribes loyal to Saul with those in the southern tribes. This reminds us that accepting the challenge of leadership often involves promoting peace in the world.

3. RESOURCEFUL IN GOVERNING. David showed great resourcefulness in knitting together all the tribes of Israel. Consider David's choice of the neutral site of Jerusalem, which was midway between Israel and Judah. This decision helped bind the two once hostile factions together.

4. RELIABLE AS A LEADER. God gave David insights that enabled him to build a strong, stable government. His nation flourished through his faithful attention to God's will and the needs of the Israelites.

FOR ADULTS

■ **TOPIC:** The Challenge of Leadership
■ **QUESTIONS:** 1. Why did David seek the Lord's guidance? 2. What did the leaders of Judah do when they came to Hebron? 3. How did David try to win the support of the inhabitants of Jabesh-gilead? 4. What observations did the leaders of Israel's tribes make about David? 5. How did David and the leaders of Israel's tribes formalize their new relationship?

■ **ILLUSTRATIONS:**

True Leadership. Kirby Puckett was the star centerfielder for the Minnesota Twins for 13 years. He had a batting average of .318 in his great career, and made the All-Star lineup 10 years in a row. Puckett won six Golden Gloves for defensive play, and he was respected as a leader by his teammates.

One of the best loved and most respected ballplayers ever to be in major league baseball, Kirby Puckett was also well-known as a deeply committed Christian. His devotion and leadership showed itself not only in private life but also in the ball games.

One time the left side of Kirby's face was crushed by a pitch thrown by Cleveland Indians' pitcher Dennis Martinez. Martinez assumed that Kirby would hate him and try to retaliate. After all, this was how others acted when struck and injured by a pitcher. But Kirby called Martinez "my good friend," and blamed himself for not ducking when Martinez's fastball came at him. Kirby's teammates and other ball players knew that he meant it. His words matched his life, and his life reflected his faith.

Challenged to Show Compassionate Leadership. On December 13, 1862, at Fredericksburg, Virginia, General Robert E. Lee positioned his soldiers behind a stone wall on Marye's Heights, which was a ridge above the city. It was an ideal position from which to halt General Ambrose E. Burnside's Union attack. Even when Burnside's flanking attack failed at Prospect Hill, he went ahead with his assault. The general sent wave after wave of Union soldiers across the open under terrible fire and then up the hill toward the wall.

Not a single Federal soldier reached the wall! By nightfall, over 8,000 Union soldiers lay on the ground in the freezing air.

On the Confederate side of the wall, the cries of the Federal troops aroused the pity of Sergeant Richard R. Kirland of the Second South Carolina Regiment. He found himself unable to bear the sounds of the wounded and dying and thus decided to respond. Kirland asked for and received permission to take water to the blue-coats.

Loaded down with borrowed canteens, Kirland climbed over the wall and began to give each soldier a drink. Without a flag of truce to guarantee his safety, the sergeant moved among the wounded for over 90 minutes. He distributed water and words of comfort to the surviving soldiers. He was dubbed "The Angel of Marye's Heights" by surviving Union troops. He is remembered by both sides today by a statue beside the stone wall. The inscription on the monument reads "An American Soldier of Sublime Compassion."

Courageous Leadership. Frederick Douglass was one of the great African-American leaders of the United States. Born a slave, young Douglass ran away to freedom. The great self-emancipated slave tells how his owner, Thomas Auld, sought to prevent him from learning to read because he knew that literacy would make Douglass restless. Douglass imagined Auld saying, "It would forever unfit him to be a slave. He would at once be unmanageable, and of no value to his master. As to himself, it could do him no good, but a great deal of harm. It would make him discontented and unhappy."

In some ways, Auld was correct. Learning to read made Douglass fiercely discontented with his lot as a slave. And literacy opened him to a world of freedom that left him unwilling to accept the idea that God was pleased with him being shackled. That's why, in 1838, at the age of 20, Douglass made his daring escape from the Maryland plantation where he was enslaved. He soon became the century's most famous black orator, writer, and abolitionist.

More than 40 years later, despite objections from many of his supporters, Douglass agreed to visit his old master as he lay dying. Both men wept when they met. "The sight of him," wrote Douglass, "the changes that time had brought upon him, his tremulous hands constantly in motion, and all the circumstances of his condition affected me deeply, and for a time choked my voice and made me speechless." The unchanging Gospel is evident in Douglass's forgiveness of the man who had once enslaved him.

FOR YOUTH

■ TOPIC: Working as a Team
■ QUESTIONS: 1. Who went with David to Hebron? 2. What kind of support did David initially enjoy as king of Judah? 3. Why did all the tribes of Israel meet with David at Hebron? 4. What reasons did the Israelites give for submitting to David's rule? 5. How did the Israelites describe the nature of their relationship to David?

■ **ILLUSTRATIONS:**

Team Work. Thomas Jefferson High School (TJHS) won the Pennsylvania State Hockey honors in 1998. On their way to that championship, they beat some good teams with larger and more talented players. TJHS was coached by Don Powell, whose team system emphasized pinpoint passing and tough tight positional hockey rather than rink rushes. The young men worked together well because they put the objectives of the team ahead of their own personal desires.

Like Powell and his hockey players, David used a team approach to establish Israel as a great nation. In his case it took years to accomplish, but it was well worth the effort. Similarly, many young people have experienced the benefits of working together as a team. It has helped them to grow personally and mature spiritually.

Filled a Need. On October 27, 1998, the School Board of Clairton, Pennsylvania, and the state board of control approved Carol Gelet to be the girl's high school basketball coach. The approval of Carol was unique, for she was already coaching the boy's high school team, a team that she had led to two Western Pennsylvania championships. Now she would have a dual role.

The girl's job opened when the former coach died in September of that year. The girls felt they needed someone whom they could trust, talk to, and rely upon for both athletic and academic help. They also believed that Gelet, a special education instructor at the high school, would support them.

These high school girls were typical youth. They were willing to follow a leader who cared for them and was knowledgeable, fair, and would do what was best for everyone. Those around David felt similarly about him as their leader. They believed he was someone who cared for them and could be trusted. Most importantly, David was an individual whom God had chosen to lead His people.

Costly Action. The University of Pittsburgh's Zeta Beta Tau fraternity was disbanded on December 6, 1995, as a result of a pledge prank. The fraternity charter was revoked, and the university ceased all support. Officials also evicted the members in the university-owned housing.

The harsh punishment resulted when young pledges followed orders of the fraternity's senior members. The recruits had been sent into female dormitories and told to photograph coeds as they showered.

While the offenders argued that they were only following their leaders' orders, the university disagreed. Officials stated that the fraternity's action violated the respect and dignity due everyone on a university campus.

David saw the harmful potential in poor leadership. He also understood that the people would follow the wrong leaders as these pledges did on the campus. Eventually, the politicians and leaders, like the fraternity leaders, would violate the respect and dignity of everyone and bring disaster to the nation.

GOD'S COVENANT WITH DAVID

BACKGROUND SCRIPTURE: 2 Samuel 7; 1 Chronicles 17
DEVOTIONAL READING: 1 Kings 8:15-21

KEY VERSE: Your house and your kingdom shall be made sure forever before me; your throne shall be established forever. 2 Samuel 7:16.

KING JAMES VERSION

2 SAMUEL 7:1 And it came to pass, when the king sat in his house, and the LORD had given him rest round about from all his enemies;

2 That the king said unto Nathan the prophet, See now, I dwell in an house of cedar, but the ark of God dwelleth within curtains.

3 And Nathan said to the king, Go, do all that is in thine heart; for the LORD is with thee.

4 And it came to pass that night, that the word of the LORD came unto Nathan, saying,

5 Go and tell my servant David, Thus saith the LORD, Shalt thou build me an house for me to dwell in?

6 Whereas I have not dwelt in any house since the time that I brought up the children of Israel out of Egypt, even to this day, but have walked in a tent and in a tabernacle.

7 In all the places wherein I have walked with all the children of Israel spake I a word with any of the tribes of Israel, whom I commanded to feed my people Israel, saying, Why build ye not me an house of cedar?

8 Now therefore so shalt thou say unto my servant David, Thus saith the LORD of hosts, I took thee from the sheepcote, from following the sheep, to be ruler over my people, over Israel:

9 And I was with thee whithersoever thou wentest, and have cut off all thine enemies out of thy sight, and have made thee a great name, like unto the name of the great men that are in the earth.

10 Moreover I will appoint a place for my people Israel, and will plant them, that they may dwell in a place of their own, and move no more; neither shall the children of wickedness afflict them any more, as beforetime,

11 And as since the time that I commanded judges to be over my people Israel, and have caused thee to rest from all thine enemies. Also the LORD telleth thee that he will make thee an house.

12 And when thy days be fulfilled, and thou shalt sleep with thy fathers, I will set up thy seed after thee, which shall proceed out of thy bowels, and I will estab-lish his kingdom.

13 He shall build an house for my name, and I will stablish the throne of his kingdom for ever.

NEW REVISED STANDARD VERSION

2 SAMUEL 7:1 Now when the king was settled in his house, and the LORD had given him rest from all his enemies around him, 2 the king said to the prophet Nathan, "See now, I am living in a house of cedar, but the ark of God stays in a tent." 3 Nathan said to the king, "Go, do all that you have in mind; for the LORD is with you."

4 But that same night the word of the LORD came to Nathan: 5 Go and tell my servant David: Thus says the LORD: Are you the one to build me a house to live in? 6 I have not lived in a house since the day I brought up the people of Israel from Egypt to this day, but I have been moving about in a tent and a tabernacle. 7 Wherever I have moved about among all the people of Israel, did I ever speak a word with any of the tribal leaders of Israel, whom I commanded to shepherd my people Israel, saying, "Why have you not built me a house of cedar?" 8 Now therefore thus you shall say to my servant David: Thus says the LORD of hosts: I took you from the pasture, from following the sheep to be prince over my people Israel; 9 and I have been with you wherever you went, and have cut off all your ene-mies from before you; and I will make for you a great name, like the name of the great ones of the earth. 10 And I will appoint a place for my people Israel and will plant them, so that they may live in their own place, and be disturbed no more; and evildoers shall afflict them no more, as formerly, 11 from the time that I appointed judges over my people Israel; and I will give you rest from all your enemies. Moreover the LORD declares to you that the LORD will make you a house. 12 When your days are fulfilled and you lie down with your ancestors, I will raise up your offspring after you, who shall come forth from your body, and I will estab-lish his kingdom. 13 He shall build a house for my name, and I will establish the throne of his kingdom forever.

Monday, October 23	2 Samuel 7:1-11	*Nathan's Prophecy*
Tuesday, October 24	1 Chronicles 17:1-10	*Nathan Reveals God's Word*
Wednesday, October 25	2 Samuel 7:12-17	*God's Promise to David through Nathan*
Thursday, October 26	1 Chronicles 17:11-15	*God Responds to David through Nathan*
Friday, October 27	2 Samuel 7:18-29	*David's Prayer*
Saturday, October 28	1 Chronicles 17:16-27	*David's Thanksgiving*
Sunday, October 29	1 Kings 8:15-21	*God's Promise to David Fulfilled*

BACKGROUND

In this week's lesson we will learn about the *ark of God* (2 Sam. 7:2), which is also known as the *ark of the covenant* (1 Sam. 4:5). This religious object was built under Moses' supervision at Mount Sinai, shortly after God made His covenant with His people and gave them instructions for building the tabernacle.

The ark was made out of acacia (a dark, hard, and durable desert wood) and located within the Most Holy Place of the tabernacle. It was entirely covered with pure gold (that is, with all of its alloys and impurities carefully removed) and carried on poles inserted in rings in the four lower corners (Exod. 25:10-15). The ark served as the place where the Lord met with His people and provided them with guidance (vs. 22).

The ark was Israel's national treasure and was ordinarily kept in the tabernacle. This was a portable, tent-like structure that the Israelites carried around on their wilderness wanderings. The northern, western, and southern sides of the tabernacle were constructed on a wooden framework to give it greater stability and security than ordinary tent poles could give. Only the eastern side or front of the structure was essentially a linen screen. A tent covered the entire tabernacle, and over the tent there were further coverings.

When the ark was returned to Israel after a brief Philistine captivity (1 Sam. 4:1—7:2), it was kept in the home of Abinadab for 20 years. David saw how blessed Abinadab was, and thus the king decided to bring the ark to Jerusalem to ensure God's blessing on the entire nation (2 Sam. 6:1-15). As we will learn in this week's lesson, David then focused his attention on replacing the tabernacle with a temple to house the ark.

NOTES ON THE PRINTED TEXT

While only a few physical remains of Jerusalem from David's time exist, there are vivid descriptions of the city's fortifications and the king's palace of cedar. Following the completion of these building projects, David planned an even bigger one that would truly focus the nation's religious and political attention toward the capital.

David wanted to replace the tabernacle with a magnificent temple to God. *Now when the king was settled in his house, and the LORD had given him rest from all his enemies around him, the king said to the prophet Nathan, "See now, I am living in a house of cedar, but the ark of God stays in a tent"* (7:1-2).

Nathan, a prophet and a counselor, initially agreed with David's plan. The building project and its purpose made sense, and thus Nathan approved it. He said to the king, *"Go, do all that you have in mind; for the LORD is with you"* (7:3).

Nathan had spoken on the basis of his own understanding, for he had not consulted the Lord on the matter. But the prophet was quick to reverse himself when ordered to do so by the Lord.

Nathan told David that up until this time in Israel's history God had manifested His presence in the ark, or tent. *But that same night the word of the LORD came to Nathan: Go and tell my servant David: . . . Are you the one to build me a house to live in? I have not lived in a house since the day I brought up the people of Israel from Egypt to this day, but I have been moving about in a tent and a tabernacle* (7:4-6).

Nathan stated that not once did God complain to Israel's leaders—the shepherds of His people—to build Him a beautiful cedar temple. *Whenever I have moved about among all the people of Israel, did I ever speak a word with any of the tribal leaders of Israel, whom I commanded to shepherd my people, Israel, saying, "Why have you not built me a house of cedar?"* (7:7).

Nathan related that the Lord had taken David from being a shepherd boy and made him the king of Israel. Throughout this period, God had remained with David. *Now therefore thus you shall say to my servant David: Thus says the LORD of hosts: I took you from the pasture, from following the sheep to be prince over my people Israel; and I have been with you wherever you went, and have cut off all your enemies from before you* (7:8-9).

God had not only enabled David to subdue his enemies but also promised to make his name famous. *I will make for you a great name, like the name of the great ones of the earth* (7:9). In addition, the Lord used David to enable the Israelites to dwell in peace in Canaan. *And I will appoint a place for my people Israel and will plant them, so that they may live in their own place, and be disturbed no more; and evildoers shall afflict them no more as formerly, from the time that I appointed judges over my people Israel; and I will give you rest from all your enemies* (7:10-11).

The Lord next said He would establish David and his descendants as a dynasty forever. The word rendered *house* (7:11) lies at the heart of this passage. David saw his own house (or palace) and desired to build a house (or temple) for the Lord. But God declared that He would build a house (or dynasty) for David. And the king's son would build a house (or temple) for the Lord.

God also promised to give David an eternal throne and an eternal kingdom. After the king's death, the Lord would allow David's son, Solomon, to sit on his throne. And God would be merciful and fair in His dealings with David's successor. The Lord would also give permanence to David's rule. Though David and his descendants would pass away, the reign of his greatest descendant—Jesus Christ—would be unbroken (7:12-13).

SUGGESTIONS TO TEACHERS

David was troubled by the fact that while he lived in a magnificent home, the ark of God was housed in a tent. The king thus decided to build a temple for the Lord. But God did not want the king to do this for Him. Perhaps at first David was saddened by the Lord's decision. But then David could take comfort in knowing that God was using him to unify the nation and subdue Israel's enemies. Likewise, God would give David a lasting dynasty.

1. DAVID'S DECISION. What finer desire could there be than to build a beautiful temple for the Lord! David's motive was noble and his plan was commendable. Our intentions sometimes seem to fit in with what we imagine God would have us to do. But for various reasons, we are not able to accomplish what we had planned. Encourage the students to share personal episodes of disappointment and how they handled them.

2. NATHAN'S DECLARATION. David and Nathan had assumed that it would be proper for the king to build a temple in Jerusalem to house the ark of the covenant. However, neither David nor Nathan had consulted the Lord. Thankfully, when God revealed to Nathan His real intent for David, the prophet had the courage to declare the same to the king.

3. DAVID'S DEVOTION. Rather than lash out in anger, David graciously accepted God's word through Nathan. David learned that God did not want him to build a temple for the ark. Though he would not have the honor of completing this project, he had other enormous tasks to finish as Israel's king.

4. GOD'S DECREE. God had accomplished significant things through David. He had given David a great name. The Lord had also given Israel a place of rest. Moreover, God had given David peace from all his enemies. In addition to these, God declared that the king's descendants would become an enduring dynasty over Israel.

The New Testament reveals that God's promises to David are fulfilled in Christ. Through Jesus' death and resurrection, we have the hope of eternal life. We can count on God to keep His promises to us. Regardless of our current problems, God's love for us remains unshakable.

FOR ADULTS

■ **TOPIC:** The Challenge of God's Promise

■ **QUESTIONS:** 1. Why did David want to build a temple? 2. Who was Nathan, and what was his message to David? 3. What was God's perspective on housing the ark in a magnificent temple? 4. What was God's promise to David at this time? 5. How can you encourage other believers who are struggling with disappointment to find comfort in God's promises through Christ?

■ ILLUSTRATIONS:
Relying on the Promise. Arthur Ashe, the champion American tennis player, acquired AIDS through a blood transfusion at the time he underwent heart surgery. The hospital did not suspect or inspect the unit of H.I.V. contaminated blood.

Ashe did not realize that he was infected with the dreaded virus until five years later when he first suffered numbness and then growing paralysis in his playing arm. The diagnosis was a brain tumor. This stay in the hospital for surgery revealed that he had contracted AIDS. After being released from the hospital, the seventh-ranked tennis star had to face rumors about his condition as well as deal with retirement from his beloved sport.

Arthur Ashe resisted the temptation to be angry at the Lord. In 1992, he addressed the students at the Niagara County Community College and testified that despite having his disease, his trust in God was firm. Ashe knew that regardless of the outcome, God would remain with him in his ordeal.

Challenge of a Promise. Ricky Hoyt has cerebral palsy. He is confined to a wheelchair. His disability is classified technically as a spastic quadriplegic. He cannot even talk, and has to communicate through a voice synthesizer. Nonetheless, Ricky Hoyt has been able to compete in over 600 sports events, including 111 triathlons, a 45-day cross country odyssey in 1992, and nearly 20 Boston Marathons. He can do these things because of his father's promise and the way he has kept his pledge.

Ricky's father, Dick, is a retired military officer who has devoted himself to compete with Ricky to fulfill his son's dreams. Ricky is the heart and his father is the body. Together they compete. Dick pushes the wheelchair, fulfilling his promise to his son to let him participate even in big-time marathons.

How much more does God fulfill His promises to those who trust Him? Believers know that the Lord will remain faithful to them and accomplish all that He has planned.

Commitment to God's Promise. Habitat for Humanity has provided affordable housing for millions throughout the world. But few know the story of its origins. A young millionaire named Millard Fuller had amassed a fortune by the age of 29, and was able to buy anything he fancied. However, he discovered that his marriage had collapsed because of his greed and attention only to business.

Shocked at having his wife, Linda, leave him, Fuller began to take stock of his life. He located Linda in New York and listened to her tell him that she didn't care about having him buy her things. He heard her describe how her life was barren of meaning with a materialistic way of living. They talked and wept together. Then they knelt and prayed.

That night in a hotel room in New York City, the couple promised God and each other that they would stop living merely for themselves and commit their lives to helping the oppressed and homeless. The Fullers' promise has been fulfilled in ways they never anticipated. For example, countless chapters of Habitat for Humanity now exist in North American communities and in many developing countries around the world.

FOR YOUTH

■ **TOPIC:** Building a Family
■ **QUESTIONS:** 1. What was troubling David about the ark being housed in the tabernacle? 2. How do Nathan's first and second responses to David differ? 3. What had God done for David to make him king of Israel? 4. What did God plan to do for David in the future? 5. How have you handled disappointments in your life?

■ **ILLUSTRATIONS:**

Lost Tradition. Judith Martin, better known as Miss Manners, noted that contemporary houses contain a room with a large table that is usually set with a 500 piece jigsaw puzzle or is used as a desk. The space, which once was called the family dining room, is now often used for other purposes. This suggests that modern society has deemphasized the importance of the traditional practice of the family meal.

Many would acknowledge that the family meal has been helpful in keeping households together. It is a time when relationships are built, especially as news of each member's day is exchanged, manners are taught, and social skills are developed. Miss Manners laments that family members often eat by themselves, and then they wonder why they feel alone.

David saw the temple as a way of bringing the people of his nation together. He wanted to expand and reinforce a tradition of worship so that God's people would become a strong and united faith community. Though the Lord did not allow David to build the temple, He did affirm the king's idea by allowing Solomon—David's son—to do the job.

Ingredient for Traditional Family. A strong economy providing employment and money positively affects the family structure. Research conducted by Gail M. Johnson, a sociologist at Penn State University, demonstrates a correlation between economic status and the family structure. Johnson's findings showed that job loss resulted in higher divorce rates and out of wedlock births, and this in turn changed the family concept and structure. The percentage of families headed by women with children grew, while married couples with families declined.

According to Johnson, 42 percent of white children and 86 percent of black children will spend part of their lives in a female headed household. In 1960, the figure was 5.1 million. In 1993, the number of children living only with their mother had tripled to 15.6 million. Female headed households are also more likely to be poor because women are forced to take lower paying jobs.

Johnson says that unemployment is the leading cause of female-headed households. Women tend to marry men who have a good job. In contrast, they tend to avoid marrying men who are unemployed. Clearly, when the economy is good, there are many more employed men than unemployed men who are married.

Strangely, one ingredient is missing from Johnson's research. Scripture teaches that God is supposed to be a part of family life. Consider David. The king had palaces, prestige, power, and wealth. Stability existed throughout his kingdom. But he also sensed the importance of God being present in his life and in the lives of his family members.

Traditional Family Changes. The so-called traditional family image is gone. In previous generations the mother would have been a full-time homemaker and the father would have been the major wage earner. The norm would have been for them to stay married to each other for life and have children. Now, only 10 percent of the families in the United States fit that mold, according to Danielle Lichter, Director of Penn State University's Population Institute. The traditional family has been replaced by single parent families.

The kind of family in which we live is not the most important factor from God's point of view. Of greater concern is whether He reigns supreme among all the family members. Regardless of how many possessions a family may have, God wants to see healthy relationships being cultivated in which the love of Christ is displayed through all the circumstances of life.

DAVID AND BATHSHEBA

BACKGROUND SCRIPTURE: 2 Samuel 11:1—12:25
DEVOTIONAL READING: Numbers 15:30-31

KEY VERSE: Why have you despised the word of the LORD,
to do what is evil in his sight? 2 Samuel 12:9a.

KING JAMES VERSION

2 SAMUEL 11:2 And it came to pass in an eveningtide, that David arose from off his bed, and walked upon the roof of the king's house: and from the roof he saw a woman washing herself; and the woman was very beautiful to look upon.

3 And David sent and enquired after the woman. And one said, Is not this Bath-sheba, the daughter of Eliam, the wife of Uriah the Hittite?

4 And David sent messengers, and took her; and she came in unto him, and he lay with her; for she was purified from her uncleanness: and she returned unto her house.

5 And the woman conceived, and sent and told David, and said, I am with child. . . .

14 And it came to pass in the morning, that David wrote a letter to Joab, and sent it by the hand of Uriah.

15 And he wrote in the letter, saying, Set ye Uriah in the forefront of the hottest battle, and retire ye from him, that he may be smitten, and die.

16 And it came to pass, when Joab observed the city, that he assigned Uriah unto a place where he knew that valiant men were.

17 And the men of the city went out, and fought with Joab: and there fell some of the people of the servants of David; and Uriah the Hittite died also.

18 Then Joab sent and told David all the things concerning the war; . . .

26 And when the wife of Uriah heard that Uriah her husband was dead, she mourned for her husband.

27 And when the mourning was past, David sent and fetched her to his house, and she became his wife, and bare him a son. But the thing that David had done displeased the LORD. . . .

12:13 And David said unto Nathan, I have sinned against the LORD. And Nathan said unto David, The LORD also hath put away thy sin; thou shalt not die.

14 Howbeit, because by this deed thou hast given great occasion to the enemies of the LORD to blaspheme, the child also that is born unto thee shall surely die.

15 And Nathan departed unto his house. And the LORD struck the child that Uriah's wife bare unto David, and it was very sick.

NEW REVISED STANDARD VERSION

2 SAMUEL 11:2 It happened, late one afternoon, when David rose from his couch and was walking about on the roof of the king's house, that he saw from the roof a woman bathing; the woman was very beautiful. 3 David sent someone to inquire about the woman. It was reported, "This is Bathsheba daughter of Eliam, the wife of Uriah the Hittite." 4 So David sent messengers to get her, and she came to him, and he lay with her. (Now she was purifying herself after her period.) Then she returned to her house. 5 The woman conceived; and she sent and told David, "I am pregnant." . . .

14 In the morning David wrote a letter to Joab, and sent it by the hand of Uriah. 15 In the letter he wrote, "Set Uriah in the forefront of the hardest fighting, and then draw back from him, so that he may be struck down and die." 16 As Joab was besieging the city, he assigned Uriah to the place where he knew there were valiant warriors. 17 The men of the city came out and fought with Joab; and some of the servants of David among the people fell. Uriah the Hittite was killed as well. 18 Then Joab sent and told David all the news about the fighting. . . .

26 When the wife of Uriah heard that her husband was dead, she made lamentation for him. 27 When the mourning was over, David sent and brought her to his house, and she became his wife, and bore him a son. . . .

12:13 David said to Nathan, "I have sinned against the LORD." Nathan said to David, "Now the LORD has put away your sin; you shall not die. 14 Nevertheless, because by this deed you have utterly scorned the LORD, the child that is born to you shall die." 15 Then Nathan went to his house.

The Lord struck the child that Uriah's wife bore to David, and it became very ill.

10

HOME BIBLE READINGS

BACKGROUND

After David received God's covenant promises, he attacked and subdued the Philistines by conquering Metheg-ammah. Israel's king also defeated the Moabites and destroyed the forces of Hadadezer, king of Zobah. Moreover, when Arameans from Damascus came to help Hadadezer, David's troops routed them. The Edomites likewise crumbled beneath the weight of David's military machine (2 Sam. 8:1-8, 13-14).

Israel's victories on the field of battle were not due exclusively to the brilliant military planning of David or the courage of his troops. Scripture makes it clear that *the LORD gave victory to David wherever he went* (8:14). God was fulfilling His promise to make David's name great and to give the Israelites rest from all their enemies (7:9-11).

The Lord enabled David to reign *over all Israel* (8:15). And the king's administration of *justice and equity to all his people* was positive proof that David truly was *"a man after [God's] own heart"* (1 Sam. 13:14). This means that though he had many faults, his spirit was sensitive to God's will.

Consider the way in which David dealt with Mephibosheth, a son of Jonathan who was crippled in his feet (2 Sam. 4:4). When the business of the kingdom had settled down, David sought to fulfill his oath to Jonathan by showing favor to a member of his friend's household (1 Sam. 20:15). David handed over Saul's estate to Mephibosheth and invited him to eat daily at the royal table (2 Sam. 9).

Some time after this, David sent some ambassadors to the land of Ammon. Rather than treat the representatives of Israel with respect, the Ammonites disgraced them. This in turn led to an all-out conflict in which the forces of Ammon, along with Aramean mercenaries, battled against David's troops. Despite the enemy's best efforts, they proved no match against the Israelites. In fact, David's forces soundly defeated their foes in each battle (10:1-19).

Against the backdrop of these great military victories and acts of personal kindness we read the sordid account of David's affair with Bathsheba, his murder of her husband, Uriah the Hittite, and the king's attempt to cover up his crimes. When confronted by Nathan the prophet, David confessed his wrongdoing and experienced God's forgiveness, though the harsh consequences of his sin would reverberate for years to come.

NOTES ON THE PRINTED TEXT

A gifted and attractive young man had aged. Many of David's earlier qualities remained but in the later years of his life less desirable traits emerged in his character, particularly sexual immorality. David had been phenomenally successful on the field of battle, but he would experience defeat in his war against sin.

Spring had arrived, and it was the typical time in the ancient Near East when kings went to war. David sent Joab and the Israelite army to ravage the Ammonites. Meanwhile, the king stayed behind in Jerusalem (11:1).

Late one afternoon, David got out of bed after taking a nap and went for a stroll on the flat roof of his palace. The higher elevation of the palace roof allowed David to see into the courtyards of nearby houses. One view was particularly enticing. He saw a woman of striking beauty taking a bath (11:2).

At this point David could have stopped and turned away from the forbidden desires swelling up inside him. But instead he *sent someone to inquire about the woman. It was reported, "This is Bathsheba, daughter of Eliam, the wife of Uriah the Hittite"* (11:3). Uriah was one of the king's mighty men (23:39). Uriah's loyalty and honesty would sharply contrast with David's infidelity and duplicity.

David gave in to his lustful passions by having some servants escort Bathsheba to the palace. She thus *came to him, and he lay with her* (11:4). This was a blatant misuse of the king's power and position.

David's one-night stand led to a problem, namely, that Bathsheba became pregnant. *The woman conceived; and she sent and told David, "I am pregnant"* (11:5). The fact that Bathsheba had just experienced menstruation makes it plain that she was not pregnant by Uriah when she came to lie with David. Bathsheba's situation was risky, for it would have been known that her husband was off at war.

David's attempt to cover-up his crime began in earnest. He summoned Uriah home from the battlefront and hoped that he could get Bathsheba's husband to have relations with her. But Uriah refused to even see his wife as long as his fellow soldiers were fighting the enemy (11:6-13).

Thus David's initial cover up plan failed. That's when the king resorted to a more sinister plot, namely, murder. *In the morning David wrote a letter to Joab, and sent it by the hand of Uriah. In the letter he wrote, "Set Uriah in the forefront of the hardest fighting, and then draw back from him, so that he may be struck down and die"* (11:14-15).

David arranged Uriah's death in order to conceal his affair with Bathsheba. Joab carried out David's orders. Uriah, along with additional Israelite troops, were killed in action. News of Uriah's death not only reached David but also Bathsheba (11:16-25). Out of genuine sorrow, Bathsheba *made lamentation for him* (11:26).

When the period of mourning was over, David had some servants escort Bathsheba to the palace, and she became one of his wives. She then gave birth to a son as a result of her adulterous union with David. We also learn that *the thing that David had done displeased the* LORD (11:27). In other words, God was aware of David's crimes and would soon execute judgment.

The Lord used Nathan to confront David. Nathan told a parable that drew in David and prompted him to offer a judgment on the offender. Nathan helped the king recognize that he was the real villain behind the parable (12:1-12). When confronted with his misdeeds, David repented (12:13).

Sensing the genuineness of David's repentance, Nathan announced that God had forgiven the king. He would not die, though the newborn baby would not survive. Here we find God judging David for his sin. The death of his beloved child undoubtedly caused the king great anguish (12:14).

David wrote Psalms 32 and 51 as a result of committing adultery with Bathsheba and arranging for the murder of her soldier-husband, Uriah. Both poems are known as penitential psalms because in them, David fully acknowledged his sin.

SUGGESTIONS TO TEACHERS

Scripture says, *Like a roaring lion your adversary the devil prowls around, looking for someone to devour* (1 Pet. 5:8). Sadly, this proved true in the life of David. Rather than shun his sinful passions, David caved in to them (2 Tim. 2:22). Though David had violated the rights of others, his treachery ultimately was against the Lord. In fact, the king was guilty of breaking at least four of the Ten Commandments, namely, coveting, adultery, lying, and murder.

1. COMPLACENCY. David had reached the pinnacle of his reign, for he had successfully established his kingdom. Perhaps at this point he felt as if he could relax and do as he pleased. Or maybe he just became bored. Regardless of the reasons, his complacency opened the way to sin.

2. COMPROMISE. David gave in to the temptation to indulge in an affair with Bathsheba. The king thus sinned against the Lord. Adultery, regardless of the easygoing morality of our times, breaks trust with God and others.

3. CORRUPTION. Bathsheba's pregnancy underscores the truth that every affair corrupts relationships. David's darkest side showed itself as he schemed to make Bathsheba's husband, Uriah, appear to be the father. But David's problems only got worse.

4. CONSPIRACY. David's cover-up ended with the murder of Uriah, his trusted soldier. David had succeeded in concealing his crime from others. But he had forgotten that the Lord knew everything about him, including his sin (Ps. 139:7-12).

5. CONFRONTATION. Nathan fearlessly confronted David with the enormity of his sin by telling a heartbreaking parable. David's indignation mirrored that of God against him for his transgressions.

6. CONDEMNATION. We can only imagine David's dismay as Nathan declared to him, *"You are the man!"* (2 Sam. 12:7). The king may have forgotten about his crimes, but God remembered them. And He used Nathan to censure David for his wrongdoing.

7. CONFESSION. David's acknowledgement of his transgression was clear and forceful: *"I have sinned against the LORD"* (12:13). His candor reminds us of Paul's statement concerning him in Acts 13:22, *"I have found David, son of Jesse, to be a man after my heart."* Remind the class that if *we confess our sins, he who is faithful and just will forgive us our sins and cleanse us from all unrighteousness* (1 John 1:9). Though our sins may be large and numerous, the grace of God through Christ abounds *all the more* (Rom. 5:20).

FOR ADULTS	■ **TOPIC:** When Believers Fall ■ **QUESTIONS:** 1. What things did David do wrong in the episode with Bathsheba? 2. What things did David do wrong in the episode

with Joab and Uriah? 3. What was the implication of God's displeasure with David? 4. How can the church use David's account to help believers remain faithful to their loved ones? 5. What is the duty of believers toward those who have fallen into sin, confessed it, and received God's forgiveness in Christ?

■ **ILLUSTRATIONS:**

Confronting a King. Just as Nathan confronted King David, a modern spokesperson for morality confronted a powerful monarch. William M. Morrison was a missionary in Africa in what was then called the Congo Free State, but which was actually a colony under the king of Belgium. Morrison and his fellow-missionary, William Sheppard, witnessed the mistreatment of Congolese workers in rubber plantations.

The missionaries protested the brutal practices of the Belgian plantation bosses. Among other atrocities, they were guilty of cutting off of the hands of workers who failed to make production quotas. Morrison informed his mission board back in the United States about the matter. Meanwhile, Sheppard was charged with libel because of his reports to the American public.

Morrison finally went to Brussels and confronted King Leopold of Belgium. The missionary boldly declared the following to the powerful ruler: "I can assure Your Majesty that nothing has ever given me greater pain than to be compelled to lose confidence in the government's real desire to do justice according to the spirit of the treaties of Berlin and Brussels. And it is after the most careful deliberation that I have reached the conclusion that our only hope lies in arousing the public opinion of the world against the iniquities which you know that your system must produce in Africa."

The results of Morrison's words were a groundswell of public opinion and pressures for change. Even the U.S. State Department was roused to protest the Belgian king's labor practices in his African colony. Colonial Africa was changed forever. Sheppard was acquitted in the libel suit. And Leopold's successor—his nephew King Albert—showed much more humanitarian concern.

Football Star's Fidelity. David's affair with Bathsheba and subsequent attempts to cover up his misdeeds brought heartache and sorrow to his family. The king's experience is a reminder for us to keep *the marriage bed . . . undefiled; for God will judge fornicators and adulterers* (Heb. 13:4).

In contrast to David, Roger Staubach, the former superstar of the Dallas Cowboys football team, remained faithful to his wife and to God. Staubach was being interviewed by Phyllis George, who asked him how he felt in comparison to Joe Namath. Namath is another former football superstar who had a series of well-publicized affairs. With the same cool that Staubach had shown as a quarterback under pressure, he replied, "Phyllis, I'm sure that I'm as sexually active as Joe. The difference is that all of mine is with one woman, my wife!"

Affected by Judgment. Marcia Miller graduated with a teaching degree and finally found employment in the school system of Charlottesville, Virginia. Because she was the youngest and newest hired, she was assigned to a sixth grade class of unruly boys in a tough ghetto school.

All of the students in the class had repeated grades so many times that they were of high school age. Also, all had been known as severe discipline problems by the school authorities. In fact, most had police records. Tragically, the boys in Marcia's class all came from broken homes where drug abuse, drunkenness, and violence were commonplace.

Marcia received no cooperation from any of her students' parents. Other teachers in the school refused to have anything to do with the boys in her class. Also, school officials lamely stated that all they wanted Miller to do was make some attempt to preserve a semblance of discipline during the school hours.

Marcia taught these boys for four years, and won such respect from everyone that she received the Student Teacher of the Year award. She admitted that trying to teach such a group of undisciplined repeaters in her classroom was challenging.

How did Marcia manage to discipline such a group of disorderly ruffians from the dregs of the ghetto, young men who were seemingly impervious to physical and legal threats and who defied all those in authority? Marcia's method had nothing to do with the usual forms of punishment. When one of the boys caused any trouble in her class, Miller would lead him out the door to the hallway, look intently into his face, and state repeatedly, "I am so disappointed in you! I'm so disappointed in you!" Her fervent sense of caring expressed in her obvious disappointment over the offender's behavior broke through the defenses of the toughest and most incorrigible boy in her class.

Sometimes we think of God as being all judgment and no mercy. But Scripture portrays Him differently. Yes, God is holy, righteous, and just. But He's also merciful, loving, and caring. When we sin against Him, we *grieve the Holy Spirit of God* (Eph. 4:30).

The solution is not to continue sinning against the Lord and thereby disappoint Him further. Rather, we should confess and forsake our misdeeds and experience His mercy (Prov. 28:13). If we consistently live in this way, we can rest assured that at the end of the age God will say to us, *"'Well done, good and trustworthy slave; . . . enter into the joy of your master'"* (Matt. 25:21).

FOR YOUTH

■ TOPIC: What Will It Hurt?

■ QUESTIONS: 1. What were the circumstances that led up to David's committing adultery with Bathsheba? 2. When David's initial attempts to cover up his crime failed, what did he do next? 3. What specific things had David done to displease the Lord? 4. How did Nathan confront David with his transgressions, and what was the king's response? 5. What can Christians do to build a defensive wall against such sins as adultery and murder?

■ ILLUSTRATIONS:

Devastating Consequences. Does sexual immorality have devastating consequences? Aside from pregnancy (which the account of David and Bathsheba highlights), consider AIDS (Auto Immune Deficiency Syndrome). A seven-year study of 350,000 youth in the Federal Jobs Program, which was conducted by the Centers for Disease Control and Prevention, noted that while the average rate of infection has slowly declined, women between the ages of 16 and 21 have a 50 percent higher infection rate than men. Young, poor, African American women are infected at a higher rate than men, closely followed by Hispanic women. The difference was attributed to young women having illicit sexual contact with older male partners.

Time magazine reported that 1.5 million people in the United States have been infected by the deadly AIDS virus, and 25 to 50 percent of these will develop the actual disease. Almost 50,000 people die each year from AIDS. And we must not forget the ravages of other sexually transmitted diseases. For instance, about 13 million new cases of venereal diseases (genital herpes, syphilis, pelvic inflammation, and others) will be diagnosed each year.

As the above indicates and as David discovered, sexual immorality is not a casual matter. It's a terrible sin that can lead to devastating consequences.

Mesmerizing Effect. A youth in a sophomore biology class recounted how the teacher allowed his students to watch him feed a live mouse to a boa constrictor that he kept in a case in the room. At first the snake rested peacefully in a corner of its cage. Then the teacher put the small mouse into the cage. The creature scampered furiously around the cage and clambered over and around the boa constrictor. The mouse even stopped and peered at the face of the snake. For a time the large green animal was motionless.

But then the boa constrictor began to uncurl its body. The snake's movement was so quiet and deliberate that the mouse paid no attention at first. But as the snake slithered closer, the mouse seemed to become fascinated. It didn't scamper away, but sat up on its haunches watching the boa gradually move toward it. The mouse showed no sign of fear but seemed mesmerized by the reptile. Then suddenly, before any onlooker anticipated anything, the snake had wrapped its coils around the mouse, crushed it, and eaten it.

This incident illustrates how sexual immorality has a way of slithering toward people and mesmerizing those who are unwary. For example, pornography, prostitution, and exploitative relationships have a serpent-like way of suddenly engulfing the unsuspecting. It's no wonder that Paul declared, *Shun fornication!* (1 Cor. 6:18).

No Desire for Commitment. Columnist Ellen Goodman laments that young people postpone marriage and simply use one another sexually without commitment. Her words were echoed by William H. Willimon, whose quotes were carried in a *New York Times* article. The piece, which is entitled "The Uncommitted Generation," says that sexual intimacy is nothing more than two adults enjoying one another in a brief physical encounter. In other words, young people have no desire for the commitment of marriage.

David's affair with Bathsheba indicates that he simply wanted to use her to satisfy his physical desires. The Lord, however, used Nathan to confront David with his sin. From this we learn that sexual intimacy outside the commitment of marriage is wrong. But in marriage it is blessed by God (Prov. 5:15-20).

SOLOMON SUCCEEDS DAVID

BACKGROUND SCRIPTURE: 1 Kings 2:1-4; 3:1-15; 1 Chronicles 29:22-25; 2 Chronicles 1:1-13
DEVOTIONAL READING: Psalm 119:10-19

KEY VERSE: Give your servant therefore an understanding mind to govern your people, able to discern between good and evil. 1 Kings 3:9a.

KING JAMES VERSION

1 KINGS 2:1 Now the days of David drew nigh that he should die; and he charged Solomon his son, saying,

2 I go the way of all the earth: be thou strong therefore, and shew thyself a man;

3 And keep the charge of the LORD thy God, to walk in his ways, to keep his statutes, and his commandments, and his judgments, and his testimonies, as it is written in the law of Moses, that thou mayest prosper in all that thou doest, and whithersoever thou turnest thyself:

4 That the LORD may continue his word which he spake concerning me, saying, If thy children take heed to their way, to walk before me in truth with all their heart and with all their soul, there shall not fail thee (said he) a man on the throne of Israel. . . .

3:3 And Solomon loved the LORD, walking in the statutes of David his father: only he sacrificed and burnt incense in high places.

4 And the king went to Gibeon to sacrifice there; for that was the great high place: a thousand burnt offerings did Solomon offer upon that altar.

5 In Gibeon the LORD appeared to Solomon in a dream by night: and God said, Ask what I shall give thee.

6 And Solomon said, Thou hast shewed unto thy servant David my father great mercy, according as he walked before thee in truth, and in righteousness, and in uprightness of heart with thee; and thou hast kept for him this great kindness, that thou hast given him a son to sit on his throne, as it is this day.

7 And now, O LORD my God, thou hast made thy servant king instead of David my father: and I am but a little child: I know not how to go out or come in.

8 And thy servant is in the midst of thy people which thou hast chosen, a great people, that cannot be numbered nor counted for multitude.

9 Give therefore thy servant an understanding heart to judge thy people, that I may discern between good and bad: for who is able to judge this thy so great a people?

10 And the speech pleased the Lord, that Solomon had asked this thing.

NEW REVISED STANDARD VERSION

1 KINGS 2:1 When David's time to die drew near, he charged his son Solomon, saying: 2 "I am about to go the way of all the earth. Be strong, be courageous, 3 and keep the charge of the LORD your God, walking in his ways and keeping his statutes, his commandments, his ordinances, and his testimonies, as it is written in the law of Moses, so that you may prosper in all that you do and wherever you turn. 4 Then the LORD will establish his word that he spoke concerning me: 'If your heirs take heed to their way, to walk before me in faithfulness with all their heart and with all their soul, there shall not fail you a successor on the throne of Israel.' . . ."

3:3 Solomon loved the LORD, walking in the statutes of his father David; only, he sacrificed and offered incense at the high places. 4 The king went to Gibeon to sacrifice there, for that was the principal high place; Solomon used to offer a thousand burnt offerings on that altar. 5 At Gibeon the LORD appeared to Solomon in a dream by night; and God said, "Ask what I should give you." 6 And Solomon said, "You have shown great and steadfast love to your servant my father David, because he walked before you in faithfulness, in righteousness, and in uprightness of heart toward you; and you have kept for him this great and steadfast love, and have given him a son to sit on his throne today. 7 And now, O LORD my God, you have made your servant king in place of my father David, although I am only a little child; I do not know how to go out or come in. 8 And your servant is in the midst of the people whom you have chosen, a great people, so numerous they cannot be numbered or counted. 9 Give your servant therefore an understanding mind to govern your people, able to discern between good and evil; for who can govern this your great people?"

10 It pleased the LORD that Solomon had asked this.

HOME BIBLE READINGS

BACKGROUND

We previously learned that after Saul's death, the tribe of Judah, to whom David belonged, anointed him as their king and placed him on the throne in Hebron. Meanwhile, the rest of the tribes of Israel set up Ishbaal, Saul's son, as their king at Mahanaim (2 Sam. 2:1-11). For the next several years civil war raged between these two factions. It ended in the assassination of Ishbaal, an event that saddened David (2:12—4:12).

After the death of Ishbaal, David was appointed king over all the people of Israel (5:1-5). He immediately began the work of establishing a united kingdom. One of his first acts was to capture the fortified city of Jerusalem and make it his capital (5:6-9). He then proceeded to reestablish and strengthen the worship of God by moving the ark of the covenant to Jerusalem and placing it within the tabernacle (6:12-15). The king next began plans to build a temple for the Lord (7:1-3). Though God did not permit David to construct the sanctuary, his successor was permitted to do so (7:13).

Despite David's great accomplishments at home and abroad, his reign was tainted by sin. The most noteworthy offense was his adultery with Bathsheba and David's attempt to cover up the crime (11:3-27). Though God forgave David after he had repented, the consequences of his sin continued to plague him (12:13-14). For instance, the child born to David and Bathsheba died (12:15-19).

Also, the example David set as a father was a bad influence on his sons. One son, Ammon, raped and humiliated his half-sister, Tamar (13:1-19). Another of David's sons, Absalom, rebelled against David and tried to take away his kingdom by force (15:1—17:29). The insurrection ended with Absalom's death (18:1-18).

David's kingdom may have been restored, but he had to put down a northern revolt (20:1-22). The last act of David recorded in 2 Samuel concerns his unlawful census of the people. This resulted in judgment from God (24:1-25).

Despite the ups and downs of David's reign, Scripture remembers him as being a good and wise king. For instance, as the end of his life drew near, David made plans for the peaceful and smooth transition of power from himself to Solomon. As we will learn in this week's lesson, David wanted to ensure that before his death, his son was solidly established on the throne of Israel.

NOTES ON THE PRINTED TEXT

As David neared death, Adonijah (his fourth son) decided to make himself king in the place of his aged father. The upstart enlisted the help of Joab and Abiathar the priest. But others remained loyal to David and worked behind the scenes to undermine Adonijah's bid for the throne. Their efforts paid off, for David had Solomon officially anointed as king (1 Kings 1:1-40).

Once Solomon had been installed on the throne, David passed on final instructions to his successor (2:1). He urged Solomon to *"be strong, be courageous, and keep the charge of the LORD your God, walking in his ways and keeping his statutes, his commandments, his ordinances, and his testimonies, as it is written in the law of Moses, so that you may prosper in all that you do and wherever you turn"* (2:2-3).

Perhaps more than anything else, David wanted Solomon to be obedient to God. In every action he took or decision he made, the young king's commitment to the Lord was to be demonstrated unflinchingly and without shame or reservation. The covenant was to be upheld for the good of the nation.

David also reiterated God's promise of an eternal dynasty (2:4). Solomon and his descendants would remain in office as kings only when they honored and obeyed the Lord. However, if they failed to do this, they would lose the throne. Despite this, David's line would continue forever, most notably through Jesus Christ, the king's greatest descendant.

Solomon's reign was not free from problems. Adonijah remained a source of contention, and when he made another attempt to undermine the king's rule, Solomon had him executed (2:13-25). The new ruler also eliminated others who had been sympathetic to Adonijah's bid for the throne (2:26-45). This helped Solomon to firmly establish his control over the kingdom.

Solomon *loved the Lord* and sought to follow *the statutes of his father David* (3:3). Nevertheless, the young king continued to worship at the high places. These hilltop shrines were havens of pagan worship, and that's why God wanted His people to destroy them. Solomon's failure to completely follow the Lord would eventually lead to his downfall (11:1-13).

Gibeon (located about five miles northwest of Jerusalem) was the most important hilltop shrine in Israel, and that's why Solomon went there to offer sacrifices and burn incense. On the altar at Gibeon, he offered *a thousand burnt offerings* (3:4). These were the most common type of sacrifice, and they were often used for giving thanks and atoning for sin. The animal was burned completely, except for the hide, which was taken by the priest (Lev. 7:8).

While Solomon was at Gibeon, the Lord appeared to him *in a dream by night* (1 Kings 3:5). In Bible times, God often gave revelation in dreams. This dream was unique in that there was a two-way conversation between the Lord and Solomon. This dream set the stage for the first major period in Solomon's tenure as king.

God said to the king, *"Ask what I should give you"* (3:5). Solomon began by noting the amazing kindness God had shown to David. Solomon's father had been honest, true, and faithful to the Lord, and He in turn continued to bless David by allowing his son to succeed him. *"And you have kept for him this great and steadfast love, and have given him a son to sit on his throne today"* (3:6).

Solomon saw himself as being relatively young and inexperienced to shoulder the awesome responsibility of ruling Israel. (He was possibly 20 years old when he became king.) His willingness to admit his lack of qualification was a demonstration of true humility. *"O LORD my God, . . . I do not know how to go out or come in"* (3:7).

Solomon was prudent in asking the Lord for wisdom to be an effective and godly leader (3:8-9). The youthful king could have asked for wealth, power, and fame. But he did not, and this pleased the Lord (3:10). God not only gave Solomon what he had requested (namely, wisdom) but also what he had not sought (namely, riches and honor; 3:11-14).

SUGGESTIONS TO TEACHERS

Wisdom is not the same as knowledge. While knowledge can be obtained through formal learning, wisdom is acquired over time through the rough and tumble of life. All of us have known people who had little formal education yet were blessed with wisdom in living. Such individuals had the common sense and prudence to shoulder tasks that seemed overwhelming. Godly wisdom (namely, the ability to live in an upright and virtuous manner) comes from a relationship with the Lord.

1. HOLY REQUIREMENT. David's deathbed advice to his son Solomon may be heeded by everyone. Solomon was wise enough to listen to his dying parent. The words about faith passed on by previous generations are never out of date! Invite the students to recall words or examples of Christian commitment from parents, grandparents, or other older people, and have them share these thoughts with the rest of the class.

2. HONEST RELIGION. Examine the way in which Solomon heeded his father's counsel. Solomon showed trust in the Lord. As you use Solomon as an example of a sincere worshiper, have the students consider different ways that believers can give praise and adoration to God.

3. HUMBLE REQUEST. Pay particular attention to the request that Solomon put before the Lord. The young king asked God for *"an understanding mind . . . to discern between good and evil"* (1 Kings 3:9). Take a few moments to discuss the purpose of praying and the contents of prayers.

4. HAPPY RESULTS. Solomon was young and inexperienced, and he faced many challenges in ruling his father's kingdom. In fact, Solomon was succeeding a man who had ruled successfully for years and had held together a far-flung empire. Nevertheless, the huge tasks that Solomon had to bear did not overwhelm him, for he relied on the Lord's strength and guidance. The youthful king's humble and honest prayer was in light of God's promise of mercy and help.

5. HONORABLE REPUTATION. First Chronicles 29:25 notes the honor and fame that Solomon enjoyed. God had highly exalted him.

■ **TOPIC:** When Tasks Overwhelm

■ **QUESTIONS:** 1. Why did David urge Solomon to heed God's commandments? 2. What would result for Solomon and his successors if they remained faithful to the Lord? 3. How did Solomon demonstrate his love for God? 4. What request did Solomon make before God, and how did the Lord respond? 5. Why is it important for all believers to obtain godly wisdom?

■ **ILLUSTRATIONS:**

Minister's Assurance. Oscar Romero, a minister in San Salvador, became the most revered martyr of the twentieth century for millions of Christians in Latin America and the United States. Romero was a gentle pastor who occupied a high leadership position in his church. As he and his fellow Christians studied God's Word, they recognized the importance of promoting justice for the oppressed.

Romero and other sympathetic believers challenged the ruling elite and powerful landowners of their nation. However, opponents of the reform movement accused Romero and other Christian leaders of being revolutionaries. Tragically, the charges led to a terrible level of violence in El Salvador. A number of church leaders were assassinated by death squads.

Despite the threats, Romero continued his weekly parish responsibilities. His messages of love, peace, and hope were broadcast by a religious radio station and heard by nearly every household in El Salvador. Though the station was bombed off the air, Romero continued preaching to a packed congregation each Sunday. He told his audience, "Each of you who believe must become a microphone, a radio station, a loudspeaker, not to talk, but to call for faith."

The warnings that Romero could be killed grew more frequent. A week before the minister was assassinated, a journalist asked him what kept him going in the midst of so much danger and turmoil. Romero, who had just returned from a religious retreat, replied, "If it were not for the message of grace through Christ, I would not be more than what St. Paul says, 'clanging metal.' "

Hand It On. Tom Anderson was one of Scotland's most talented and best known fiddle players. Born and raised in the Shetland Islands, where the fiddling tradition has been cherished for generations, Anderson performed widely and won acclaim for his brilliant playing. He wrote many popular fiddle tunes, taught countless students, and led several fiddle orchestras.

In Anderson's old age, while suffering from what would be his final illness, he called young Jacqueline Sinclair to his home. He had trained Jacqueline, a crippled girl who had become a promising expert fiddler. Handing her his own treasured violin, Anderson said, "You, too, have a special gift of music. I want to give you my precious fiddle. I hand it over to you. Play it well, play it often, and give joy to others." Jacqueline prizes that instrument, and carries on the Tom Anderson legacy today as one of the premier Scottish fiddlers. She teaches others and leads an orchestra.

David passed on instructions to Solomon in which he urged his son to walk in the way of the Lord. This was David's lasting legacy to future generations. What kind of legacy are we leaving to the next generation?

Sermon in a Sentence. The renowned missionary and speaker Dr. E. Stanley Jones, once stated, "I don't know what the future holds, but I do know who hold's the future!" That kind of trust, springing from worship, is the secret of success for every Christian leader.

■ TOPIC: Which Way to Go?

■ QUESTIONS: 1. What promise had God made to David concerning his descendants? 2. As Solomon began his reign as king, what characterized his relationship with God? 3. What did Solomon do at Gibeon? 4. Why did Solomon ask for wisdom? 5. Who are some godly Christians you know who would be willing to share their wisdom with you?

■ ILLUSTRATIONS:

Life's Priority. In October, 1997, Goodwill CEO Fred Gandy encouraged the nation to clean out its closets and help change people's lives. Toronto, Ohio newspaper boy Adam Chesnut responded by asking his 50 customers to donate clothing and household items. After achieving this goal, he asked the entire town to join in the campaign, claiming that he wanted to make a difference.

Here's a young man who has made serving and helping others a priority in his life. Solomon also wanted to serve the Lord and the people of Israel. This was the king's foremost priority. Rather than seek wealth and prestige, Solomon asked God for wisdom so that he could do a better job of leading others. You, too, should determine your priorities so that you can be a better servant for the Lord.

Ability to Distinguish. In September, 1998, the Commonwealth Foundation unveiled a 63-page study that reviewed the curricula of Pennsylvania's State System of Higher Education. The study criticized the state's higher education requirements, pointing out that almost half the students graduate without taking courses in literature, history, philosophy, foreign languages, and mathematics. Instead of essential academic subjects, students trade for courses in "Star Trek and

Modern Man," "Pistol 1," "Jewelry 1," "Craft Studio," and "Television Workshop." The report calls for more rigorous core courses of study to replace the irrelevant subjects now being offered.

Some students may boast that they aced a course such as Star Trek 101. Sadly, they may be unprepared when the circumstances of life force them to distinguish between what is superficial and ordinary and what is profound and vital. For this reason such a course as Star Trek 101—though interesting—will not greatly enhance a young person's post academic life. A good composition or math course, though, may help.

Solomon also had to decide between what was superficial and what would enhance his ability to serve God and others. The king was prudent in choosing wisdom. We also are discerning if we make the same choice.

Carefully Considered Choice. Gillette claims that the Mach 3 is a "total shaving system." According to *USA Today*, it took Gillette seven years to develop the product at a cost of $750 million. The marketing team considered 87,000 names before making the selection. Apparently, it was a well made choice. Even at seven dollars each, the Mach 3 outsells all other razors by 4 to 1.

If a company can appreciate a worthwhile goal, how much more can we as followers of Christ? For instance, this week's lesson encourages us to follow Solomon's goal of pursuing the knowledge and wisdom of God. What better aim in life could we have?

SOLOMON BUILDS THE TEMPLE

BACKGROUND SCRIPTURE: 1 Kings 5:1-8; 6:1-22, 37-38; 8:4—9:5
DEVOTIONAL READING: Psalm 84:1-4

KEY VERSE: Will God indeed dwell on the earth? Even heaven and the highest heaven cannot contain you, much less this house that I have built! 1 Kings 8:27.

KING JAMES VERSION

1 KINGS 6:37 In the fourth year was the foundation of the house of the LORD laid, in the month Zif:

38 And in the eleventh year, in the month Bul, which is the eighth month, was the house finished throughout all the parts thereof, and according to all the fashion of it. So was he seven years in building it. . . .

8:22 And Solomon stood before the altar of the LORD in the presence of all the congregation of Israel, and spread forth his hands toward heaven: . . .

27 But will God indeed dwell on the earth? behold, the heaven and heaven of heavens cannot contain thee; how much less this house that I have builded?

28 Yet have thou respect unto the prayer of thy servant, and to his supplication, O LORD my God, to hearken unto the cry and to the prayer, which thy servant prayeth before thee to day:

29 That thine eyes may be open toward this house night and day, even toward the place of which thou hast said, My name shall be there: that thou mayest hearken unto the prayer which thy servant shall make toward this place.

30 And hearken thou to the supplication of thy servant, and of thy people Israel, when they shall pray toward this place: and hear thou in heaven thy dwelling place: and when thou hearest, forgive. . . .

9:1 And it came to pass, when Solomon had finished the building of the house of the LORD, and the king's house, and all Solomon's desire which he was pleased to do,

2 That the LORD appeared to Solomon the second time, as he had appeared unto him at Gibeon.

3 And the LORD said unto him, I have heard thy prayer and thy supplication, that thou hast made before me: I have hallowed this house, which thou hast built, to put my name there for ever; and mine eyes and mine heart shall be there perpetually.

4 And if thou wilt walk before me, as David thy father walked, in integrity of heart, and in uprightness, to do according to all that I have commanded thee, and wilt keep my statutes and my judgments:

5 Then I will establish the throne of thy kingdom upon Israel for ever, as I promised to David thy father, saying, There shall not fail thee a man upon the throne of Israel.

NEW REVISED STANDARD VERSION

1 KINGS 6:37 In the fourth year the foundation of the house of the LORD was laid, in the month of Ziv. 38 In the eleventh year, in the month of Bul, which is the eighth month, the house was finished in all its parts, and according to all its specifications. He was seven years in building it. . . .

8:22 Then Solomon stood before the altar of the LORD in the presence of all the assembly of Israel, and spread out his hands to heaven. . . .

27 "But will God indeed dwell on the earth? Even heaven and the highest heaven cannot contain you, much less this house that I have built! 28 Regard your servant's prayer and his plea, O LORD my God, heeding the cry and the prayer that your servant prays to you today; 29 that your eyes may be open night and day toward this house, the place of which you said, 'My name shall be there,' that you may heed the prayer that your servant prays toward this place. 30 Hear the plea of your servant and of your people Israel when they pray toward this place; O hear in heaven your dwelling place; heed and forgive." . . .

9:1 When Solomon had finished building the house of the LORD and the king's house and all that Solomon desired to build, 2 the LORD appeared to Solomon a second time, as he had appeared to him at Gibeon. 3 The LORD said to him, "I have heard your prayer and your plea, which you made before me; I have consecrated this house that you have built, and put my name there forever; my eyes and my heart will be there for all time. 4 As for you, if you will walk before me, as David your father walked, with integrity of heart and uprightness, doing according to all that I have commanded you, and keeping my statutes and my ordinances, 5 then I will establish your royal throne over Israel forever, as I promised your father David, saying, 'There shall not fail you a successor on the throne of Israel.' "

BACKGROUND

God denied David's request to erect a temple but promised that his son Solomon, would do so (2 Sam. 7:13). God enabled this king to carry out one of history's most magnificent building projects.

Solomon's temple (the first of three edifices on the site in Jerusalem) was the crowning achievement of his extensive construction program throughout his kingdom. Taking seven years to build, this great sanctuary used the services of the best craftspersons and artisans in the ancient Near East (1 Kings 6:37-38).

The king conscripted an enormous work force to bring the project to completion within a relatively short period of time (5:13-18). Engineers today would marvel at the skills of Solomon's masons who quarried, shaped, dressed, moved, and erected huge blocks of stones in the temple (6:7). Likewise, modern steelworkers would respect the molding, smelting, casting, and polishing abilities of Solomon's metalworkers, who could fashion such bronze pieces as the molten sea, which was a huge receptacle holding large quantities of water (7:23-26). People would also be amazed at the costly aromatic wood panels that lined the walls and ceiling of the sanctuary's interior, and the pure gold that was added for decorative purposes (7:8-22).

The purpose of the temple was to provide a suitable abode for the ark of the covenant. This signified that God was manifesting His holy presence among His people. The temple became the center of Israel's worship and national identity.

A great temple dedication service brought heads of the tribes and foreign dignitaries to Jerusalem. The ark was moved with impressive ceremony to the Holy of Holies, which was the innermost area of the newly-completed sanctuary. Solomon himself presided at the impressive rites of dedication, offering a moving prayer in which he asked God to always look with favor on His people. Solomon's words acknowledged that God's presence was not limited to the temple (8:1-53).

It was after Solomon had finished building the temple, as well as his royal palace, that God appeared again to him in a dream (the first time was at Gibeon; 3:4-15). God informed the monarch that he had been blessed. The Lord also promised him that he would never lack a descendant on the throne as long as God's commands were being heeded. However, if the king or his subjects rebelled against the Lord, He would uproot them and destroy the temple (9:1-9).

NOTES ON THE PRINTED TEXT

*I*n the fourth year the foundation of the house of the LORD was laid. . . . [Solomon] was seven years in building it (6:37-38). The period of time was due to the greatness of the task. While we do not know exactly what the sanctuary looked like, it may have been similar in appearance to those excavated at ancient Phoenician sites, given that architects and builders from Tyre worked on Solomon's temple (7:13-14).

A huge platform had to be constructed over a series of rocky slopes. The temple most likely was rectangular in shape and had a maximum height of about 45 feet. The entire structure possibly rested on a raised terrace of carefully cut stone. The sanctuary was divided into three chambers: a vestibule (or portico), the Holy Place, and the Most Holy Place.

The floors of the temple were cypress, while much of the rest of the interior was made from olive wood. Gold was everywhere. Two massive bronze pillars stood in front of the doors. A bronze altar and other bronze pieces were in the courtyard. Worshipers would have entered the temple from the east.

At the temple's completion in 959 B.C., Solomon held a huge dedication ceremony. First, the priests placed the ark in the sanctuary. Next, the king gave a blessing to those present (8:1-21). *Then Solomon stood before the altar of the LORD in the presence of all the assembly of Israel, and spread out his hands to heaven* (8:22).

In Solomon's prayer, he acknowledged the uniqueness of God and that He had faithfully kept all His promises to His people. For example, the Lord had allowed David's son to succeed him on the throne of Israel. Solomon requested that God would allow David's dynasty to endure for all time (8:23-26).

Then the king asked his audience, *"But will God indeed dwell on the earth? Even heaven and the highest heaven cannot contain you, much less this house that I have built!"* (8:27). This verse underscores the truth that God is infinite. In contrast, all that He has made—vast as creation may be—has its limits. Thus, no mere building, regardless of how wonderful it may be, could contain the Lord.

The fact that God manifested His holy presence in the temple was an act of grace. Perhaps this is why Solomon humbly asked the Lord to heed his request to watch over the temple and hear the prayers of himself and the rest of the Israelites concerning their nation.

Solomon said, *"Regard your servant's prayer and his plea, O LORD my God, heeding the cry and the prayer that your servant prays to you today; that your eyes may be open night and day toward this house, the place of which you said, 'My name shall be there,' that you may heed the prayer that your servant prays toward this place"* (8:28-29). Then the king prayed, *"Hear the plea of your servant and of your people Israel when they pray toward this place; O hear in heaven your dwelling place; heed and forgive"* (8:30).

After Solomon had finished the temple, his palace, various fortifications around Israel, and other building projects, the Lord appeared to him again in a dream. *When Solomon had finished building the house of the LORD and the king's house and all that Solomon desired to build, the LORD appeared to Solomon a second time, as he had appeared to him at Gibeon* (9:1-2).

The Lord assured Solomon that He had heard the king's prayer. God promised to be present and accessible in the temple. *The LORD said to him, "I have heard your prayer and your plea, which you made before me; I have consecrated this house that you have built, and put my name there forever; my eyes and my heart will be there for all time"* (9:3).

The Lord shifted His focus to the conduct of Solomon and his descendants. The future dominion of David's line over Israel was contingent on their fidelity to the Mosaic covenant. *"As for you, if you will walk before me, as David your father walked, with integrity of heart and uprightness, doing according to all that I have commanded you, and keeping my statutes and my ordinances, then I will establish your royal throne over Israel forever, as I promised your father David saying, 'There shall not fail you a successor on the throne of Israel'"* (9:4-5). The Lord's warning was a necessary reminder for Solomon, who would eventually compromise the conditions required for enjoying God's blessing (11:1-13).

SUGGESTIONS TO TEACHERS

The work ethic in the United States is based on the virtues of thrift, commitment, and perseverance. To some extent these are derived from ideas in the Bible. Yes, such a work ethic tends to bring financial gain. Nevertheless, there are dangers associated with it. The life of Solomon reminds us that regardless of how much we accomplish, obeying God is foremost in priority. As 1 Samuel 15:22 says, *"Surely, to obey is better than sacrifice."*

1. PLAN FOR CONSTRUCTION. To honor God, Solomon hired the best craftspersons and used the finest materials. When we honor the Lord, we should give Him our best. This applies to our time, energy, and possessions.

2. PRESENTATION OF CONDITIONS. Have the students consider God's words to Solomon regarding his ambitious plans for the temple. *"If you walk in my statutes, obey my ordinances, and keep all my commandments by walking in them, then I will establish my promise with you"* (1 Kings 6:12-13). Here we see that all our plans in life are under God's scrutiny. Therefore, *whether we are at home or away, we make it our aim to please him. For all of us must appear before the judgment seat of Christ* (2 Cor. 5:9-10).

3. PROGRAM FOR COMPLETION. Solomon finished the building of the Jerusalem temple within seven years. The sanctuary was amazingly grand and beautiful, which made it a suitable tribute to God. Solomon mobilized all his energies, organizational skills, and material resources to achieve his goal of honoring the Lord with a temple. Worthwhile projects and programs that endure beyond our lifetime require such a high level of commitment.

4. PRAYER OF CONSECRATION. A great dedication service, climaxed by Solomon's prayer, set apart the temple for worship. Talk with the class members about the importance of setting apart a special place for worship in their lives. Also discuss what spiritual significance a church building may have in the life of a community.

5. PROMISE OF COMMITMENT. God promised to establish Solomon's royal throne over Israel forever if he and his successors heeded the Mosaic covenant (1 Kings 9:5-9). Solomon understood that his actions affected future generations. Emphasize to the students that the way in which we live can either adversely or positively affect people who are yet to be born.

FOR ADULTS

■ TOPIC: When Goals are Reached

■ QUESTIONS: 1. Why do you think it took Solomon seven years to complete the temple? 2. What was Solomon implying when he asked, *"But will God indeed dwell on the earth"* (8:27)? 3. Why do you think Solomon was concerned that the Lord would *"hear the plea of your servant and of your people Israel"* (8:30)? 4. When God appeared to Solomon a second time, what did He urge the king to do? 5. Why is a life of obedience to God most desirable from an eternal perspective?

■ **ILLUSTRATIONS:**

Proclamation to the Pilgrims. In the autumn of 1623, members of Plymouth Plantation were finally able to reach their goal of securing sufficient food to keep themselves alive for a long winter. Governor William Bradford declared the following Thanksgiving Proclamation to the residents of the community, who were also known as *Pilgrims*.

> Inasmuch as the great Father has given us this year an abundant harvest of Indian corn, wheat, beans, squashes, and garden vegetables, and has made the forests to abound with game and the sea with fish and clams, and inasmuch as He has protected us from the ravages of savages, has spared us from pestilence and disease, has granted us freedom to worship Him according to the dictates of our own conscience; I, your magistrate, proclaim that all ye Pilgrims, with your wives and little ones, gather at the meetinghouse on the hill and render thanksgiving to the Almighty God for all His blessings.

William Bradford captured the spirit of Thanksgiving. He thanked God with enthusiasm for specific blessings. Bradford wasn't too proud to praise God even for small manifestations of His grace. Bradford knew that all good gifts—including the "squashes" and "clams"—come from God (Jas. 1:17).

Glorifying God on Main Street. Lord George MacLeod, the late great Scottish minister who founded the Iona Community, told about a boy who hurled a stone through a church window. The stone smashed one of the letters in a glass inscription so that the words no longer read "GLORY TO GOD IN THE HIGHEST," but rather said "GLORY TO GOD IN THE HIGH ST." (In Scottish towns, High Street is usually the main thoroughfare).

MacLeod regretted that the church members restored the window to its original wording. He wanted the letter "E" mounted on a swivel so that everyone would be able to read both versions: GLORY TO GOD IN THE HIGHEST and GLORY TO GOD IN THE HIGH ST. MacLeod's point was that Christians may glorify God in a church building only as they also glorify Him out in the world. Solomon's prayer indicated this type of balanced perspective.

Purpose of the Temple and Worship. Isaac Bashivis Singer, who is a well regarded author, told how his grandfather, who was a rabbi, once embarrassed his congregation by asking why God was so eager to be praised. The elderly rabbi went on to point out that devout people were expected to bow three times a day and tell the Lord how great and wonderful He is. After making a few more comments, Singer's grandfather explained, "The Almighty knows that when people stop praising Him, they begin praising one another and praising themselves."

Solomon was aware of the same truth. That's why he wanted to build a great temple for the praise of God. This king also realized that when people do not spend time worshiping God, they begin idolizing themselves, other people, and things in the world. Applicable here are the words of Paul: *They exchanged the glory of the immortal God for images resembling a mortal human being or birds or four-footed animals or reptiles* (Rom. 1:23).

FOR YOUTH

■ TOPIC: What Is True Worship?
■ QUESTIONS: 1. Why was Solomon's completion of the temple a significant event in Israel's history? 2. In Solomon's prayer of dedication, what did he note about God and His promises? 3. When did the Lord appear a second time to Solomon? 4. What condition did God place on Solomon for the continuance of his royal dynasty? 5. How do the public prayers of our spiritual leaders set the tone for the church?

■ ILLUSTRATIONS:
Worship and the Heisman Trophy. Ricky Williams, the star fullback at the University of Texas, was the nation's leading rusher in his junior year during the 1997 season. Disappointed at not being invited to New York for the Heisman ceremony that fall, he thought about dropping out of college and becoming a professional football player.

During the Christmas break, however, Williams attended his church in San Diego. He listened intently to the pastor's sermon that Sunday, and found himself receiving insights and guidance during the worship service that changed his thinking. Williams realized that he enjoyed going to school. He thus resolved to return to his studies and play football during his senior year. That Sunday's worship experience convinced him to play for the Longhorns for a final season.

The gifted athlete may have looked like an art student off the field with the dreadlocks and tattoo of Mickey Mouse on his forearm. But on the field, the 6-foot-1-inch, 225 pound fullback won awards for rushing the most yards. He even broke the record Tony Dorsett held for 22 years.

In December, 1998, the Longhorn star received the Heisman Trophy, which is college football's most coveted individual award. Ricky Williams also earned respect for the way in which he tried to change what the Heisman Trophy signified. When told that the Heisman is the greatest personal honor, Williams shook his head vigorously in dissent. "I disagree," he said. "It's a team award. You can't become a finalist without the effort and hard work of the whole team. The best part of this whole season is that I was part of a Texas team that won eight games." Some would say that Williams's practice of regularly worshiping God is the reason for his humble spirit.

Finding God, or Being Found by God? We sometimes hear someone speaking of trying to find God. The words imply that God is elusive, trying to hide or remain aloof. The question is not so much "How can I find God?" but rather "How can I let myself be found by Him?"

Remember, this great and gracious God has already sought out us in the person of Jesus (1 John 4:10). Like the shepherd seeking out his lost sheep in the wilderness or the housewife searching for that lost coin in the dark recesses of her house (see Luke 15), God has relentlessly sought out us. This Lord wants to find us as much as we may want to find Him. In the person of the crucified, risen one, the search process has ended!

Priorities. John Wannamaker, founder of Wannamaker's Department Store, had a sign that still hangs in the actual office he occupied years ago. It reads, "God First. Family Second. Shoes Third." It was a reminder to both him and his employees of life's priorities.

Each of us must decide what role the Lord will play in our life. We should follow Wannamaker's lead by putting God first.

SOLOMON'S MISTAKES

BACKGROUND SCRIPTURE: 1 Kings 11
DEVOTIONAL READING: Nahum 1:2-8

KEY VERSE: The LORD was angry with Solomon, because his heart had turned away from the LORD, the God of Israel. 1 Kings 11:9a.

KING JAMES VERSION

1 KINGS 11:1 But king Solomon loved many strange women, together with the daughter of Pharaoh, women of the Moabites, Ammonites, Edomites, Zidonians, and Hittites;

2 Of the nations concerning which the LORD said unto the children of Israel, Ye shall not go in to them, neither shall they come in unto you: for surely they will turn away your heart after their gods: Solomon clave unto these in love.

3 And he had seven hundred wives, princesses, and three hundred concubines: and his wives turned away his heart.

4 For it came to pass, when Solomon was old, that his wives turned away his heart after other gods: and his heart was not perfect with the LORD his God, as was the heart of David his father.

5 For Solomon went after Ashtoreth the goddess of the Zidonians, and after Milcom the abomination of the Ammonites.

6 And Solomon did evil in the sight of the LORD, and went not fully after the LORD, as did David his father.

7 Then did Solomon build an high place for Chemosh, the abomination of Moab, in the hill that is before Jerusalem, and for Molech, the abomination of the children of Ammon.

8 And likewise did he for all his strange wives, which burnt incense and sacrificed unto their gods.

9 And the LORD was angry with Solomon, because his heart was turned from the LORD God of Israel, which had appeared unto him twice,

10 And had commanded him concerning this thing, that he should not go after other gods: but he kept not that which the LORD commanded.

11 Wherefore the LORD said unto Solomon, Forasmuch as this is done of thee, and thou hast not kept my covenant and my statutes, which I have commanded thee, I will surely rend the kingdom from thee, and will give it to thy servant.

12 Notwithstanding in thy days I will not do it for David thy father's sake: but I will rend it out of the hand of thy son.

13 Howbeit I will not rend away all the kingdom; but will give one tribe to thy son for David my servant's sake, and for Jerusalem's sake which I have chosen.

NEW REVISED STANDARD VERSION

1 KINGS 11:1 King Solomon loved many foreign women along with the daughter of Pharaoh: Moabite, Ammonite, Edomite, Sidonian, and Hittite women, 2 from the nations concerning which the LORD had said to the Israelites, "You shall not enter into marriage with them, neither shall they with you; for they will surely incline your heart to follow their gods"; Solomon clung to these in love. 3 Among his wives were seven hundred princesses and three hundred concubines; and his wives turned away his heart. 4 For when Solomon was old, his wives turned away his heart after other gods; and his heart was not true to the LORD his God, as was the heart of his father David. 5 For Solomon followed Astarte the goddess of the Sidonians, and Milcom the abomination of the Ammonites. 6 So Solomon did what was evil in the sight of the LORD, and did not completely follow the LORD, as his father David had done. 7 Then Solomon built a high place for Chemosh the abomination of Moab, and for Molech the abomination of the Ammonites, on the mountain east of Jerusalem. 8 He did the same for all his foreign wives, who offered incense and sacrificed to their gods.

9 Then the LORD was angry with Solomon, because his heart had turned away from the LORD, the God of Israel, who had appeared to him twice, 10 and had commanded him concerning this matter, that he should not follow other gods; but he did not observe what the LORD commanded. 11 Therefore the LORD said to Solomon, "Since this has been your mind and you have not kept my covenant and my statutes that I have commanded you, I will surely tear the kingdom from you and give it to your servant. 12 Yet for the sake of your father David I will not do it in your lifetime; I will tear it out of the hand of your son. 13 I will not, however, tear away the entire kingdom; I will give one tribe to your son, for the sake of my servant David and for the sake of Jerusalem, which I have chosen."

13

Monday, November 20	1 Kings 9:10-25	*Acts of Solomon*
Tuesday, November 21	1 Kings 11:1-8	*Solomon's Idolatry*
Wednesday, November 22	1 Kings 11:9-13	*God's Judgment on Solomon*
Thursday, November 23	Nahum 1:2-8	*The Wrath of God*
Friday, November 24	1 Kings 11:14-25	*Adversaries of Solomon*
Saturday, November 25	1 Kings 11:26-37	*Jereboam's Rebellion against Solomon*
Sunday, November 26	1 Kings 11:38-43	*A Conditional Promise and Solomon's Death*

BACKGROUND

Solomon was born to David and Bathsheba after the death of their first son (2 Sam. 12:24). Though Solomon was not David's oldest living son, he was crowned king after his mother and Nathan the prophet intervened with David. They had worked behind the scenes to convince the elderly monarch to have Solomon succeed him as ruler (1 Kings 1—2).

Scripture reveals that Solomon composed 3,000 proverbs, and he also had 1,005 songs in his repertoire (1 Kings 4:32). While Solomon's temple is the most famous of his construction projects, it is by no means the only one (chaps. 5—8). He also fortified a number of cities that helped provide protection to Jerusalem, built storage cities for stockpiling the materials required for his kingdom, and established military bases for contingents of charioteers (9:15-19).

As we will learn in this week's lesson, Solomon had faults in addition to elements of greatness. His 700 princesses and 300 concubines came from many of the kingdoms with which he had treaties (11:1). He evidently allowed his wives to worship their pagan deities and even had altars to these idols constructed in Jerusalem (11:7-8). Thus, despite the splendor of Solomon's royal court and the vastness of his wisdom, much of what he did proved futile (at least from an eternal perspective), for the powerful king failed to *fear God and keep his commandments* (Eccl. 12:13).

NOTES ON THE PRINTED TEXT

Solomon's reign, which had such promise, ended tragically. Contrary to the Mosaic law, he married many foreign women who did not believe in Israel's God (Deut. 7:1-4). Perhaps the most significant marriage was to the daughter of Egypt's Pharaoh. (Egyptians seldom married foreigners. However, Egypt was somewhat weak at this time.) Solomon's wives also included Moabite, Ammonite, Edomite, Hittite, and Phoenician women. It's clear that the writer of 1 Kings had a jaundiced view of Solomon's policy (11:1-2).

What the Lord had foretold in the Mosaic law occurred in the life of Solomon. His initial toleration of his wives' pagan religions grew as he aged, and he was lured into the worship of their false gods. Unlike David, Solomon was no longer wholeheartedly devoted to the Lord (11:4).

Scripture explains why Solomon abandoned his religious heritage. *For Solomon followed Astarte the goddess of the Sidonians, and Milcom the abomination of the Ammonites* (11:5). Astarte, the reputed sister and wife to Baal (the supreme fertility god of the Canaanites), was the goddess of love, war, and fertility. Numerous ancient clay plaques and figurines depicting naked women testify to her popularity. Astarte worship usually involved temple prostitution. Milcom's worship also often involved child sacrifice by fire. Both of these practices were abhorrent to God (11:6).

On a hill east of Jerusalem and south of the Mount of Olives, Solomon constructed shrines to honor the pagan deities of his wives. Undoubtedly their presence lured many Israelites away from the Lord. Today this spot is called the "hill of shame." While no archaeological evidence of any such shrines has been found, there is ample mention of them in Scripture (11:7-8).

The worship of Chemosh and Molech also involved the sacrifice of children as burnt offerings. It's no wonder that Solomon's endorsement of these pagan practices earned him the censure of God. The Lord was angry that Solomon had failed to heed His warnings about slipping into idolatry (11:9-10).

The Lord is holy and righteous, and this is why He had to discipline Israel's wayward king. Because Solomon had acted irresponsibly as Israel's ruler, God would tear away part of the kingdom and give it to one Solomon's servants (namely, Jeroboam; 11:26-39). However, for the sake of David, God would not divide Israel while Solomon was still alive. Rather, the Lord would take away the kingdom from his son, Rehoboam (11:43).

God's mercy is evident in that He would let Rehoboam remain in control of Judah and Jerusalem (11:11-13). The result was the division of Solomon's united kingdom into two separate nations—the southern kingdom of Judah and the northern kingdom of Israel (12:16-19).

SUGGESTIONS TO TEACHERS

Involvement with wrongdoing inevitably brings ruin. Whether it's through relationships that lure us away from the Lord or lesser loyalties that displace our primary loyalty, compromise costs us dearly. Solomon's account is a sobering example.

1. DISMAYING FAILURE. Not only was Solomon's heart turned away from the Lord but also his example led the Israelites astray. What perhaps seemed like an innocent way of placating his wives contributed to the eventual downfall of Solomon's kingdom.

2. DISAPPOINTING FLAW. The Lord had appeared twice to Solomon to warn him about about slipping into idolatry. It's thus understandable why God became angry with Solomon for his unfaithfulness.

3. DANGEROUS FOES. Solomon's luxury-loving ways and extravagant building programs created severe problems in Israel by the time of his death. For instance, he had overtaxed and overworked his subjects, and this led to deep discontent (12:4). But Solomon's failure to heed the Mosaic law was the main reason for the dissolution of his kingdom (11:11).

4. DIRE FUTURE. Jeroboam, a persuasive leader from the 10 northern tribes, emerged to set up a rival kingdom when Solomon's son, Rehoboam, obstinately refused to listen to the Lord or to the wise counsel of his elders. God's punishment came in the form of a divided kingdom in which Solomon's son ruled over a greatly reduced realm (12:6-15).

FOR ADULTS	■ TOPIC: When Compromise Ruins

■ QUESTIONS: 1. How many wives did Solomon have? 2. Why did Solomon depart from his rich spiritual heritage? 3. What are some of the challenges to our faith that often confront us? 4. What steps can we take to keep from falling into sin? 5. What part does God's discipline of us serve in helping us to remain faithful to Him?

■ **ILLUSTRATIONS:**

Blew His Chances. In 1994, Bam Morris was a rookie running back for the Pittsburgh Steelers. During that season, Morris rushed for over 800 yards. In one game against the Giants, he gained 146 yards for his team. Although a hefty 240 pounds, he showed such agility and bursts of speed that he was being hailed as the next Earl Campbell (a legendary running back).

The following year, Morris's performance was even better. In the post-season alone, he rushed for 188 yards, including 73 in the Super Bowl against the Dallas Cowboys. Morris moved to the Baltimore Ravens in 1996, and led the conference with a spectacular 618 yards rushing in the course of the final games of the season.

Despite his successes on the football field, Morris was having problems off the field, especially with drug abuse. However, he was such a talented player that he received a second chance, then another, and still another. He was warned by Art Modell, the owner of the Ravens, that if there were any more incidents relating to substance abuse, Morris would have to be dropped from the team. Then Morris was arrested on drug charges. In a display of leniency, the judge put him on probation. But Morris violated his probation, and received a jail sentence in early 1998.

Solomon also had a brilliant beginning. But his life was tainted by severe moral compromise. This could have been avoided had Israel's king remained wholehearted in his devotion to the Lord.

Ruinous Compromise. In the late 1950s, millions of people in the United States watched a popular quiz show entitled "The $64,000 Question." The star competitor on the program was a brilliant young scholar named Mark Van Doren. His father and family members were distinguished leaders in the academic world, and young Mark had a promising future as an acclaimed professor.

The quiz show posed difficult questions to contestants, and Van Doren seemed to be a whiz in coming up with the correct answers week after week. Ever increasing numbers of people marveled as Van Doren addressed a wide array of subjects episode after episode. He was soon hailed as the century's greatest intellect. Then rumors spread that the quiz show was rigged. Reporters discovered that Van Doren had been given the answers to questions in advance and coached on how to make it look if he was struggling to come up with the correct responses.

Van Doren later testified that at first he had objected to the gimmick. But then he was told that the program was merely entertainment. Supposedly giving help to quiz contestants was a common practice and simply part of show business. Van Doren evidently believed his cheating would increase society's appreciation of higher education and intellectual pursuits.

But these were lame excuses for Van Doren's moral compromise. His questionable acts eventually ruined his academic career and disgraced his family.

FOR YOUTH

■ TOPIC: The Cost of Compromise

■ QUESTIONS: 1. Why did the Lord forbid Israel's king from entering into marriages with foreign women? 2. What caused Solomon to slip into idolatry? 3. What things did Solomon do that the Lord considered evil? 4. What was the main reason for God's anger with Solomon? 5. What can we do to ensure that our hearts and lives remain fully devoted to the Lord?

■ ILLUSTRATIONS:

Forgotten Loyalties. *Boston Globe* columnist Mike Barnicle resigned under pressure for fabricating a 1995 tear-jerker column about a black child and a white child who both had been hospitalized with cancer and who became friends. When the black child died, Barnicle said that the parents of the white child gave $10,000 to the bereaved family.

The situation for Barnicle, however, began to unravel when *Reader's Digest* prepared to reprint the story. Despite the publication's best efforts, its fact-checking editors could not verify the account. This eventually forced the columnist to leave the *Boston Globe* in disgrace.

Some people—whether youth or adults—forget their loyalties and values. Barnicle forgot his loyalty to the truth. And Solomon forgot his loyalty to God. We are wise if we avoid making such tragic mistakes.

Measure of Success. On Saturday, August 29, 1998, an unusual auction took place in Penn Hills, Pennsylvania. The toys owned by H. Carlin Hulick were auctioned. The short salesman, who was known for his easygoing manner, had died suddenly of cancer.

Hulick's home, along with a separate garage, was jammed from basement to attic with boxes of toys. There were thousands of items, and almost all were in the original boxes with the price tags still on them. This man, who loved buying, building, and collecting planes, cars, and ships, had spent 59 years at his hobby. As 30-foot long moving trucks were unloaded, those who remembered Hulick laughed at the bumper sticker on his car, which read, "He who dies with the most toys wins!"

Here's an example of someone who thought that success is measured in terms of material accumulation. But Scripture says it's not. Solomon also amassed a fortune, yet he ultimately was a moral failure as Israel's king. He didn't realize that a strong relationship with the Lord is far more important from an eternal perspective.

Devastating Consequences. Jeremy P. Spinneweber and Matthew E. Belfoure, both 18, wanted to depart Trinity High School in Washington, Pennsylvania, with a bang during the school's commencement on June 5, 1998. The two had 70 projectiles under mulch and in a bush near the stage where graduation was to be held. Each projectile was inside a 10-inch long cardboard cylinder with powder at the bottom. When the projectiles were ignited, a small fireball would first soar into the sky and then undergo a second ignition that would release small parachutes. However, a janitor preparing the graduation area tripped over the wires, foiling the plan.

The two youths were arrested and arraigned on felony charges of risking a catastrophe. They were also charged with criminal conspiracy and a misdemeanor charge of disorderly conduct. Both eventually pled guilty when confronted by the authorities. They never realized the potential devastating consequences of their action. (People could have been burned, or struck by the projectiles or the clay weighted canisters as they fell from the sky, or injured during the ensuing panic.)

Like these two youths, Solomon failed to seriously consider the devastating consequences of his actions. His idolatry brought division to the nation and encouraged the Israelites to abandon their commitment to the Lord.

GOOD NEWS OF JESUS
(THE GOSPEL OF LUKE)

PREPARING THE WAY

BACKGROUND SCRIPTURE: Luke 1:5-25; 3:1-18
DEVOTIONAL READING: Isaiah 40:1-5

KEY VERSE: The voice of one crying out in the wilderness:
"Prepare the way of the Lord, make his paths straight." Luke 3:4.

KING JAMES VERSION

LUKE 3:2 Annas and Caiaphas being the high priests, the word of God came unto John the son of Zacharias in the wilderness.

3 And he came into all the country about Jordan, preaching the baptism of repentance for the remission of sins. . . .

7 Then said he to the multitude that came forth to be baptized of him, O generation of vipers, who hath warned you to flee from the wrath to come?

8 Bring forth therefore fruits worthy of repentance, and begin not to say within yourselves, We have Abraham to our father: for I say unto you, That God is able of these stones to raise up children unto Abraham.

9 And now also the axe is laid unto the root of the trees: every tree therefore which bringeth not forth good fruit is hewn down, and cast into the fire.

10 And the people asked him, saying, What shall we do then?

11 He answereth and saith unto them, He that hath two coats, let him impart to him that hath none; and he that hath meat, let him do likewise.

12 Then came also publicans to be baptized, and said unto him, Master, what shall we do?

13 And he said unto them, Exact no more than that which is appointed you.

14 And the soldiers likewise demanded of him, saying, And what shall we do? And he said unto them, Do violence to no man, neither accuse any falsely; and be content with your wages.

15 And as the people were in expectation, and all men mused in their hearts of John, whether he were the Christ, or not;

16 John answered, saying unto them all, I indeed baptize you with water; but one mightier than I cometh, the latchet of whose shoes I am not worthy to unloose: he shall baptize you with the Holy Ghost and with fire:

17 Whose fan is in his hand, and he will throughly purge his floor, and will gather the wheat into his garner; but the chaff he will burn with fire unquenchable.

18 And many other things in his exhortation preached he unto the people.

NEW REVISED STANDARD VERSION

LUKE 3:2 During the high priesthood of Annas and Caiaphas, the word of God came to John son of Zechariah in the wilderness. 3 He went into all the region around the Jordan, proclaiming a baptism of repentance for the forgiveness of sins. . . .

7 John said to the crowds that came out to be baptized by him, "You brood of vipers! Who warned you to flee from the wrath to come? 8 Bear fruits worthy of repentance. Do not begin to say to yourselves, 'We have Abraham as our ancestor'; for I tell you, God is able from these stones to raise up children to Abraham. 9 Even now the ax is lying at the root of the trees; every tree therefore that does not bear good fruit is cut down and thrown into the fire."

10 And the crowds asked him, "What then should we do?" 11 In reply he said to them, "Whoever has two coats must share with anyone who has none; and whoever has food must do likewise." 12 Even tax collectors came to be baptized, and they asked him, "Teacher, what should we do?" 13 He said to them, "Collect no more than the amount prescribed for you." 14 Soldiers also asked him, "And we, what should we do?" He said to them, "Do not extort money from anyone by threats or false accusation, and be satisfied with your wages."

15 As the people were filled with expectation, and all were questioning in their hearts concerning John, whether he might be the Messiah, 16 John answered all of them by saying, "I baptize you with water; but one who is more powerful than I is coming; I am not worthy to untie the thong of his sandals. He will baptize you with the Holy Spirit and fire. 17 His winnowing fork is in his hand, to clear his threshing floor and to gather the wheat into his granary; but the chaff he will burn with unquenchable fire."

18 So, with many other exhortations, he proclaimed the good news to the people.

HOME BIBLE READINGS

BACKGROUND

During this quarter, we will do a series of studies from the Gospel of Luke. The writer addressed his work to Theophilus. Perhaps this person, whose name means "lover of God," was an important government official who had converted to Christianity and wanted to learn more about his new faith. Or perhaps Theophilus was a spiritual seeker who wanted to explore the facts about Christ so he could decide for himself what to believe.

In either case, Luke wrote his Gospel to create an accurate, dependable account of the works, teachings, and life of Jesus. Luke sought to present Jesus as the Son of Man, the answer to the needs and hopes of the human race, and the one who came to seek and save the lost.

Luke was a Gentile physician and possibly came from Antioch of Syria (Col. 4:14). His own Gentile roots and Gentile audience explain why his Gospel has a universal perspective. It speaks to the condition of the entire human race, not just to Jews. Luke either omitted Jewish phrases and practices found in the other Gospels or explained them carefully. This makes his account readable for those less familiar with Jewish ways.

This week's lesson introduces us to John the Baptist. We will learn that he preached a baptism of repentance in order to prepare the way for Jesus. We will also discover that when large crowds came to hear John, he warned them that they had better be sincere about repenting and living righteously.

NOTES ON THE PRINTED TEXT

John the Baptist began his ministry when Tiberius was emperor of Rome, Pontius Pilate was governor of Judea, and Caiaphas was high priest (Luke 3:1-2). John *went into all the region around the Jordan, proclaiming a baptism of repentance for the forgiveness of sins* (3:3). In the desolate area where the Jordan empties into the Dead Sea, John called candidates for baptism to repent and be cleansed spiritually. His baptism was not just for the ceremonially unclean or Gentiles. It was also for everyone who repented, including Jews.

In calling people to repent, John was urging them to abandon their evil ways and turn to God in faith. This represented a complete change in the way one lived. John was concerned about the sincerity of those who repented. He challenged his listeners by comparing some of them to evil snakes fleeing a rapidly spreading brush fire. The idea is that they were seeking baptism only to escape the coming judgment. *John said to the crowds that came out to be baptized by him, "You brood of vipers! Who warned you to flee from the wrath to come?"* (3:7). John also urged the crowds to live in a manner worthy of their new commitment to God. *"Bear fruits worthy of repentance"* (3:8).

Evidently some within the crowds felt confident they had God's grace. They presumed they were righteousness before God because of being descended from Abraham. John warned them, *"Do not begin to say to yourselves, 'We have Abraham as our ancestor; for I tell you, God is able from these stones to raise up children to Abraham"* (3:8). In other words, their birthright did not exclude them from the need to renounce their sin and get right with the Lord.

John declared that divine wrath was imminent. He noted that the ax of God's judgment was poised, ready to sever the roots of the unrepentant. In fact, He would chop down every tree that failed to bear good fruit and throw it *"into the fire"* (3:9).

John's preaching caused many people to respond favorably. Verses 10 through 14 contain a series of three questions asked by the crowds and answers from John. Here we have a sampling of John's moral instructions, all having to do with material things.

And the crowds asked [John], "What then should we do?" (3:10). In response, John directed the attention of the people to those who lacked clothing and food and urged them to ease the suffering by making personal sacrifices. *"Whoever has two coats must share with anyone who has none; and whoever has food must do likewise"* (3:11).

John next addressed the tax collectors. In that day these people, who worked for the Romans, often overcharged others and pocketed the extra. When tax collectors came to be baptized, *they asked [John], "Teacher, what should we do?"* (3:12). John urged them to be honest and fair. *He said to them, "Collect no more than the amount prescribed for you"* (3:13).

John then spoke to some soldiers, who no doubt were members of the occupying Roman army. In ancient times, soldiers would abuse their power for personal gain. When the *soldiers asked [John], "And we, what should we do?"* (3:14), he told them to be content with their pay (3:14).

The impact John had on the people caused some to wonder *whether he might be the Messiah* (3:15). But John made it plain that he was insignificant compared to the one yet to come. In those days the lowliest servants generally removed the sandals of their masters and household guests. But John didn't feel qualified even to be the lowliest servant of the Messiah (3:16)

John also pointed out the limitations of what he could do. He could administer the symbol of spiritual baptism (water baptism), but he could do nothing about the reality of sin within. Jesus, however, would cleanse hearts. The reference to fire may mean that Christ would burn out the sin of the repentant (thus purifying them) and would burn (judge) people who did not repent.

John conjured up a harvest image in the minds of his hearers to show what he meant (3:17). Sin (or unrepentant sinners) was like chaff and Christ's everlasting judgment was like *unquenchable fire.* Despite John's severe words, his message was still good news of hope about the coming Messiah (3:18).

SUGGESTIONS TO TEACHERS

The annual buying spree is underway! Many streets, houses, and stores have been decorated with Christmas ornaments (some since Halloween). Also, advertisers are busy urging us to get ready for the festive season. Following this advice might get us ready for the holiday, but will we be morally and spiritually prepared to honor the birth of Christ?

Only those who are genuinely prepared for the coming of the Savior can celebrate His birth in a meaningful way. That's why in teaching this week's lesson, you'll want to avoid spotlighting the commercialized aspect of Christmas, and instead stress the spiritual truth that Jesus calls all people to repent and believe.

1. PROMISED PREPARER. Before discussing John the Baptist's role, have the students consider the account of his birth and the skepticism of Zechariah, his father. Though Zechariah, a devout priest, was told that God would intervene to enable his elderly wife, Elizabeth, bear a child, Zechariah doubted. The point to stress is that he should have unconditionally trusted God. Like Zechariah, some students in your class may have trouble believing in God's promises. This would be a good time to talk about what faith really means.

2. PERSUASIVE PREACHER. Have the class consider John the Baptist's message and what it means to repent. In light of the shallow ideas that some in our society have about repentance, it's important to note that turning to God is never a casual matter. Then ask the students to consider why God was just in punishing the wicked.

3. PARTICULAR PROMISE. John the Baptist announced to the crowd of people that God was sending the long-promised Deliverer. The baptism He would perform would be different in kind and emphasis from that done by John. In addition to cleansing people from their sins, Jesus would bring forgiveness and peace to those who repented and believed.

4. PEERLESS PERSON. Have the students contrast the personalities of John the Baptist, who embodied the best of the ancient covenant with Israel, and Jesus the Messiah, who inaugurated God's new era of redemption. Discuss what we must do to prepare to receive the Savior of the world. In the face of the cynicism and despair that's so prevalent these days, some in your class may not be expecting anything from God during the holiday season. Remind them that when they turn away from sin and come to Christ in faith, God keeps His promise to redeem them. They can rest assured that He will remain faithful to His promises.

■ **TOPIC:** Preparing for Christ's Birth

■ **QUESTIONS:** 1. When did the "word of God" (Luke 3:2) come to John? 2. Why did John refer to some in the crowds as a brood of vipers (3:7)? 3. How did John portray the baptism offered by Christ? 4. How do you think you would have responded had John spoken to you personally? 5. How has the presence and power of Christ in your life made a difference in the way you relate to others?

■ **ILLUSTRATIONS:**

More Than a Pile of Loot. Just whispering the word "Thanksgiving" gives some retailers a strong sense of anticipation. It's the day when they can finally unleash products on the public in the hope of making lots of money. (Russell Baker once suggested renaming Thanksgiving "Thunderherd Day," for it's used to kick off a nationwide shopping spree.)

But if you venture this week to a Dutch town called Assen, you'll never know the annual shopping frenzy has descended. This year Assen said *Enough!*, and banned any sign of Christmas until the sixth of December. That's when, according to tradition, the people of the community fully set their minds and hearts on the holiday season. And they wouldn't have it any other way. In fact, one Dutch woman said of the American version of Christmas, "It's just some pile of loot!"

Unprepared Teacher. A couple of years ago, a local newspaper reported a bomb scare in a church in western Kentucky. The police dispatcher received a 911 call around 6:30 P.M. one Sunday evening from the youth minister, who stated that there was a bomb in the sanctuary.

The Kentucky State Police patrol cars and bomb disposal experts promptly arrived. After evacuating the building, they searched the church and found no explosive device on the premises. This made the police suspicious, and so they quizzed the youth pastor. Eventually, they learned that the bomb threat was a hoax. The young man confessed that he had called 911 that Sunday night. It seems that he was scheduled to preach that evening and was not prepared. Because of his prank, no worship service was held that evening.

Being unprepared for the time when we celebrate the birth of Christ will not bring police charges or personal embarrassment to us. Nevertheless, we will miss out on all the spiritual joy associated with the advent of the Savior. John's message of repentance and faith thus is for all of us to take seriously.

What to Give? After complaining that I never knew what to give people for Christmas, my pastor sent me the following recommendations. To your enemy offer forgiveness. To an opponent give tolerance. To a friend give your heart. To a customer offer service. To all people give charity. To every child offer a good example. And to yourself give respect.

■ **TOPIC:** Preparing the Way

■ **QUESTIONS:** 1. What does it mean to repent, and why did John urge the crowds to do so? 2. How can we tell whether a person has sincerely repented? 3. Why do you think John told the crowds to be loving and kind to others? 4. Why is it a privilege for us to serve Jesus? 5. Who are some people you know who need to hear the good news of Christ?

■ **ILLUSTRATIONS:**

Opening Act. When country music superstar Hank Williams, Jr., performed at Pittsburgh's Civic Arena, he began by singing the popular tune, "Restless Heart." The purpose of his opening act was to prepare the audience for the main attraction by building anticipation and excitement.

In a spiritual sense, John was the "opener" for Jesus. In other words, he prepared the people for Jesus' arrival by building their anticipation. He wanted to make sure that they (as well as all of us) were prepared to meet the Savior.

Where Are the Fruits? Knowing that many are afraid of talking about their spiritual problems, a well-known religious leader in Philadelphia launched a toll-free hotline in December 1998. A weeklong blitz of television and radio commercials, bought at a cost of $225,000, produced floods of calls, most of which began, "Pastor, I'm in need of spiritual help."

The line, staffed Monday through Friday from 8 A.M. to 8 P.M., receives about 100 calls each day, while a message machine records calls coming in at other times. In 1999, a Spanish language line was added. More than 140 volunteers listened to people talk about their spiritual problems.

Some think the ministry does not really fulfill John's call to repentance. According to these critics, John stressed the importance of spiritual fruit that demonstrated the reality of one's faith commitment. He also emphasized that personal actions should accompany one's feelings and words.

Genuine Repentance. The members of a local church in the southern part of the United States listened to their pastor read aloud a hand written two-page letter from one of their members. In this document, the writer expressed his sorrow for what he had done wrong. It was clear that the person was truly repentant and wanted to get right with God and His people. Though some were skeptical, the majority of church members were responsive to the repentant believer's request and gladly received him back into their fellowship.

This forgiving spirit mirrors God's willingness to pardon those who genuinely repent. He can forgive sin because of what Christ did at Calvary.

RESPONDING TO GOD

BACKGROUND SCRIPTURE: Luke 1:26-38
DEVOTIONAL READING: Matthew 1:18-25

KEY VERSE: "Here am I, the servant of the Lord;
let it be with me according to your word." Luke 1:38a.

KING JAMES VERSION

LUKE 1:26 And in the sixth month the angel Gabriel was sent from God unto a city of Galilee, named Nazareth,

27 To a virgin espoused to a man whose name was Joseph, of the house of David; and the virgin's name was Mary.

28 And the angel came in unto her, and said, Hail, thou that art highly favoured, the Lord is with thee: blessed art thou among women.

29 And when she saw him, she was troubled at his saying, and cast in her mind what manner of salutation this should be.

30 And the angel said unto her, Fear not, Mary: for thou hast found favour with God.

31 And, behold, thou shalt conceive in thy womb, and bring forth a son, and shalt call his name JESUS.

32 He shall be great, and shall be called the Son of the Highest: and the Lord God shall give unto him the throne of his father David:

33 And he shall reign over the house of Jacob for ever; and of his kingdom there shall be no end.

34 Then said Mary unto the angel, How shall this be, seeing I know not a man?

35 And the angel answered and said unto her, The Holy Ghost shall come upon thee, and the power of the Highest shall overshadow thee: therefore also that holy thing which shall be born of thee shall be called the Son of God.

36 And, behold, thy cousin Elisabeth, she hath also conceived a son in her old age: and this is the sixth month with her, who was called barren.

37 For with God nothing shall be impossible.

38 And Mary said, Behold the handmaid of the Lord; be it unto me according to thy word. And the angel departed from her.

NEW REVISED STANDARD VERSION

LUKE 1:26 In the sixth month the angel Gabriel was sent by God to a town in Galilee called Nazareth, 27 to a virgin engaged to a man whose name was Joseph, of the house of David. The virgin's name was Mary.
28 And he came to her and said, "Greetings, favored one! The Lord is with you." 29 But she was much perplexed by his words and pondered what sort of greeting this might be. 30 The angel said to her, "Do not be afraid, Mary, for you have found favor with God.
31 And now, you will conceive in your womb and bear a son, and you will name him Jesus. 32 He will be great, and will be called the Son of the Most High, and the Lord God will give to him the throne of his ancestor David. 33 He will reign over the house of Jacob forever, and of his kingdom there will be no end."
34 Mary said to the angel, "How can this be, since I am a virgin?" 35 The angel said to her, "The Holy Spirit will come upon you, and the power of the Most High will overshadow you; therefore the child to be born will be holy; he will be called Son of God. 36 And now, your relative Elizabeth in her old age has also conceived a son; and this is the sixth month for her who was said to be barren. 37 For nothing will be impossible with God." 38 Then Mary said, "Here am I, the servant of the Lord; let it be with me according to your word." Then the angel departed from her.

Monday, December 4	Luke 1:26-33	*The Birth of Jesus Foretold*
Tuesday, December 5	Luke 1:34-38	*Mary Says Yes to God*
Wednesday, December 6	Psalm 16	*The Joy of God's Presence*
Thursday, December 7	Psalm 121	*The Lord Helps Me*
Friday, December 8	Matthew 1:18-25	*The Miraculous Conception*
Saturday, December 9	Matthew 1:1-17	*The Genealogy of Jesus the Messiah*
Sunday, December 10	Lamentations 3:22-26	*The Mercies of God*

BACKGROUND

When Gabriel appeared to Mary of Nazareth, she was perhaps no more than 15 years old. The angel's startling announcement that she would soon become the mother of the Christ child meant the end of a normal life.

From that time on Mary's name would be on the lips of gossips and rumor-mongers. Joseph, her husband-to-be, could have decided to end their betrothal through a public, humiliating divorce. Even if he did so, she would still have to return in shame to her father's home or else survive on her own by whatever means she could.

Thankfully, God intervened to prevent this tragic possibility from happening (Matt. 1:18-25). Nevertheless, faced with an extraordinary turn of events that she had neither caused nor sought, Mary would have had plenty of reason to balk at Gabriel's message. Instead, she willingly and humbly accepted her assignment as the bearer of the Christ child (Luke 1:38).

The social customs of the day form the backdrop of this week's lesson. As noted above, Mary was betrothed to Joseph (1:27). In ancient times, this was a mutual promise or contract for a future marriage (Deut. 20:7; Jer. 2:2). This custom is not to be mistaken with the modern concept of engagement. Betrothal followed the selection of the bride by the prospective husband. The contract was negotiated by a friend or agent representing the bride. It was confirmed by oaths and was accompanied with presents to the bride and often to the bride's parents.

Betrothal was celebrated by a feast. In some instances, it was customary for the bridegroom to place a ring on the bride's finger as a token of love and fidelity. In Jewish culture, betrothal was actually part of the marriage process. A change of intention by one of the partners after he or she was betrothed was a serious matter, subject in some instances to a fine.

It's true that betrothal was much more closely linked with marriage than our modern engagement. Nevertheless, the actual marriage took place only when the bridegroom took the bride to his home. Then the marriage was consummated through physical intimacy. In the case of Mary and Joseph, this didn't occur until after the birth of Jesus (Matt. 1:25).

NOTES ON THE PRINTED TEXT

Two of the most frequently used illustrations of this week's lesson were painted by Flemish artist Jan van Eyck (1380–1441) and Italian artist Sandro Botticelli (1444–1510). They differ in their interpretations of Gabriel's announcement to Mary concerning the Christ child.

In van Eyck's portrayal, Mary has been reading Scripture, and she raises her head and hands in a gentle gesture of reverent acceptance at the news that a smiling Gabriel delivers. Botticelli's angel appears in a commanding pose and is towering over Mary, who seems to be in a trance-like state of awe. Perhaps the truth of Mary's response lies somewhere in between these two depictions.

In the sixth month the angel Gabriel was sent by God to a town in Galilee called Nazareth, to a virgin engaged to a man whose name was Joseph, of the house of David. The virgin's name was Mary (Luke 1:26-27). Six months after Gabriel made his announcement about John the Baptist, God sent him to Nazareth, which was a tiny Galilean village located about 90 miles north of Jerusalem. There a young woman was engaged to Joseph, a descendant of David. The two had made a verbal marriage covenant, and perhaps sealed it with a financial pledge. While they had not yet consummated their relationship, the agreement was every bit as binding as marriage.

And he came to her and said, "Greetings, favored one! The Lord is with you" (1:28). Gabriel announced to Mary that she had found favor with God and that the Lord was with her. The angel's announcement left Mary feeling confused and distressed, and she tried to figure out what the angel could have meant. Gabriel, sensing Mary's fear, reassured her that God was going to bless her. *But she was much perplexed by his words and pondered what sort of greeting this might be* (1:29). Gabriel offered more comforting words when he said, *"Do not be afraid, Mary, for you have found favor with God"* (1:30).

Then Gabriel made a startling announcement to Mary. He declared that she was going to become pregnant and give birth to a male child, whom she would name Jesus. *"And now, you will conceive in your womb and bear a son, and you will name him Jesus"* (1:31). The name, which means "the Lord saves," was apt, for this child would be God's anointed Deliverer. *"He will be great, and will be called the Son of the Most High, and the Lord God will give to him the throne of his ancestor David. He will reign over the house of Jacob forever, and of his kingdom there will be no end"* (1:32-33).

Mary was still perplexed. How could she, an unwed virgin, become the mother of the promised King? *Mary said to the angel, "How can this be, since I am a virgin?"* (1:34).

The angel revealed that the Holy Spirit would bring about the conception of Jesus in Mary's womb. In other words, her pregnancy was the special and unique work of God. *The angel said to her, "The Holy Spirit will come upon you, and the power of the Most High will overshadow you; therefore the child to be born will be holy; he will be called the Son of God"* (1:35).

Gabriel offered to Mary a sign of confirmation. He announced that her older relative, Elizabeth, was in her sixth month of pregnancy. The angel's intent was to underscore how powerfully God had worked in Elizabeth's life to enable her to conceive. Nothing was impossible with God, even Mary's conception of the Christ child (1:37).

In faith, Mary responded to God and accepted the responsibility given to her. *Then Mary said, "Here am I, the servant of the Lord; let it be with me according to your word"* (1:38). Following Mary's statement and with Gabriel's mission completed, the angel departed from the young woman.

SUGGESTIONS TO TEACHERS

Some religious traditions are reluctant to pay much attention to Mary the mother of Jesus. At best, she is relegated to being a passive figure in a children's manger scene. This is tragic. Thankfully, in this week's lesson, we will give more serious attention to her as a person of extraordinary faith. Her humble and compliant attitude is worthy of emulation in all believers.

1. ANNOUNCEMENT. Gabriel's God-given message to Mary was undoubtedly the most momentous one she would ever receive. It also should be taken seriously by the members of your class. This young Jewish woman from an ordinary village would bring forth the Christ child. And through her baby, whom she would name *Jesus*, God would provide salvation for all humanity! With the advent of Christ, none of your students have to conjecture about how God might free them from sin. Through the atoning sacrifice of His Son, salvation is possible for all who believe.

2. ASTONISHMENT. Though Mary was initially surprised by the news that God wanted her to be the bearer of the Christ child, she neither doubted the Lord nor flinched from the assignment. Some in your class may be struggling with trying to find a scientific explanation for the virgin birth of Christ. Let them know that Scripture doesn't try to solve the mysterious way in which God brought about this miracle. Be sure to note that the conception of Jesus underscored how uniquely set apart—that is, holy and sinless—He was in God's eyes. That's why Jesus would be called the Son of God!

3. ACKNOWLEDGEMENT. Mary trusted the Lord, despite the potential risks involved (such as being misunderstood and rejected by others). This is the essence of true faith in God. It requires no proofs and makes no demands of God. The person of faith calmly rests in the Lord's wise and loving hand.

4. ACCEPTANCE. Mary willingly accepted and obeyed her God-given task of bearing the Christ child, saying, *"Let it be with me according to your word"* (Luke 1:38). This is the kind of response that God also wants from every student in your class. Take a few moments to talk about occasions when it is hardest to say *yes* to the Lord and *no* to oneself and others.

■ **TOPIC:** Obeying God's Call

■ **QUESTIONS:** 1. What do we learn about Mary from Luke 1:26-28? 2. What feelings was Mary experiencing as she listened to Gabriel's announcement? 3. What explanation did Gabriel offer to Mary concerning her pregnancy? 4. How does Jesus' amazing birth remind you of God's power? 5. In what way is Mary an example of unconditional faith for all of us who believe?

■ **ILLUSTRATIONS:**

Your Favorite Holiday? Deborah A. Bruce wrote an article entitled "Monday Morning" (Dec. 21, 1998). It states that if you're like most Americans, your favorite holidays include Christmas (in a recent national survey, 85 percent named Christmas as one of their favorites), Thanksgiving (50 percent), and Easter (24 percent). Furthermore, when asked to name the "most significant Christian holiday to you personally," 70 percent named Christmas and 19 percent named Easter. Moreover, 72 percent reported that celebrating the birth of Jesus was "very important" to them.

How do Americans celebrate Christmas? Three quarters of them exchange gifts, attend family gatherings, cook holiday meals, and decorate Christmas trees. Religious ways of celebrating the holiday are somewhat less common: 63 percent attend a worship service, 57 percent take time out for spiritual reflection, and 51 percent read the Bible or some other religious book. Caring for the poor and homeless at Christmas is more likely to take the form of giving food, money, or clothing (68 percent do this) than giving time (36 percent volunteer for charitable activities at Christmas).

Misunderstanding the Message. Have you ever listened to children sing Christmas carols? Sometimes their zestful singing will lead us to realize that we are not clearly communicating the Christmas message. They hear and picture things that even our most creative imaginations could never conceive.

Consider some of the familiar lines of Christmas carols from a child's perspective (as noted by John B. Barker). How about a buttered and green paste Jesus who can "sleep in heavenly peas"? And what about the weather? It's "joy to the world, the Savior rains!" Other young children puzzle over the strange grooming habits of old: "For lo, the days are hastening on, by prophet beards foretold." Quite a few are mystified by the laundry practices: "While shepherds washed their socks by night."

Or, while the family waits for relatives to arrive at the airport, what three year old doesn't entertain himself or herself by singing, "Angels we have heard on high, sweetly singing o'er the plane." Perhaps a youngster wonders whether an uncle or aunt is looking out the plane's window at those singing angels. The same confusion arises over the international arrivals: "This is He whom Sears of old time chanted of with one accord."

Each of these examples illustrate some of the confusion young children have about Christmas and the Gospel. As we sing holiday carols, we can clarify things by emphasizing the birth of Jesus. For instance, we can explain that the Christmas songs are about God's promise to provide salvation through Jesus. The joy and wonder of His coming are cause for everyone—whether young or old—to sing and celebrate.

Responding to God's Call. In Sir Walter Scott's novel entitled *Old Mortality,* the main character by that name wanders about the Scottish countryside with a tool kit to search out old cemeteries. Old Mortality was an eighteenth century eccentric in many ways, but he felt he was obeying God's call by locating forgotten burial places of Scottish covenanters who had died martyrs' deaths a century earlier.

After dismounting from his horse, Old Mortality would scrutinize the weathered tombstones. When he located the graves of people who had given their lives for their faith, he would painstakingly restore the inscriptions. He would scrape away moss and dirt, and then he would carefully sharpen the lines with his chisel so that the names, deeds, and dates of the past would not be forgotten. Old Mortality wanted to have his generation and the ones to come remember what had happened in the past.

For us, responding to God may not take the form of restoring old gravestones. But we are wise to show others some ways of obeying God's call.

FOR YOUTH

■ TOPIC: Saying Yes to God

■ QUESTIONS: 1. What did Gabriel reveal about the child whom Mary would bear? 2. What was Mary's condition when Gabriel made his announcement to her? 3. What was unique about the son whom Mary would bear? 4. How might you praise God for the miraculous birth of His Son? 5. Why is Jesus' amazing birth important for you to remember?

■ ILLUSTRATIONS:

Undue Fascination with Angels. A renewed interest in angels can be traced back to 1975 when a well known evangelist preached a television sermon about them. He was bombarded with 200,000 requests for reprints. Fascination with angels has increased ever since, and it hasn't diminished because of Christmas.

Just take a look around and you'll see that books on angels and guardian angels continue to dominate the best-seller lists this holiday season. Workshops abound to help you unleash your own "angel experiences" or your "inner angel," while others claim to put people on talk shows in touch with angels. Television's *Touched by an Angel* consistently receives high ratings. And Hollywood has produced movies such as the venerable *It's a Wonderful Life* to newer releases such as *The Preacher's Wife* or *City of Angels.*

Mary was certain that the angel Gabriel had visited her. She also knew that he wasn't supposed to be the object of her fascination and worship. Rather, God was to be the subject of her praise. This is good to remember the next time we meet others who are obsessed with angels.

A Name to Live Up To. Peerless Price was named for a moving company. But this wasn't his claim to fame. On January 4, 1999, the receiver for the Tennessee Volunteers college football team caught four passes and returned a pair of kick-offs for 43 yards. This enabled his fellow players to win the Orange Bowl and a national championship. Years earlier his mother saw the name Peerless Price and liked it. After giving it to her son, she raised him to live up to its literal meaning, which is "without equal."

Gabriel told Mary to give the Christ child an eternally significant name—Jesus. His whole mission in life was summarized by that name. He came to save the lost from their sins.

Fulfilled Hope. On January 16, 1942, Robert Trumbell, Gene Aldrich, and Tony Pastula took off on a carrier-based bomber on what was supposed to be a submarine reconnaissance mission. On their return the plane missed the ship. The radio malfunctioned. Forced to ditch the plane in the sea, the three men barely had time to inflate the life raft before the bomber sank.

For 34 scorching days and cold nights, the three drifted in a four-by-eight-foot raft in the middle of the Pacific Ocean. However, the three never abandoned their hope of being picked up. In fact, hope sustained them throughout their ordeal and eventually enabled them to experience a new beginning after they were rescued.

The good news of this season is that salvation came through the birth of Christ in a Bethlehem stable. This birth gave the world a new hope and a new beginning, one that none of us should refuse to take.

PRAISING GOD

BACKGROUND SCRIPTURE: Luke 1:39-56
DEVOTIONAL READING: Psalm 34:1-3

KEY VERSE: "My soul magnifies the Lord, and my spirit rejoices in God my Savior, for he has looked with favor on the lowliness of his servant." Luke 1:46-48.

KING JAMES VERSION

LUKE 1:39 And Mary arose in those days, and went into the hill country with haste, into a city of Juda;

40 And entered into the house of Zacharias, and saluted Elisabeth.

41 And it came to pass, that, when Elisabeth heard the salutation of Mary, the babe leaped in her womb; and Elisabeth was filled with the Holy Ghost:

42 And she spake out with a loud voice, and said, Blessed art thou among women, and blessed is the fruit of thy womb.

43 And whence is this to me, that the mother of my Lord should come to me?

44 For, lo, as soon as the voice of thy salutation sounded in mine ears, the babe leaped in my womb for joy.

45 And blessed is she that believed: for there shall be a performance of those things which were told her from the Lord.

46 And Mary said, My soul doth magnify the Lord,

47 And my spirit hath rejoiced in God my Saviour.

48 For he hath regarded the low estate of his handmaiden: for, behold, from henceforth all generations shall call me blessed.

49 For he that is mighty hath done to me great things; and holy is his name.

50 And his mercy is on them that fear him from generation to generation.

51 He hath shewed strength with his arm; he hath scattered the proud in the imagination of their hearts.

52 He hath put down the mighty from their seats, and exalted them of low degree.

53 He hath filled the hungry with good things; and the rich he hath sent empty away.

54 He hath holpen his servant Israel, in remembrance of his mercy;

55 As he spake to our fathers, to Abraham, and to his seed for ever.

NEW REVISED STANDARD VERSION

LUKE 1:39 In those days Mary set out and went with haste to a Judean town in the hill country, 40 where she entered the house of Zechariah and greeted Elizabeth. 41 When Elizabeth heard Mary's greeting, the child leaped in her womb. And Elizabeth was filled with the Holy Spirit 42 and exclaimed with a loud cry, "Blessed are you among women, and blessed is the fruit of your womb. 43 And why has this happened to me, that the mother of my Lord comes to me? 44 For as soon as I heard the sound of your greeting, the child in my womb leaped for joy. 45 And blessed is she who believed that there would be a fulfillment of what was spoken to her by the Lord."

46 And Mary said,

"My soul magnifies the Lord,
47 and my spirit rejoices in God my Savior,
48 for he has looked with favor on the lowliness of
his servant.
Surely, from now on all generations will call me
blessed;
49 for the Mighty One has done great things for me,
and holy is his name.
50 His mercy is for those who fear him
from generation to generation.
51 He has shown strength with his arm;
he has scattered the proud in the thoughts of
their hearts.
52 He has brought down the powerful from their
thrones,
and lifted up the lowly;
53 he has filled the hungry with good things,
and sent the rich away empty.
54 He has helped his servant Israel,
in remembrance of his mercy,
55 according to the promise he made to our ancestors,
to Abraham and to his descendants forever."

Monday, December 11	Psalm 34:1-4	*Gratitude*
Tuesday, December 12	Psalm 92:1-4	*It Is Good to Give Thanks*
Wednesday, December 13	Luke 1:39-45	*Mary Visits Elizabeth*
Thursday, December 14	Luke 1:46-56	*Mary's Song of Praise*
Friday, December 15	Psalm 96	*Sing to the Lord*
Saturday, December 16	Psalm 103:1-5, 19-22	*Bless the Lord*
Sunday, December 17	Daniel 2:17-23	*Daniel's Prayer and Praise*

BACKGROUND

The consistent message of Scripture is that God sent His Son to make salvation available to the lost. For example, Hebrews 1:1-2 says that long ago God's prophets declared His message in many ways (such as through visions, dreams, and puzzling sayings) and at various times. Though their proclamations were incomplete and fragmentary, they nevertheless were inspired and authoritative.

But with the coming of Christ, things are noticeably different. The Father sent His Son to bring His saving message to us. Jesus' superiority over the prophets is underscored by the fact that God created the universe through Him. In fact, Christ will one day inherit all things.

No one else can compare to Jesus. He is the one who died on the cross to atone for humanity's sin. His high priestly act makes it possible for God to spiritually cleanse and forgive the believing sinner.

The grace and pardon of God toward the repentant is the theme of Mary's song of praise recorded in Luke 1:46-55. It is one of the few praise psalms in the New Testament. The traditional name for the hymn is the *Magnificat*. This is a translation of the first word in the Latin version of verse 46. For centuries Mary's song has been incorporated into the liturgies, hymns, and art of many Christian traditions.

In her song, Mary noted that the Lord had taken notice of her by bringing about the miraculous conception of Jesus in her womb. God did this despite the fact that Mary was a poor peasant girl from Nazareth in Galilee. She realized that God had not chosen other much more prominent women to be the mother of the Messiah. This underscored even more for Mary the gracious way in which God was working in her life.

NOTES ON THE PRINTED TEXT

At first Mary was confused by the message she had received from Gabriel. But then when the angel explained that God had chosen Mary to bear the Christ child, her confusion was replaced with joy and excitement. In fact, after Gabriel had departed, Mary went in a hurry to the hill country of Judea. She was eager to relate the good news of her pregnancy to Elizabeth. If Mary was in

Nazareth at the time, she would have traveled south (perhaps a distance of 50 to 70 miles) to reach Elizabeth's home. Judah is about a three-day trip from Nazareth (Luke 1:39-40).

At the sound of Mary's greeting, Elizabeth felt her unborn baby move within *her womb* (1:41). The context of the verse suggests that the child's response was due to the prompting of the Holy Spirit. Elizabeth, who was also filled with the Spirit, celebrated Mary's pregnancy. Elizabeth declared that both Mary and her child were the object of God's favor.

Elizabeth considered it an honor that Mary, who would give birth to the Messiah, would visit her. Elizabeth's attitude is one of humility and piety. She was thankful that Mary decided to share the miraculous way in which God was working in her life. As a woman of faith, Elizabeth could see that Mary had believed the promises of God concerning her. It's no wonder that Elizabeth's unborn baby was filled with joy at the sound of Mary's greeting (1:42-45).

Mary responded with a song of praise. Her initial words were personal. She exalted, rejoiced, and praised the Lord for His choice of choosing her—a poor, Nazarene woman —to bear the Christ child. *"My soul magnifies the Lord, and my spirit rejoices in God my Savior, for he has looked with favor on the lowliness of his servant"* (1:46-48). Mary declared that future generations would marvel at the role God wanted her to have in His plan of salvation. *"Surely, from now on all generations will call me blessed; for the Mighty One has done great things for me, and holy is his name"* (1:48-49).

Mary next praised God for showing mercy to all who worshiped Him. *"His mercy is for those who fear him from generation to generation"* (1:50). This was evident in the dramatic reversals that would affect the proud and the humble. Those who were self-confident and arrogant would be brought low. *"He has shown strength with his arm; he has scattered the proud in the thoughts of their hearts"* (1:51). While God deposes the world's rulers, He lifts up (or exalts) the lowly. And while He satisfies the hungry with good things, He sends the rich away with empty hands (1:52-53).

Finally, Mary noted that God's mercy extended even to the nation of Israel. She affirmed that God's people had a special role in serving Him and making Him known to the world. The righteous would rejoice in the fact that the promise of salvation that God had made to Abraham and His descendants was being fulfilled in the miraculous conception and birth of Christ (1:54-55).

SUGGESTIONS TO TEACHERS

A four-year-old girl visiting a lavishly decorated shopping mall studied the scene where miniature hot-air balloons hung from the roof three stories above her head. She was fascinated by the mechanical clowns arrayed in a dazzling toyland layout, and by a jolly Santa enthroned on an altar-like platform. Suddenly the girl asked her parents, "But where's the baby Jesus?"

The child's question is revealing. A trip to any mall makes it clear that the focus during the holidays is on everything else but the Savior. This week's lesson will help your class to place the remaining time before Christmas in a better perspective. The key idea is praise to God for the gift of His Son.

1. RECOGNITION. Begin the class time by noting how Elizabeth welcomed Mary. Elizabeth humbly acknowledged what the Lord was doing through Mary and shared in her joy. Of course, this was also a time of great change for both women. In the midst of not knowing what the future might bring, Elizabeth affirmed that God was in control and was carrying out His perfect will. Perhaps some of your students also feel uneasy about the future. Let them know that God will guide them and watch over them even through turbulent times.

2. REJOICING. How much joy do your students feel amid the hustle and bustle of the holiday season? Remind the class that gladness and rejoicing should be a part of their Christmas experience. Let them know that joy stems not from the manufactured feelings of cheer generated by chirpy jingles and warm eggnog, but rather from the knowledge of Christ's arrival.

3. RESPECTFUL. Mary could have become arrogant and smug over the fact that she would give birth to the Messiah. But thankfully she remained humble. And even though she was the object of God's favor, she praised Him, not herself. In our "celebrate me!" culture, such a self-effacing attitude is rarely seen. Mary's disposition reminds us that true humility comes from respecting God and keeping Him at the center of our lives.

4. REMEMBRANCE. Ask your students to think about the Lord's concern for the poor and hurting in society. Then note that Christmas often finds people showing concern for the hungry and homeless, and sending food baskets and toys to those in need. But what about the plight of these persons after the holiday has ended? Take a few moments to discuss how believers can help the disadvantaged throughout the year, not just during Christmas.

 FOR ADULTS

■ TOPIC: Praising God

■ QUESTIONS: 1. What do we learn from Luke 1:41 about the child in Elizabeth's womb? 2. What explanation did Mary offer for wanting to praise God? 3. What future plans did God have for Israel? 4. Why is it important for us to rejoice in the way God has blessed our fellow believers? 5. What are some ways we can reach out to those in need with the love of Christ?

■ **ILLUSTRATIONS:**

The True Source of Joy. Unsaved people normally think of happiness as a fleeting emotion that ebbs and flows with changing circumstances. But this concept is not taught in Scripture. Genuine and lasting happiness, or joy, has a staying power that enables it to endure despite the harshest of situations.

For Christians, Jesus is the true source of joy (John 15:11). Just as obeying the Father was the basis for the Savior's joy, so also when believers obey Jesus, they experience unspeakable joy. Such gladness comes from the Spirit and enables believers to see even hardships as opportunities for rejoicing (Gal. 5:22; Jas. 1:2).

The early followers of Jesus radiated that joy. The old Welsh monk, Saint Cadoc, frequently commented, "No one is pious who is not cheerful." Saint Francis and his early associates were known as "God's Happy People." John Wesley's Methodist societies displayed intense gladness. Even dour John Calvin and his Scottish followers turned Psalm 100 it into a joyous anthem of praise to God.

Child's Praise. The story is told of some first graders who presented their version of the Christmas account. For the most part, the children stuck reasonably close to the narrative in the Gospels. But they also added a couple of unexpected touches. For example, at the manger, the first graders showed a doctor coming to examine Mary with a toy stethoscope. Then he led her behind a bale of straw. A few groans signifying childbirth followed.

Next, the little guy portraying the doctor in the children's version of the Nativity scene reappeared. While he proudly held up a doll-size baby Jesus, the boy turned to another lad playing Joseph and shouted, "It's God!" Now that's true praise!

Praising God in New Haven. In New Haven, Connecticut, a young mother said to her minister, "I have a little problem about my child's prayers. She loves to talk to God every night and repeat the Lord's Prayer. But she doesn't say the correct version, and I want to ask you whether I should correct her."

The minister said, "What does your little girl say that you think is incorrect?" "Well," said the mother, "every night she asks, 'Our Father who art in New Haven, how did you know my name?' " The minister replied, "I wouldn't correct her. She's voiced two deep theological truths that most adults should remember. First, God is everywhere, even in New Haven. Second, He knows everyone— even your daughter—by name."

FOR YOUTH

■ TOPIC: Sing Praise

■ QUESTIONS: 1. What tone permeates Elizabeth's comments to Mary? 2. In what way had God been mindful of Mary? 3. How did Mary see the life circumstances of the strong and weak being reversed? 4. What are some ways that God has recently shown His favor on you? 5. How has God's mercy enabled you to remain faithful to Him?

■ ILLUSTRATIONS:

In Awe. While trips to Disney World and Disneyland are still by far the most frequently made requests to the *Make a Wish Foundation*, another often made wish is to meet a sports personality or visit an entertainer. Many baseball, hockey, and football players regularly grant these wishes and make innumerable trips to hospitals in the West.

Entertainers often do the same too. For instance, San Lan, a Chinese gymnast, fell on July 30, 1998 at the Good Will Games in New York. She was paralyzed from the neck down. Her wish was for a visit from her favorite movie star, Leonardo DiCaprio. DiCaprio complied and visited the adolescent at Mount Sinai Hospital.

Like many young people, San Lan was in awe of someone who is famous and well known. Mary, however, got it right when she expressed awe and gratitude to God for His mercy to her. We, too, should worship the Lord for His grace to us in Christ.

Celebrate. Confederate General George E. Pickett had his soldiers and cavalry lined up on a two-mile front at Gettysburg. The Confederate and Union forces were drawn up for battle when word was received that Pickett's wife had given birth to their first son. The news excited and softened the hearts of the troops. All along their lines bonfires were lit and there were shouts and cheers of celebration.

Across the field, Grant was curious as to what was happening. Scouts reported that the Confederates were celebrating the birth of Pickett's son. Grant immediately had Union forces light bonfires in celebration of General Pickett's son.

Soon both armies were watching the fires burn. No shots were fired. Only the lights of joy burned. In addition, soon thereafter, a baby's silver service (engraved to "George E. Pickett, Jr.") was delivered to the Confederate general, a gift from Grant and two other Union generals.

On one hand, this is what the birth of Jesus was meant to bring—peace and joy. On a broader scale, His birth is a cause for celebration. If soldiers at war can pause and take time out to joyously celebrate a birth, how much more should we celebrate the birth of the Prince of Peace, especially through our worship?

The Biggest Christmas Party Ever. The *Guinness Book of Records* (1998) claimed that the biggest Christmas party ever held was put on by the Boeing Corporation on December 15, 1979. Boeing invited and entertained 103,152 guests for an enormous celebration that day. But on December 25, 2000, over one billion people will participate in what will truly be the biggest Christmas party ever, one in honor of the birth of the Savior! Though we won't all be in one place at one time, believers everywhere will celebrate that event.

A SAVIOR IS BORN

BACKGROUND SCRIPTURE: Luke 2:1-20
DEVOTIONAL READING: Matthew 16:13-16

KEY VERSE: "To you is born this day in the city of David a Savior, who is the Messiah, the Lord." Luke 2:11.

4

KING JAMES VERSION

LUKE 2:4 And Joseph also went up from Galilee, out of the city of Nazareth, into Judaea, unto the city of David, which is called Bethlehem; (because he was of the house and lineage of David:)

5 To be taxed with Mary his espoused wife, being great with child.

6 And so it was, that, while they were there, the days were accomplished that she should be delivered.

7 And she brought forth her firstborn son, and wrapped him in swaddling clothes, and laid him in a manger; because there was no room for them in the inn.

8 And there were in the same country shepherds abiding in the field, keeping watch over their flock by night.

9 And, lo, the angel of the Lord came upon them, and the glory of the Lord shone round about them: and they were sore afraid.

10 And the angel said unto them, Fear not: for, behold, I bring you good tidings of great joy, which shall be to all people.

11 For unto you is born this day in the city of David a Saviour, which is Christ the Lord.

12 And this shall be a sign unto you; Ye shall find the babe wrapped in swaddling clothes, lying in a manger.

13 And suddenly there was with the angel a multitude of the heavenly host praising God, and saying,

14 Glory to God in the highest, and on earth peace, good will toward men.

15 And it came to pass, as the angels were gone away from them into heaven, the shepherds said one to another, Let us now go even unto Bethlehem, and see this thing which is come to pass, which the Lord hath made known unto us.

16 And they came with haste, and found Mary, and Joseph, and the babe lying in a manger.

17 And when they had seen it, they made known abroad the saying which was told them concerning this child.

18 And all they that heard it wondered at those things which were told them by the shepherds.

19 But Mary kept all these things, and pondered them in her heart.

20 And the shepherds returned, glorifying and praising God for all the things that they had heard and seen, as it was told unto them.

NEW REVISED STANDARD VERSION

LUKE 2:4 Joseph also went from the town of Nazareth in Galilee to Judea, to the city of David called Bethlehem, because he was descended from the house and family of David. 5 He went to be registered with Mary, to whom he was engaged and who was expecting a child. 6 While they were there, the time came for her to deliver her child. 7 And she gave birth to her firstborn son and wrapped him in bands of cloth, and laid him in a manger, because there was no place for them in the inn.

8 In that region there were shepherds living in the fields, keeping watch over their flock by night. 9 Then an angel of the Lord stood before them, and the glory of the Lord shone around them, and they were terrified. 10 But the angel said to them, "Do not be afraid; for see—I am bringing you good news of great joy for all the people: 11 to you is born this day in the city of David a Savior, who is the Messiah, the Lord. 12 This will be a sign for you: you will find a child wrapped in bands of cloth and lying in a manger." 13 And suddenly there was with the angel a multitude of the heavenly host, praising God and saying,

14 "Glory to God in the highest heaven, and on earth peace among those whom he favors!"

15 When the angels had left them and gone into heaven, the shepherds said to one another, "Let us go now to Bethlehem and see this thing that has taken place, which the Lord has made known to us." 16 So they went with haste and found Mary and Joseph, and the child lying in the manger. 17 When they saw this, they made known what had been told them about this child; 18 and all who heard it were amazed at what the shepherds told them. 19 But Mary treasured all these words and pondered them in her heart. 20 The shepherds returned, glorifying and praising God for all they had heard and seen, as it had been told them.

121

BACKGROUND

No one knows precisely when Jesus was born. Even His year of birth is only an educated guess based on the information available. The intention of the medieval creators of our calendar was to set the date of Jesus' birth at A.D. 1. But they obviously miscalculated. The Jewish historian Josephus places the death of Herod the Great in 4 B.C., and both Matthew and Luke state that Herod was king at the time of Jesus' birth (Matt. 2:1; Luke 1:5). But it's unclear how much before Herod's death Jesus was born.

We know that Herod became king of the Jews in 37 B.C. Apart from Matthew 2:16, no historical record mentions Herod's slaughter of the infants in Bethlehem. Josephus wrote that Herod ordered the murders of members of his own family to protect his throne. So it's not surprising that some peasant children in Bethlehem went unnoticed among Herod's many atrocities, leaving us no help with dating. Since Herod's calculations led him to target children under two years old, Jesus' birth most likely occurred one or two years before Herod's death.

A date of either in 6 or 5 B.C. would fit with Luke's note that Augustus (who reigned from 27 B.C. to A.D. 14) was the Roman emperor when Jesus was born (Luke 2:1). Luke's mention of Quirinius (2:2), however, creates a problem. After Herod died, Rome divided his territory among his surviving sons. Archelaus ruled in Judea until he was deposed by the Romans in A.D. 6. Only then was Quirinius appointed governor, after serving for more than a decade as commander of the Roman troops in the area. Perhaps Luke simply identified him by his later office. Or it may be that Quirinius was in office for two separate terms, first 6–4 B.C. and then A.D. 6–9.

Despite these lingering questions, there is no doubt about the integrity and accuracy of Luke's narrative. His historical approach underscores the fact that at Christ's birth the eternal God invaded temporal human affairs. In addition, the Lord used pagan rulers and events to accomplish His purposes.

NOTES ON THE PRINTED TEXT

Luke introduced Jesus' birth by setting it in its historical context. He mentioned two officials—the emperor of Rome, Caesar Augustus, and the governor of Syria, Publius Sulpicius Quirinius. Luke also mentioned a political event—the Roman census that drew Mary and Joseph to Bethlehem (Luke 2:1-3).

People were required to go to their ancestral homes for registration. This would have made it easier to list families. Because Joseph (and most likely Mary) was a descendant of David, the couple went to their tribal home in Judea to be registered (2:4). This was a difficult trek of more than 70 miles through mountainous terrain, especially for Mary, who was *expecting a child* (2:5). Evidently there was no way Joseph could delay the trip.

Since Bethlehem was filled to overflowing with travelers, there was *no place for [Joseph and Mary] in the inn* (2:7). Thus, according to ancient tradition, Mary gave birth to the Christ child in a cave that had been made into a stable (2:7). Another possibility is that Joseph and Mary stayed in the open courtyard of a crowded inn, where there would have been a series of stalls along the walls.

In either case, it's clear that Jesus was born amid humble circumstances. This reminds us of how low God stooped to lift fallen humanity. Because Jesus identified with the lowliest, He gives hope today to those who have no other source of hope.

After Mary gave birth to Jesus, she wrapped the infant *in bands of cloth* (2:7) and laid Him in a trough used for feeding animals. Perhaps Mary wondered how the angel's words concerning the Christ child would come true (1:32-33).

Luke directed his readers' attention to other poor and marginalized persons. *In that region there were shepherds living in the fields, keeping watch over their flock by night* (2:8). Since they lived out in the open and were unable to maintain strict obedience to the law, shepherds generally were considered ceremonially unclean. As a result, they were despised by religious legalists.

Ironically, God didn't announce the birth of the Savior to the rich and powerful, but rather to ordinary shepherds. *Then an angel of the Lord stood before them, and the glory of the Lord shone around them, and they were terrified* (2:9). Perhaps this was God's way of telling the world that there are no second-class people, for all need His salvation.

The sight of the angel terrified the shepherds. But he reassured them that he came to bring a message of hope, not condemnation. *"Do not be afraid; for see— I am bringing you good news of great joy for all the people: to you is born this day in the city of David a Savior, who is the Messiah, the Lord"* (2:10-11). In other words, the Anointed One, the Messiah, had come to bring forgiveness and deliverance from sin.

The angel encouraged the shepherds to find the Christ child. *"This will be a sign for you: you will find a child wrapped in bands of cloth and lying in a manger"* (2:12). The shepherds could verify the angel's announcement by traveling to Bethlehem. There they would find the newborn King.

Suddenly the night sky was filled with the sounds of many angels singing praise to God. They declared peace to all who receive God's favor (that is, through faith in His Son). *And suddenly there was with the angel a multitude of* the heavenly host, praising God and saying, "Glory to God in the highest heaven, and on earth peace among those whom he favors!" (2:13-14).

Undoubtedly the angel's announcement was overwhelming to the shepherds. They stopped what they were doing and hurried to see what they had heard about (2:15). They weren't disappointed, for they found the baby just as they had been told. *So they went with haste and found Mary and Joseph, and the child lying in the manger* (2:16). Afterward, the enthusiastic shepherds *made known what had been told them about this child; and all who heard it were amazed at what the shepherds told them* (2:17-18).

The shepherds returned to their fields, but they were changed forever (2:20). Meanwhile, Mary *treasured all these words and pondered them in her heart* (2:19). In other words, she reflected on the events so that she could more fully appreciate the way in which God was working in her life and that of her Son.

SUGGESTIONS TO TEACHERS

Perhaps some students in your class think they know all about the birth of Jesus. They may have participated in so many Christmas pageants that they struggle with getting interested in this week's lesson. Your challenge is to help them take a fresh look at what the Bible teaches and to encourage them to rejoice in the coming of God's Son.

1. DATE IN HISTORY. Some occasionally voice doubts about whether an actual person named Jesus really lived. Luke's references to various historical figures clearly show that Jesus was no mythological person but rather someone who was born at a specific point in time. God did not remain aloof or allow Himself to be considered in the abstract. Instead, the Lord of glory took on flesh and was born in the city of Bethlehem.

2. DEPARTURE TO BETHLEHEM. The harsh realities of the Christmas narrative are sometimes overlooked. At great personal inconvenience, a poor peasant couple was forced to make a long and tiresome journey. The two lived in a turbulent time and were subjected to the dictates of a powerful distant emperor. Augustus ruled through callous local underlings who were backed by a ruthless occupying army. Emphasize to your students that God enabled Mary and Joseph to prevail over their circumstances. Similarly, God can help the class deal with their problems.

3. DEPRESSING CIRCUMSTANCES. Jesus was born in the most humble of settings. The eternal King did not appear in a grandiose Roman palace, but rather in a dark and dirty place in an obscure corner of the empire. No matter how futile our circumstances might seem, we can find strength in knowing that God cared enough to send His Son to experience life as we know it.

4. DISCLOSURE TO THE SHEPHERDS. Lowly shepherds were the first to learn the momentous news and the first to gaze upon the infant Jesus. From this we see that God sent His Son to even the least significant of humans! No one can rightfully claim that he or she is unimportant to the Lord after hearing that shepherds were Jesus' first audience.

what he had declared? 3. How did Mary's response to the shepherds' story contrast with the response of others? 4. What new perspective on Jesus' birth have you gained as a result of studying Luke 2:4-20? 5. Why should celebrating the birth of Christ be a joyous occasion for believers?

■ **ILLUSTRATIONS:**

The First Creche. A legend has it that in December of 1223, Francis of Assisi was on his way to preach in the village of Greccio, Italy. As he walked, he pondered how he could bring home to the poor illiterate peasants the real meaning of Christmas. He wanted the account of the Savior's birth to live in their hearts.

Suddenly Francis had an idea. He would recreate the manger scene for his audience. First, he went to a friend in the village, and between them they fashioned the first creche, or Nativity scene. Then, when the peasants came to the church on Christmas eve, they stopped in amazement and fell on their knees in adoration. There they saw a live donkey and ox. They also noticed real people playing the parts of Joseph, Mary, and the shepherds. Moreover, in a crude manger lay a representation of the infant Jesus.

Francis proceeded to tell the onlookers the wonderful account of the birth of Christ. This enabled the peasants to feel as if they were actually in ancient Bethlehem. This experience helped them never to forget the message of hope and gladness they heard that night.

Poet's Longing. Thomas Hardy's poem, "The Oxen," describes an old English rural folk legend in which the oxen are said to kneel in their stalls every Christmas Eve at the stroke of midnight in memory of Jesus' birth in Bethlehem. At the end of the poem, Hardy imagines someone telling him that in a remote farm the animals were kneeling that night. If he were invited to see this, the agnostic Hardy said he would "go with the person in the . . . hope that it might be so."

Perhaps you, like the poet Hardy, have wished that there might be some cause for hoping, some reason for worshiping, and some evidence for believing the truth of Christ's birth. Consider again Luke 2:11, *"to you is born this day in the city of David a Savior, who is the Messiah, the Lord."*

The Father has come to us in the person of His Son, Jesus. And at the manger, God has reached out to us in love. All of us are residents of this planet where Jesus made His home! This is the reason for hoping, worshiping, and believing.

Startling Realization. As Astronaut Edgar Mitchell sped away from the moon, he looked through the window of his capsule at the small distant planet called Earth. This sight reminded him that all people are part of the same human family and in need of redemption in Christ. William Sloan Coffin, Jr., commenting on Mitchell's experience wrote, "I was thrilled once to hear him tell his tale, but I couldn't help thinking, 'You shouldn't have had to go to the moon to come to that realization. It's enough to go to Bethlehem.'"

FOR YOUTH	■ **TOPIC:** An Awesome Announcement ■ **QUESTIONS:** 1. What conditions did Mary have to endure? 2. What was the response of the shepherds when they saw the

angel? 3. What did the shepherds do after the angel had departed from them? 4. Which truths from this week's lesson are most precious to you? 5. Why is it important to remember the humble circumstances surrounding Jesus' birth?

■ **ILLUSTRATIONS:**

Lost Roots. "Where are you from?" That is one of the most frequently asked questions in a conversation between adults. Many older people grew up in one place with family roots in a particular town or city. But this isn't true for younger people today. They don't have a strong sense of family roots that links them to one specific place. A child may have been born in one state, spent his or her preschool years in another state, and then the grade school and middle school years in a third state. Meanwhile, the grandparents live across the country.

Joseph undoubtedly had a sense of family roots and heritage, and that's why Bethlehem was important to him and his family. This reminds us that Jesus knew His background and heritage. We too share in that same heritage, regardless of our past and present life circumstances.

New Norms. There were over 4,000,000 babies born in the United States in 1998. Most of these infants began their lives in a hospital. The delivery room or birthing suite is the norm. Fifty years ago, however, a delivery outside the hospital would have been commonplace. And it's still the norm for much of the world.

There wasn't anything extraordinary about the place of Jesus' birth. It was humble and ordinary. Nevertheless, it was one of the most spectacular events in human history, and thus worthy of our remembrance and celebration!

Strange Contrast. The leaders of Bethlehem have been busy with preparations to celebrate Christmas this year. The town expects millions of tourists to converge on the city during the holiday season. What a strange contrast this is from that first Christmas! Then only a handful of people witnessed the birth of Jesus, whom God sent to make salvation possible for the lost.

PRESENTED IN THE TEMPLE

BACKGROUND SCRIPTURE: Luke 2:21-40
DEVOTIONAL READING: Isaiah 52:7-10

KEY VERSE: "For my eyes have seen your salvation, which you have prepared in the presence of all peoples, a light for revelation to the Gentiles and for glory to your people Israel." Luke 2:30-32.

KING JAMES VERSION

LUKE 2:25 And, behold, there was a man in Jerusalem, whose name was Simeon; and the same man was just and devout, waiting for the consolation of Israel: and the Holy Ghost was upon him.

26 And it was revealed unto him by the Holy Ghost, that he should not see death, before he had seen the Lord's Christ.

27 And he came by the Spirit into the temple: and when the parents brought in the child Jesus, to do for him after the custom of the law,

28 Then took he him up in his arms, and blessed God, and said,

29 Lord, now lettest thou thy servant depart in peace, according to thy word:

30 For mine eyes have seen thy salvation,

31 Which thou hast prepared before the face of all people;

32 A light to lighten the Gentiles, and the glory of thy people Israel.

33 And Joseph and his mother marvelled at those things which were spoken of him.

34 And Simeon blessed them, and said unto Mary his mother, Behold, this child is set for the fall and rising again of many in Israel; and for a sign which shall be spoken against;

35 (Yea, a sword shall pierce through thy own soul also,) that the thoughts of many hearts may be revealed.

36 And there was one Anna, a prophetess, the daughter of Phanuel, of the tribe of Aser: she was of a great age, and had lived with an husband seven years from her virginity;

37 And she was a widow of about fourscore and four years, which departed not from the temple, but served God with fastings and prayers night and day.

38 And she coming in that instant gave thanks likewise unto the Lord, and spake of him to all them that looked for redemption in Jerusalem.

NEW REVISED STANDARD VERSION

LUKE 2:25 Now there was a man in Jerusalem whose name was Simeon; this man was righteous and devout, looking forward to the consolation of Israel, and the Holy Spirit rested on him. 26 It had been revealed to him by the Holy Spirit that he would not see death before he had seen the Lord's Messiah.

27 Guided by the Spirit, Simeon came into the temple; and when the parents brought in the child Jesus, to do for him what was customary under the law, 28 Simeon took him in his arms and praised God, saying,

29 "Master, now you are dismissing your servant in peace,
according to your word;

30 for my eyes have seen your salvation,

31 which you have prepared in the presence of
all peoples,

32 a light for revelation to the Gentiles
and for glory to your people Israel."

33 And the child's father and mother were amazed at what was being said about him. 34 Then Simeon blessed them and said to his mother Mary, "This child is destined for the falling and the rising of many in Israel, and to be a sign that will be opposed 35 so that the inner thoughts of many will be revealed—and a sword will pierce your own soul too."

36 There was also a prophet, Anna the daughter of Phanuel, of the tribe of Asher. She was of a great age, having lived with her husband seven years after her marriage, 37 then as a widow to the age of eighty-four. She never left the temple but worshiped there with fasting and prayer night and day. 38 At that moment she came, and began to praise God and to speak about the child to all who were looking for the redemption of Jerusalem.

5

HOME BIBLE READINGS

Monday, December 25	Exodus 13:11-16	*The Consecration of the Firstborn*
Tuesday, December 26	Luke 2:21-24	*According to the Law*
Wednesday, December 27	Deuteronomy 6:1-9	*Our Love for God*
Thursday, December 28	Luke 2:25-35	*Adoration and Prophecy of Simeon*
Friday, December 29	Isaiah 52:3-10	*The Good News of Peace*
Saturday, December 30	Luke 2:36-38	*Adoration of Anna*
Sunday, December 31	1 Timothy 5:3-8	*Honor Widows Who Hope in God*

BACKGROUND

In this week's lesson we read about two elderly individuals, Simeon and Anna. Simeon was a devout Jew who encountered the infant Jesus when Joseph and Mary brought Him to the temple to be circumcised (Luke 2:25-35). Under the inspiration of the Spirit, Simeon recognized Jesus as the Messiah of Israel and the Savior of all humankind. Simeon also uttered prophecies concerning both Jesus and Mary.

Simeon is perhaps best known for his song, which has been called the *Nunc Dimittis* [nuhnk-dih-MITT-iss], and which comes from the opening phrase in Latin, "*now you are dismissing*" (2:29; in other words, "now permit [me] to die"). The idea is that Simeon could die in peace because he had seen the Messiah.

The song bears many of the essential characteristics of Hebrew praise. For instance, it rejoices in the goodness of God, states the reason for that rejoicing, and expands poetically on that statement. Simeon's song is also filled with allusions to the Old Testament.

Anna was a widow, the daughter of Phanuel of the tribe of Asher, and thus a Galilean. The mention of Anna's lineage indicates that she came from a family of some distinction. She was living in Jerusalem at the time of Jesus' birth. In fact, she could be found in the temple courtyards day and night worshiping God through fasting and prayer (2:36-38).

Anna, like Simeon, was familiar with the period of war and national oppression that her nation had gone through in the not too distant past. (The reign of Herod the Great was especially characterized by much violence and bloodshed.) This undoubtedly is one reason why Anna had an intense longing for the redemption promised through the Messiah. This hope of national deliverance sustained her through many years of patient waiting. In the birth of Jesus, Anna's faith was abundantly rewarded, and she became a grateful and continual witness of the spiritual deliverance that had come to Israel.

Sadly, Anna's testimony as a woman would have counted for little in Jewish courts of the day. But thankfully Luke included her witness in his Gospel, perhaps to highlight one of the changes that Jesus the Redeemer wanted to bring about among His followers. No longer would they regard women as untrustworthy witnesses, but as full members of a new community of faith in Christ (Gal. 3:28).

NOTES ON THE PRINTED TEXT

Jesus was born into a devout Jewish home. In accordance with the Mosaic law, His parents had Him circumcised when He was eight days old (Lev. 12:3; Luke 2:21). This marked Jesus as a child of the covenant and reminded Him of His Jewish heritage.

Mary and Joseph also observed the purification rites for a woman following the birth of her male child. According to Leviticus 12:2, Mary remained ceremonially unclean seven days after Jesus' birth. Verse 3 says she then had to wait 33 days until the time of her purification was completed.

When Mary's time of waiting had ended, she was required to bring a year-old lamb for a whole burnt offering and a young pigeon or turtledove for a sin offering (13:6). But since Mary could not afford to bring a sheep, she was allowed to bring two turtledoves or two young pigeons. One would be for the whole burnt offering and the other for the sin offering (13:8). Luke 2:21-24 indicates that Mary chose the second option.

At the time of Jesus' birth, there was a pious Jew named Simeon who lived in Jerusalem (2:25). His devotion to God was evident in the way in which he observed the law of Moses. His upright way of living, however, went far beyond a mere external heeding of various rules and regulations. Simeon was also filled with (or controlled and guided by) the Holy Spirit.

Another interesting fact about Simeon is that he was *looking forward to the consolation of Israel* (2:25). In other words, he eagerly expected the Messiah to come and rescue His people. Undoubtedly Simeon was well acquainted with the Old Testament and its many prophecies that spoke of the Messiah bringing spiritual peace and rest (Isa. 9:6-7).

The Spirit had disclosed to Simeon that before he died he would see the Christ (Luke 2:26). The title *Christ* comes from a Greek word meaning "anointed one." It is equivalent to Messiah, a word derived from Hebrew. The Jews believed that a man would appear as the Lord's anointed prophet, priest, and king to bring salvation to the people of God. Sadly, most of them failed to recognize Jesus, who fulfilled the most comprehensive definition of the Messiah (John 1:10-11).

While Joseph and Mary were in the temple precincts with the infant Jesus, the Spirit led Simeon there as well. The couple allowed the elderly man to take the child in his arms. He then offered praise to God (Luke 2:27-28).

In Simeon's song, he thanked the Lord for letting him see the Redeemer. Simeon noted that the child would be a light to all peoples, whether Jew or Gentile (2:29-32). Many Jews knew of God's promises to bless their nation. But sadly they did not always give equal attention to the prophecies saying that God would bring salvation to the entire world (Isa. 49:6). Simeon, however, knew that Jesus had come to save all who believe.

Mary and Joseph were *amazed at what was being said about [Jesus]* (Luke 2:33). Simeon told them that Jesus would be rejected by many in Israel and that this would lead to their downfall. Nevertheless, He would be a source of joy to others (2:34). As a result, *"the inner thoughts of many will be revealed"* (2:35). The idea here is that a person's reasonings and motives would be exposed by the way in which he or she responded to the Savior. Even Mary herself would experience anguish and suffering because of what would happen to Jesus.

Luke noted that a prophetess named Anna was also in the temple (2:36-37). While Simeon was talking with Mary and Joseph, Anna came along and began praising God. She also talked about the infant Jesus to everyone who had been waiting for the *redemption of Jerusalem* (2:38).

SUGGESTIONS TO TEACHERS

Several years ago *Unplug the Christmas Machine* was the startling title that appeared in bookstores. The main idea behind the book was that the day after Christmas, people are no longer caught in the gears and pulled by the levers of a commercialized holiday. This week's lesson may be the first opportunity your students have to pause and recognize the true significance of the Christ.

1. SIGNIFICANT NAME. Luke 2:21 says that the newborn babe *was called Jesus.* This is the Greek form of Joshua, which means "the Lord saves." Take a few moments to discuss what it means to be saved. Be sure to go beyond the pat answers to talk seriously about how Jesus liberates us from relying on violence and revenge, and from living in destructive ways. Likewise, Jesus liberates us to serve others and promote justice. Trusting in Jesus means, for starters, that we recognize Him as our only Savior from sin.

2. SACRED OBSERVANCES. Note how Mary and Joseph observed the traditions of their faith both before and after Jesus was born. Our religious practices are also important to us, and they can have a tremendous positive effect on our children. Likewise, regular times of worship are essential to our spiritual health. Have your students discuss some religious traditions they find uplifting.

3. SIMEON'S FULFILLMENT. God lavished His mercy and grace on Simeon by allowing him to see the infant Jesus. From Simeon we learn three important truths. First, Jesus is a gift from God. Second, Jesus is the Messiah promised in the Old Testament. And third, Jesus is a light of salvation and truth to the entire world.

4. SOLEMN PRONOUNCEMENT. Simeon realized that in seeing the infant Jesus, he was privileged to behold the fulfillment of God's promise of the heaven-sent Deliverer. We have a similar opportunity when we look to Jesus with the eyes of faith. We can smile at whatever might happen to us in the future, for we know that in Christ we have the hope of eternal life.

5. SENIOR'S DISCERNMENT. End the class time by having your students examine Anna's joyful response to meeting Jesus. She both gave thanks and spoke about Him *to all who were looking for the redemption of Jerusalem* (2:38). Here is a good summary of how one responds to Jesus—with praise and testimony!

■ **TOPIC:** Recognizing the Christ

■ **QUESTIONS:** 1. What characterized Simeon's relationship with the Spirit? 2. What specific information did Simeon share with Mary and Joseph about Jesus? 3. What was the hope to which Anna clung? 4. What are some ways we can demonstrate our devotion to God? 5. What are some ways you have seen Jesus transform the lives of other believers?

■ **ILLUSTRATIONS:**

The XMAS of Christmas. A chaplain friend of mine noted that when people use Xmas, they really mean Xhaustion, Xcuses, Xchanges, Xcesses, Xtravagances, Xasperations, Xhibitions, and worldly Xcitement. How much better it is to make Jesus the center of our Christmas observances and thereby know the joy, happiness, sharing, and contentment found only in Him.

The Open Door. Each year at Christmastime, radio commentator Paul Harvey tells a story that wonderfully illustrates the necessity of the incarnation of Jesus. One Christmas Eve a devout mother dressed her children and asked her nonbelieving husband if he would attend the special holiday service with them. He said *no*, stating that he'd rather read the paper and enjoy the evening at home.

Shortly after his family had gone, the man noticed a repeated sound on one of his house windows. He put down his paper and found a small flock of birds shivering in the falling snow and attempting to hurl themselves through his window. Feeling compassion for the birds, he dressed and headed outside to open the door to his warm barn, where the birds could weather the storm. The birds, however, refused to enter.

Frustrated because of all his attempts to encourage the birds had failed, the man heard himself saying, "If only I could become one of them and lead them to where it's warm and safe." Just as the words left his lips, he heard the church bells ring out, "O Come, O Come, Emmanuel." He immediately sank to his knees in the snow.

For centuries people have wondered why it was necessary for Christ to become human. Harvey's story is a clear illustration of Jesus' purpose, namely, to redeem the lost.

Time to Recognize Jesus' Presence. A researcher named Michael Fortino has made a careful study of hundreds of people across North America for over a year. By using a stopwatch, he has clocked the ways persons use their time. He has also reported the cumulative effects of these ways.

Fortino states that most people spend five years of their lives waiting in lines. Other totals of time include six months sitting at traffic lights, one year searching for misplaced objects, six years eating, eight months opening junk mail, four years doing housework, and two years trying to return telephone calls to people who never seem to be available.

This evening will conclude the span of time called the year 2000. Also, we will have a new measure of 365 days to use during 2001. In light of this, let's commit ourselves to recall each day in the coming year that Christ lives in us and is a foremost part of our lives.

FOR YOUTH

■ TOPIC: A Time of Promise

■ QUESTIONS: 1. What kind of person was Simeon? 2. What was Simeon's view of the Messiah? 3. What did Anna do when she saw the Savior? 4. How can you help your friends understand Jesus better? 5. If you had the opportunity, what are some things about Jesus you would want to share with others?

■ ILLUSTRATIONS:

Two Portraits. "Madonna and Child" the headline read, proclaiming the news of a birth that ended months of anticipation and national interest that bordered on obsession. Readers were treated to a story that began with conception and ended with a cesarean section.

The crowds before the hospital were huge, and the media attention was enormous as word of Lourdes Maria Ciccone's birth was released. The little 6-pound, 9-ounce girl was born on October 14, 1996, in Los Angeles to singer-entertainer Madonna and her personal trainer, Carlos Leon. Hundreds of thousands of dollars were offered for a photograph of Madonna and her child.

What a contrast this is to another portrait, similarly titled "Madonna and Child." This one is by Crivelli, a fifteenth-century artist. It depicts a quiet barn, some shuffling animals, and a pair of reverential parents. In this painting there are no crowds, no media satellite dishes, just a simple view of the incarnation of Jesus depicted in medieval fashion and grandeur.

Perhaps this second portrait highlights the essence of the Advent, namely, that God has come in the form of a baby. God touches each of us through this humble birth in Bethlehem. As a citizen of heaven, you can join countless other believers in praising God for sending His Son.

True Homage. Audrey Wetherell Johnson (1907–1984) had been raised in England in a Christian home. Under a skeptical tutor in France, however, she came to the conclusion as a young person that she "no longer believed in the bodily resurrection of Jesus, nor in His virgin birth." She penned: "My attitude of agnosticism resulted in months of desperation as I considered the meaninglessness of life without any philosophy in which I could believe."

After returning to England, Wetherell finally arrived at a psychological crisis point. She desperately prayed that God would give her "some philosophy that makes reasonable sense." As a result of her desperate plea, "in a mysterious way that Wetherell could not explain even years later, God met her, and with tears of joy Wetherell worshiped Jesus as Savior and Lord" (Susie Hilstrom in *Worldwide Challenge*). Later she became responsible for Bible Study Fellowship, a Christian group that would eventually flourish in over 20 countries with 17,000 leaders.

Filling Father's Shoes. Thomas Watson, Jr., the man who built International Business Machines (IBM) into a computer giant, spent much of his early life worrying about filling his father's shoes. Tortured by self-doubts, Thomas was a depressed child. He was also upset that his sister, Jane, was his father's favorite.

Thomas spent much of his younger years pulling pranks, drinking, dancing, and challenging authority. After a stint in the armed forces, he began to work in the company that his father ran. Thomas succeeded by building the company into what it is today, an industrial powerhouse. At the same time, Thomas has far outgrown the shadow of his demanding father.

Perhaps like Thomas Watson, you know what it is like to grow up frustrated and unable to live up to the expectations of others. After going to the temple courts, both Joseph and Mary must have left with huge expectations for Jesus. The record of Scripture, though, indicates no frustration on His part. He simply trusted God for the future, and this enabled Jesus to do great things for the Lord. This can also be true of you!

JESUS IN NAZARETH

BACKGROUND SCRIPTURE: Luke 4:14-30
DEVOTIONAL READING: Isaiah 61

KEY VERSE: "The Spirit of the Lord is upon me, because he has anointed me to bring good news to the poor. He has sent me to proclaim release to the captives and recovery of sight to the blind, to let the oppressed go free, to proclaim the year of the Lord's favor." Luke 4:18-19.

6

KING JAMES VERSION

LUKE 4:16 And he came to Nazareth, where he had been brought up: and, as his custom was, he went into the synagogue on the sabbath day, and stood up for to read.

17 And there was delivered unto him the book of the prophet Esaias. And when he had opened the book, he found the place where it was written,

18 The Spirit of the Lord is upon me, because he hath anointed me to preach the gospel to the poor; he hath sent me to heal the brokenhearted, to preach deliverance to the captives, and recovering of sight to the blind, to set at liberty them that are bruised,

19 To preach the acceptable year of the Lord.

20 And he closed the book, and he gave it again to the minister, and sat down. And the eyes of all them that were in the synagogue were fastened on him.

21 And he began to say unto them, This day is this scripture fulfilled in your ears.

22 And all bare him witness, and wondered at the gracious words which proceeded out of his mouth. And they said, Is not this Joseph's son?

23 And he said unto them, Ye will surely say unto me this proverb, Physician, heal thyself: whatsoever we have heard done in Capernaum, do also here in thy country.

24 And he said, Verily I say unto you, No prophet is accepted in his own country.

25 But I tell you of a truth, many widows were in Israel in the days of Elias, when the heaven was shut up three years and six months, when great famine was throughout all the land;

26 But unto none of them was Elias sent, save unto Sarepta, a city of Sidon, unto a woman that was a widow. . . .

28 And all they in the synagogue, when they heard these things, were filled with wrath,

29 And rose up, and thrust him out of the city, and led him unto the brow of the hill whereon their city was built, that they might cast him down headlong.

30 But he passing through the midst of them went his way,

NEW REVISED STANDARD VERSION

LUKE 4:16 When he came to Nazareth, where he had been brought up, he went to the synagogue on the sabbath day, as was his custom. He stood up to read, 17 and the scroll of the prophet Isaiah was given to him. He unrolled the scroll and found the place where it was written:

18 "The Spirit of the Lord is upon me,
　because he has anointed me
　　to bring good news to the poor.
He has sent me to proclaim release to the captives
　and recovery of sight to the blind,
　　to let the oppressed go free,
19 to proclaim the year of the Lord's favor."

20 And he rolled up the scroll, gave it back to the attendant, and sat down. The eyes of all in the synagogue were fixed on him. 21 Then he began to say to them, "Today this scripture has been fulfilled in your hearing." 22 All spoke well of him and were amazed at the gracious words that came from his mouth. They said, "Is not this Joseph's son?" 23 He said to them, "Doubtless you will quote to me this proverb, 'Doctor, cure yourself!' And you will say, 'Do here also in your hometown the things that we have heard you did at Capernaum.' " 24 And he said, "Truly I tell you, no prophet is accepted in the prophet's hometown. 25 But the truth is, there were many widows in Israel in the time of Elijah, when the heaven was shut up three years and six months, and there was a severe famine over all the land; 26 yet Elijah was sent to none of them except to a widow at Zarephath in Sidon. . . . 28 When they heard this, all in the synagogue were filled with rage. 29 They got up, drove him out of the town, and led him to the brow of the hill on which their town was built, so that they might hurl him off the cliff. 30 But he passed through the midst of them and went on his way.

Monday, January 1	Luke 4:1-13	*Tempted as We Are*
Tuesday, January 2	Luke 4:14-21	*A Mission to the People*
Wednesday, January 3	Isaiah 61	*The Good News of Deliverance*
Thursday, January 4	Luke 4:22-30	*Jesus' Own Received Him Not*
Friday, January 5	2 Kings 5:1-14	*The Healing of Naaman*
Saturday, January 6	Matt. 13:54-58	*The Rejection of Jesus*
Sunday, January 7	Mark 3:31-35	*Whoever Does the Will of God*

BACKGROUND

The Gospel accounts were not written as mere biographies; rather, they were evangelistic tracts. Biographers usually delve into the childhood of their subjects. But the Gospel writers mostly skipped over the years when Jesus was growing up, except for one reference in Luke to Jesus accompanying His parents to the temple (2:41-50).

Like the other Gospel writers, Luke's main intent was to show what Jesus' life, death, and resurrection meant to believers. Luke thus proceeded quickly in his narrative to the start of Jesus' ministry. First, we learn about the preparatory work of John the Baptist (3:1-22). Then we find information about the genealogy of Christ (3:23-38).

The next section concerns Jesus' encounter with the devil and how the Savior resisted Satan's repeated enticements to sin (4:1-13). Following this, Christ returned to Galilee, being filled with the Spirit's power. Soon Jesus became well known throughout the surrounding country, and He won acclaim from those who heard Him teach in their synagogues (4:14-15).

Jesus then returned to His hometown of Nazareth to deliver His manifesto. It is important to note that He worshiped regularly as part of God's people, and was no soloist purposely separating Himself from the faith community. Likewise, Jesus was quite familiar with Scripture, and readily found the passage from the scroll of Isaiah, which He read to the those in the Nazareth synagogue.

Synagogues served a key role in Jewish life in the time of Jesus. Wherever 10 Jewish families lived, they formed a synagogue (literally, "congregation" or "assembly"). Sacrifices could be made only at the temple, but from the time of the Exile, teaching of the law and worship took place in synagogues situated wherever Jews had been scattered throughout the world.

After recitation of the Shema [sh-MAH] ("Hear, O Israel, the Lord is our God, the Lord is One"), prayers, Scripture readings, and teaching followed. Since there was no professional clergy (rabbis held secular trades to earn their living), the synagogue leader could invite anyone considered qualified to teach.

Typically, seven members of the congregation would stand to read Scripture. The designated teacher would then sit down to teach. In this week's lesson, we find that Jesus' reading from Isaiah 61:1-2 caused quite a stir in Nazareth.

NOTES ON THE PRINTED TEXT

Jesus' initial preaching took place in Galilee. After returning to His childhood home, the Savior went to worship in the synagogue, *as was his custom* (Luke 4:16). While attendance was stipulated for every devout Jew, worship for Jesus was more than a mere formality. He longed to commune with and give praise to His heavenly Father.

Those taking a lead role in a synagogue worship service often varied. While any devout Jewish male was allowed to participate, usually a priest, Levite, or visiting rabbi would have been the most likely choice. In this case, Jesus was asked to read from the Hebrew Scriptures.

Jesus was given a scroll containing the Book of Isaiah. He unrolled the document to 61:1-2, which says, *"The Spirit of the Lord is upon me, because he has anointed me to bring good news to the poor. He has sent me to proclaim release to the captives and recovery of sight to the blind, to let the oppressed go free, to proclaim the year of the Lord's favor"* (Luke 4:18-19).

Isaiah pictured the deliverance of Israel from exile in Babylon as a year of Jubilee when all debts were cancelled, all slaves were freed, and all property was returned to its original owners (Lev. 25:8-23). Of course, the release from Babylonian exile did not bring the fulfillment the Jews had expected, for they were still a conquered and oppressed people.

Jesus understood this, which makes His declaration all the more profound. After rolling up the scroll, handing it back to the attendant, and sitting down, Jesus declared to His audience that He fulfilled the messianic prophecies made by Isaiah (Luke 4:20-21). In other words, Jesus would bring this good news to pass, though in a way that many of His fellow Jews were not yet able to grasp.

At first those in attendance were amazed by the *gracious words that came from [Jesus'] mouth* (4:22). But then some began to get suspicious. They asked, *"Is not this Joseph's son?"* In other words, how is it possible for the son of an ordinary carpenter to be the Messiah?

Jesus bluntly responded by quoting the maxim, *"Doctor, cure yourself!"* (4:23) This proverb underscored the people's demand that Jesus repeat the type of miracles He had performed in Capernaum (Mark 1:21-27). It was not enough for them to believe what Jesus had claimed in the synagogue. Perhaps this is why He declared that prophets are usually not accepted by the residents in their hometown (Luke 4:24).

Jesus next gave two examples of two Gentiles whom God chose to help in Old Testament times, namely, the widow of Zarephath (1 Kings 17:8-16) and Naaman the Syrian (2 Kings 5:1-14). Jesus made it clear that God had anointed Him to bring salvation to all people, whether Jews or Gentiles (Luke 4:25-27).

Jesus' comments enraged His listeners (4:28). In fact, *they got up, drove him out of the town, and led him to the brow of the hill on which their town was built* (4:29). The intent of the mob was to push Jesus over the cliff. Amazingly, however, this didn't happen, for Jesus *passed through the midst of them and went on his way* (4:30). Though the biblical text doesn't say this escape was a miracle, it probably was.

Why did Jesus' comments so enrage the people of Nazareth? They were upset because Jesus claimed that God sometimes chose to reach Gentiles rather than Jews. The Savior implied that His hearers were as unbelieving as the citizens of the northern kingdom of Israel in the days of Elijah and Elisha, a time notorious for its widespread injustice and immorality.

Apparently those in Jesus' audience were concerned with preserving the ethnic reputation and customs of their religious tradition. If so, Jesus' words might well have represented a threat to the image they wanted to project to the watching world. Once Jesus' neighbors realized what He was really saying, they determined to reject Him.

The reaction of Jesus' hometown crowd moves us to ask whom we are reaching out to with the good news about Christ. Also, what issues does Jesus' Gospel address in our times? Are we, like the Nazareth listeners, so committed to preserving the status quo that the Lord has to go around us to accomplish His work? Perhaps nothing could be more tragic than this!

SUGGESTIONS TO TEACHERS

Some congregations in the United States have the custom of making a cross out of the Christmas tree they displayed during the holidays. They then place it in the front of their sanctuary during Lent. The purpose is to show the tie between the manger of Bethlehem and the cross of Calvary. In other words, the infant Jesus eventually grew up and sacrificed Himself for others.

Realizing this truth helps us to transition from a busy Christmas season centering on the birth of Jesus to lessons dealing with His mission and ministry. We note that from the start of His ministry, He was aware that God had anointed Him to bring the good news of the kingdom to all people, regardless of their race, nationality, gender, or social status. We also learn from Jesus that God wants us to be His ambassadors to the lost.

1. CUSTOMARY PRACTICE. Jesus studied God's Word and gathered regularly with the community of faith. Though He was the perfect Son of God and His local synagogue was far less than perfect, Jesus attended services every week. His example underscores how important it is for us to make regular worship a part of our lives (Heb. 10:25).

2. CLEAR PROCLAMATION. Take a few moments to discuss Isaiah 61:1-2 with your students, and be sure to consider ways in which this passage applies to them. For instance, ordained clergy are not the only ones whom God wants to accomplish His work. All of God's people are to do whatever they can to serve Him. This includes reaching out the poor and homeless in the community with the good news of salvation and compassionate involvement.

The unconditional love of God is at the heart of such ministry. It's easy, of course, to talk about love, but it's much harder to do the tough work of living it. Love as God intended it is more than just passion, romantic feelings, or sentimental expressions. It involves commitment, sacrifice, and service—the kind of things that benefit both the giver and the receiver.

3. COMMANDING PERSONAGE. Jesus went against popular expectations in His Nazareth sermon and stirred up such severe opposition that His townsfolk wanted to murder Him. Despite this, He had the courage to speak up for and show compassion to those whom society despised. Even when threatened, Jesus didn't sidestep issues. This high level of trust in God, which was evident from the start of Jesus' ministry, should also be characteristic of our lives.

4. CONTEMPTIBLE PATRIOTISM. At first we might think that the fury of the people of Nazareth was an extreme example from the dark ages of the past. The sad truth, however, is that such rage still exists today among those who are unbelieving and wicked. This is not surprising, for Jesus said in John 15:18, *"If the world hates you, be aware that it hated me before it hated you."*

FOR ADULTS

■ TOPIC: Discovering Your Mission

■ QUESTIONS: 1. Why do think Jesus accepted the invitation from the leader of the synagogue to read the Scriptures? 2. What did Jesus say that caused the people of Nazareth to reject Him? 3. How do you think Christ handled the rejection He experienced? 4. Why are we sometimes surprised when our Christian life and faith are not easily understood or accepted by those who know us well? 5. What are some things we can do when others reject us because of our faith?

■ **ILLUSTRATIONS:**

Pleasing God. In *Sold Out*, Promise Keepers founder Bill McCartney wrote the following:

> Recently I spoke at a large arena. The moment I stepped off the stage, I began asking friends and associates how I'd done. There were high fives, back slaps, and encouraging compliments to the effect that I'd "hit a home run." I went back to the hotel quite pleased with myself.

> The next morning, early, I went to my knees. God wasn't to be found. I asked, "Lord, where are You? I rose early to meet with You. I spoke of Your wonder and glory last night. I praised You with all of my heart. I thought You would be pleased. What have I done? Where are You?"

> In that very instant, I sensed God was asking me a direct question: "Last night, when you finished your message, why didn't you ask *Me* how you did? You came to Me for anointing to speak, but you went to your friends seeking their opinions. Why did you not seek *Mine* first?"

It broke my heart to hear. But it was true. I'd spent weeks seeking God's heart for that message. And it *was* a home run; the power of the Holy Spirit fell upon that arena—not because of anything I said, but because *God* showed up. And yet I didn't seek *God's* affirmation first. I sought the approval of people. I confessed my sin and repented. Immediately God's sweetness returned. It shocked me into seeing that the only one I've ever needed to please is God.

Reminder of Mission. In the old House of Representatives in the capitol in Washington, D.C., there once stood a clock made by an elderly New Englander. Prominent in the decoration of the clock was a large carving of the "gatekeeper of history." The people in the House of Representatives were reminded constantly by the clock's carving that history would judge what they said and did. They came to see that more important than the time of day was whether their lives and actions in that chamber would stand the scrutiny of time.

Today there is no such symbol in the House of Representatives. Now there is only the television camera. This prompts many leaders to pose and perform before a fickle public. What reminders of God's mission do we as believers have in our daily lives?

Challenged to Serve. God wants us to make the good news of salvation known throughout the world, especially among the impoverished of our planet. But few of us really know what these people have to endure on a daily basis. One reason is that their living conditions are beyond what most of us have ever experienced.

In *Nine Steps to Third World Living*, John Nelson made the following observations about the reality of life among the poor:

> First, take out the furniture. Leave a few old blankets, a kitchen table, and maybe a wooden chair. You've never had a bed, remember? Second, throw out your clothes. Each person in the family may keep their oldest suit or dress and a shirt or blouse. The head of the family has the only pair of shoes. Third, all kitchen appliances have vanished. Keep a box of matches, a small bag of flour, some sugar and salt, a handful of onions, and a dish of dried beans. Rescue the moldy potatoes from the garbage can, for those are tonight's meal.
>
> Fourth, dismantle the bathroom, shut off the running water, and take out the wiring and the lights and everything that runs by electricity. Fifth, take away the house and move the family into the tool shed. Sixth, no more letter carrier, firefighters, or government services. The two-classroom school is three miles away, but only two of your seven children attend anyway, and they have to walk.
>
> Seventh, throw out your bankbooks, stock certificates, pension plans, and insurance policies. You now have a cash hoard of only $5. Eighth, get

out and start cultivating your three acres. Try hard to raise $300 in cash crops because your landlord wants one-third and your moneylender 10 percent. Ninth, find some way for your children to bring in a little extra money so you have something to eat tomorrow. But it won't be enough to keep your family healthy, so lop off 25 to 30 years of your life.

Contrast the above with the percentage of American adults who say this is what they would spend money on first, especially if they suddenly became wealthy: their house, 31%; education for kids and/or self, 30%; a vacation, 10%; a new car, 9%; help for kids and extended family, 3%; charity, 2%; household help, 2%; paying off debt, 2%; boat, 2%; investments, 1%; clothes/jewelry, 1%; other miscellaneous items, 7%.

This reminds us that virtually every American is already wealthy compared to the impoverished people of the world. Given the conditions in which hundreds of millions of people live, it's scandalous that only two percent of Americans would first give to charity, while the vast majority would spend their wealth only on themselves.

■ **TOPIC:** Challenged to Serve
■ **QUESTIONS:** 1. What point was Jesus making by reading from Isaiah 61:1-2? 2. What was Jesus' point by mentioning the widow of Zarephath? 3. How was Jesus able to slip away from the angry mob? 4. How can we make regular worship a part of our lives? 5. How do people sometimes show their rejection of Christians?

■ **ILLUSTRATIONS:**

Strange Irony. A 64 million-dollar project, financed by American donations, is rapidly transforming modern Nazareth—a congested city of 60,000—into a biblical era village. Nazareth draws on its connection to the past and its obvious tourist appeal.

Visitors to the heart of the city now can stroll along donkey paths into a replica of the ancient village in which Jesus lived. One-room stone houses and courtyards have actors playing the part of first-century peasants and laborers. The actors describe the news of Jesus as if He were a contemporary. And storytellers take tourists on the "parable walk." For the truly devout, there are communion services, foot washings, and Bible readings. The hope is to draw millions of visitors to the city over the next few years.

What a strange irony that modern Nazareth is capitalizing on its association with Jesus. The Gospel of Luke reminds us that the ancient residents of the city rejected the Messiah. His contemporaries refused to listen to anything He had to say.

Hometown Boy at Death. Andy Warhol is best remembered for his parodies of the consumerism and pop culture of the 1960's. His revolutionary silk-screened likenesses of Jackie Kennedy, Chairman Mao, and Marilyn Monroe are well known, as are the Campbell's Soup cans, Brillo Pads, and the Coca-Cola bottles. Lesser known are his religious paintings that reflect his strict spiritual upbringing.

Warhol preferred to live and work in New York City. In fact he died there at age 58 due to an infection he received after undergoing routine surgery. But it was his hometown of Pittsburgh that created the Andy Warhol Museum. The city, which has a blue-collar outlook, and which abhorred his outlandish outfits and lifestyle, nonetheless wanted the museum within its boundaries.

Jesus, too, was initially rejected and abhorred by the people of Nazareth. Sadly, the city's residents were negative toward Him when He ministered among them centuries ago.

Heard Call to Free the Captives. Barbara Vogel's fifth grade American history class at a public school in Colorado had finished a unit on slavery when the students were shocked to discover that the slave trade still continued in the Sudan. One student wanted to stop the trade in human lives. He convinced the class to start collecting change in jars with the hope of buying the freedom of two slaves.

The local newspaper heard about the project and ran a story on it. Soon other newspapers and radio and television stations were sharing the story. The checks began pouring in to the class. Within the first year, the students sent over $50,000 to a charitable organization, which in turn arranged for over 1,000 people to be set free.

These students are just a few of those who are striving to improve the lot of others around the world. Jesus had even loftier goals not only for His hometown of Nazareth but also for the rest of the world. As His faithful followers, we are given the task of fostering hope, peace, and joy through the liberating message of the Gospel.

THE COST OF DISCIPLESHIP

BACKGROUND SCRIPTURE: Luke 9:18-25, 57-62; 14:25-33
DEVOTIONAL READING: Matthew 10:34-39

KEY VERSE: "Whoever does not carry the cross and
follow me cannot be my disciple." Luke 14:27.

KING JAMES VERSION

LUKE 9:57 And it came to pass, that, as they went in the way, a certain man said unto him, Lord, I will follow thee whithersoever thou goest.

58 And Jesus said unto him, Foxes have holes, and birds of the air have nests; but the Son of man hath not where to lay his head.

59 And he said unto another, Follow me. But he said, Lord, suffer me first to go and bury my father.

60 Jesus said unto him, Let the dead bury their dead: but go thou and preach the kingdom of God.

61 And another also said, Lord, I will follow thee; but let me first go bid them farewell, which are at home at my house.

62 And Jesus said unto him, No man, having put his hand to the plough, and looking back, is fit for the kingdom of God. . . .

14: 25 And there went great multitudes with him: and he turned, and said unto them,

26 If any man come to me, and hate not his father, and mother, and wife, and children, and brethren, and sisters, yea, and his own life also, he cannot be my disciple.

27 And whosoever doth not bear his cross, and come after me, cannot be my disciple.

28 For which of you, intending to build a tower, sitteth not down first, and counteth the cost, whether he have sufficient to finish it?

29 Lest haply, after he hath laid the foundation, and is not able to finish it, all that behold it begin to mock him,

30 Saying, This man began to build, and was not able to finish.

31 Or what king, going to make war against another king, sitteth not down first, and consulteth whether he be able with ten thousand to meet him that cometh against him with twenty thousand?

32 Or else, while the other is yet a great way off, he sendeth an ambassage, and desireth conditions of peace.

33 So likewise, whosoever he be of you that forsaketh not all that he hath, he cannot be my disciple.

NEW REVISED STANDARD VERSION

LUKE 9:57 As they were going along the road, someone said to him, "I will follow you wherever you go." 58 And Jesus said to him, "Foxes have holes, and birds of the air have nests; but the Son of Man has nowhere to lay his head." 59 To another he said, "Follow me." But he said, "Lord, first let me go and bury my father." 60 But Jesus said to him, "Let the dead bury their own dead; but as for you, go and proclaim the kingdom of God." 61 Another said, "I will follow you, Lord; but let me first say farewell to those at my home." 62 Jesus said to him, "No one who puts a hand to the plow and looks back is fit for the kingdom of God." . . .

14:25 Now large crowds were traveling with him; and he turned and said to them, 26 "Whoever comes to me and does not hate father and mother, wife and children, brothers and sisters, yes, and even life itself, cannot be my disciple. 27 Whoever does not carry the cross and follow me cannot be my disciple. 28 For which of you, intending to build a tower, does not first sit down and estimate the cost, to see whether he has enough to complete it? 29 Otherwise, when he has laid a foundation and is not able to finish, all who see it will begin to ridicule him, 30 saying, 'This fellow began to build and was not able to finish.' 31 Or what king, going out to wage war against another king, will not sit down first and consider whether he is able with ten thousand to oppose the one who comes against him with twenty thousand? 32 If he cannot, then, while the other is still far away, he sends a delegation and asks for the terms of peace. 33 So therefore, none of you can become my disciple if you do not give up all your possessions."

BACKGROUND

Jesus quickly made a name for Himself as a preacher and healer. Crowds thronged to Him. Rumors circulated that He was the long-awaited Messiah. Some people were eager to attach themselves to His messianic cause, perhaps expecting to receive privileges and rewards in return. Others, curious and enjoying the spectacle of fearless preaching and striking healings, followed Jesus as He moved throughout the region.

The world has seen countless leaders with big egos and sensational messages, but never anyone as humble, genuine, and trustworthy as Jesus. He refused to ride a wave of popularity, build an ever-greater crowd of followers, or promote Himself. Instead, Jesus rejected the world's trappings of power and success and set His sights on the cross. Jesus knew that serving in love meant a costly renunciation of worldly ways. He thus taught the crowds that if they were serious about getting right with God, they had to live completely for Him.

The cost of such discipleship is high. To those who glibly announced that they wished to be Jesus' followers, the Savior stated He couldn't offer them fame and wealth. And to those who said they intended to become His followers in the future—but only after various family obligations were first met—Jesus underscored the urgency of following Him without delay.

To everyone today who ponders Jesus and His messianic claims, this week's lesson serves as a reminder that absolute devotion to Him is of foremost importance. Most of us commit ourselves to a great many things. When we take a look at our commitments and our motivations behind them, we begin to see a pattern. This pattern points to where our main commitment, or treasure, really is. Perhaps this is why Jesus said, *"For where your treasure is, there your heart will be also"* (Luke 12:34).

When you stop and think about it, the most valuable treasure a person can seek is Christ. After all, He is Lord of all creation, and He died in our place to bring us back to God. He is the only one worthy of our highest commitment. When this fragile life is over and eternity begins for us in heaven, only the things we did in Jesus' honor will retain any enduring value. Thus, the only valuable way to live is to be fully devoted to Christ. As Jesus said in Matthew 6:24, *"You cannot serve God and wealth."*

Notes on the Printed Text

In 1991 and 1992, the Pittsburgh Penguins won back-to-back Stanley Cups. But amazingly on October 13, 1998, the team filed for bankruptcy protection. The fan base had eroded after big stars such as Mario Lemieux retired or were traded to other teams. What were once sell-out games now had plenty of seats available. The fans and followers had lost their enthusiasm for the Penguins.

Jesus knew well the fickleness of the crowds of people who followed Him. The Gospel of Luke reveals that Jesus, while on His way to Jerusalem, encountered three would-be disciples. As the Savior talked with them, He underscored the high cost of discipleship.

As they were going along the road, someone said to him, "I will follow you wherever you go" (Luke 9:57). Here we find an enthusiastic volunteer stopping Jesus. He had been immensely impressed by the Lord's teaching and wanted to join His group. With lofty praise, the would-be disciple announced his willingness to go anywhere with Jesus.

Our Lord quickly sized up this person. Perhaps he looked like a couch potato who lacked any stamina and vitality (whether physical, mental, or spiritual). Or maybe he enjoyed a wealthy life of ease. In either case, Jesus wanted him to understand the nature of the commitment he would be making. The Savior declared there wouldn't be a huge salary or worldly fame for those who followed Him. *And Jesus said to him, "Foxes have holes, and birds of the air have nests; but the Son of Man has nowhere to lay his head"* (9:58).

Jesus saw potential in another bystander and tried to recruit him. *To another he said, "Follow me"* (9:59). The man, however, wanted to delay becoming a disciple. He said he would follow Jesus at a later date. The man claimed that he had ongoing commitments to his parents. Only after they were dead and buried (which could have been years away) would he accept Jesus' invitation. *But he said, "Lord, first let me go and bury my father."*

The Lord told the man that his first duty lay with God. Let those who had rejected God's grace—namely, the spiritually dead—perform the burial duties on those who were physically dead. The issue here is one of getting priorities straight. While social obligations cannot be ignored, they must always take a backseat to serving Christ. *But Jesus said to him, "Let the dead bury their own dead; but as for you, go and proclaim the kingdom of God"* (9:60).

Another person stepped forward and offered to follow Jesus. But first this person wanted to go home and say goodbye to his family (9:61). Jesus made it clear that fitness for service in the kingdom required staying with the task at hand. No distractions were allowed. *Jesus said to him, "No one who puts a hand to the plow and looks back is fit for the kingdom of God"* (9:62).

At some other point in His ministry, Jesus again talked about the cost of discipleship. Perhaps some of those traveling with Him were thinking about following Him. *Now large crowds were traveling with him; and he turned and said to them,*

"Whoever comes to me and does not hate father and mother, wife and children, brothers and sisters, yes, and even life itself, cannot be my disciple" (14:25-26).

Jesus used hyperbole (or intentional exaggeration) to urge His followers to leave everything behind. True discipleship meant loving the Savior so much that all other loves were hatred by comparison. Obviously Jesus was not telling people to hate those dearest to them. Rather, He was underscoring the importance of setting priorities. In this case, the Lord had to be first, even ahead of one's family.

The Savior declared, *"Whoever does not carry the cross and follow me cannot be my disciple"* (14:27). The point is that following Jesus means total submission, perhaps even to the point of death. In fact, it is a death to a whole way of sinful living, for it means renouncing our selfish ambitions.

Jesus again reminded His listeners that they had to consider carefully the cost of discipleship. No wise individual would try to construct a watch tower or a farm building without first making sure the project could be completed. Otherwise they would surely invite the ridicule of everyone in town (14:30). *"For which of you, intending to build a tower does not first sit down and estimate the cost, to see whether he has enough to complete it? Otherwise, when he has laid a foundation and is not able to finish, all who see it will begin to ridicule him"* (14:28-29).

Jesus offered a second parable about a king who met with his counselors to determine whether they had enough soldiers to defeat their enemy in battle. If it became clear that victory was not on his side, the king would then send a delegation to discuss terms of peace (Luke 14:31-32).

Jesus concluded by declaring that a disciple had to be willing to give up everything in order to follow Him. Only those who were willing to invest all they had in God's kingdom were serious about being Jesus' follower. *"So therefore, none of you can become my disciple if you do not give up all your possessions"* (14:33).

SUGGESTIONS TO TEACHERS

We live in a culture that craves personal comfort and commends maintaining personal safety. Sadly, the idea of making and honoring long-term commitments is not an ideal upheld by many. It therefore should not surprise us that the demands Jesus places on His followers run counter to popular thinking. The cost of discipleship is often more than most people will pay.

1. RADICAL COMMITMENT. Look carefully at the Scripture text in this week's lesson. Start with Jesus' words about His messiahship. He warned that He would be a suffering Deliverer, not a popular conquering hero. His rule would come through sacrificial love and costly caring for others, not through hoarding life. These truths are key to understanding the Savior's life and message.

2. RELUCTANT CAMPAIGNERS. Talk with the students about the people described in Luke 9:57-62. What similarities can be observed between these people and us?

3. RESOLUTE CROSS-BEARING. Move on to Luke 14:25-27 and discuss the implications of bearing one's cross. Remind the class that there was nothing sentimental or pleasant about carrying a cross in Jesus' time. Then note that self-denial is the idea behind the metaphor. By this Jesus meant a willingness to obey His commands, serve one another, and suffer—perhaps even die—for His sake.

4. REQUISITE COST. Finally, examine the two parables about building a tower and embarking on a military campaign without first considering the cost. Draw the students into some thoughtful conversation about what changes in their lives might be in order or what new priorities they might have to make if they are serious about being Jesus' devoted followers.

FOR ADULTS

■ **TOPIC:** Counting the Cost

■ **QUESTIONS:** 1. How much did Jesus say one had to give up to be His disciple? 2. Why did Jesus insist that our love for Him must be even greater than our love for our immediate family? 3. Why is halfhearted commitment not an option for Jesus' followers? 4. In what ways does Jesus' teaching about discipleship run counter to the thinking of the world? 5. How has being a follower of Christ recently challenged you in your faith?

■ **ILLUSTRATIONS:**

Keeping in Training. Karen Phelps, the marathon runner, knows the need for daily running if she is to remain in competition as a champion athlete. In an interview she recently stated, "On this particular day, I didn't feel like running at all, but I made myself do it, because running is a sport you have to practice every day. I wanted to win races, so I had a detailed plan for training. First, run daily, even if you don't feel like it. Second, run daily, even if you sometimes have to skip fun and pleasure. Third, run daily, even in bad weather, and even if people think you're weird. Fourth, run daily, even when it gives you aches and pains and you feel like quitting. Fifth, run daily, even if you don't feel it's doing you any good."

"One day," Phelps continued, "as I jogged along on my training run, it came to me that daily practice—training—was what my spiritual life needed, too. Do you know what I've learned? Sometimes you may not feel like praying or reading the Bible or going out of your way to help others. But if you're in training—whether physical or spiritual—you'll do it."

In Memorium. I was reading through the newsletter of the seminary where I did graduate studies and noticed the sterling legacies of those who had recently passed away. One believer had served as a Bible school teacher for two decades, and then as a missionary for another two decades. The last years of her life were spent serving in a church in the Midwest of the United States.

Another Christian served as a missionary for 15 years in Central America. Then for 12 years he was a religious professor in a college on the East coast of the United States. He spent most of his later years as a missionary-at-large.

Then there's the believer who began serving the Lord as a Sunday school teacher and then as a Bible college professor. But the majority of his life was spent serving a small congregation in the southern United States. There he helped to train others to do the work of the ministry.

What is the key to the success of these believers? It's their unwavering commitment to Christ. Their lifelong desire wasn't to become famous, rich, or powerful. Rather, they simply wanted to honor the Lord through their faithful service.

Words of the Commission. For over two centuries, starting with George Washington, the officer's commission in the armed forces of the United States of America has carried almost the same words. The main changes have to do with who originates and signs the document, and where and when the commission is given. But the words otherwise are almost identical for officers' commissions given throughout the nation's history.

The solemn phrases carry heavy responsibilities, as any person who has been commissioned as an officer knows. You pledge to "repose special trust and confidence in your patriotism . . . diligently discharge the duties of (your rank) by doing and performing all manner of things, thereunto belonging . . . to observe and follow such orders . . . This commission is to continue in force indefinitely."

These words could be applied to the commission that Jesus Christ gives each of His followers. Of course, Jesus demands even more. His disciples are to take up their cross and following Him absolutely.

FOR YOUTH ■ TOPIC: Is Discipleship for Me?
■ QUESTIONS: 1. What excuses do people often make for not following Jesus? 2. Why is it important to count the cost before making a commitment to Jesus? 3. How is it possible to give up everything in order to follow Christ? 4. Why can't Jesus' disciples afford to be halfhearted in their commitment? 5. Why is it sometimes hard for us to give Jesus complete control of our lives?

■ **ILLUSTRATIONS:**
Fan or Follower? A well-known religious leader decided to make a stop in a major midwestern city of the United States. It's not surprising that when news spread of his anticipated arrival, many people wanted to see him. One person, in particular, wanted a private audience with the religious leader.

This champion athlete felt that he, of all people, should be given a private audience. After all, the sports figure was known for his physical strength and skill and for the impressive records he had set during his career. Certainly he should have been granted his request.

Remarkably, however, the religious leader's staff said he would not be able to meet with the athlete. Perhaps the leader was too busy to fit the athlete into his schedule for the day. Or maybe the leader sensed the athlete was more of a fan who was seeking to boost his own image by being seen with the leader.

When Jesus ministered on earth, there were many people who wanted to see and be seen with Him. But Jesus didn't want fans. Rather, He wanted followers who would commit themselves wholeheartedly to Him!

Demonstrated Understanding. Just before Christmas 1998, former light-heavyweight boxing champion, Archie Moore, died in San Diego. "The Mongoose" was the only boxer to face both Rocky Marciano and Mohammed Ali. At the funeral Moore was eulogized by George Foreman, a former student who later became a world heavyweight boxing champion, and who is now an ordained minister.

Foreman said, "When I think of Archie Moore, an old proverb comes to mind. Suppose you want to build a tower. First you sit down and figure the cost. Then you see if you have enough money to finish it. Otherwise, if you lay a foundation and can't complete the building, everyone will make fun of you. In all the years we talked while Archie was teaching me, he made it clear. 'I love God and my family, and I will love you if you work hard.' So Archie laid the foundation, and today he stands as a tower for all athletes, saying, 'If you want it, leave your excuses behind and come get it.' "

Moore and Foreman both understood Jesus' parable regarding priorities. For Jesus' followers, He must come first. No excuses will be accepted.

Setting Priorities. Many high school students take a course in study skills and acquire the tools for active learning. One of those tools is time management. As part of the course, students learn to prioritize their time. For instance, they must decide between wise and unwise activities. Wise use of time aids in production, while unwise use of time is wasted. Students learn to figure out which tasks have to be accomplished and which don't really matter. Time is budgeted so that they learn to see whether an assignment is due tomorrow, next week, or next month.

Jesus called His followers to get their priorities straight. Certain decisions, such as accepting His call to discipleship, were the best and wisest choices. Everything else was less important from an eternal perspective.

LOST AND FOUND

BACKGROUND SCRIPTURE: Luke 15
DEVOTIONAL READING: Ephesians 1:15—2:2

KEY VERSE: "This son of mine was dead and is alive
again; he was lost and is found!" Luke 15:24.

KING JAMES VERSION

LUKE 15:1 Then drew near unto him all the publicans and sinners for to hear him.

2 And the Pharisees and scribes murmured, saying, This man receiveth sinners, and eateth with them. . . .

11 And he said, A certain man had two sons:

12 And the younger of them said to his father, Father, give me the portion of goods that falleth to me. And he divided unto them his living.

13 And not many days after the younger son gathered all together, and took his journey into a far country, and there wasted his substance with riotous living.

14 And when he had spent all, there arose a mighty famine in that land; and he began to be in want.

15 And he went and joined himself to a citizen of that country; and he sent him into his fields to feed swine.

16 And he would fain have filled his belly with the husks that the swine did eat: and no man gave unto him.

17 And when he came to himself, he said, How many hired servants of my father's have bread enough and to spare, and I perish with hunger!

18 I will arise and go to my father, and will say unto him, Father, I have sinned against heaven, and before thee,

19 And am no more worthy to be called thy son: make me as one of thy hired servants.

20 And he arose, and came to his father. But when he was yet a great way off, his father saw him, and had compassion, and ran, and fell on his neck, and kissed him.

21 And the son said unto him, Father, I have sinned against heaven, and in thy sight, and am no more worthy to be called thy son.

22 But the father said to his servants, Bring forth the best robe, and put it on him; and put a ring on his hand, and shoes on his feet:

23 And bring hither the fatted calf, and kill it; and let us eat, and be merry:

24 For this my son was dead, and is alive again; he was lost, and is found. And they began to be merry.

NEW REVISED STANDARD VERSION

LUKE 15:1 Now all the tax collectors and sinners were coming near to listen to him. 2 And the Pharisees and the scribes were grumbling and saying, "This fellow welcomes sinners and eats with them." . . .

11 Then Jesus said, "There was a man who had two sons. 12 The younger of them said to his father, 'Father, give me the share of the property that will belong to me.' So he divided his property between them. 13 A few days later the younger son gathered all he had and traveled to a distant country, and there he squandered his property in dissolute living. 14 When he had spent everything, a severe famine took place throughout that country, and he began to be in need. 15 So he went and hired himself out to one of the citizens of that country, who sent him to his fields to feed the pigs. 16 He would gladly have filled himself with the pods that the pigs were eating; and no one gave him anything. 17 But when he came to himself he said, 'How many of my father's hired hands have bread enough and to spare, but here I am dying of hunger! 18 I will get up and go to my father, and I will say to him, "Father, I have sinned against heaven and before you; 19 I am no longer worthy to be called your son; treat me like one of your hired hands." ' 20 So he set off and went to his father. But while he was still far off, his father saw him and was filled with compassion; he ran and put his arms around him and kissed him. 21 Then the son said to him, 'Father, I have sinned against heaven and before you; I am no longer worthy to be called your son.' 22 But the father said to his slaves, 'Quickly, bring out a robe—the best one—and put it on him; put a ring on his finger and sandals on his feet. 23 And get the fatted calf and kill it, and let us eat and celebrate; 24 for this son of mine was dead and is alive again; he was lost and is found!' And they began to celebrate."

8

HOME BIBLE READINGS

BACKGROUND

This week's lesson concerns the parable of the lost son. Generally speaking, parables are brief stories and sayings drawn from everyday life (for example, anecdotes about the planting of crops, the settling of debts, the hiring of workers, and the wise use of money). Parables comprise more than one-third of the recorded teachings of Jesus. In fact, Mark 4:34 says that at one time Jesus *did not speak to them except in parables.*

In His parables, Jesus first would comment on something in the physical world and then compare it to something in the spiritual world. (The word parable literally comes from "to cast alongside.") The Savior did this to clarify truths relating to the kingdom of God. Jesus' parables motivated interested listeners (for example, the disciples) to find out more about what was being taught. At the same time, these stories concealed truth from uninterested listeners (for example, the religious leaders). Jesus explained His parables to those who genuinely desired to understand His teaching. The truths He proclaimed, however, remained obscure to those who were antagonistic to His message and ministry.

Luke presented a trio of parables spoken by Jesus in reply to the accusation that He associated with tax collectors and sinners. Luke underscored Jesus' concern for the outcasts of society by recording the parables of the lost sheep, the lost coin, and the lost son. Each story underscored the Lord's intense desire for the spiritually lost to be saved. Luke's delight in presenting these beloved parables has led scholars to call his writings "The Gospel for the Outcasts."

NOTES ON THE PRINTED TEXT

The Pharisees and scribes took the law of Moses seriously and followed strict spiritual disciplines designed to promote holiness. In an earlier day they may have represented the pure lifestyle God had wanted His people to follow, but by the time of Jesus, their sincere love of God had become heavily intermixed with lifeless legalism.

As a result of being caught up in keeping humanly made rules, the religious leaders removed themselves from those who would not or could not meet their standards or keep their rituals. Their hearts became hard toward tax collectors and other people who broke their laws (Luke 15:1).

The term *"sinners"* (15:2) would cover the irreligious who for varied reasons did not follow the customs and rituals of pharisaic Judaism. This group might include donkey drivers, shepherds, tanners, peddlers, and prostitutes. For the religious leaders to associate with such types was unthinkable, and to eat with them, as Jesus did, seemed outrageous.

Rather than confront the Pharisees and scribes directly, Jesus told them a series of parables. In the parable of the lost son, He noted that there was a *"man who had two sons"* (15:11). We learn that *"the younger of them said to his father, 'Father, give me the share of the property that will belong to me'"* (15:12). In making this demand, the youth was being selfish and impatient with his father. In fact, the young man wanted his third (the amount specified by law) right then. Rather than punish him for his insolence, the father granted the request. *"So he divided his property between them."* Most likely, the inheritance was in livestock and land.

Normally, the sale of livestock and land took months of haggling between the seller and buyer. But in the case of the younger son, he somehow was able to liquidate his inheritance quickly (perhaps at bargain-basement rates). Awash in cash, he went to a far country to get away from his family and enjoy himself. *"A few days later the younger son gathered all he had and traveled to a distant country, and there he squandered his property in dissolute living"* (15:13).

Perhaps a drought occurred not longer after the youth had spent his money. If so, this explains why there was a devastating famine in the land. Crop failures then, as now, produced food shortages. *"When he had spent everything, a severe famine took place throughout that country, and he began to be in need"* (15:14).

So desperate and hungry was the youth that he broke Jewish law by associating with people and animals the Jews considered to be ceremonially unclean (15:15). The lad became so hungry that he *"would gladly have filled himself with the pods that the pigs were eating; and no one gave him anything"* (15:16).

At this low point in his life, the youth did some deep soul searching. He sensed that life could not get much worse, for even his father's servants had enough food to eat. *"But when he came to himself he said, 'How many of my father's hired hands have bread enough and to spare, but here I am dying of hunger!'"* (15:17).

The youth formulated a plan of action. He would return home, admit his wrongdoing, and ask that his father employ him as a cheap day laborer. *"Father, . . . treat me like one of your hired hands"* (15:18-19).

The father had been eagerly waiting for the younger son's return. Ordinarily an older adult would never run in public, for doing so required lifting one's long robes, which in turn exposed one's legs and underwear (a socially taboo action). But the father was willing to endure such humiliation in order to welcome his son back into the family. *"But . . . his father saw him and was filled with compassion; he ran and put his arms around him and kissed him"* (15:20).

The youth began his confession, but his father cut him off abruptly (15:21).

"The father said to his slaves, 'Quickly, bring out a robe—the best one—and put it on him; put a ring on his finger and sandals on his feet'" (15:22). The best robe belonged to the father. The ring was a symbol of trust and authority. And expensive sandals marked the child as a free person, not a servant. All were given to demonstrate that the youth had been restored to his former position as a son in the family.

To further underscore the son's reconciliation, the father ordered that a calf be slaughtered for a great banquet. " *'And get the fatted calf and kill it, and let us eat and celebrate; for this son of mine was dead and is alive again, he was lost and is found!'"* (15:23-24).

SUGGESTIONS TO TEACHERS

A "prodigal" is someone who is "recklessly extravagant" and "characterized by wasteful living" (*Merriam Webster's Collegiate Dictionary*). This would certainly be true of the youth in Jesus' story (traditionally known as the parable of the prodigal son). But despite the lad's immoral behavior, his father still loved him and longed for him to abandon his sinful ways. This story is a powerful illustration of God's unconditional love for the lost.

1. CRITICISM OF THE LEGALISTIC SELF-RIGHTEOUS. Let the students know that Jesus deliberately associated with the lost, even though the religious elite of His day refused to do so. Then discuss who the "lost" might be today. Why are some in the church displeased when Christians show concern for the outcasts of society? Why is such an uncaring attitude offensive to God?

2. CONCERN FOR THE LOST SHEEP. In this parable the owner highly valued every sheep in his flock, even the one that had been lost (Luke 15:3-7). Likewise, we are never regarded by God as nameless members of the human race but rather as individuals whom He wants to redeem. If a cherished part of a flock of sheep was worth the risk and effort of the owner to seek and find, how much more has our Lord valued us and sought to bring us back into fellowship with Him through His Son, Jesus Christ?

3. CELEBRATION OVER THE LOCATED COIN. In this parable, a woman expressed intense delight in finding a coin she had lost (15:8-10). This reflected the joy that God feels when a lost person is reconciled to Him through faith in His Son. The theme of God's rejoicing when the lost are found should be discussed. Using the words of the familiar hymn, "Amazing Grace," talk together about what the following line means: "Once I was lost, but now I am found."

4. CARING OF THE LIVING PARENT. Devote ample lesson time to discuss this familiar parable (15:11-32). Remind your students that both sons in Jesus' story were spiritually lost and in need of redemption. In the parable, the father welcomed the repentant younger son, and remained compassionate toward the uncaring older son. The story ends with only the younger son experiencing a true change of heart, one that is well pleasing to God.

■ **TOPIC:** Celebrating Reconciliation

■ **QUESTIONS:** 1. Why did the religious leaders criticize and oppose Jesus? 2. Why did the younger son decide to return home? 3. What was the main point of Jesus' parable? 4. What are some ways believers can share the Gospel with those who are spiritually lost? 5. How has God used one of the humiliating moments of your life to do something good?

■ **ILLUSTRATIONS:**

Found by God. The late Isaac Asimov was renowned for his science fiction. He also said he was an atheist. He disclaimed any notion of the existence of God, and he made no place for any kind of faith in his life.

When Asimov was interviewed one time by David Frost on television, the famous writer tried to dismiss a question about God by replying, "Whose God?" When Frost persisted in talking about the God of the Bible, Asimov deflected the topic by claiming that he hadn't given much thought to the subject. But Frost persevered, telling Asimov that a person with his intelligence would surely have given some thought to the meaning of God. Asimov replied that God was smarter than him and thus should try to find him (rather than the other way around).

Then, on the day in which the interview appeared on television (including the flippant remark about letting God find him), Isaac Asimov was struck with a severe attack of kidney stones. While groaning with pain, the famed science fiction writer could only mutter, "All right, God. You've found me. Now let me go!" (Isaac Asimov, *Asimov Laughs Again,* Harper-Collins).

Found Feline. In July, 1994, Carol Ann Timmel carefully placed her beloved cat, Tabitha, in a special pet carrier provided by the airliner for the flight from New York to Los Angeles. But when Timmel arrived in Los Angeles and tried to pick up her cat, she could not find the animal. The airline staff could not explain how Tabitha could be missing.

Timmel then filed a lawsuit to force the airliner to conduct a thorough search, but finally dropped it when the company agreed to ground the plane for 24 hours. Meanwhile, 12 days had elapsed. The aircraft had flown from New York to Los Angeles, New York to San Juan, Puerto Rico, and New York to Miami. Newspapers picked up the story of Timmel's determined effort to find her pet, and some ran a daily "Cat Watch" with photos of Tabitha.

Finally, 12 days and 12,000 miles after Tabitha had gotten lost in the belly of a jumbo jet, the high-flying cat was found. After being retrieved from a hiding place in the drop ceiling of the jet's cargo area, Tabitha emerged into the arms of its joyful owner. The pet had been without food or water for the entire time and lost two pounds, though was otherwise fine.

The airline president estimated the company had invested 100 staff hours in fruitless searches for Tabitha, but recognized Timmel's love for her cat and backed her tireless effort to find the animal. Everyone celebrated finding Tabitha! God is even more determined to bring us back to Him. And the celebration in heaven is far more joyous when we are reconciled to Him through Christ.

Only One Door Away, but Lost. A young man traveled to Chicago and registered at a hotel in the city. Then, while taking a walk around the nearby business district, he became lost. He couldn't remember the name, location, and appearance of the hotel and thus was unable to find it.

It became necessary to secure a second room, and so the young man chose another nearby hotel. Then for five days he tried to find the place where he had deposited his baggage. At first the young man was too embarrassed to acknowledge to the authorities that he was lost. But then, after failing to solve his problem, he finally asked the police for help.

The police soon found the young man's original registration. They told him that for five days he had been lodging right next door to the place where he had left his baggage. He lost five days' peace of mind, five days' time, and five days' use of his baggage, all because he wouldn't tell the authorities he was lost.

The young man should not have delayed in asking the police for help. After all, it was their duty to assist those who had lost their way. Similarly, no one should put off coming to the Lord in repentance and faith. After all, Jesus Himself said, *"the Son of Man came to seek out and to save the lost"* (Luke 19:10).

■ **TOPIC:** Seeking Another Chance

■ **QUESTIONS:** 1. Why did the father's youngest son demand his share of the inheritance? 2. Why was the father's response to his son's return so amazing? 3. What can we do to be as grace-oriented as God is toward the lost? 4. What caused you to turn to God in repentance and seek His forgiveness? 5. In what ways has God made His influence obvious in your life?

■ **ILLUSTRATIONS:**

In the Wrong Place. One Thanksgiving morning, an elderly couple placed their luggage in the trunk of their car and departed for their son's home some distance away. They planned to have dinner with him and his family.

Tragically, the elderly couple never arrived. Eventually the police search widened to cover a large portion of the state in which they lived. Television and newspapers carried the couple's pictures and story. Finally, one week later, a security guard asked the police to come to a motel in a nearby state. There they found the two elderly persons. The couple had become disoriented and lost, and ended up hundreds of miles off course.

In this case "lost" meant "being in the wrong place." Though the elderly couple had gotten lost, a concerned group of people did all that they could to find and restore them to their loved ones. In the same way, God seeks out the lost so that they might be restored to Him in faith.

Came to Themselves. On November 23, 1998, two teenagers ran away from their homes near a major midwestern city in the United States. They then jumped a train and were off on what seemed to be the adventure of their lives.

A few hours later the youths decided to switch to another train, which was heading for a brewing company on the east coast. Somehow the boxcar's door slammed shut and locked, trapping the two teenagers. For eight days the adolescents survived by drinking the drops of stale beer left in the mostly empty bottles. Finally, a brewery employee, while taking inventory in the rail yard and after hearing the youths pounding on the boxcar's side, freed them.

The two, already on probation at an institution for suspended students and having already run away once before, vowed that their lives would be different. One of the youths exclaimed, "I decided I've got to get a new crew to hang out with so that I can change my ways and stay out of trouble!" The other youth similarly echoed, "I'm going to straighten up my life and go to church!" The younger son in Jesus' parable also came to himself after a trying situation.

Searching. In May, 1998, Dr. Robert Ballard found the *USS Yorktown*. Ballard, who 10 years before had discovered the lost ocean liner *Titanic*, had been searching for the *Yorktown*, a World War II aircraft carrier that sank 56 years earlier after a Japanese torpedo attack.

The expedition was the largest and most technologically challenging undersea search ever mounted by the United States Navy and the National Geographic Society. For several weeks while aboard the research vessel *Laney Chouset*, Ballard and his crew crisscrossed 300 square miles of the Pacific ocean north of Midway Island. They watched and waited as a towed mapping device and an underwater drone scanned the ocean bottom miles below. The wreckage was finally discovered 16,650 feet down, which is nearly one mile further down than the wreckage of the *Titanic*.

If people will go to such extremes to find an old sunken aircraft carrier, imagine the extent to which God has gone to seek and save us! Though lost, we can be found and reconciled to Him by trusting in Christ.

THREAT OF RICHES

BACKGROUND SCRIPTURE: Luke 16
DEVOTIONAL READING: Luke 12:15-21

KEY VERSE: "You cannot serve God and wealth." Luke 16:13b.

9

KING JAMES VERSION

LUKE 16:1 And he said also unto his disciples, There was a certain rich man, which had a steward; and the same was accused unto him that he had wasted his goods.

2 And he called him, and said unto him, How is it that I hear this of thee? give an account of thy stewardship; for thou mayest be no longer steward.

3 Then the steward said within himself, What shall I do? for my lord taketh away from me the stewardship: I cannot dig; to beg I am ashamed.

4 I am resolved what to do, that, when I am put out of the stewardship, they may receive me into their houses.

5 So he called every one of his lord's debtors unto him, and said unto the first, How much owest thou unto my lord?

6 And he said, An hundred measures of oil. And he said unto him, Take thy bill, and sit down quickly, and write fifty.

7 Then said he to another, And how much owest thou? And he said, An hundred measures of wheat. And he said unto him, Take thy bill, and write fourscore.

8 And the lord commended the unjust steward, because he had done wisely: for the children of this world are in their generation wiser than the children of light.

9 And I say unto you, Make to yourselves friends of the mammon of unrighteousness; that, when ye fail, they may receive you into everlasting habitations.

10 He that is faithful in that which is least is faithful also in much: and he that is unjust in the least is unjust also in much.

11 If therefore ye have not been faithful in the unrighteous mammon, who will commit to your trust the true riches?

12 And if ye have not been faithful in that which is another man's, who shall give you that which is your own?

13 No servant can serve two masters: for either he will hate the one, and love the other; or else he will hold to the one, and despise the other. Ye cannot serve God and mammon.

NEW REVISED STANDARD VERSION

LUKE 16:1 Then Jesus said to the disciples, "There was a rich man who had a manager, and charges were brought to him that this man was squandering his property. 2 So he summoned him and said to him, 'What is this that I hear about you? Give me an accounting of your management, because you cannot be my manager any longer.' 3 Then the manager said to himself, 'What will I do, now that my master is taking the position away from me? I am not strong enough to dig, and I am ashamed to beg. 4 I have decided what to do so that, when I am dismissed as manager, people may welcome me into their homes.' 5 So, summoning his master's debtors one by one, he asked the first, 'How much do you owe my master?' 6 He answered, 'A hundred jugs of olive oil.' He said to him, 'Take your bill, sit down quickly, and make it fifty.' 7 Then he asked another, 'And how much do you owe?' He replied, 'A hundred containers of wheat.' He said to him, "Take your bill and make it eighty.' 8 And his master commended the dishonest manager because he had acted shrewdly; for the children of this age are more shrewd in dealing with their own generation than are the children of light. 9 And I tell you, make friends for yourselves by means of dishonest wealth so that when it is gone, they may welcome you into the eternal homes.

10 "Whoever is faithful in a very little is faithful also in much; and whoever is dishonest in a very little is dishonest also in much. 11 If then you have not been faithful with the dishonest wealth, who will entrust to you the true riches? 12 And if you have not been faithful with what belongs to another, who will give you what is your own? 13 No slave can serve two masters; for a slave will either hate the one and love the other, or be devoted to the one and despise the other. You cannot serve God and wealth."

BACKGROUND

In ancient times people did not use slips of paper (like dollar bills) as a medium of exchange. Instead, they used various kinds of metals (for example, gold, silver, and copper) to measure value or worth. These coins were well suited for such a purpose since they could be stored and transported more easily than the items for which they were exchanged.

Since silver was more widely available than gold, it became the most common precious metal used in business dealings, general trade, and the payment of tribute. Before the introduction of coins, payment in the form of gold and silver was weighed out in predefined amounts on balances. The talent was the largest unit of weight and measure. It was equivalent to about 3,000 silver shekels (the basic Israelite weight unit).

From the above we see that the use of money was prominent in New Testament times. Though we sometimes think that western society is the most materialistic in history, a study of other cultures—whether ancient or modern—discloses that the desire for money and possessions has dominated the minds of people in every part of the world down through the centuries.

Consider the Pharisees of Jesus' day. They were members of a Jewish sect that had risen to prominence during the two centuries before the Savior's birth. Their goal was to increase the righteousness of society. They insisted on strict obedience to the law of Moses. They believed they had received the spirit of Moses and claimed to know the divine will in legal matters.

Theoretically, the Pharisees believed in righteousness and love, but all too often they practiced legalism and hypocrisy. For instance, though they said they were worshipers of God, they were really *lovers of money* (Luke 16:14). Perhaps this is one reason why Jesus warned His disciples (most of whom owned little and had little hope of ever being well off) about the dangers of wanting to be rich. Jesus called His followers to refuse to be enslaved by the desire for more wealth. Rather, they were to use their possessions responsibly (16:13).

The parable of the dishonest manager is the focus of study in this week's lesson. Jesus did not tell the story to encourage fraud or deceit, but rather to urge His disciples to be wise managers of their wealth and possessions. They were to remember that they were stewards of what God had entrusted to their care.

NOTES ON THE PRINTED TEXT

The Pharisees were notorious for their greed and for using wealth to gratify their selfish desires (Luke 16:14). Jesus wanted His followers to live differently. The issue was not whether to have wealth but rather how to use it. The Savior wanted His disciples to use their material means to advance the cause of righteousness in the world. For instance, by using wealth in a prudent and discerning manner, believers could ease the affliction of those in need.

Undoubtedly it was with these principles in mind that Jesus told His disciples a parable about a dishonest manager. A wealthy landowner had heard that his overseer was dishonest. Because accurate records were not always kept in ancient times, the mismanagement of funds and property was possible. *"There was a rich man who had a manager, and charges were brought to him that this man was squandering his property"* (16:1).

The manager received payments from those who had outstanding debts with the landowner. In this case, the bills were written in terms of commodities rather than cash. Perhaps on top of the interest the landowner charged, the manager charged an extra amount, which he then kept for himself.

Somehow the landowner learned about the manager's dishonest ways. The rich man thus called the manager in and questioned him about his fraudulence. The landowner ordered the dishonest steward to give him *"an accounting of your management, because you cannot be my manager any longer"* (16:2). In other words, because the overseer was about to be fired from his cushy "desk job," he needed to get his financial records in order.

The manager did not challenge the accusations made against him, perhaps because he knew they were true. Recognizing that he was about to be dismissed, he considered what other kind of work he could do. He first thought about ditch digging, but decided he couldn't do that because he wasn't strong enough. He also rejected the idea of begging because he was too proud to do it. *"Then the manager said to himself, 'What will I do, now that my master is taking the position away from me? I am not strong enough to dig, and I am ashamed to beg'"* (16:3).

The manager then devised a shrewd plan. He would win the friendship of his master's debtors by reducing the amount they owed. Then, the steward reasoned, after he lost his job as manager, he would be able to receive favors from them in return. *"I have decided what to do so that, when I am dismissed as manager, people may welcome me into their homes"* (16:4).

Some think the manager may have done nothing illegal by reducing the debts. Since Mosaic law prohibited the charging of interest (Deut. 23:19), it is claimed that the steward simply cut the interest the master had added to the original loan. This view might have some merit, except for the fact that Jesus called the steward dishonest.

In the parable, the overseer invited each person who owed money to his employer to come and discuss the situation. When the manager asked the first person how much he owed (Luke 16:5), the debtor replied, "*a hundred jugs of olive oil*" (16:6). The shrewd steward told him to "*Take your bill, sit down quickly, and make it fifty.*"

The manager then asked the next debtor how much he owed the landowner. The man replied, "*A hundred containers of wheat*" (16:7). In response, the steward told him to "*Take your bill and make it eighty.*" Some think these differences in the percentage of reduction was due to the difference in the relative value of olive oil and wheat.

When the landowner found out what the steward had done, "*his master commended the dishonest manager because he had acted shrewdly*" (16:8). On the surface we might think that Jesus was giving His approval to the overseer's dishonest ways. But this would be an incorrect conclusion. Rather, Jesus was spotlighting the manager's act of prudence.

Jesus explained that "*the children of this age are more shrewd in dealing with their own generation than are the children of light*" (16:8). The idea is that the manager used foresight in preparing for his future. Similarly, Jesus wanted His followers to be prudent in the way they prepared for their eternal future.

Jesus then said, "*I tell you, make friends for yourselves by means of dishonest wealth, so that when it is gone, they may welcome you into the eternal homes*" (16:9). The idea is that believers are to use their material resources to benefit others. As a result, such generosity would lead to an eternal reward in heaven.

It's true that money and possessions will not last forever. Nevertheless, believers who are generous and used their material resources to help others are making spiritual investments. Perhaps the idea here is to use our wealth in a way that will foster faith and obedience (12:33-34).

Jesus next observed that unless His disciples were faithful in small matters, they wouldn't be faithful in large ones. In other words, if believers cheat even a little, they won't be honest with greater responsibilities (16:10). Also, those who were untrustworthy with earthly wealth couldn't be trusted with heavenly riches (16:11). "*And if you have not been faithful with what belongs to another, who will give you what is your own?*" (16:12).

Jesus concluded by noting that if His disciples became enslaved to material things, they wouldn't be able to serve God. Ultimately, an unchecked desire for worldly riches pushes believers away from the Lord. "*You cannot serve God and wealth*" (16:13).

SUGGESTIONS TO TEACHERS

Some religious people take vows of poverty. Though they have no wealth or private property, they know they must guard against being enslaved by the desire for comfort and possessions. Jesus' warning about wealth thus applies to everyone! Through this week's lesson, you can stress to your students the importance of using their material resources wisely for God's glory.

1. RESOURCEFUL STEWARDSHIP. The parable of the dishonest manager may be difficult for your students to understand. Emphasize that Jesus was not winking at wasteful actions or condoning dishonest behavior. Rather, He was commending the foresight and resourcefulness of the steward. Note that we should use our wealth prudently because it belongs to God, not us. Also, money is neither good nor evil, but rather the way in which we use it. We thus should use our money for good. Moreover, because people see money as having a lot of power, we should use our wealth thoughtfully and carefully.

2. RESPONSIBLE SERVICE. Don't forget to spend some time considering Jesus' statements in Luke 16:10-13. Stress that faithful use of our possessions is expected of us as Jesus' followers. Someone once said, "It's not what you'd do if a million were your lot. Rather, it's what you do with the nickel that you've got!" God will not entrust us with heavenly responsibilities if we are irresponsible in using the material resources He has given us in this world.

3. REVEALING STORY. When Jesus said no one can serve two masters— God and money—the Pharisees sneered. Jesus pointed out that though the religious leaders may have hidden their hypocrisy from others, they had not hidden it from God. Christ noted that many of the things they highly valued were detested by the Lord (Luke 16:13-15).

Encourage your students to mention some things people value that God detests. As the class responds, have one of the students create a list on a chalkboard or a sheet of newsprint. Then ask them why they think the items listed are detestable to the Lord.

FOR ADULTS

■ TOPIC: Preparing for the Future

■ QUESTIONS: 1. Why did the owner plan to dismiss the manager of his estate? 2. What points of application are evident from the parable Jesus told? 3. Which is more challenging for you, how you earn money or spend it? Why? 4. What are some of the things you are doing to prepare financially for the future? 5. What are some of the things you are doing to prepare spiritually for the future?

■ ILLUSTRATIONS:

Money Neuroses. For some people, the booming economy in the United States has been a real bust. In fact, one mental health therapist practicing on the east coast has discovered that many of his patients can't tell the difference between pathological greed and smart financial thinking.

Some of these patients are among the most successful people in the country— Wall Street traders and bankers, independently wealthy market daredevils, and many self-made men and women. But their risk-taking has become destructive. Many of them, while rich and successful, are self-centered, insecure, unsatisfied, and unhappy. These people have what the therapist calls "a market value" of themselves; in other words, "What I possess determines my value."

The neuroses of these patients often create within them an inability to sleep at night, fears that their wealth will suddenly disappear, excessive concerns about financial mistakes, crippling self-doubt, and illusions of infallibility. Despite long and expensive periods of treatment, these people remain preoccupied with money. Clearly, Jesus' teachings on wealth and its wise use could prove relevant to them.

Worthless Digging. In the spring of 1608, the settlers at Jamestown, Virginia, did nothing but dig for gold. They neglected to plant crops, erect buildings, and prepare for the cold of winter. Instead, they were more concerned about washing the precious metal they had found. If it had not been for the native Americans who fed them, these greedy colonists would have died from starvation.

After working all spring, the colonists loaded their cargo onto a ship heading for England. They smugly told themselves they were rich. To their chagrin, however, their "gold" turned out to be worthless iron pyrite, sometimes known as "fool's gold." Sadly, the Jamestown settlers wasted all their time and energy on that which had neither temporal nor eternal value.

Life's Goals. Legend has it that Henry Ford once met with a young engineer he was considering hiring. The automobile genius asked the man what his goals in life were. "To make a million dollars!" the young man declared. Ford told the man to come back in a couple of days. When he interviewed the engineer that time, Ford handed the man a pair of glasses in which silver dollars had been fitted into the lens frame. Insisting the man put them on, Ford asked, "Now, what do you see?" The man scowled and squinted, and finally replied that he couldn't see anything because the dollars were in the way. "Exactly!" said Henry Ford. "I want you to learn the lesson that if your goal is only to get money, you'll miss out on life. You must invest yourself and think about serving others."

 FOR YOUTH ■ TOPIC: Money Madness
■ QUESTIONS: 1. How do you think the manager handled his dire situation? 2. Why is it important for us to use our material resources wisely? 3. What are some ways that we, as Christians, can use our money to help those in need? 4. How can we use the things God has given us to foster faith and obedience in others? 5. Which principle from Jesus' parable would most likely prompt you to make changes in your lifestyle? Why?

■ ILLUSTRATIONS:
Priorities. Eddie sat in a chair and refused to get dressed before the bus arrived to take him to school. The 12 year old didn't want to go. When his mother asked

him why, Eddie explained that the yellow shirt she had laid out for him to wear would draw taunts from his classmates. He also told his mother, "They'll throw stones at me again." Finally, after much coaxing from his mother, Eddie put on the yellow shirt and went to school.

Eddie lived in rural part of the eastern United States. Enormous poverty existed because many coal and manufacturing companies had left the region years earlier. Tragically, Eddie's family couldn't escape the destitution. Even more tragic was the fact that his classmates who were better off financially teased him because he wore the same clothes every week. He supposedly was "odd" because he didn't have designer shirts, pants, and shoes.

Eddie's classmates placed more value on having lots of money and possessions than on forming personal relationships. Jesus, however, saw things differently. He taught that serving God and others is more important than being rich.

Values. The United Nations reported that in 1998, 1.5 billion people got by on less than one dollar day. Also, half the world's children under the age of five were malnourished. Moreover, only one-third of the world's children would live past the age of 40.

In contrast, the average American nine year old has more than four compact discs, which he or she purchased at a cost of more than 10 dollars apiece. Perhaps young people in the United States should spend less money on themselves and use their wealth to help ease the poverty of children in other parts of the world.

Wall Street to Holy Land. The 1998 stock market frenzy reached epic heights in December of that year when Christianity became part of a website's sales strategy. The Internet company was launched earlier that year by a foreign developer. The website bills itself as a virtual pilgrimage to the holy land. While it receives over a million hits per day, the owner says the real money is made in the on-line "Shopping Mall." Here one will find religious mementos for sale. These include olive wood crosses, beads, water from the Jordan River and the Sea of Galilee, jewelry, and videos.

This is an example of someone who wants to exploit religion for his own financial gain. But according to Luke 16:13, this way of thinking is warped. No matter how hard someone may try, *"You cannot serve God and wealth."*

GOING TO JERUSALEM

BACKGROUND SCRIPTURE: Luke 18:15—19:10
DEVOTIONAL READING: Matthew 10:34-39

KEY VERSE: "The Son of Man came to seek out and to save the lost." Luke 19:10.

KING JAMES VERSION

LUKE 18:31 Then he took unto him the twelve, and said unto them, Behold, we go up to Jerusalem, and all things that are written by the prophets concerning the Son of man shall be accomplished.

32 For he shall be delivered unto the Gentiles, and shall be mocked, and spitefully entreated, and spitted on:

33 And they shall scourge him, and put him to death: and the third day he shall rise again.

34 And they understood none of these things: and this saying was hid from them, neither knew they the things which were spoken. . . .

19:1 And Jesus entered and passed through Jericho.

2 And, behold, there was a man named Zacchæus, which was the chief among the publicans, and he was rich.

3 And he sought to see Jesus who he was; and could not for the press, because he was little of stature.

4 And he ran before, and climbed up into a sycomore tree to see him: for he was to pass that way.

5 And when Jesus came to the place, he looked up, and saw him, and said unto him, Zacchaeus, make haste, and come down; for to day I must abide at thy house.

6 And he made haste, and came down, and received him joyfully.

7 And when they saw it, they all murmured, saying, That he was gone to be guest with a man that is a sinner.

8 And Zacchæus stood, and said unto the Lord; Behold, Lord, the half of my goods I give to the poor; and if I have taken any thing from any man by false accusation, I restore him fourfold.

9 And Jesus said unto him, This day is salvation come to this house, forsomuch as he also is a son of Abraham.

10 For the Son of man is come to seek and to save that which was lost.

NEW REVISED STANDARD VERSION

LUKE 18:31 Then he took the twelve aside and said to them, "See, we are going up to Jerusalem, and everything that is written about the Son of Man by the prophets will be accomplished. 32 For he will be handed over to the Gentiles; and he will be mocked and insulted and spat upon. 33 After they have flogged him, they will kill him, and on the third day he will rise again." 34 But they understood nothing about all these things; in fact, what he said was hidden from them, and they did not grasp what was said. . . .

19:1 He entered Jericho and was passing through it. 2 A man was there named Zacchaeus; he was a chief tax collector and was rich. 3 He was trying to see who Jesus was, but on account of the crowd he could not, because he was short in stature. 4 So he ran ahead and climbed a sycamore tree to see him, because he was going to pass that way. 5 When Jesus came to the place, he looked up and said to him, "Zacchaeus, hurry and come down; for I must stay at your house today." 6 So he hurried down and was happy to welcome him. 7 All who saw it began to grumble and said, "He has gone to be the guest of one who is a sinner." 8 Zacchaeus stood there and said to the Lord, "Look, half of my possessions, Lord, I will give to the poor; and if I have defrauded anyone of anything, I will pay back four times as much." 9 Then Jesus said to him, "Today salvation has come to this house, because he too is a son of Abraham. 10 For the Son of Man came to seek out and to save the lost."

10

HOME BIBLE READINGS

BACKGROUND

Many people in Palestine assumed that the long-awaited Messiah would be a conquering military hero. The popular scenario for the messianic age was a great victory over the Roman occupation army. This would be followed by the establishment of an independent Jewish state presided over by the great Deliverer. This would usher in a perpetual era of peace and prosperity for God's chosen people (John 6:15; Acts 1:6).

Jesus, however, had other ideas about what He would do as the Messiah. He didn't come to earth to be the chieftain of an army or political statesman, for He was no earthly ruler but rather the King of heaven (John 18:36). The Savior knew that it was God's will for Him to die on the cross in self-giving love to atone for the sins of humanity (12:27-33).

Luke wrote his Gospel to demonstrate that Jesus not only was executed at Calvary but also rose from the dead. Luke also stressed that these events were the greatest news of all time and thus to be proclaimed to everyone. Luke devoted considerable space to show the way Jesus accepted the burden of being a suffering Messiah and why He deliberately traveled to Jerusalem to fulfill His mission.

Beginning with the material in this week's lesson, our studies for the remainder of the quarter will center on Jesus' decision to *set his face to go to Jerusalem* (Luke 9:51). God would vindicate Jesus' crucifixion by raising Him from the dead. The encounters of Jesus with a despised tax collector named Zacchaeus (the topic of this week's lesson) serve to underscore that the Messiah's salvation is to be offered to all people, not just the religious elite.

NOTES ON THE PRINTED TEXT

Jesus' ministry was entering its last and most crucial phase—the events leading up to the cross. That's why, while on the way to Jerusalem, He spoke privately with His disciples. He knew that His words were filled with eternal importance. *"We are going up to Jerusalem, and everything that is written about the Son of Man by the prophets will be accomplished"* (Luke 18:31).

Jesus' true identity is evident from the names He used to describe Himself. The title *"Son of man"* (Matt. 16:13) underscored Jesus' deity (Daniel 7:13-14; Mark 2:10), messiahship, and humanity (Mark 8:31; 10:45). The titles *"Son of the liv-*

ing God" (Matthew 16:16) and *"only Son"* (John 3:16) indicate that a unique and intimate relationship exists between Jesus and the Father (Luke 1:35). As the great *"I am"* (John 8:58), Jesus was claiming eternal existence (Exod. 3:14). Not only was He sent by the Father, but also He was to be considered fully equal with Him (John 5:18; 10:30, 36).

Jesus explained that the gruesome events awaiting Him in Jerusalem would fulfill Old Testament messianic prophecies. *"For he will be handed over to the Gentiles; and he will be mocked and insulted and spat upon. After they have flogged him, they will kill him, and on the third day he will rise again"* (Luke 18:32-33). Though wicked people would succeed in executing Jesus, He would conquer death through His resurrection (Acts 2:24).

Despite two previous predictions, Jesus' disciples still did not understand the significance of His words concerning His suffering, death, and resurrection. *But they understood nothing about all these things; in fact, what he said was hidden from them, and they did not grasp what was said* (Luke 18:34).

As Jesus continued His journey to Jerusalem, He came near to the town of Jericho. There He met and healed a blind beggar (18:35-43). Jesus then *entered Jericho and was passing through it* (19:1).

Jericho is one of the oldest inhabited cities in the world and the first city the Israelites conquered under Joshua's command. The climate of Jericho was conducive to the groves of date palms and balsam trees growing there. The city was also famous for its olive oil, which people dubbed the "balm of Gilead." Being situated on the main north-south trade route between Egypt and Judea, Jericho was a key customs post for taxes. It was there that Jesus found *a man . . . named Zacchaeus; he was chief tax collector and was rich* (19:2).

In Jesus' day, the Romans often employed residents from the local population as tax collectors. Those who wanted the job had to bid for it. The person with the highest offer was allowed to collect tariffs and tolls in a designated area. In order to make a profit, tax collectors would charge several times more than what the Roman government required. The desire for personal gain would invariably lead to the inflation of tolls and customs.

A tax collector such as Zacchaeus would have been held in disdain by the Jews because he served as an agent of the despised Roman government. The people would also resent the fact that Zacchaeus had gotten rich at their expense. No doubt the religious elite would have regarded Zacchaeus as being ceremonially unclean because of his frequent contact with Gentiles.

When Zacchaeus heard that Jesus was passing through Jericho, he wanted to see the Savior, whose name undoubtedly was on everyone's lips. *He was trying to see who Jesus was, but on account of the crowd he could not, because he was short in stature* (19:3).

Zacchaeus decided to run ahead and climb a sycamore tree (19:4). Jesus saw him and stopped. Jesus wanted the tax collector to get down and take Him to his home. *When Jesus came to the place, he looked up and said to him, "Zacchaeus, hurry and come down; for I must stay at your house today." So he hurried down and was happy to welcome him* (19:5-6).

The crowd grumbled in disbelief. How could Jesus make a personal visit to the home of a despised sinner? The people complained that Jesus was breaking the laws of cleanliness and purity by associating with one who was so impure. *All who saw it began to grumble and said, "He has gone to be the guest of one who is a sinner."* (19:7).

Zacchaeus both acknowledged his sin and repented of it. The genuineness of his conversion is seen by his announcement that he would sell half his possessions and donate the proceeds to the poor. He would also make generous restitution to those whom he had cheated. *"Look, half my possessions, Lord, I will give to the poor; and if I have defrauded anyone of anything, I will pay it back four times as much"* (19:8).

Unlike the religious elite, whom Jesus knew were hypocrites (Matt. 23:13), Jesus knew that Zacchaeus was sincere. Jesus announced that the tax collector had been saved. *"Today salvation has come to this house, because he too is a son of Abraham"* (Luke 19:9).

The people of Jericho had criticized Jesus for associating with Zacchaeus. However, in 19:10, the Savior declared that He had come to earth *"to seek out and to save the lost."* In other words, His mission wasn't to please Himself but rather to redeem sinners from divine judgment (Mark 10:45).

SUGGESTIONS TO TEACHERS

The overarching theme of this week's lesson is that Jesus was going to Jerusalem to lay down His life for humanity. This is also a central truth emphasized in Luke's Gospel. In fact, the accounts of the blind beggar and Zacchaeus were recorded to portray Jesus as the Messiah. He didn't fit the conventional idea of the Messiah because He came to bring light and life even to the outcasts of society.

1. **UNCOMPROMISING MESSIAH.** Let your students know that Jesus deliberately chose to go to Jerusalem. He knew that it would eventually lead to His death, but He did not falter. He could have dodged the cross, but then He would not have accomplished His redemptive work. Also note that Jesus was not a helpless victim of tragic events. Rather, He fearlessly traveled to Jerusalem and openly declared to His followers that He would suffer and die.

2. **UNCOMPREHENDING FOLLOWERS.** Though Jesus informed His disciples of what awaited Him, they failed to grasp the significance of His words. Perhaps they were distracted by the incorrect assumption that Jesus would liberate their nation from Rome. If so, they had a distorted view of why Jesus had come to earth. Discuss how believers today sometimes tune out Jesus and also try to fit Him into skewed ways of thinking.

3. UNCONSCIONABLE SHYSTER. Though we may chuckle at parts of the narrative of Zacchaeus, his townsfolk in Jericho saw nothing amusing about him. Most loathed this rich, selfish man who had sold out to the Romans and unscrupulously gouged his fellow Jews as a tax collector in Jericho. But Jesus deliberately stopped to reach out to this despicable character! Have your students consider why Jesus singled out this person from the crowd.

4. UNCONGENIAL AUDIENCE. The bystanders were shocked and offended that Jesus chose to associate with Zacchaeus. The religious elite were especially upset and questioned whether Jesus was a true observer of the Old Testament customs and rites. Despite their objections, Jesus knew that traditionalism and legalism were not substitutes for serving God.

5. UNCOMPLAINING SAVIOR. Jesus extended God's undeserved mercy to a greedy social outcast named Zacchaeus. Again, Jesus showed that He came to seek and save the lost. Here was love in action, and here was grace enacted!

FOR ADULTS

■ TOPIC: Reclaiming the Lost

■ QUESTIONS: 1. Why do you think it was hard for the Twelve to accept Jesus' teaching about His death and resurrection? 2. Why was Zacchaeus so despised by others, and why did Jesus choose to associate with him? 3. Why is it important to live by the same standards that we expect others to maintain? 4. Why was Zacchaeus so happy to entertain Jesus in his home (Luke 19:9)? 5. Have you ever been surprised by God's grace for you? 6. Why is a person's changed behavior a good indicator that he or she has made a genuine profession of faith?

■ ILLUSTRATIONS:

The Need for Love. In the prologue to *Leadership Jazz*, Max DePree writes:

> Esther, my wife, and I have a granddaughter named Zoe, the Greek word for life. She was born prematurely and weighed one pound, seven ounces, so small that my wedding ring could slide up her arm to her shoulder. . . . When Esther and I scrubbed up for our first visit and saw Zoe in her isolette in the neonatal intensive care unit, she had two IV's in her navel, one in her foot, a monitor on each side of her chest, and a respirator tube and a feeding tube in her mouth.
>
> To complicate matters, Zoe's biological father had jumped ship the month before Zoe was born. Realizing this, a wise and caring nurse named Ruth gave me my instructions. "For the next several months, at least, you're the surrogate father. I want you to come to the hospital every day to visit Zoe, and when you come, I want you to rub her body and her legs and arms with the tip of your finger. While you're caressing her, you should tell her over and over how much you love her, because she has to

be able to connect your voice to your touch."

God knew that we also needed His voice and His touch. God has spoken to us through His Word and He has touched us through His Son and His body, the church. . . . God has called us not only to proclaim His love but also to touch people with it. May we always be available to do both.

Afraid of God. The picture some people have of God is similar to the view that the German subjects had of their emperor, Frederick William. Legend has it that he was once out walking in a town when he was seen by one of the residents. To his surprise, the man tried to slip quickly inside a doorway in order not to be seen. The emperor roared, "Where are you going?" The man, realizing that he had been spotted, timidly said that he was going into the house. "Your house?" demanded the ruler. Quaking, the man said it wasn't. "Then why are you trying to enter it? You're a burglar, aren't you?"

The man feared that he would be seized and jailed. Deciding that his only hope was to tell the truth, he stammered, "I was trying to avoid you, your majesty." The emperor bristled. "Avoid me. Why?" "Because I fear you, your majesty," replied the now-shaken man. Frederick then grabbed his heavy stick and struck the citizen on the chest, shouting, "You are not supposed to fear me. You are supposed to love me! Now love me, you swine. Love me!"

Thankfully, this isn't God's way. Jesus came to earth to provide salvation for those who are alienated and separated from Him because of sin.

FOR YOUTH ■ **TOPIC:** Plucked Out of the Crowd
■ **QUESTIONS:** 1. How can we keep the cross and resurrection at the heart of what we teach about Jesus? 2. In what sense had salvation come to the home of Zacchaeus (Luke 19:9)? 3. Have you ever been surprised by God's grace for you? 4. How do you respond when people who are different from you visit your church? 5. Why is it important to share the good news of God's love with all people, regardless of their status in society?

■ **ILLUSTRATIONS:**

Changed Person. His nickname, the "plucky little ruler," did not do justice to Jordan's King Hussein. When he died on February 7, 1999, the world, and especially the Middle East, lost a giant of a leader.

Hussein became king as a teenager, having stood beside his grandfather (the monarch at the time) when he was shot to death in Jerusalem in 1952. Like many Arabs, Hussein was initially opposed to Israel and participated in several wars against the Jewish state. Hussein also survived a civil war with the Palestine Liberation Army.

The king, however, realized that if there was to be a lasting peace in the region, he and his nation had to change. Despite widespread disappointment within Jordan, Hussein participated in the 1994 peace treaty with Israel. He then shocked the world by traveling to Jerusalem and weeping at the funeral of Israel's Prime Minister Yitzhak Rabin, who had been assassinated. A year later, after a deranged Jordanian soldier gunned down Israeli school children on a field trip to Jordan, Hussein traveled to Israel to each of the victims' homes to apologize and console the parents.

The account of Hussein, like that of Zacchaeus, shows how much people can change. In the case of the tax collector, the dramatic turnaround of his life was due to the grace God offered him through faith in Christ.

Following the Footsteps. Thirty-seven seventh and eighth graders from a middle school in eastern Pennsylvania struggled up the steep slope of the towering bluff called Mount Washington. Each one was trying to reach the faint light of a flickering lantern on the back door of the Bigham House. They were helped through the mud and slippery leaves by a rope. They were retracing the steps of runaway slaves from the mid-nineteenth century. But unlike the middle school children, the fugitives didn't have the luxury of a rope. If someone slipped, he or she would have fallen down the near-vertical slope.

The students were following part of the route of the Underground Railroad. Slaves moving northward made their way to the house of Thomas Bigham, a journalist, lawyer, and abolitionist. Along with members of *Generations Together* (a cross-generational program that pairs senior citizens and students), the children were discovering what runaway slaves experienced. The visitors found themselves shivering in the cold damp December air while standing on the back porch of the house. They were shocked to learn that many fugitives arrived barefoot. Several of the students felt proud of the slaves and themselves for making the trip.

The path to spiritual freedom is even more important. Like Zacchaeus, we must leave the darkness of slavery to sin and turn our hearts in faith to Christ.

Small Stature but Big Person. Tyrone "Mugsy" Bogues plays in the National Basketball Association (NBA). In contrast to his other teammates, the Wake Forest alumnus is only 5' 3" tall and weighs 140 pounds. In 1987, Bogues was drafted twelfth in the first round by the Charlotte Hornets. Though a person of small stature, he has become a powerhouse player in the field of towering giants. His height has not held him back whatsoever.

Zacchaeus was a short person too. But despite his small stature, he didn't let it keep him from seeing Jesus. The actions of Zacchaeus showed he was a big person with an equally large heart!

ONE WHO SERVES

BACKGROUND SCRIPTURE: Luke 22:1-30
DEVOTIONAL READING: Mark 10:35-45

KEY VERSE: "The greatest among you must become like
the youngest, and the leader like one who serves." Luke 22:26.

KING JAMES VERSION	*NEW REVISED STANDARD VERSION*

KING JAMES VERSION

LUKE 22:14 And when the hour was come, he sat down, and the twelve apostles with him.

15 And he said unto them, With desire I have desired to eat this passover with you before I suffer:

16 For I say unto you, I will not any more eat thereof, until it be fulfilled in the kingdom of God.

17 And he took the cup, and gave thanks, and said, Take this, and divide it among yourselves:

18 For I say unto you, I will not drink of the fruit of the vine, until the kingdom of God shall come.

19 And he took bread, and gave thanks, and brake it, and gave unto them, saying, This is my body which is given for you: this do in remembrance of me.

20 Likewise also the cup after supper, saying, This cup is the new testament in my blood, which is shed for you.

21 But, behold, the hand of him that betrayeth me is with me on the table.

22 And truly the Son of man goeth, as it was determined: but woe unto that man by whom he is betrayed!

23 And they began to enquire among themselves, which of them it was that should do this thing.

24 And there was also a strife among them, which of them should be accounted the greatest.

25 And he said unto them, The kings of the Gentiles exercise lordship over them; and they that exercise authority upon them are called benefactors.

26 But ye shall not be so: but he that is greatest among you, let him be as the younger; and he that is chief, as he that doth serve.

27 For whether is greater, he that sitteth at meat, or he that serveth? is not he that sitteth at meat? but I am among you as he that serveth.

28 Ye are they which have continued with me in my temptations.

29 And I appoint unto you a kingdom, as my Father hath appointed unto me;

30 That ye may eat and drink at my table in my kingdom, and sit on thrones judging the twelve tribes of Israel.

NEW REVISED STANDARD VERSION

LUKE 22:14 When the hour came, he took his place at the table, and the apostles with him. 15 He said to them, "I have eagerly desired to eat this Passover with you before I suffer; 16 for I tell you, I will not eat it until it is fulfilled in the kingdom of God." 17 Then he took a cup, and after giving thanks he said, "Take this and divide it among yourselves; 18 for I tell you that from now on I will not drink of the fruit of the vine until the kingdom of God comes." 19 Then he took a loaf of bread, and when he had given thanks, he broke it and gave it to them, saying, "This is my body, which is given for you. Do this in remembrance of me."
20 And he did the same with the cup after supper, saying, "This cup that is poured out for you is the new covenant in my blood. 21 But see, the one who betrays me is with me, and his hand is on the table. 22 For the Son of Man is going as it has been determined, but woe to that one by whom he is betrayed!" 23 Then they began to ask one another which one of them it could be who would do this.

24 A dispute also arose among them as to which one of them was to be regarded as the greatest. 25 But he said to them, "The kings of the Gentiles lord it over them; and those in authority over them are called benefactors. 26 But not so with you; rather the greatest among you must become like the youngest, and the leader like one who serves. 27 For who is greater, the one who is at the table or the one who serves? Is it not the one at the table? But I am among you as one who serves.

28 "You are those who have stood by me in my trials; 29 and I confer on you, just as my Father has conferred on me, a kingdom, 30 so that you may eat and drink at my table in my kingdom, and you will sit on thrones judging the twelve tribes of Israel.

Monday, February 5	Luke 22:1-6	*The Plot to Kill Jesus*
Tuesday, February 6	Luke 22:7-13	*The Preparation of the Passover*
Wednesday, February 7	Exodus 12:14-20	*The Feast of Unleavened Bread*
Thursday, February 8	Luke 22:14-23	*The Institution of the Lord's Supper*
Friday, February 9	John 13:18-30	*Jesus Foretells His Betrayer*
Saturday, February 10	Luke 22:24-30	*The Dispute about Greatness*
Sunday, February 11	Mark 10:35-45	*The Request of James and John*

BACKGROUND

The Passover (along with the Feast of Unleavened Bread) was the first of three great festivals of the Hebrews (Luke 22:7). The name "Passover" recalls the deliverance of Israel from slavery in Egypt (Exod. 12:1—13:16). God sent His angel to kill all the firstborn sons of the Egyptians in order to persuade Pharaoh to let His people go. Hebrew families were instructed to sacrifice a lamb and smear its blood on the doorpost of their house as a signal to God that His angel should "pass over" them during the judgment.

Passover was observed on the fourteenth day of the first month, Abib (March-April), with the service beginning in the evening (Lev. 23:5). It was on the evening of this first day that Israel left Egypt in a hurry. Unleavened bread was used in the celebration as a remainder that the people had no time to leaven their bread before they ate their final meal as slaves in Egypt.

In New Testament times, Passover became a pilgrim festival. Large numbers gathered in Jerusalem to observe the annual celebration. Thus an usually large crowd was on hand to take part in the events surrounding Jesus' entry into the city (Luke 19:37-39), and His arrest, trial, and crucifixion (23:18, 27, 35, 48). Apparently many stayed on until the Feast of Pentecost, when they heard Peter's persuasive sermon (Acts 2:1-41).

The Passover meal was usually eaten with family members and close friends. Jesus wanted His closest associates, the 12 disciples, to share the meal with Him. He knew, of course, that the authorities would soon arrest, try, and execute Him. The meal we know as the Last Supper was the setting for the heartbreaking episode of Judas's betrayal and the dismaying scene of the disciples squabbling over who was the greatest among them.

NOTES ON THE PRINTED TEXT

The Synoptic Gospels present Jesus sharing the Passover meal as His last supper with the disciples. He reinterpreted the common elements of the celebration in the light of a new covenant. The unleavened bread symbolized His body and the wine represented His blood (Luke 22:19-20).

In New Testament times, Jews normally sat in chairs for meals, but they reclined on cushions in typical Greek fashion when eating at banquets like the

Passover. With their feet pointed away from the center of the room and their heads more toward the center, they generally reclined on one elbow, using the other arm to reach the food on the table beside them (Luke 7:38; John 13:23).

Jesus noted that He had looked forward to this time of fellowship and eating with His disciples prior to His suffering and death. He vowed that He would not eat the Passover meal again until it came to fulfillment in the kingdom of God (Luke 22:14-16). The Savior's words remind us that this event foreshadowed His work on the cross. As the spotless Lamb of God, His blood was spilled in order to save the lost from the penalty of death brought by sin (John 1:29; Rev. 5:6).

Luke 22:17 says that Jesus took a cup of wine (which was known as the "cup of blessing") and uttered a prayer of thanks to God. The Savior then invited His disciples to *"Take this and divide it among yourselves."* Uppermost in Jesus' thoughts was the cross. He noted that He would not *"drink of the fruit of the vine until the kingdom of God comes"* (22:18).

Customarily, the head of a Jewish household would explain each of the elements of the Passover meal. For instance, when explaining the bread, he would announce, "This is the bread of affliction that our ancestors ate when they came from the land of Egypt." Similarly Jesus, after taking some bread and giving thanks to God, broke the bread in pieces, gave it to His disciples, and said, *"This is my body, which is given for you. Do this in remembrance of me"* (22:19).

Luke mentions two cups of wine, while Matthew and Mark mention only one. In the traditional Passover meal, the wine is served four times. Jesus spoke the words, *"This cup that is poured out for you is the new covenant in my blood"* (Luke 22:20), when He offered the fourth and last cup. His remark about the *"blood of the covenant"* (Mark 14:24) looked back to when God redeemed Israel from Egypt (Exod. 24:8). By His shed blood, Jesus undoubtedly alluded to the suffering Servant pouring out His life (Isa. 53:12). Jesus saw Himself as making redemption possible for the lost by His own death.

During this solemn occasion, Jesus declared that one of the Twelve would betray Him. In fact the traitor was in their midst. *"But see, the one who betrays me is with me, and his hand is on the table"* (Luke 22:21). John 13:26 clearly identifies the turncoat as *"Judas son of Simon Iscariot."*

Neither Jesus nor His heavenly Father were caught off guard by the treachery of Judas. It was part of God's overall plan to bring about the Crucifixion. Nevertheless, Jesus still underscored the atrocity of the crime. *"For the Son of Man is going as it has been determined, but woe to that one by whom he is betrayed!"* (Luke 22:22).

Jesus' words upset His followers. Perhaps suspicious and accusing glances were exchanged. *Then they began to ask one another, which one of them it could be who would do this* (22:23). We can imagine the disciples drifting from the topic of betrayal to a debate about loyalty. If so, this soon degenerated into an argument about who was the best, or greatest, disciple (22:24).

Jesus, though undoubtedly disappointed with His bickering disciples, remained calm. He noted that the great and powerful kings of the world ordered their subjects around. Ironically, these rulers still wanted to be known as friends of the people. *"The kings of the Gentiles lord it over them; and those in authority over them are called benefactors"* (22:25).

Jesus declared that this hypocritical and self-centered way of leading was not to exist among His followers. Greatness was not defined in terms of how many people one ordered around but by how many people one humbly served. *"But not so with you; rather the greatest among you must become like the youngest, and the leader like one who serves"* (22:26).

Jesus used Himself an example. He had humbly served His followers. This was to remind them that their greatness would be equal to the services they rendered to others. *"For who is greater, the one who is at the table or the one who serves? Is it not the one at the table? But I am among you as one who serves"* (22:27).

Having gently rebuked His disciples, Jesus then praised them. God would eternally reward their faithfulness and commitment. In fact, their reward would be greater than they could ever imagine. *"You are those who have stood by me in my trials; and I confer on you, just as my Father has conferred on me, a kingdom, so that you may eat and drink at my table in my kingdom, and you will sit on thrones judging the twelve tribes of Israel"* (22:28-30).

SUGGESTIONS TO TEACHERS

So much material is packed into this week's lesson that you may find it difficult to cover all of it, especially if your students get sidetracked in discussing relatively insignificant matters. Be sure to keep the main goal of the lesson in focus, namely, that there is eternal joy in serving others unconditionally and unselfishly.

1. AUTHORITIES' SCHEMING. It's ironic that the chief priests and scribes conspired to silence Jesus (Luke 22:2). From this we see that even religious people sometimes stoop to do ungodly things. We must guard ourselves against the proud attitude that leads us to think we can impose our will on others in the church and claim that it is God's will.

2. JUDAS'S SELLOUT. Stick to the facts presented here, and don't let the class members drift into unproductive psychologizing and theorizing about Judas. Be sure to point out that the sinful motives and acts of Judas can be found in all of us. For instance, have not all of us betrayed our Lord at various times?

3. JESUS' SUPPER. This portion of the lesson is an opportunity for your students to think about the meaning of the Lord's Supper. Let them know that it enables believers to bring to remembrance—in a visibly dynamic and dramatic way—the Messiah's past sacrifice for our sins, His present sustaining of our life, and His future return. The Lord's Supper serves as a message to both the saved and the unsaved that Christ's atoning sacrifice is for all who are lost.

4. DISCIPLES' SERVANTHOOD. People are often confused about the way to achieve true greatness. Ask your students, "What does popular culture tell us about who is great?" Then note that Jesus' teaching runs counter to society's notions by stressing that true greatness is found in humbly serving others. End the teaching time by talking about the joy of serving others unconditionally and unselfishly.

FOR ADULTS	■ TOPIC: Service—The Way to Greatness ■ QUESTIONS: 1. Why was Jesus so eager to eat the Passover meal with the Twelve? 2. How did Jesus respond when the disciples

argued about who was the greatest among them? 3. Using Jesus' definition of greatness, who are some of the greatest people in your life? 4. Why is it important for us to serve others unconditionally and unselfishly? 5. Why do we sometimes struggle to serve in this way?

■ **ILLUSTRATIONS:**

Humility. John Hunt led the expedition that enabled Sir Edmund Hillary of New Zealand and Tenzing Norgay of Nepal to conquer Mount Everest on May 29, 1953. Other expedition members later noted how Hunt had to work with a group of egotistical expert climbers, each wanting to be the first to climb to the top of the world's highest mountain.

Hunt set the example of humbly setting pride aside and putting the team first. In fact, he and two other team members made the first attempt for the summit but stopped 400 feet short to leave their equipment and supplies for Hilary and Tenzing to make the second attempt.

"It was my ambition just as much as everybody else's in the party to be first at the top," Hunt later reported in an interview. "I thought about it a lot and concluded that it was important for the leader to be in a position where he could exercise some control if necessary. It did not seem that I could do both."

Hunt sacrificed the glory of being the first to the top of the mighty peak for the sake of others on the team. "What he achieved with us on Everest," said expedition member George Lowe, "was that he had a group of prima donnas who all wanted to be first to the top and he made us a team." Hunt's humility was summed up when he told a reporter for *The Guardian* newspaper, "The relationship between a person and what he or she does on a mountain is one of humility."

Paragliding Evangelizing. A preacher thought he could serve the Lord by trying a dramatic stunt. One day in December 1998, he went up in a motored paraglider over a town in southern England, and soared over a crowd of spectators. Bellowing through a bullhorn, he preached a hellfire sermon. Police arrested the man, and the court fined him about $1700. The preacher defended his sensationalism by saying, "I thought that maybe if they heard this voice booming out from the sky, they would think it was God!"

The preacher failed to understand that God doesn't work that way. Rather than shout at us from the sky, the Lord came among us as one who serves. And He calls us to serve one another humbly. Thus service, not shouting, is the way to greatness in the divine kingdom.

True Greatness? Ty Cobb was undoubtedly one of the great players of baseball. During his 24 seasons, 22 with the Detroit Tigers (1905–26) and 2 with the Philadelphia Athletics (1927–1928), he all but wrote baseball's record books. He finished his career with a lifetime batting average of .367, still highest in the history of the game. In 1936, he was the first man to be elected to the Baseball Hall of Fame.

Cobb was also noted for his fierce competitive spirit. He reportedly had a violent temper and an abusive personality that endeared him to almost no one. He was described as "ruthless and mean-spirited" and had a "no holds barred" style of play.

Cobb and his wife, Charlie, had five children. But his focus on baseball took its toll on the family. Off the field, Cobb's family had to deal with his turbulent disposition and sarcastic manner. Charlie finally divorced Ty in 1947, charging extreme cruelty throughout their marriage. Cobb remarried again in 1949, but it also failed, ending in divorce seven years later.

On the field, Casey Stengel said in 1975, "No one even came close to Ty as the greatest all-time ball player. That guy was superhuman, amazing." But off the field, Cobb was pathetic. While obviously a remarkably talented ballplayer, he wrestled with an extremely combative nature. And though he was a success in baseball, Cobb failed in other more important areas of life, perhaps because he didn't understand the meaning of true greatness.

FOR YOUTH

■ **TOPIC:** Who Is the Greatest?
■ **QUESTIONS:** 1. What did Jesus say was the significance of the bread and cup? 2 What promise to the disciples did Jesus make about the future kingdom? 3. How does understanding the Passover meal help you more fully appreciate the significance of Communion? 4. What criteria do you use to determine greatness? 5. What forms of serving others bring you the greatest satisfaction? Why?

■ **ILLUSTRATIONS:**

Understanding Artist. Flemish artist Dieric Bouts (1415–1475) was contracted by a church in Belgium to paint a large mural measuring 6 feet by 5 feet. Aided by consultants, Bouts painted in the traditional Northern Renaissance style. Jesus sits at the center of a rectangular table covered by a white tablecloth. His disciples sit upright, eyes riveted on the Savior, with their hands folded in reverential prayer. Pewter plates, a pewter chalice, and glasses sit prominently on the table. A candelabra hangs above Jesus, whose right hand points upward as He instructs His disciples. Meanwhile, His left hand holds a thin wafer.

What is interesting is that behind Jesus, Bouts has added members of the church to the interior of the Flemish room. They peer at Jesus through a kitchen window and stand behind the table's seated participants, acting as servants.

Bouts understood that God has called us to be His servants. He also wants us to serve one another. According to Jesus, this is the path to true greatness.

Importance of a Meal. Thanksgiving weekend is the heaviest travel period in the United States. In fact, the day before and the Friday after rank as the peak times of travel. Families, college students, and grandparents crowd the nation's airport terminals, bus stations, train depots, and highways in an effort to be with their loved ones for the holiday. Is the traffic due to a desire to eat stuffed turkey and mashed potatoes? Most likely the answer is *no*. People are expending all that energy and effort because they want to see their family and friends.

For many of us, sharing a meal with our loved ones is a joyous occasion. This was also true for Jesus and His disciples. They planned to eat the Passover meal together because they cared for each other.

Ultimate Mark of Greatness. By now the newest class to the Pro Football Hall of Fame will have been announced. Each of those elected in this group will be enshrined, along with the other greats of the game, at Canton, Ohio's Pro Football Hall of Fame. Perhaps you have read about their achievements on the field— games played, touchdowns achieved, yardage run, passes caught or completed, and so on.

It's a great honor to be considered one of football's greatest players. But Jesus said that an even higher level of greatness existed among those who humbly serve others. To be a servant of the King is the ultimate mark of greatness.

DYING ON A CROSS

BACKGROUND SCRIPTURE: Luke 23:13-49
DEVOTIONAL READING: Luke 23:50-56

KEY VERSE: Jesus, crying with a loud voice, said, "Father, into your hands
I commend my spirit." Having said this, he breathed his last. Luke 23:46.

KING JAMES VERSION

LUKE 23:33 And when they were come to the place, which is called Calvary, there they crucified him, and the malefactors, one on the right hand, and the other on the left.

34 Then said Jesus, Father, forgive them; for they know not what they do. And they parted his raiment, and cast lots.

35 And the people stood beholding. And the rulers also with them derided him, saying, He saved others; let him save himself, if he be Christ, the chosen of God.

36 And the soldiers also mocked him, coming to him, and offering him vinegar,

37 And saying, If thou be the king of the Jews, save thyself.

38 And a superscription also was written over him in letters of Greek, and Latin, and Hebrew, THIS IS THE KING OF THE JEWS.

39 And one of the malefactors which were hanged railed on him, saying, If thou be Christ, save thyself and us.

40 But the other answering rebuked him, saying, Dost not thou fear God, seeing thou art in the same condemnation?

41 And we indeed justly; for we receive the due reward of our deeds: but this man hath done nothing amiss.

42 And he said unto Jesus, Lord, remember me when thou comest into thy kingdom.

43 And Jesus said unto him, Verily I say unto thee, To day shalt thou be with me in paradise.

44 And it was about the sixth hour, and there was a darkness over all the earth until the ninth hour.

45 And the sun was darkened, and the veil of the temple was rent in the midst.

46 And when Jesus had cried with a loud voice, he said, Father, into thy hands I commend my spirit: and having said thus, he gave up the ghost.

47 Now when the centurion saw what was done, he glorified God, saying, Certainly this was a righteous man.

48 And all the people that came together to that sight, beholding the things which were done, smote their breasts, and returned.

49 And all his acquaintance, and the women that followed him from Galilee, stood afar off, beholding these things.

NEW REVISED STANDARD VERSION

LUKE 23:33 When they came to the place that is called The Skull, they crucified Jesus there with the criminals, one on his right and one on his left. 34 Then Jesus said, "Father, forgive them; for they do not know what they are doing." And they cast lots to divide his clothing. 35 And the people stood by, watching; but the leaders scoffed at him, saying, "He saved others; let him save himself if he is the Messiah of God, his chosen one!" 36 The soldiers also mocked him, coming up and offering him sour wine, 37 and saying, "If you are the King of the Jews, save yourself!" 38 There was also an inscription over him, "This is the King of the Jews."

39 One of the criminals who were hanged there kept deriding him and saying, "Are you not the Messiah? Save yourself and us!" 40 But the other rebuked him, saying, "Do you not fear God, since you are under the same sentence of condemnation? 41 And we indeed have been condemned justly, for we are getting what we deserve for our deeds, but this man has done nothing wrong." 42 Then he said, "Jesus, remember me when you come into your kingdom." 43 He replied, "Truly I tell you, today you will be with me in Paradise."

44 It was now about noon, and darkness came over the whole land until three in the afternoon, 45 while the sun's light failed; and the curtain of the temple was torn in two. 46 Then Jesus, crying with a loud voice, said, "Father, into your hands I commend my spirit." Having said this, he breathed his last. 47 When the centurion saw what had taken place, he praised God and said, "Certainly this man was innocent." 48 And when all the crowds who had gathered there for this spectacle saw what had taken place, they returned home, beating their breasts. 49 But all his acquaintances, including the women who had followed him from Galilee, stood at a distance, watching these things.

12

BACKGROUND

As Jesus prayed in Gethsemane, Judas and his companions were setting their plot in motion. The religious leaders probably could have found a way to arrest Jesus without the help of Judas, but his cooperation made their job easier. Knowing Jesus' habits, Judas could guide an armed crowd to Him at a time when He could be arrested without many of His supporters on hand to observe (Luke 22:1-6).

When the arresting party arrived, the disciples were still groggy from sleep. Yet Peter managed to take a swing with his sword at a nearby man named Malchus, a servant of the high priest (John 18:10). But Malchus ducked, and Peter only sliced off his ear. Jesus then rebuked Peter for trying to stand in the way of God's will for Him, namely, His crucifixion (Luke 22:47-51).

Seeing that Jesus was determined not to resist arrest, the disciples began to think of their own safety. As Jesus had predicted, His followers scattered. However, at least two disciples, Peter and John ran only a short distance, and then followed the crowd back to Jerusalem (22:54-62).

It was to the religious leaders' advantage that Jesus be arrested, tried, and convicted before the people in Jerusalem awakened. So that night the Sanhedrin met in an upstairs room of the house of the high priest Caiaphas to hear accusations against Jesus. They were already convinced that He should be executed. All they needed were witnesses to confirm their opinion of His guilt.

In actuality, Jesus had two trials—one Jewish and one Roman. Each of these trials had three parts. The Jewish trial began with a preliminary hearing before Annas, a former high priest (John 18:12-14, 19-23). Next, the Sanhedrin tried Jesus in the quarters of the current high priest, Caiaphas (Mark 14:53-65). This trial ended with an official condemnation of Jesus at daybreak (Mark 15:1; Luke 22:66-71).

The Jews then took Jesus to the Roman governor of Judea, Pontius Pilate, who questioned Him (Luke 23:1-5). Pilate next sent Jesus to be examined by Herod Antipas, the ruler of Jesus' home territory—Galilee (23:6-12). Finally, Pilate sentenced Jesus to be crucified (23:13-25).

Why did the religious leaders have to take Jesus to Pilate? The reason is that only a Roman ruler could approve a death sentence and carry out capital punishment. The Jewish authorities knew that Pilate had come up from Caesarea with his troops to keep order in the city during Passover. These religious leaders also realized that Pilate's reputation back in Rome was not good. This made it imperative for him to do whatever he could to remain in good standing with the Jewish authorities.

One of the charges against Jesus was insurrection against Rome, an accusation that Pilate could not ignore. At first the governor tried to dismiss all the charges against Jesus on the basis of flimsy evidence. But he finally caved in to the pressures of the street-mob and allowed Jesus to be executed in the most hideous way known. Undoubtedly Pilate, the crowd, and the religious leaders thought Jesus' crucifixion would silence Him permanently.

NOTES ON THE PRINTED TEXT

At a small hill outside Jerusalem, dubbed the Skull, the early morning sunlight shown on three holes. Beside them were some rocks and three wooden uprights. The execution squad was efficiently finishing their preparations when the procession of guards and the condemned, each carrying their crosspieces, arrived.

The victims were quickly stripped (except for a loincloth) and stretched out on their crosses. The victims were positioned so that the saddle (nothing more than a wooden peg) was positioned between the legs of the condemned. This peg supported one's weight. When the cross was raised, this would cause excruciating pain to the victim.

The arms and legs of the condemned were stretched and held while executioners drove spikes through wrists and ankles, as evidenced by skeletons discovered by archaeologists. In one motion, the cross was raised and dropped into the prepared hole. Meanwhile soldiers jammed rocks into the hole to keep the execution device upright.

By 9 A.M., Jesus was hanging on a cross. Perhaps to further humiliate Him, the people in charge had Him executed with two common criminals (Luke 23:32). This would serve as a warning to any who might challenge the authority of the government. *When they came to the place that is called The Skull, they crucified Jesus there with the criminals, one on his right and one on his left* (23:33).

Often those being executed would make venomous remarks to the crowds or their executioners. Jesus, though, prayed for the forgiveness of His killers. *Then Jesus said, "Father, forgive them; for they do not know what they are doing"* (23:34).

Public executions always drew the curious, and this one was no exception. Perhaps as the *people stood by, watching* (23:35), the Roman soldiers cast lots for Jesus' clothes (23:34). (This was foretold in Psalm 22:18.) Also, the gloating religious leaders mocked and taunted Jesus saying, *"He saved others; let him save himself if he is the Messiah of God, his chosen one!"* (Luke 23:35).

The soldiers' reactions varied. A few offered Jesus some of the crude vinegar wine and herbs from a large clay pot. (They were forbidden to drink anything more potent while on duty.) Perhaps they were humiliating Him further by pretending to offer the King His wine. *The soldiers also mocked him . . . saying, "If you are the King of the Jews, save yourself!"* (23:36).

To serve as a warning to any spectator or passerby, the Romans posted the charge over the heads of the condemned. Jesus' crime was inscribed on a sign, perhaps to further humiliate Him. All four Gospels report the inscription, though the wording varies among the accounts (Matt. 27:37; Mark 15:26; Luke 23:38; John 19:19). Putting them all together, the statement would read, "This is Jesus of Nazareth, the King of the Jews."

One of the felons being crucified *kept deriding [Jesus] and saying, "Are you not the Messiah? Save yourself and us!"* (Luke 23:39). But the second criminal rebuked such behavior. He reminded the first thief of God's wrath. They were justly paying for their crimes. Jesus, though, was innocent. *"Do you not fear God, since you are under the same sentence of condemnation? And we indeed have been condemned justly, for we are getting what we deserve for our deeds, but this man has done nothing wrong"* (23:40-41).

The penitent felon made a remarkable request, especially in light of the fact that Jesus was dying on a cross. *"Jesus, remember me when you come into your kingdom"* (23:42). The Savior granted the request. The dying lawbreaker would be with his Lord in paradise, which is another way of referring to heaven, the believer's place of eternal peace and rest (23:43).

Three hours later, at noon, the sky darkened, as if God were expressing His displeasure. Another significant event also occurred. The expensive woven tapestry that shielded the Most Holy Place split down the middle (23:44-45). This curtain separated the Holy Place from the Most Holy Place. The torn fabric meant that Jesus had opened the way to God. Repentant sinners now had direct access to God through Jesus, their great High Priest (Heb. 10:19-22).

Jesus' final words before His death were the prayer recorded in Psalm 31:5, which expressed confidence in God's care. *Then Jesus, crying with a loud voice, said, "Father, into your hands I commend my spirit"* (Luke 23:46). Here we are reminded that no one took Jesus' life from Him; rather, He voluntarily gave it up (John 10:17-18).

Jesus' death produced a variety of reactions. The centurion, undoubtedly a witness to many executions, glorified God and testified to Jesus' innocence. *When the centurion saw what had taken place, he praised God and said, "Certainly this man was innocent"* (Luke 23:47). Others went away *beating their breasts* (23:48), which was a way of expressing deep remorse and anguish.

Among the eyewitnesses were some of Jesus' followers, several of whom were *women . . . from Galilee* (23:49). They watched from a distance, either out of fear or respect for Jesus' privacy.

SUGGESTIONS TO TEACHERS

This week's lesson deals with Jesus' crucifixion. Sometimes, in teaching about this historic event, students can become sidetracked by discussing interesting but less-important details of the account. You should keep the focus on the significance of what Jesus did for us as believers. Perhaps by developing your lesson around some of the main characters—especially Jesus—you will be able to underscore that Christ died at Calvary to atone for our sins.

1. THE OFFICIAL WHO PLEASED THE CROWD BUT PERMITTED JESUS' DEATH. Pilate dismissed Jesus as a troublemaking provincial rabbi, and finally gave in to the shrieks of the crowd (Luke 23:1-6). Explain to your students that such a cowardly, self-serving attitude has no place among believers. The Lord wants us to be courageous in our commitment to Him.

2. THE MAN WHO MISSED THE CELEBRATION BUT FOUND THE SAVIOR. Simon of Cyrene was forced to shoulder Jesus' cross (23:26). Perhaps from this incident Simon discovered that becoming Jesus' companion in His pain and humiliation brought a heightened awareness of the Savior's significance. When we follow Jesus in sacrificial service, we gain a new appreciation for His presence and power in our lives.

3. THE CRIMINAL WHO RECOGNIZED JESUS AND RECEIVED FORGIVENESS. Deathbed conversions are possible for any who turn to Christ in faith (23:42-43). But why wait? Why miss out on a life of forgiveness through the redeeming love of Jesus? Now is the time to renounce sin and be saved!

4. THE REDEEMER WHO SUFFERED DEATH AND SUCCEEDED IN HIS MISSION. Jesus died to atone for the sins of humanity (23:46). Take time to discuss how Jesus' death met God's perfect demands and paid the penalty for our sin. In the Crucifixion, we are confronted with such costly sacrificial love that we shouldn't ever question or deny God's intent to redeem us.

FOR ADULTS

■ TOPIC: Fulfilling One's Mission

■ QUESTIONS: 1. What is the significance of Jesus' being executed with criminals? 2. What do you think motivated the Roman soldiers to be cruel and humiliate Jesus? 3. Why did Jesus, who is the Son of God, have to die on the cross? 4. Why did Jesus allow Himself to be executed in such an agonizing, brutal, and public way? 5. What positive differences has Jesus' death on the cross made in your life?

■ ILLUSTRATIONS:

Mission Completed Successfully. The Berlin airlift was one of the great triumphs of the Cold War. On June 24, 1948, Joseph Stalin, the dictator of the former Soviet Union, began a siege of the three western zones surrounding Berlin. He held the city hostage by blocking all roads, rail lines, and canals to Berlin.

Britain and the United States responded by flying in supplies of food and fuel to Berlin. Day and night over the next 15 months, British and American planes flew 277,569 missions, delivering over 2,000,000 tons of food and coal to the city's inhabitants. Finally, in May 1949, Stalin relented and lifted the blockade. The West had won. The city was saved.

The airlift continued until the end of September to build up supplies. The final plane, a British Dakota, landed on September 23, 1949. On it's nose was painted "Psalm 21, Verse 11." The verse reads, *If they plan evil against you, if they devise mischief, they will not succeed."*

This verse could also be applied to the cross of Christ. His enemies tried to destroy Him, but they failed, for God brought victory. Thus, Jesus' mission was completed successfully.

Sacrificing for Others. In 1946, scientists at Los Alamos, New Mexico, were putting together materials they would use in one of the early tests of the atomic bomb. Everyone knew the deadly hazards of radiation.

One of the brilliant young researchers engaged in the project was Louis Slotkin. One afternoon, he was carrying out a procedure that he had done many times before. It involved bringing together two hemispheres of uranium in order to learn precisely how much U-235 would produce a chain reaction. The dangerous part was to have the two bits of uranium near each other but using a screwdriver to prevent them from touching (thus preventing a fatal chain reaction from starting).

That afternoon Slotkin's screwdriver accidentally slipped. The two hemispheres of uranium nudged too close to each other. Suddenly there was a blinding blue light. The scientist instantly knew the danger. He could have dived quickly aside and probably saved himself. But he knew there were seven others in the lab with him. He deliberately reached with his bare hands and yanked apart the uranium hemispheres. The lethal reaction stopped.

But Slotkin realized that he would pay a terrible price for his courageous act. While standing with the others as they waited to be taken to the hospital, he calmly informed them that it was unlikely he would survive such a high dose of radiation. Nine days later, Slotkin died a painful death because of his self-sacrificing act for his co-workers.

Jesus could have rescued Himself from the cross. But He willingly died an excruciating and humiliating death so that the lost might be saved.

Nothing Counts but the Cross. Robert Capon, in *The Foolishness of Preaching: Proclaiming the Gospel Against the Wisdom of the World* (Eerdmans, 1998), made the following observation:

> For one thing, our preachers tell us the wrong story entirely, saying not a word about the dark side—no, that's too weak—about the dark *center* of

the Gospel. They can't bring themselves to come within a country mile of the horrendous truth that we are saved in our *deaths*, not by our efforts to lead a good life. Instead, they mouth the canned recipes for successful living they think their congregations want to hear. It makes no difference what kind of success they urge on us: "spiritual" or "religious" success is as irrelevant to the Gospel as is success in health, money, or love. Nothing counts but the cross.

FOR YOUTH

■ TOPIC: A Decisive Moment

■ QUESTIONS: 1. What attitude did Jesus display when others mocked and slandered Him? 2. Why did Jesus refuse to rescue Himself from the cross? 3. Do you think Jesus' mockers would have believed in Him if God had delivered Him from the cross? Why or why not? 4. What does Jesus' willingness to endure humiliation teach us about Him? 5. How has Jesus helped you through times when you felt alone and abandoned?

■ ILLUSTRATIONS:

One of the Crowd. In a painting of Jesus' crucifixion by the Dutch artist, Rembrandt, attention immediately focuses on the cross and the one hanging on it. Then the viewer's eyes fall on the crowd gathered around the cross. At the edge of the painting—at the very fringe of the crowd—one figure stands in the shadows. That person is the artist himself! Rembrandt stands at the crucifixion, watching silently.

The Gospels record various responses of the crowd. Some mocked. Some wept. Others, like Rembrandt, watched silently. What is your response?

Crux of the Cross. In January, 1997, an emergency excavation of a fifth century A.D. house at Jerusalem's Jaffa Gate unearthed a cross. While many crosses have been found before, this one was unique. The tiny bronze object was inlaid with two pieces of wood.

Archaeologists dated the cross to the Byzantine period (between the fifth to the eighth century A.D.). They pointed out that the object probably was a relic sold to pilgrims who came to Jerusalem. However, some insisted that the wood was from the "true cross" of Jesus. Experts responded that it was impossible to identify the real cross, let alone the wood from which it was made. And historians pointed out that thousands of crosses were made in the ancient world. Nevertheless, some continued to assert that the wood came from the cross on which Jesus died.

The solution was to determine the age of the wood by scientific testing. The only catch was that in order to pinpoint its age through radiocarbon tests, a sample of the wood had to be used. Otherwise, no accurate date could be established. The outcry against doing this has prevented the test from happening.

Despite all the statements made by the experts, some are still trying to link the wood in this tiny object to Jesus' cross. Their emphasis, however, seems to be misguided. The Christian faith doesn't rest on having physical evidence of the cross on which Jesus died. Rather, it is based but on the testimony of eyewitnesses, who declared that He both died and rose again from the dead (John 20: 30-31).

Wrongly Penalized. A junior in a high school in the eastern part of the United States had hopes of winning the 189-pound weight class wrestling title. The top ranked athlete seemed like the favorite, that is, until he was told he would have to forfeit all his victories.

Each year wrestlers must be examined by a doctor before the season begins. During the physical, the doctor writes a minimum weight at which the individual can wrestle. In mid-fall, the high school physician certified the junior for the 189-pound class. (The student still had that original form from the physician.) However, when the athletic department secretary prepared the eligibility form for the state, she inadvertently typed in 275 pounds.

State rules gave the district's coaches, athletic directors, and principals 34 days to check each form for clerical errors. No official from the high school, however, bothered to proofread the form, which was mailed to the state athletic association.

School personnel discovered the error on February 3, 1999. (The deadline for any clerical correction was December 19, 1998.) When notified, the athletic association announced that the student could not compete at the 189-pound weight class, but rather only at the heavyweight division (which was over 275 pounds).

The athlete felt crushed. School officials and the student's parents were upset, pointing out that he "was an innocent victim . . . being crucified for an adult's mistake." Here is a case where a young person was penalized for someone else's error.

Pilate found Jesus innocent of any of the charges the religious leaders brought against Him (Luke 23:13-15). Also, Jesus had never sinned against God (Heb. 7:26). Nevertheless, He was punished for our transgressions (Isa. 53:5). Because Jesus willingly paid the price for our sins, we can have new life through faith in Him (Acts 4:12).

Witnesses to the Resurrection

Background Scripture: Luke 24:13-49
Devotional Reading: Matthew 28:16-20

Key Verse: "Repentance and forgiveness of sins is to be proclaimed in his name to all nations. . . . You are witnesses of these things." Luke 24:47-48.

KING JAMES VERSION

LUKE 24:33 And they rose up the same hour, and returned to Jerusalem, and found the eleven gathered together, and them that were with them,

34 Saying, The Lord is risen indeed, and hath appeared to Simon.

35 And they told what things were done in the way, and how he was known of them in breaking of bread.

36 And as they thus spake, Jesus himself stood in the midst of them, and saith unto them, Peace be unto you.

37 But they were terrified and affrighted, and supposed that they had seen a spirit.

38 And he said unto them, Why are ye troubled? and why do thoughts arise in your hearts?

39 Behold my hands and my feet, that it is I myself: handle me, and see; for a spirit hath not flesh and bones, as ye see me have.

40 And when he had thus spoken, he shewed them his hands and his feet.

41 And while they yet believed not for joy, and wondered, he said unto them, Have ye here any meat?

42 And they gave him a piece of a broiled fish, and of an honeycomb.

43 And he took it, and did eat before them.

44 And he said unto them, These are the words which I spake unto you, while I was yet with you, that all things must be fulfilled, which were written in the law of Moses, and in the prophets, and in the psalms, concerning me.

45 Then opened he their understanding, that they might understand the scriptures,

46 And said unto them, Thus it is written, and thus it behoved Christ to suffer, and to rise from the dead the third day:

47 And that repentance and remission of sins should be preached in his name among all nations, beginning at Jerusalem.

48 And ye are witnesses of these things.

49 And, behold, I send the promise of my Father upon you: but tarry ye in the city of Jerusalem, until ye be endued with power from on high

NEW REVISED STANDARD VERSION

LUKE 24:33 That same hour they got up and returned to Jerusalem; and they found the eleven and their companions gathered together. 34 They were saying, "The Lord has risen indeed, and he has appeared to Simon!" 35 Then they told what had happened on the road, and how he had been made known to them in the breaking of the bread.

36 While they were talking about this, Jesus himself stood among them and said to them, "Peace be with you." 37 They were startled and terrified, and thought that they were seeing a ghost. 38 He said to them, "Why are you frightened, and why do doubts arise in your hearts? 39 Look at my hands and my feet; see that it is I myself. Touch me and see; for a ghost does not have flesh and bones as you see that I have." 40 And when he had said this, he showed them his hands and his feet. 41 While in their joy they were disbelieving and still wondering, he said to them, "Have you anything here to eat?" 42 They gave him a piece of broiled fish, 43 and he took it and ate in their presence.

44 Then he said to them, "These are my words that I spoke to you while I was still with you—that everything written about me in the law of Moses, the prophets, and the psalms must be fulfilled." 45 Then he opened their minds to understand the scriptures, 46 and he said to them, "Thus it is written, that the Messiah is to suffer and to rise from the dead on the third day, 47 and that repentance and forgiveness of sins is to be proclaimed in his name to all nations, beginning from Jerusalem. 48 You are witnesses of these things. 49 And see, I am sending upon you what my Father promised; so stay here in the city until you have been clothed with power from on high."

13

HOME BIBLE READINGS

BACKGROUND

The Gospels agree that Jesus was raised bodily on Sunday, the first day of the week. They also agree that Mary Magdalene was the first witness of the empty tomb, and most probably of the resurrected Lord. This is an important piece of historical evidence, for the testimony of a woman was of no legal value in ancient Jewish society. Had some early church writers invented a story of the Resurrection, they would not have emphasized Mary's witness in the narrative.

Like the crucifixion accounts, the resurrection narratives diverge in a number of particulars. Only Matthew reports an earthquake and the rolling away of the stone from the tomb (Matt. 28:2). Matthew and Mark speak of one angel at the tomb (Matt. 28:5; Mark 16:5), whereas Luke and John speak of two (Luke 24:4; John 20:12). Matthew and Mark report only the women visiting the empty tomb, while Luke and John tell of a visit by Peter, with John relating a footrace between Peter and the beloved disciple to the tomb (Luke 24:12; John 20:3-8).

Luke and the other Gospel writers emphasized that no one expected to encounter Jesus alive from the dead. In fact, the disciples not only grieved for their deceased leader but also struggled to make sense of the apparent disgrace and defeat surrounding His crucifixion.

The report that God raised Jesus from the dead was more than hearsay to Luke and the earliest Christians. Reliable eyewitnesses attested to seeing the risen Lord. Luke carefully presented some of these accounts as evidence that Jesus truly was alive from the dead. And for Luke and the other New Testament writers, Jesus' resurrection was more than a mere report. Rather, they regarded it as good news worth believing.

NOTES ON THE PRINTED TEXT

While Luke 23 records Jesus' sacrifice, chapter 24 shows God's acceptance of that sacrifice. The grand confirming act of the life and death of Christ is His resurrection. He was buried late on Friday afternoon. After sunset on Saturday, when the Sabbath was over, some women purchased aromatic oils for anointing Jesus' body. But by then it was too late for them to do the anointing (Mark 16:1; Luke 23:55-56).

Thus early the next morning the women headed for the tomb. Their main concern on this trip was who they could find to roll away the massive stone blocking the tomb's entrance (Mark 16:3). But the women worried in vain, for the stone had already been rolled aside by an angel (Matt. 28:2).

Jesus first appeared to these women and Mary Magdalene. The Savior also appeared to Peter sometime on Sunday (Luke 24:34; 1 Cor. 15:5). Jesus' appearance to the two travelers on the road to Emmaus was around midday on Sunday (Mark 16:12-13).

The Gospel of Luke describes this last encounter in considerable detail (24:13-32). These two disciples thought Jesus would set up a political kingdom. Thus, His death seemed like a tragedy to them. But Jesus explained that it was necessary for the Messiah to die on the cross before entering into His glory. The Savior also *interpreted to them the things about himself in all the scriptures* (24:27).

When the two disciples finally reached Emmaus, they invited Jesus to stay with them, which He did. At the start of a meal, the Savior opened their eyes, which enabled them to recognize Him. He then *vanished from their sight* (24:31). They in turn immediately *got up and returned to Jerusalem; and they found the eleven and their companions gathered together* (24:33).

The two disciples learned from the group that the Lord was really alive and had appeared to Peter (24:34). The disciples from Emmaus then told what happened on the road and how they knew, when Jesus broke the bread, that He was the risen Lord. *Then they told what had happened on the road, and how he had been made known to them in the breaking of the bread* (24:35).

While Jesus' followers were still talking about what had happened, He appeared and greeted them. But they were frightened, for they thought they were seeing a ghost (24:36-37). In response, Jesus asked His followers, *"Why are you frightened, and why do doubts arise in your hearts?"* (24:38).

Jesus then offered proof that He was actually alive from the dead. He invited the group to examine His hands and feet to verify that it was truly Him. If they touched Him, they would see that He wasn't a ghost, for the latter didn't have flesh and bones as they could see He had (24:39). *And when he had said this, he showed them his hands and his feet* (24:40).

The disciples' initial fear was replaced by joy. But they were so amazed to see Jesus that they had trouble believing it was actually Him. He then asked them, *"Have you anything to eat?"* (24:41). In response the group gave the Savior a piece of baked fish, which He took and ate while they watched (24:42-43).

Jesus then reminded His disciples that before His crucifixion, He had told them that everything written about Him *"in the law of Moses, the prophets, and the psalms must be fulfilled"* (24:44). (These were the three parts of the Hebrew [Old] Testament.) In other words, Jesus' death and resurrection had been predicted centuries earlier.

Apparently the meaning of the biblical texts was not self-evident to the disciples. Jesus had to explain them in light of His death and resurrection (24:45). He noted that it was necessary for the Messiah to die on the cross (in order to atone for humanity's sin), and then on the third day to rise again from the dead. *"Thus it is written, that the Messiah is to suffer and to rise from the dead on the third day"* (24:46).

Jesus next stated that all people of every nation had to be urged to repent of their sin and turn to God in faith for forgiveness. The disciples were to begin heralding the good news of salvation to those living in Jerusalem. From there the Gospel was to be declared far and wide. *"Repentance and forgiveness of sins is to be proclaimed in his name to all nations, beginning from Jerusalem"* (24:47).

Jesus was appointing His followers as His representatives. They would be His *"witnesses of these things"* (24:48). Perhaps the thought of doing this left some of the disciples feeling overwhelmed. Jesus reassured them by saying, *"I am sending upon you what my Father promised"* (24:49). By this Christ meant the Holy Spirit. By waiting for Him, they would receive the power they needed to witness effectively for Christ to the lost. The Savior's comments anticipate the outpouring of the Spirit on the day of Pentecost (Acts 2:1-4).

SUGGESTIONS TO TEACHERS

State it boldly! If God had not raised Jesus from the dead, your class would not be gathering to study this week's lesson. In fact, there would be no church building, no congregation, and no hope of heaven. Notable scholars maintain that without the resurrection of Jesus, the shape and direction of all subsequent history would have been different. The news of the Savior's resurrection is the pivotal event not only for us as His followers but also for all humankind!

1. REAPPEARANCE TO THE UNSUSPECTING. Be sure to stress that Jesus' disciples were not expecting to see Him alive from the dead. This fact rules out any rumors that His resurrection was a story concocted by the early church. Those who may be skeptical of the statement that God raised Jesus from the dead should carefully examine Luke 24.

2. REMINDER OF SCRIPTURE'S PROMISE. Have your students spend some time considering Jesus' encounter with the two disciples going to Emmaus. Note that as Jesus walked with them, He explained how the events of the past few days had been prophesied in the Old Testament. Also stress that because the two disciples opened their hearts to Christ, He in turn opened their understanding. This can also be true for your students, especially when they read their Bibles in light of Jesus' resurrection.

3. REVELATION AT THE TABLE. When Jesus and the two disciples sat together to eat the evening meal, Jesus broke the bread and gave thanks for it. In that moment *their eyes were opened, and they recognized him* (Luke 24:31). We can only guess what triggered their recognition. Was it the way Jesus prayed for the meal? Did they suddenly recall how He had broken bread for over five thousand? Did they see the nail scars in His hands? Give the class an opportunity to discuss this further.

4. RESOLVE OF JOYFUL DISCIPLES. In each of the appearances of the risen Lord, His followers were filled with joy. In the case of His appearance among the disciples gathered in Jerusalem, they welcomed His command to herald the good news of His resurrection far and wide. The Lord also wants the believers in your class to tell others about the risen Lord. They don't do this in their own power. Rather, the Spirit abides in all Christians and enables them to be potent witnesses for Jesus.

FOR ADULTS

■ TOPIC: You Are a Witness!

■ QUESTIONS: 1. How do you think Jesus was able to appear among the disciples despite the fact they were in a room protected by locked doors? 2. How did Jesus open the understanding of the disciples to what the Old Testament said about Him? 3. What Old Testament passages might Jesus have referred to? 4. How does the news of Jesus' resurrection affect your view of death? 5. Why do some people refuse to follow Christ despite the overwhelming evidence of His resurrection?

■ **ILLUSTRATIONS:**

Easter in the Cemetery. A visitor to Paris decided to attend an Easter celebration. The worship started in a small chapel with a beautiful service at midnight. The following day, on Sunday, the faithful gathered again. This time they assembled in the main sanctuary. Then, while being led by the pastor, the worshipers walked out to a nearby cemetery.

The pastor waited until the participants gathered nearby, then announced dramatically, *"Christos voskres!"* (which means, "Christ is risen!"). While the group stood among the graves of deceased loved ones, they responded enthusiastically *"Voistennu voskres!"* (which means, "Yes, He is risen!"). Despite the fact that beloved family members and friends had died, these Christians faithfully and joyously affirmed the truth of Jesus' resurrection and the hope of eternal life that it holds for all believers.

What a Hoax! A rich Englishman died and left most of his estate to a London hospital. He had sat on the board of directors of the hospital for many years. In his will, the deceased attached a strange condition to his generous bequest. He stipulated that he had to be in attendance at each monthly meeting of the board of directors!

The board of the hospital thus arranged to have the Englishman's body embalmed and preserved in a suitable storage place in the hospital. Every month for over 100 years, at meetings of the hospital's board of directors, attendants routinely bring in the mummified form and carefully place the man's remains at the head of the table. In this way the minutes of the meetings are able to report that the Englishman is "present." What a hoax!

The Gospels present a drastically different account of Jesus. His corpse was not propped up so that gullible followers could be fooled into thinking He was somehow with them. Rather, many saw Jesus alive from the dead. Of this there is no doubt! Though we can't see, hear, or touch Jesus physically now, we can draw near to Him through the Holy Spirit, who abides in all Christians.

FOR YOUTH

■ TOPIC: Seeing is Believing
■ QUESTIONS: 1. Why did the disciples at first doubt that Jesus was truly among them? 2. Why did the disciples need the Spirit to be effective witnesses for Christ? 3. Why do others need to know that Jesus has risen from the dead? 4. What resources do we have to help us understand the Scriptures? 5. How can the Spirit help us to be faithful witnesses to the death and resurrection of Jesus?

■ ILLUSTRATIONS:

Final Rites? On July 17, 1918, Czar Nicholas II and his family were executed by Bolshevik revolutionaries in the cellar of the Ipatiev house near Yakaterinburg. The bodies of Russia's last Czar, his wife (Alexandra), their five children, and four servants were dumped in a mass grave in a forest outside the city and doused with acid. There they lay until they were unearthed in 1991.

Once discovered, the "Yekaterinburg Remains" were housed in glass cases. Even after positive DNA testing and other conclusive scientific evidence was presented, religious leaders and government officials refused to acknowledge that the bones were those of the former royal family. Seven years passed before the remains were finally buried in a modest ceremony at Saint Peter's Cathedral.

On Wednesday, July 15, 1998, hundreds of ministers carried banners and flags. President Boris Yeltsin and other government leaders joined them. They viewed the wooden gold-lined caskets, each with an ornately etched nameplate, upon which was the yellow flag of the Romanov family. The ceremony was designed to be an act of repentance for the murder of the innocent.

Centuries earlier, there was no such pomp, ceremony, or repentance among the religious and political leaders at the death of another King. In fact, the authorities felt relieved that Jesus was no longer a threat. However, the grave was unable to hold this Ruler. He rose from the dead and presented Himself to His disciples. He then empowered them to share the good news of His resurrection to all the world.

Grave Will Not Reveal Myth. In September 1998, a large humanly-made hill—which is 18 feet high and 177 feet in diameter, and 50 miles northwest of Oslo,

Norway—experienced a huge sinking problem. The hill is a Viking burial mound, believed to be that of the ninth century King Halvdan the Black. (Halvdan was a powerful regional king who drowned in A.D. 860 when his horse-drawn sleigh plunged through the ice of Rands Fjord. He was buried in a mound in Ringerike.) The king couldn't fulfill his dream of uniting Norway. However, his son, Harold Fairhair, did succeed in becoming the first ruler of the unified nation.

Archaeologists brought in ground radar and other equipment to examine the burial mound. The equipment indicated the presence of a 75-foot long Viking ship and other treasures. Such a find had the potential for unlocking the early history of Norway. The team of experts stated that the sinkage of the mound was related to the decomposition of the large artifacts. They thus urged immediate excavation in order to save the treasures for future Norwegians.

Some scholars and government officials, however, feared that the excavation could traumatize Norwegians by "puncturing" their founding lore. Norway's history was chronicled in Snorri Sturluson's *Heimskringla*, the colorful and bloody saga of the nation's early kings. The Icelandic sage wrote his book in the early 1200's, and it's the country's historical record. It starts with the legends of Odin, but turns concrete with Halvdan the Black, who was named for his dark hair.

Historians have speculated that Snorri embellished the medieval account to strengthen Halvdan's rule. They fear that excavating the mound might prove Halvdan never existed. Others think the site was plundered centuries ago and is empty. They feel that any tampering with the site might severely damage the nation's image.

What a contrast this is with Christianity! An open grave is the basis for our faith in Christ. There's no doubt of Jesus' resurrection, for many people saw Him alive from the dead. God has called us to share the good news of the Resurrection with others. We present the truth, not an ancient myth.

CONTINUING JESUS' WORK (ACTS)

THE PROMISE OF THE SPIRIT'S POWER

BACKGROUND SCRIPTURE: Acts 1
DEVOTIONAL READING: John 16:7-14

KEY VERSE: "You will receive power when the Holy Spirit has come upon you; and you will be my witnesses in Jerusalem, in all Judea and Samaria, and to the ends of the earth." Acts 1:8.

KING JAMES VERSION

ACTS 1:3 To whom also he shewed himself alive after his passion by many infallible proofs, being seen of them forty days, and speaking of the things pertaining to the kingdom of God:

4 And, being assembled together with them, commanded them that they should not depart from Jerusalem, but wait for the promise of the Father, which, saith he, ye have heard of me.

5 For John truly baptized with water; but ye shall be baptized with the Holy Ghost not many days hence.

6 When they therefore were come together, they asked of him, saying, Lord, wilt thou at this time restore again the kingdom to Israel?

7 And he said unto them, It is not for you to know the times or the seasons, which the Father hath put in his own power.

8 But ye shall receive power, after that the Holy Ghost is come upon you: and ye shall be witnesses unto me both in Jerusalem, and in all Judæa, and in Samaria, and unto the uttermost part of the earth.

9 And when he had spoken these things, while they beheld, he was taken up; and a cloud received him out of their sight.

10 And while they looked stedfastly toward heaven as he went up, behold, two men stood by them in white apparel;

11 Which also said, Ye men of Galilee, why stand ye gazing up into heaven? this same Jesus, which is taken up from you into heaven, shall so come in like manner as ye have seen him go into heaven.

12 Then returned they unto Jerusalem from the mount called Olivet, which is from Jerusalem a sabbath day's journey.

13 And when they were come in, they went up into an upper room, where abode both Peter, and James, and John, and Andrew, Philip, and Thomas, Bartholomew, and Matthew, James the son of Alphæus, and Simon Zelotes, and Judas the brother of James.

14 These all continued with one accord in prayer and supplication, with the women, and Mary the mother of Jesus, and with his brethren.

NEW REVISED STANDARD VERSION

ACTS 1:3 After his suffering he presented himself alive to them by many convincing proofs, appearing to them during forty days and speaking about the kingdom of God. 4 While staying with them, he ordered them not to leave Jerusalem, but to wait there for the promise of the Father. "This," he said, "is what you have heard from me; 5 for John baptized with water, but you will be baptized with the Holy Spirit not many days from now."

6 So when they had come together, they asked him, "Lord, is this the time when you will restore the kingdom to Israel?" 7 He replied, "It is not for you to know the times or periods that the Father has set by his own authority. 8 But you will receive power when the Holy Spirit has come upon you; and you will be my witnesses in Jerusalem, in all Judea and Samaria, and to the ends of the earth." 9 When he had said this, as they were watching, he was lifted up, and a cloud took him out of their sight. 10 While he was going and they were gazing up toward heaven, suddenly two men in white robes stood by them. 11 They said, "Men of Galilee, why do you stand looking up toward heaven? This Jesus, who has been taken up from you into heaven, will come in the same way as you saw him go into heaven."

12 Then they returned to Jerusalem from the mount called Olivet, which is near Jerusalem, a sabbath day's journey away. 13 When they had entered the city, they went to the room upstairs where they were staying, Peter, and John, and James, and Andrew, Philip and Thomas, Bartholomew and Matthew, James son of Alphaeus, and Simon the Zealot, and Judas son of James. 14 All these were constantly devoting themselves to prayer, together with certain women, including Mary the mother of Jesus, as well as his brothers.

HOME BIBLE READINGS

Monday, February 26	Acts 1:1-5	*The Promise of the Holy Spirit*
Tuesday, February 27	Acts 1:6-11	*The Ascension of Jesus*
Wednesday, February 28	Mark 3:13-19	*Jesus Appoints the Twelve*
Thursday, March 1	Acts 1:12-20	*The Acts of the Apostles Begin*
Friday, March 2	Psalm 29	*The Voice of God's Spirit*
Saturday, March 3	Matthew 27:3-10	*The Suicide of Judas Iscariot*
Sunday, March 4	Acts 1:21-26	*Matthias Chosen to Replace Judas Iscariot*

BACKGROUND

In his Gospel account, Luke told about God's life-transforming news to all persons through the ministry, death, and resurrection of Jesus. Luke followed that piece of writing with another account that described the dynamic spread of that good news beyond Jerusalem to distant lands through the community of believers in the first century A.D.

This second volume traditionally has been called *The Acts of the Apostles*. Though the apostles Peter and Paul receive considerable attention, the Holy Spirit is the principal character in Acts. It was through the Spirit's power in the lives of Jesus' followers that the Gospel was proclaimed throughout the Roman Empire. That's why some think "The Acts of the Spirit" is the best title for the book.

Acts 1:8 is the theme verse, giving the book a three-part structure. In the first part, Luke detailed the witness of the church in Jerusalem (1:1—8:3). In the second part, he discussed the witness of the church in Judea and Samaria (8:4—12:24). And in the third part, Luke related the witness of the church to the farthest corners of the earth (12:25—28:31).

While the first half of Acts predominantly concerns the ministry of Peter to the Jews (1:1—12:24), the second half of the book is mostly focused on Paul's ministry to the Gentiles (12:25—28:31). Chapters 1 and 2 detail the ascension of Christ and the outpouring of the Spirit on the Day of Pentecost. Chapters 3 through 8 concern the ministry of such individuals as Peter and John in the face of opposition from the Jewish religious leaders. In chapters 8 through 12, Luke related the witness of Philip, the conversion of Paul (Saul), and the conversion of Cornelius. Chapters 12 through 28 detail Paul's three missionary journeys and his voyage to Rome.

NOTES ON THE PRINTED TEXT

Luke opened his account of the early Christian church by mentioning a previous manuscript dealing with the words and works of Jesus (Acts 1:1). We are left with the impression that in its original form the Book of Acts was probably the second of two large scrolls (the first being the Gospel of Luke), which together made up one large work.

As Luke wrote the sequel to his Gospel, he first summarized the contents of that work (1:1-3). He did this because the account of the infancy of the church—which is the subject of Acts—proceeds directly from the life of Christ. Then for his first new material, Luke described one post-resurrection appearance of Jesus and the Savior's ascension into heaven.

During the 40 days after His crucifixion, Jesus appeared to the apostles from time to time and proved to them in many ways that He actually was alive. On these occasions He also talked to them *about the kingdom of God* (1:3). We might wish we had more extant detailed information on this subject. Nevertheless, in some sense that kingdom is present (Luke 11:20; John 3:3; Rom. 14:17) and in another sense it is future (Matt. 6:10; 25:34).

The risen Lord next issued a command. His disciples were to remain in Jerusalem. *While staying with them, he ordered them not to leave Jerusalem, but to wait there for the promise of the Father* (1:4). The promise that Jesus described was the Holy Spirit. *"This," he said, "is what you have heard from me; for John baptized with water, but you will be baptized with the Holy Spirit not many days from now" (1:4-5).*

Jesus' disciples drew the wrong conclusion about Him, His resurrection, and His teaching. They believed He would now free Israel from the oppression of Roman rule and make the Jewish nation a powerhouse in the region. Luke gives the impression that they persistently questioned Jesus about this. *"Lord, is this the time when you will restore the kingdom to Israel?"* (1:6).

Jesus gently corrected His disciples by noting that God the Father set the timetable for all events, whether worldwide, national, or personal in nature. Jesus' followers were not to worry about these matters. *He replied, "It is not for you to know the times or periods that the Father has set by his own authority"* (1:7).

The followers of Christ were to concern themselves with spreading the good news and bringing the lost to faith. Jesus told the group that they needed outside help to fulfill His agenda. Through the presence of the Spirit, the disciples would be filled with the courage and ability to witness for Jesus.

Jerusalem was a dangerous place, for those who had caused Christ's execution still had the upper hand there. The disciples would need courage to testify in His name. But they weren't to stop with Jerusalem. They were also to take the message to Judea and Samaria, and even to the ends of the earth. *"But you will receive power when the Holy Spirit has come upon you; and you will be my witnesses in Jerusalem, in all Judea and Samaria, and to the ends of the earth"* (1:8).

It was not long after Jesus made His final statement to His disciples that He was taken up into the sky *as they were watching* (1:9). The fact that *a cloud took [Jesus] out of their sight* served as a visible reminder that God's glory was present as the apostles watched their Savior leave.

The dramatic departure of the risen Christ from His earthly, bodily ministry among His followers is known as the Ascension. To a large extent the Ascension was for the benefit of the disciples. They could no longer expect Jesus' visible presence. Instead, they must now wait for the promised Spirit, through whom the work of Christ would continue.

As the disciples were straining their eyes to see the risen Lord, two white-robed men *suddenly . . . stood by them* (1:10). These were angels, and they proclaimed that one day Jesus would return in the same way He had left, namely, bodily and visibly (1:11).

After Jesus' ascension, the disciples returned to Jerusalem, went to the upstairs room of a house where they were staying, and spent time in prayer (vss. 12-14). About 120 followers of Christ spent 10 days together. They worshiped God and encouraged each other. During that time Matthias was selected to replace Judas Iscariot, who had committed suicide after betraying Jesus (1:15-26).

SUGGESTIONS TO TEACHERS

Does your congregation sometimes seem to lack vision and energy? Is there a sense of "not much we can do about the way things are"? Do you and other church leaders occasionally feel tired and overworked in your congregation? Have you and others sometimes wished for a greater zest in serving and a closer awareness of the Lord in your lives?

Undoubtedly, you would agree that God is real and that Jesus is your Lord. And you would concur with the good news of the Resurrection. But you might ask, "How can we be empowered to follow Christ better?" This week's lesson reminds us of Jesus' continuing presence among us through the Spirit. Be sure to tell your students of the help the Spirit can give them in witnessing for Christ.

1. APPEARING TO THE DISCIPLES. Luke opened Acts by stating clearly that the risen Lord presented Himself to the disciples. The Resurrection was not a vague, secondhand report but rather a vital personal experience for them. Remind the members of your class that God raised Jesus alive from the dead. This is more than an announcement made on Easter Sunday; it's the foundation of our faith.

2. ANTICIPATING THE FUTURE. The disciples pressed Jesus for details about the future, just as we sometimes find ourselves speculating when the Second Coming will occur. Jesus, however, refocused the attention of His followers on being His faithful witnesses. Similarly, Jesus doesn't want us to become preoccupied with what God plans to do in the future. Rather, our task is to proclaim the Gospel to the lost and help our fellow believers grow in their faith.

3. ASCENDING TO THE FATHER. The Ascension is celebrated in some but not all churches. The main point to consider surrounds the significance of Jesus' departure. His ascension underscores His victory over the forces of evil and points to His present lordship over the events of history.

4. ABIDING IN THE FELLOWSHIP. This was a time of great uncertainty for Jesus' followers. Nevertheless, they stayed together to worship God, pray to Him, and fellowship with one another. They were spiritually united because of their faith in Christ. How connected do the members of your class feel to the Christian fellowship known as the church?

5. AWAITING THE FULFILLMENT. Waiting is not always easy, especially when we seem to have to wait for God to act. The disciples' way of expectant, prayerful waiting is an example for us to consider. Invite your students to recount occasions when God helped them to wait patiently for Him to answer their prayer requests. How did this strengthen their faith in Him?

■ **FOR ADULTS**	■ **TOPIC:** The Promise of the Empowered ■ **QUESTIONS:** 1. Why was it important for the disciples to wait in Jerusalem *for the promise of the Father* (Acts 1:4)? 2. Why were

the disciples preoccupied with Jesus restoring the *kingdom to Israel* (1:6)? 3. Why did the disciples remain looking upward toward heaven after Jesus departed? 4. What is the role of the Spirit in the church today? 5. Why is it important to know that witnessing includes relying on the power of God's Spirit?

■ **ILLUSTRATIONS:**

Difficulty of Waiting. Television host Hugh Downs and his wife were in Washington, D.C., preparing to return to New York. A call came telling them that their flight had been cancelled. Downs quickly checked on train schedules and discovered a train that was leaving for New York in 45 minutes.

Mrs. Downs was in the shower, so Hugh decided to speed up their departure by packing their bags. He hurriedly threw their clothing and belongings into suitcases, called the bellhop, and had their luggage sent to Union Station. A few minutes later, Mrs. Downs emerged from the bathroom, wrapped in a towel. Calling to her husband, she asked if he would bring her green dress.

Sometimes, as Hugh Downs discovered, we take matters into our own hands too hastily. Jesus' disciples may have wanted to do that before the day of Pentecost by doing the Lord's will impulsively in their own strength. But Jesus told them to wait patiently until they were *baptized with the Holy Spirit* (Acts 1:5). Being willing to wait for the Lord is not easy, but absolutely necessary!

Kinds of Waiting. Paul Tillich wrote an essay entitled, "Theology of Peace," which was published in *The Christian Century*. In the essay, Tillich said the following:

> There are two kinds of waiting, the passive waiting in laziness and the receiving waiting in openness. He who waits in laziness, passively, prevents the coming of what he is waiting for. He who waits in quiet tension, open for what he may encounter, works for its coming. Such waiting in openness and hope does what no willpower can do for our own inner development. The more seriously the great religious men took their own

transformation, using their will to achieve it, the more they failed and were thrown into hopelessness about themselves. Desperately, they asked, and many of us ask with them, "Can we hope at all for such inner renewal?" What gives us the right to such hope after all our failures? Again there is only one answer: waiting in inner stillness, with posed tension and openness toward what we can only receive. Such openness is highest activity; it is the driving force that leads us toward the growth of something new in us. And the struggle between hope and despair in our waiting is a symptom that the new has already taken hold of us.

From this we see that waiting for the fulfillment of God's promises in our lives sometimes demands us to be quiet and patient in spirit.

Lengthening Lent. This is the first Sunday of Lent. The term "Lent" comes from an old Anglo-Saxon word meaning "to lengthen," and originally referred to the lengthening of daylight hours in the northern hemisphere. For Christians, Lent became associated with the lengthening awareness of God's mercy through Jesus' crucifixion and resurrection.

From the fourth century A.D., the church observed Lent as a 40-day period for believers to deepen their faith through prayer, worship, fasting, and alms giving. Some Christian groups laid down strict rules about observing that period leading up to Easter. At the same time, others have recoiled against such demands. Many believers today simply ignore Lent.

But we all tend to be lazy and complacent. Perhaps we can use this season of Lent to strengthen our understanding of the Spirit and our commitment to our Lord.

FOR YOUTH

■ **TOPIC:** Promised Power
■ **QUESTIONS:** 1. Why did Luke stress the fact that Jesus presented Himself alive to His followers *by many convincing proofs* (Acts 1:3)? 2. Why was it important for the disciples to be empowered by the Holy Spirit? 3. In what way would Jesus one day return to earth? 4. What do you think Jesus' disciples prayed about? 5. What evidence of the Spirit's power have you seen in your own life?

■ **ILLUSTRATIONS:**
Aptly Titled. The British sitcom *Waiting For God* is a weekly dose of half-hour stories of older individuals in a retirement home who are waiting to die. Their stories are intermixed with those of Tom Bellard, Diana Trent, and the staff in a hilarious comedy. Tragically, there are some of us who are still waiting for God. Like those residents, we sit, having forgotten that that the Lord has already reached out to us through Christ. And the Spirit is continually present to touch our lives.

At Risk. A special Senate committee warned in a February 1999 report that all segments of the U. S. economy were "at risk" from the year 2000 (Y2K) computer problem. While the study concluded that government and businesses have worked hard to correct the Y2K problem, efforts began too late and were insufficient. The report predicted blackouts from unprepared electric power companies, disruptions in travel and telecommunications, and problems in the health care industry. Citizens were advised to keep copies of financial statements and stockpile small amounts of food and water.

Some, though, stockpiled and hoarded huge amounts of food, fuel, ammunition, wood burning stoves, generators, and weapons. Others bought caves in remote areas and prepared to defend themselves. For instance, a group of about 20 families in the northeast bought 420 acres and erected solar heated homes. They also stockpiled vast amounts of dehydrated food. These were but one of the 200 communities that cropped up due to the fears of the Y2K problem!

Such individuals didn't want to feel powerless at the dawn of a new millennium. In contrast, Jesus reminded His followers that real power would not be found in weapons, refuges, and stockpiles of provisions. Rather, it would come from God. This power of the Holy Spirit would be unlike anything experienced previously.

Thawed for Immortality. The *Ice Man* toy is an object that is put together and then has water poured over it before being frozen. The child then melts the *Ice Man* with warm water syringes and scalpels to remove the "organs." *Time Magazine* asked if this might not encourage belief in immortal life through cryogenics. (Cryogenics is a branch of physics concerned with the production and maintenance of extremely low temperatures, and with the effects that occur under such conditions.)

As Christians, we know that immortality does not come through cryogenics. Rather, eternal life comes through faith in Christ. Nothing we do as humans can ever alter that truth.

The Holy Spirit Comes in Power

BACKGROUND SCRIPTURE: Acts 2
DEVOTIONAL READING: John 3:5-8

KEY VERSE: Peter said to them, "Repent, and be baptized every one of you in the name of Jesus Christ so that your sins may be forgiven; and you will receive the gift of the Holy Spirit." Acts 2:38.

KING JAMES VERSION

ACTS 2:1 And when the day of Pentecost was fully come, they were all with one accord in one place.

2 And suddenly there came a sound from heaven as of a rushing mighty wind, and it filled all the house where they were sitting.

3 And there appeared unto them cloven tongues like as of fire, and it sat upon each of them.

4 And they were all filled with the Holy Ghost, and began to speak with other tongues, as the Spirit gave them utterance. . . .

37 Now when they heard this, they were pricked in their heart, and said unto Peter and to the rest of the apostles, Men and brethren, what shall we do?

38 Then Peter said unto them, Repent, and be baptized every one of you in the name of Jesus Christ for the remission of sins, and ye shall receive the gift of the Holy Ghost.

39 For the promise is unto you, and to your children, and to all that are afar off, even as many as the LORD our God shall call.

40 And with many other words did he testify and exhort, saying, Save yourselves from this untoward generation.

41 Then they that gladly received his word were baptized: and the same day there were added unto them about three thousand souls.

42 And they continued stedfastly in the apostles' doctrine and fellowship, and in breaking of bread, and in prayers.

43 And fear came upon every soul: and many wonders and signs were done by the apostles.

44 And all that believed were together, and had all things common;

45 And sold their possessions and goods, and parted them to all men, as every man had need.

46 And they, continuing daily with one accord in the temple, and breaking bread from house to house, did eat their meat with gladness and singleness of heart,

47 Praising God, and having favour with all the people. And the Lord added to the church daily such as should be saved.

NEW REVISED STANDARD VERSION

ACTS 2:1 When the day of Pentecost had come, they were all together in one place. 2 And suddenly from heaven there came a sound like the rush of a violent wind, and it filled the entire house where they were sitting. 3 Divided tongues, as of fire, appeared among them, and a tongue rested on each of them. 4 All of them were filled with the Holy Spirit and began to speak in other languages, as the Spirit gave them ability. . . .

37 Now when they heard this, they were cut to the heart and said to Peter and to the other apostles, "Brothers, what should we do?" 38 Peter said to them, "Repent, and be baptized every one of you in the name of Jesus Christ so that your sins may be forgiven; and you will receive the gift of the Holy Spirit. 39 For the promise is for you, for your children, and for all who are far away, everyone whom the Lord our God calls to him." 40 And he testified with many other arguments and exhorted them, saying, "Save yourselves from this corrupt generation." 41 So those who welcomed his message were baptized, and that day about three thousand persons were added. 42 They devoted themselves to the apostles' teaching and fellowship, to the breaking of bread and the prayers.

43 Awe came upon everyone, because many wonders and signs were being done by the apostles. 44 All who believed were together and had all things in common; 45 they would sell their possessions and goods and distribute the proceeds to all, as any had need. 46 Day by day, as they spent much time together in the temple, they broke bread at home and ate their food with glad and generous hearts, 47 praising God and having the goodwill of all the people. And day by day the Lord added to their number those who were being saved.

HOME BIBLE READINGS

BACKGROUND

The significant events recorded in Acts 2 took place on the *day of Pentecost* (vs. 1). The latter term is a rendering of the Greek noun *pentekoste* [pen-tay-koss-TAY], which literally means the "Fiftieth Day" after the Sabbath of the Passover week (Lev. 23:4-7, 15-16).

The Jews celebrated Pentecost on the first day of the week, and it was one of the three great annual feasts of Israel, being preceded by Passover (Lev. 23:4-8; Num. 28:16-25) and followed four months later by the feast of tabernacles (Lev. 23:33-43; Num. 29:12-38). Pentecost is also called the feast of weeks (for it was observed seven weeks after Passover; Exod. 34:22; Deut. 16:9-10), the feast of harvest (for at that time God's people gathered the first fruits of their harvest; Exod. 23:16), and the day of the firstfruits (Num. 28:26).

The celebration is most often referred to as the feast of weeks (literally in Hebrew, *shavuot*). This festival originally was an agricultural celebration for the nation of Israel at the time of the spring harvest. God's people expressed their joy and gratitude for the Lord's provision of an abundant ingathering of crops. In later Judaism, Pentecost became the anniversary for the giving of the law to Moses at Mount Sinai. This is a reasonable possibility in light of the time notation recorded in Exodus 19:1.

Before A.D. 70, the fiftieth day after the Sabbath of Passover week was also the first day of the week. Thus, this method of reckoning would always place Pentecost on a Sunday. This explains why the coming of the Spirit and the beginning of the church, both of which are recorded in Acts 2:1-4, occurred on a Sunday.

NOTES ON THE PRINTED TEXT

Christ ascended into heaven 40 days after His resurrection and thus 10 days before Pentecost (Acts 1:2-3). He commanded His followers to wait in Jerusalem until He had sent to them the Holy Spirit (1:4-5). Earlier in His ministry, Jesus had stated that the Spirit would not be given until He Himself had been glorified (John 7:37-39). The Spirit's unique presence and ministries thus were essential for the fulfilling of the Great Commission, in which believers would travel throughout the world and make disciples from all nations (Matt.

28:18-20). However, without the presence and power of the Spirit, Jesus' followers would not be able to obey His command, and their evangelistic efforts would have ended in failure.

During the 10 days between Christ's ascension and Pentecost, there were about 120 disciples who waited and prayed for the coming of the Spirit (Acts 1:15). While Christ did not specifically state that He would send the Spirit during Pentecost, it is possible that the apostles were looking forward to something happening on that day (2:1).

Luke noted that God's Spirit suddenly came upon the disciples. His coming sounded like the roaring of a mighty windstorm above them. There was also the appearance of flames or tongues of fire appearing and settling on each person in the room. The disciples spoke in a variety of languages to those who had gathered in Jerusalem. *All of them were filled with the Holy Spirit and began to speak in other languages, as the Spirit gave them ability* (2:4).

As the disciples praised God in other tongues, Jews from different countries marveled at what was being said. Peter, under the guidance of the Spirit, explained to the crowds the meaning of this event. This phenomenon was evidence that God was fulfilling His promise to pour out His Spirit upon people (2:5-21).

The central topic of Peter's sermon was the resurrection of Jesus. The apostle interpreted what happened to the Messiah in light of Scripture. Peter patiently explained that he and his associates were witnesses to Jesus' resurrection and power (2:22-36).

When the crowd heard Peter's remarks, *they were cut to the heart and said to Peter and to the other apostles, "Brothers, what should we do?"* (2:37). Peter never hedged the demand. He declared, *"Repent, and be baptized every one of you in the name of Jesus Christ so that your sins may be forgiven; and you will receive the gift of the Holy Spirit"* (2:38). Peter reassured his listeners, *"For the promise is for you, for your children, and for all who are far away, everyone whom the Lord our God calls to him"* (2:39).

Peter continued preaching for some time. Throughout his sermon, he urged his listeners to *"Save yourselves from this corrupt generation"* (2:40). The only way to do this was by abandoning their sinful ways and turning to God through faith in Christ. In Him they would find mercy, forgiveness, kindness, and purpose.

Three thousand people enthusiastically responded to Peter's invitation and gave their lives to Christ. Rather than let the new believers drift, the disciples immediately shared the Gospel and how it applied to each of them. Groups met together, ate together, and prayed together to demonstrate their allegiance to Christ and to one another (2:41-42).

The Spirit produced a unified body that amazed many in Jerusalem. Luke detailed some of the extraordinary unity, particularly noting the exceptional generosity of some believers (2:43-47). For instance, the disciples *would sell their possessions and goods and distribute the proceeds to all, as any had need* (2:45).

SUGGESTIONS TO TEACHERS

Mention of the Holy Spirit may seem a little strange to some in your class. Perhaps they have not understood who the Spirit is or what the Spirit's coming means. Maybe some have dismissed all mention of the Spirit as irrelevant to their religious practice.

A study of Acts, however, makes it clear that the Spirit is relevant to the church. Also, every believer needs Him to live for the Savior. This week's lesson about the coming of the Spirit on the day of Pentecost will open up to your students a new and deeper understanding of how God wants to work in their lives. It should also encourage your class members to be more faithful and obedient to Christ.

1. THE GODLY CONFLAGRATION. The disciples on the day of Pentecost vividly remembered the Spirit's presence and power in their midst. He was among them in wind and fire! The Spirit's presence came upon them in such force that they were changed forever. He kindled a burning awareness of Christ's nearness and love. Be sure to discuss how the promise of the Spirit applies to Jesus' followers today. Are the members of your class fervent in their devotion to Christ?

2. THE CRITICAL COMMENTS. Some bystanders sneered at the way the Spirit-filled disciples expressed what happened. These critics claimed that the disciples were drunk (Acts 2:13). The disciples, however, didn't allow the put-downs and criticism to stop them from proclaiming the Gospel. Christians today also encounter critics. Let the students know that the Spirit can enable them to continue witnessing for Jesus despite opposition from unbelievers.

3. THE CONFIDENT COMMUNICATOR. Note that Peter was boldly preaching to the crowd. This was the same person who had previously denied being a follower of Jesus. What prompted Peter and his associates to risk their lives by telling people in Jerusalem about Christ and His resurrection? It was the power of the Spirit! The same Spirit empowers every Christian today to share his or her faith with others.

4. THE CONSTANT COMPANION. Some today whimper that God seems absent or that He has deserted them. But this isn't true of those who have been touched by the Spirit! Those rejoicing in the Spirit know they're never alone.

When we're saved, the Spirit lives in us and helps us live for Christ. When we yield control of our lives to the Spirit, He helps us overcome our selfish impulses. And when God's Spirit is in control of our lives, we consider other people's needs above our own wants and desires.

5. THE COMMITTED COMMUNITY. Those early Spirit-filled Christians were confident that they were empowered to carry on the ministry Jesus had entrusted to them. They were also committed to each other. They continually renewed their sense of belonging to Christ by worshiping God, sharing with one another joyfully, and telling the lost about Jesus. There were no isolationist tendencies among these believers! Have your students examine Acts 2:45-47 and discuss how the early Christian community displayed God's power and love.

■ TOPIC: Empowered by the Spirit

■ QUESTIONS: 1. Why do you think the Spirit showed Himself to the disciples both audibly and visibly? 2. Why did Peter urge his listeners to repent of their sins? 3. Why was Peter's message successful in reaching his listeners with the good news about Christ? 4. How can we be sure that the Spirit is present in our lives? 5. Why do some people tend to avoid helping others in need?

■ ILLUSTRATIONS:

Helping Others in Need. In *After Loss*, Robert Digiulio, a former principal of an elementary school, wrote about the tragedy of losing his wife and oldest daughter in a car accident. In the days following the incident, Digiulio and his two surviving daughters, Katie and Aimee, had to deal with loneliness and grief. There were times when the loss seemed unbearably great and the sorrow too overwhelming to handle. Digiulio could not make it through the difficult moments alone. He needed the assistance of other people. Thankfully, friends were willing to help him through his crisis.

Looking back on those days, Digiulio wrote the following:

> I was grateful for my friends. Since the crash many offered, "If you need anything, Bob, just call." And if I did ask them to watch Katie so I could go to the dentist, or drive Aimee to day camp, or help me hoist a ladder to the roof, they jumped at the opportunity. People were wonderful. We couldn't have gotten through those weeks without them.

God also wants us to help others in need. By doing so, we show them that the Spirit is present and powerfully at work in our lives.

Walking His Walk. The Israel National Parks Authority has proposed the construction of a 262-foot-long bridge built just beneath the surface of the water in the Sea of Galilee near the site of ancient Capernaum so that tourists can "walk in the footsteps of Jesus." The contractor and entrepreneur expect to attract 80,000 visitors a year to pay to follow Jesus by walking on water. The owner assures everyone who comes that lifeguards will be on duty to assist any who stray from the underwater pathway. (Thankfully, this project has been cancelled.)

Such theme park tourist attractions tend to trivialize the power, love, and mercy of Christ. Walking in the footsteps of Jesus means allowing the Spirit to empower us to live virtuously, humbly, and sacrificially.

Jerusalem Syndrome. Occasionally visitors to Jerusalem seem to get carried away with a misguided sense of spiritual excitement. Several have burned passports and sat on the Mount of Olives as they wait for Christ's return. Others have donned robes and announced themselves to be the Messiah. One man even ran naked through the streets brandishing a sword as a self-anointed prophet.

Dr. Yair Carlos Bar-El, a Jerusalem psychiatrist who has studied and treated many such deluded persons, calls the malady "the Jerusalem Syndrome." He states that most patients snap out of it after rest and counseling, and are then extremely embarrassed about their bizarre behavior.

The believers on the day of Pentecost were not suffering from any sort of "Jerusalem Syndrome." What they saw, said, and did was the work of the Spirit in their lives. Far from being delusional, they knew that Jesus had risen from the dead, and they wanted to tell as many people as possible this good news. At one time they were timid and uncertain followers of Jesus. But now they were infused with His power and presence. They burst forth from the Upper Room on to the main streets of Jerusalem and eventually the entire Roman world!

FOR YOUTH ■ **TOPIC:** Moved by Power
■ **QUESTIONS:** 1. Why was it important for the disciples to be united in thought and purpose? 2. Why was Christ's resurrection central to Peter's sermon? 3. Why do you think the early believers felt it was important to share what they owned with one another? 4. Why do we need the Spirit in our lives? 5. How does God's Spirit help you become more sensitive to the needs of others?

■ **ILLUSTRATIONS:**

One Person's Power. What can one young person do? Kim Maschi will tell you that even a seventh grader can be empowered to do a lot. Back in 1996, Kim, a 12-year-old seventh grade student at a middle school in Massachusetts, read that soccer balls were being made by children as young as 5 to 11 years old in southeast Asia. These children were forced to work all day, six days a week.

Soccer balls, Kim learned, have to be made by hand, sewn one by one. Kim discovered that a child could only make about one soccer ball a day, and got paid about 60 cents for that day's work. Evidence turned up that many of these children are injured or crippled by the work, and when that happens, they are simply replaced with other children. Kim's research also turned up evidence that children working in soccer ball sweatshops are not going to school and get no medical benefits for their injuries.

Kim said, "American companies are some of the ones bringing these handmade soccer balls into our country and onto our soccer fields." She joined with others in a movement called "Foul-Ball Campaign" to enlighten people to the realities behind those new soccer balls bought in sporting goods shops or ordered by athletic departments of schools and colleges. Tragically, Kim and others got little response from the people she tried to contact.

Concerned that children in sweatshops were being forced to sew soccer balls for other kids to play with, and determined to use what power she had to bring her concern to those who could change things, Kim wrote to the columnist of her local newspaper. This person contacted Kim and decided to help. The columnist began by getting in touch with the national director of Foul-Ball Campaign.

The director and Kim have been working with other grassroots groups through their organization. The Foul-Ball Campaign is also pushing the Federation of International Football Associations (known as FIFA) to use soccer balls only from manufacturers who have been regularly inspected in accordance with procedures created by UNICEF. These procedures ensure that no child labor was used in the manufacturing process.

Kim and other young persons are seeking to make a difference in the world. God also wants you, as a Christian young person, to make a difference for Him. With the help of His Spirit, you have the power to make an important contribution to society.

Effects of Power. At Pittsburgh's Carnegie Science Center, the lecturer was discussing electrical energy and needed someone to touch the Van de Graff Generator. Blair volunteered to go forward and place her right hand on the large shiny silver ball. As she touched the device, her long blond hair rose up on her head. While no one in the audience could see the electrical charge, the effects were quite obvious.

On the day of Pentecost, no one could actually see the Spirit. However, His presence was powerfully evident to Jesus' followers. The Spirit enabled them to be bold in their witness and sensitive to the needs of their fellow believers.

The Holy Spirit Works with Power

BACKGROUND SCRIPTURE: Acts 3:1—4:13
DEVOTIONAL READING: 1 Corinthians 1:26-31

KEY VERSE: When they saw the boldness of Peter and John and realized that they were uneducated and ordinary men, they were amazed and recognized them as companions of Jesus. Acts 4:13.

KING JAMES VERSION

ACTS 3:1 Now Peter and John went up together into the temple at the hour of prayer, being the ninth hour.

2 And a certain man lame from his mother's womb was carried, whom they laid daily at the gate of the temple which is called Beautiful, to ask alms of them that entered into the temple;

3 Who seeing Peter and John about to go into the temple asked an alms.

4 And Peter, fastening his eyes upon him with John, said, Look on us.

5 And he gave heed unto them, expecting to receive something of them.

6 Then Peter said, Silver and gold have I none; but such as I have give I thee: In the name of Jesus Christ of Nazareth rise up and walk.

7 And he took him by the right hand, and lifted him up: and immediately his feet and ankle bones received strength.

8 And he leaping up stood, and walked, and entered with them into the temple, walking, and leaping, and praising God.

9 And all the people saw him walking and praising God:

10 And they knew that it was he which sat for alms at the Beautiful gate of the temple: and they were filled with wonder and amazement at that which had happened unto him. . . .

4:1 And as they spake unto the people, the priests, and the captain of the temple, and the Sadducees, came upon them,

2 Being grieved that they taught the people, and preached through Jesus the resurrection from the dead.

3 And they laid hands on them, and put them in hold unto the next day: for it was now eventide.

4 Howbeit many of them which heard the word believed; and the number of the men was about five thousand. . . .

13 Now when they saw the boldness of Peter and John, and perceived that they were unlearned and ignorant men, they marvelled; and they took knowledge of them, that they had been with Jesus.

NEW REVISED STANDARD VERSION

ACTS 3:1 One day Peter and John were going up to the temple at the hour of prayer, at three o'clock in the afternoon. 2 And a man lame from birth was being carried in. People would lay him daily at the gate of the temple called the Beautiful Gate so that he could ask for alms from those entering the temple. 3 When he saw Peter and John about to go into the temple, he asked them for alms. 4 Peter looked intently at him, as did John, and said, "Look at us." 5 And he fixed his attention on them, expecting to receive something from them. 6 But Peter said, "I have no silver or gold, but what I have I give you; in the name of Jesus Christ of Nazareth, stand up and walk." 7 And he took him by the right hand and raised him up; and immediately his feet and ankles were made strong. 8 Jumping up, he stood and began to walk, and he entered the temple with them, walking and leaping and praising God. 9 All the people saw him walking and praising God, 10 and they recognized him as the one who used to sit and ask for alms at the Beautiful Gate of the temple; and they were filled with wonder and amazement at what had happened to him. . . .

4:1 While Peter and John were speaking to the people, the priests, the captain of the temple, and the Sadducees came to them, 2 much annoyed because they were teaching the people and proclaiming that in Jesus there is the resurrection of the dead. 3 So they arrested them and put them in custody until the next day, for it was already evening. 4 But many of those who heard the word believed; and they numbered about five thousand. . . .

13 Now when they saw the boldness of Peter and John and realized that they were uneducated and ordinary men, they were amazed and recognized them as companions of Jesus.

HOME BIBLE READINGS

Monday, March 12	Acts 3:1-10	*Peter Heals a Crippled Beggar*
Tuesday, March 13	Acts 3:11-16	*Peter's Sermon in Solomon's Portico*
Wednesday, March 14	Acts 3:17-21	*Peter Calls for Repentance*
Thursday, March 15	Acts 3:22-26	*Jesus Is the Promised Messiah*
Friday, March 16	Acts 4:1-4	*The Rise of Persecution*
Saturday, March 17	Acts 4:8-12	*Peter and John before the Council*
Sunday, March 18	1 Cor. 1:26-31	*No Boasting in God's Presence*

BACKGROUND

Luke evidently wrote Acts as a defense of Christianity to Theophilus [thee-AH-fih-lus] to show him that there was nothing subversive or sinister about the followers of Jesus. Luke demonstrated through his narrative that the imperial officials of Rome were impartial regarding Christianity. In fact, in no instance recorded in Acts did the Roman officials persecute the church (unless we view the local officials in 16:22-23 as an exception).

The geographical framework of Acts, which details the spread of Christianity from Jerusalem to Rome, lends support to this idea. Undoubtedly, Luke saw himself as a recorder of the events surrounding Jesus' ministry and the establishment of the church. One could say that Jesus remained the active living focus of Acts, especially since the church existed to advance His cause.

Luke also detailed the work of the Spirit to continue Jesus' ministry of salvation and grace. This explains why the book is filled with transitions, such as from the ministry of Jesus to that of the apostles, from the old covenant to the new covenant, and from Israel to the church.

The writer evidenced a concern for outcasts and sinners, such as the Ethiopian official (8:26-40), Cornelius (10:1-48), and the Philippian jailer (16:22-34). Though such people might have been rejected by religious legalists in Palestine, they were accepted and redeemed by Christ. Luke likewise placed an emphasis on women. Though they did not occupy a central role in Jewish worship, they played a key role in the spread of the Gospel. The writer referred to such women as Lydia (16:11-15, 40) and Priscilla (18:18-20), not to mention the countless conversions of unnamed women at various stops on Paul's missionary journeys.

Luke also stressed the dedication of Jesus' followers. In fact, all the principal characters of Acts demonstrated great devotion to God and tremendous personal discipline in their spiritual lives. This is evident, for example, in the account of Peter's healing of the crippled beggar—the subject of this week's lesson.

NOTES ON THE PRINTED TEXT

Jesus' followers at first were centered in Jerusalem. They also considered themselves to be faithful Jews. As such, they continued to observe their traditional Jewish practices, including worshiping regularly at the temple. Of course, at that time there were no church buildings, and those who gathered in the name of Jesus met in homes. The ousting of Christians from the temple and synagogues had not yet taken place.

One day at three o'clock in the afternoon Peter and John approached the temple precincts. Most likely this was a regular practice for them and other early followers of Jesus. *Peter and John were going up to the temple at the hour of prayer, at three o'clock in the afternoon* (Acts 3:1). As the two disciples made their way forward, they saw a crippled beggar *being carried in. People would lay him daily at the gate of the temple called the Beautiful Gate so that he could ask for alms from those entering the temple* (3:2).

The great temple in Jerusalem had eight gates at the top of stairs and set within the walls. (At places, this wall was 60 feet high.) The largest of these gates was a triple gate tunnel. Each dome, some 20 feet high, was built of huge stone blocks that had been worked to a smooth finish. The domes in the ceilings of the gates were 16 feet in diameter and embossed with a variety of floral and geometric decorations, all painted in bright colors. And the doors were elaborately decorated and covered with Corinthian bronze sheeting. Perhaps it's this brilliant appearance that led to one of the gates being called *Beautiful* (3:2). (It's usually thought to be the Gate of Nicanor.)

To this gate a crippled man was brought each day by friends so that he could beg for handouts from those who passed by. On this day, the beggar spotted Peter and John and asked them for some money. *When he saw Peter and John about to go into the temple, he asked them for alms* (3:3).

The two apostles stopped, and Peter said to the man, *"Look at us"* (3:4). The cripple stopped pleading and did as he had been told, perhaps expecting Peter to give him some coins. Instead of seeing a hand thrust him some alms, the beggar heard Peter say, *"I have no silver or gold, but what I have I give you; in the name of Jesus Christ of Nazareth, stand up and walk"* (3:6).

At that moment a miracle occurred. As Peter lifted the beggar, he who had never learned to stand, let alone walk and leap, was on his feet, moving about freely, and praising God. The man was filled with joy as he accompanied the apostles inside the temple. *Immediately his feet and ankles were made strong. Jumping up, he stood and began to walk, and he entered the temple with them, walking and leaping and praising God* (3:7-8).

The man's noisy presence drew a crowd, and many people recognized him (3:9-10). Luke noted that *all the people ran together to them in the portico called Solomon's Portico* (3:11). The colonnaded corridor bordered on the east side of the outer court of the temple and rested on a massive Herodian retaining wall (which is still largely visible as the lower courses of the present temple-area wall) built out over the Kidron Valley. Solomon's Portico may have been so named because of a tradition that Solomon had once constructed a similar east wall and colonnade.

Peter, not one to pass up the opportunity to preach, explained to the crowd that the man clinging to him and John had been healed through Jesus' power. This was the same Jesus whom the authorities had killed but whom God had resurrected from the dead (3:12-26).

Peter's sermon drew the attention of the religious authorities. The priests, officers of the temple police, and the Sadducees arrived, livid that Peter was preaching the Resurrection. As a result of Pentecost, thousands had been converted, and now another large group had congregated and was actively listening to the Gospel. Though Peter and John were arrested, this didn't prevent thousands more from committing themselves to Christ (4:1-4).

Following a night in jail, the disciples were led before the Jewish high council, the same one that had condemned Jesus to death (Luke 22:66). During the trial, Peter boldly witnessed about Jesus' resurrection and the salvation He offers. The judges then released the two apostles with a warning not to preach in Jesus' name anymore (Acts 4:5-22).

SUGGESTIONS TO TEACHERS

Contrary to what some think, the Spirit is not given to make us feel warm inside. Rather, God gives us the Spirit so that we can have the power to serve the risen Lord. This week's lesson will help your students understand that the Spirit empowers them to continue the work that Jesus did.

1. EMPOWERED TO HEAL. Part of Jesus' ministry was to bring about spiritual, emotional, and physical wellness in the lives of people. According to Acts, the early Christians continued this healing ministry. Sometimes church people shy away from any talk about God's ability to heal us from our afflictions. Why not take this opportunity to briefly discuss the issue with your students? For example, how has God dramatically changed their lives or the lives of people they know?

2. EMPOWERED TO PREACH. Preaching doesn't just mean standing up in a pulpit on Sunday morning. Every believer can—and should—be able to say something about the love of God through Christ. Remind the class members that evangelism means heralding the good news. Declaring the Gospel is not an optional matter, though. God wants all Jesus' followers to be involved in this great work. "But how can I say anything?" some might ask. The answer is simple and clear. The Spirit empowers every believer who asks for help.

3. EMPOWERED TO PERSEVERE. Peter and John were undaunted by threats and jailing. They testified boldly about Jesus before the authorities. People could see that Peter and John had been with Jesus (Acts 4:13). Are those around us able to make that kind of observation? The empowering Spirit strengthened these early Christians to continue serving the Lord despite opposition. They refused to use the excuses we sometimes give (such as feeling overwhelmed or burned out). Furthermore, the early Christians persevered, not by claiming any human stamina or personal strength, but by relying on the Spirit. So must we!

■ **TOPIC:** Empowered for Service

■ **QUESTIONS:** 1. Why was what Peter gave the disabled man better than what he first expected? 2. Why were the Sanhedrin members concerned about the apostles' authorization to heal? 3. What is most striking to you about Peter's statements before the Sanhedrin? Why? 4. When might it be advisable to use the negative approach in preaching repentance? How about the positive approach? 5. What stories of changed lives have strengthened your faith in Christ's resurrection power?

■ **ILLUSTRATIONS:**

A Perseverer. The story of a man named Patrick illustrates the power of the Spirit in a Christian's life. Born into a devout family's home in ancient Britain, Patrick was carried off when he was 16 by marauding raiders and taken as a slave to Ireland. He was forced to tend pigs and endured cruel treatment at the hands of his pagan captors. His afflictions strengthened his faith in the Lord, and this enabled him to survive his ordeal.

Patrick escaped by walking 200 miles, and then he took a ship that carried him to Gaul. When he finally got home to his family in Britain, he announced that he sensed God was calling him to return to Ireland. His family couldn't understand why he'd risk his life and waste his time by going back to the brutal, rough pagans who had mistreated him. Furthermore, Patrick had little formal learning. When he started classes to be ordained, he was ridiculed by the scholarly, sophisticated church leaders for his poor skills in rhetoric and classical Latin. His rustic manners and lack of education credentials caused the snobbish upper class to hesitate to ordain him. But despite opposition, he was finally ordained and commissioned to go to Ireland as a missionary.

Patrick suffered persecution by the native Irish and false charges by British church officials, showing that they continued to regard him as being unfit for ordination. Worse was Patrick's reception by Irish kings and Druids. He narrowly escaped death several times, especially when he challenged the pagan king by lighting a fire celebrating the resurrection of Christ before the ruler started the flame of a heathen nature celebration. Patrick was imprisoned twice for long weeks by Irish enemies. But he persevered.

In one generation this great missionary brought the light of Christ and the torch of western civilization to the natives on the bleak fringe of Europe. Patrick and his colleagues are credited with preserving the ancient learning that had been almost destroyed by the Vandals, Huns, and Goths in the looting, burning, and chaos that swept the continent after the fall of Rome. Society's debt to Patrick is greater than most realize!

Freedom Fighter. Over 150 years ago, a brave woman named Harriet Tubman escaped from slavery. But her own freedom was not enough. She risked her life

19 more times to rescue other slaves. Harriet Tubman became the most famous conductor on the Underground Railroad, leading over 300 persons to freedom.

Harriet was born a slave in Bucktown, Maryland, around 1820. Her owners forced her to labor in the fields, and she became strong. When she was about 12, Harriet was struck on the head by an angry overseer because she refused to help tie up a runaway to be whipped. The blow caused her severe headaches the rest of her life. When she was about 29, she learned that she was to be sold and sent to a plantation farther south. She finally decided to escape.

Harriet walked 90 miles to reach Pennsylvania and continue to Canada. Her deep faith sustained her and motivated her to make daring trips back to the slave areas to guide others north to freedom. This won her the nickname, "Moses of her people." Slave owners feared her so much that they put out a reward of $40,000 for her capture. But not one person she led to freedom was recaptured or killed.

Later, during the Civil War, Harriet Tubman served as a nurse, guide, cook, and soldier for the Union Army. Eventually, she was able to buy a house and 26 acres in Auburn, New York. In 1903, Harriet gave the buildings and property to her church to be used as a home for the aged. This great, empowered leader passed away in 1913. She exhibited a courage akin to that of Peter in this week's Scripture text.

FOR YOUTH

■ TOPIC: Power Works

■ QUESTIONS: 1. What role do you think faith played in the healing of the lame man? 2. What transformed Peter from a coward to a courageous spokesperson for Christ? 3. How do you think the religious authorities felt when they discovered that the name of Jesus was still being invoked? 4. In what ways do you rejoice at how God has changed you? 5. Should you rejoice when the process of change is painful? If so, why?

■ ILLUSTRATIONS:

Any Correlation? Dr. Richard Sloan of Columbia University published a report in the British medical journal, *The Lancet*, that the evidence of an association between religion and health was inconsistent and weak. He questioned whether faith boosted healing. He urged fellow doctors to be cautious when recommending faith as an aid to physical recovery.

How would Peter and John have responded? With complete faith in Christ and His presence, they healed a cripple. God's power was unmistakable in this incident. The overwhelming testimony of Scripture is that the Lord can bring about spiritual, emotional, and physical wellness in the lives of people.

Support System. On Christmas Day, 1994, Kimberly's life suddenly changed. As she was about to join her family for dinner, the eighth grader from Pennsylvania suffered a seizure that caused her head to twitch to the right and drained the color from her eyes. Doctors discovered that the arteries and veins in her brain were severely tangled and that she was divinely blessed to be alive. Most cases such as Kimberly's produce a fatal stroke. In April 1995, she underwent a nine-hour surgical procedure to shrink the malformation. She also began to take an anti-seizure medication. Now she attends college and plans to become a pediatrician.

Kimberly's life was transformed by a variety of people who became her support system. Tutors volunteered to teach her at home so that she could maintain her B average and enable her to graduate with her classmates. Her swimming coach and her teammates supported her throughout the dangerous illness, even giving her a varsity letter the evening before her surgery. Kimberly's guidance counselor helped her through the long medical ordeal as did another counselor at the local Make-A-Wish Foundation.

Like all these people, God wants us to demonstrate His life-transforming love to others. After all, He says in His Word, *Little children, let us love, not in word or speech, but in truth and action* (1 John 3:18).

Taking Faith on the Road. A group of churchmen from Illinois chartered a bus to a two-day Christian men's conference in a nearby state. While going to the conference, the men were irritated by the driver, who couldn't locate their motel and insisted on smoking. "He had a kind of uncaring attitude and was in his own little world," said one of the leaders.

During the conference the men experienced a touch from God, and the trip home was like a rolling revival. "We sang some songs and asked for testimonies, and we had about three hours' worth," said a member of the group. "We almost asked the bus driver to slow down so we could get all the testimonies in!"

As they neared home, the men passed a hat and collected $100 for the driver. He had tears in his eyes and said, "The gift is great, but what I'm hearing from you guys is worth a lot more." Back in the church parking lot they formed a circle of prayer, and even the bus driver got involved.

The power of Christ brings renewal to believers as well as changing those who approach Him for the first time. (Taken from an account in the *Aurora Beacon News*.)

OBEDIENT TO THE SPIRIT

BACKGROUND SCRIPTURE: Acts 5:12-42
DEVOTIONAL READING: Psalm 103:15-18

KEY VERSE: Peter and the apostles answered, "We must obey God rather than any human authority." Acts 5:29.

KING JAMES VERSION

ACTS 5:27 And when they had brought them, they set them before the council: and the high priest asked them,

28 Saying, Did not we straitly command you that ye should not teach in this name? and, behold, ye have filled Jerusalem with your doctrine, and intend to bring this man's blood upon us.

29 Then Peter and the other apostles answered and said, We ought to obey God rather than men.

30 The God of our fathers raised up Jesus, whom ye slew and hanged on a tree.

31 Him hath God exalted with his right hand to be a Prince and a Saviour, for to give repentance to Israel, and forgiveness of sins.

32 And we are his witnesses of these things; and so is also the Holy Ghost, whom God hath given to them that obey him.

33 When they heard that, they were cut to the heart, and took counsel to slay them.

34 Then stood there up one in the council, a Pharisee, named Gamaliel, a doctor of the law, had in reputation among all the people, and commanded to put the apostles forth a little space;

35 And said unto them, Ye men of Israel, take heed to yourselves what ye intend to do as touching these men.

36 For before these days rose up Theudas, boasting himself to be somebody; to whom a number of men, about four hundred, joined themselves: who was slain; and all, as many as obeyed him, were scattered, and brought to nought. . . .

38 And now I say unto you, Refrain from these men, and let them alone: for if this counsel or this work be of men, it will come to nought:

39 But if it be of God, ye cannot overthrow it; lest haply ye be found even to fight against God.

40 And to him they agreed: and when they had called the apostles, and beaten them, they commanded that they should not speak in the name of Jesus, and let them go.

41 And they departed from the presence of the council, rejoicing that they were counted worthy to suffer shame for his name.

42 And daily in the temple, and in every house, they ceased not to teach and preach Jesus Christ.

NEW REVISED STANDARD VERSION

ACTS 5:27 When they had brought them, they had them stand before the council. The high priest questioned them, 28 saying, "We gave you strict orders not to teach in this name, yet here you have filled Jerusalem with your teaching and you are determined to bring this man's blood on us." 29 But Peter and the apostles answered, "We must obey God rather than any human authority. 30 The God of our ancestors raised up Jesus, whom you had killed by hanging him on a tree. 31 God exalted him at his right hand as Leader and Savior that he might give repentance to Israel and forgiveness of sins. 32 And we are witnesses to these things, and so is the Holy Spirit whom God has given to those who obey him."

33 When they heard this, they were enraged and wanted to kill them. 34 But a Pharisee in the council named Gamaliel, a teacher of the law, respected by all the people, stood up and ordered the men to be put outside for a short time. 35 Then he said to them, "Fellow Israelites, consider carefully what you propose to do to these men. 36 For some time ago Theudas rose up, claiming to be somebody, and a number of men, about four hundred, joined him; but he was killed, and all who followed him were dispersed and disappeared. . . . 38 So in the present case, I tell you, keep away from these men and let them alone; because if this plan or this undertaking is of human origin, it will fail; 39 but if it is of God, you will not be able to overthrow them—in that case you may even be found fighting against God!"

They were convinced by him, 40 and when they had called in the apostles, they had them flogged. Then they ordered them not to speak in the name of Jesus, and let them go. 41 As they left the council, they rejoiced that they were considered worthy to suffer dishonor for the sake of the name. 42 And every day in the temple and at home they did not cease to teach and proclaim Jesus as the Messiah.

Monday, March 19	Acts 5:1-11	*Ananias and Sapphira Sin and Die*
Tuesday, March 20	Acts 5:12-16	*The Apostles Heal Many*
Wednesday, March 21	1 Thessalonians 1	*Life and Faith of Believers*
Thursday, March 22	Acts 5:17-23	*Persecution and Relief*
Friday, March 23	Acts 5:24-28	*Arrest and Accusation*
Saturday, March 24	Acts 5:29-32	*The Answer of the Apostles*
Sunday, March 25	Acts. 5:34-42	*The Warning of Gamaliel*

BACKGROUND

The Book of Acts provides us with our best close-up look at the early days of the church. We quickly note that the spread of the Gospel was neither smooth nor easy. The opposition was formidable. The fledgling community of Jesus' followers survived only because of their unflagging obedience to the Spirit. Had it not been for His empowering presence, the movement that started on the day of Pentecost would have quickly been snuffed out.

The religious authorities in Jerusalem were able to intimidate most people by their threats and punishments. They even forced powerful Roman officials to back down on occasion. When these temple leaders dragged Peter and his associates before them under arrest, they expected Jesus' followers to knuckle under and quit stirring up the populace with their claims about the Savior. Instead, the religious leaders were confronted with prisoners who stubbornly refused to be cowed by anything or anyone. The authorities discovered that Christians were willing to accept suffering rather than give in to threats or even death.

In fact, Peter and others bravely used their appearances before the temple leaders as opportunities to speak out about Jesus. When the authorities tried to silence the disciples, these early Christians made it clear that they had to put their obedience to God ahead of obedience to everyone and everything else.

NOTES ON THE PRINTED TEXT

The religious authorities had sternly warned the apostles not to preach in the name of Jesus. The apostles, however, were not intimidated and continued to witness. This led to their arrest and jailing. That night an angel of the Lord released them. At daybreak they returned to their preaching in the temple. Meanwhile, the Jewish council met to decide what to do with the apostles. But during their formal hearing, they discovered that not only had the apostles escaped but also that they were in the temple speaking of Jesus' power (Acts 5:12-25).

The captain went with his temple guards and arrested the apostles, but without violence, for they were afraid the people would kill them if they treated the apostles roughly (5:26). Then the authorities brought the apostles before the council (5:27). The mood was tense. The high priest charged the apostles with disobedience. *"We gave you strict orders not to teach in this name, yet here you have filled*

Jerusalem with your teaching and you are determined to bring this man's blood on us" (5:28).

In response to the high priest, the apostles—with Peter as their spokesperson—did not hesitate to announce, *"We must obey God rather than any human authority"* (5:29). Peter was declaring that the apostles' ultimate allegiance was to Christ. Not even the Jewish council could usurp the Savior's authority.

Peter continued, *"The God of our ancestors raised up Jesus, whom you had killed by hanging him on a tree. God exalted him at his right hand as Leader and Savior that he might give repentance to Israel and forgiveness of sins"* (5:30-31). In other words, the same God who had bound Himself to Israel was continuing to provide salvation for His people through faith in Christ. Jesus' resurrection was proof that He was Israel's Lord and Redeemer.

Peter then declared to the council, *"And we are witnesses to these things"* (5:32). In other words, the good news about Jesus was true, not false. In fact, the Holy Spirit affirmed the truth of Christ's resurrection and exaltation. The Spirit is the one *"whom God has given to those who obey him."*

The normally staid leaders were furious. They wanted the apostles immediately executed. *When they heard this, they were enraged and wanted to kill them.* (5:33). But one council member, Gamaliel, remained calm as he rose to speak. He was a Pharisee whom the general population liked. Though the majority of the Sanhedrin were Sadducees and opponents of the Pharisees, Gamaliel was much respected.

Gamaliel ordered that the apostles be removed from the council's chambers. Then he addressed the Sanhedrin. *"Fellow Israelites, consider carefully what you propose to do to these men"* (5:35). Gamaliel then cited several examples of would-be messiahs and failed uprisings. Theudas had led his fanatics in an abortive revolt against Rome. His effort was crushed in 4 B.C. After him came Judas "the Galilean" who led a revolt in A.D. 6. He, too, was killed and his followers were scattered (5:36-37).

Gamaliel advocated a wait-and-see attitude. He urged the members of the council to leave the followers of Jesus alone. If His disciples were teaching and doing things merely on their own will, their movement would soon be overthrown (5:38). *"But if it is of God, you will not be able to overthrow them—in that case you may even be found fighting against God!"* (5:39).

Gamaliel's motion passed, and the apostles' lives were spared. But the council members refused to dismiss the apostles without some kind of punishment and warning. Out of sight of the crowds in the streets, they had the apostles flogged. *Then they ordered them not to speak in the name of Jesus, and let them go* (5:40).

Instead of leaving feeling shamed and afraid, the apostles departed joyfully, praising God that they *were considered worthy to suffer dishonor for the sake of the name* (5:41). Difficult circumstances could not conquer them, for they belonged to the Lord.

In addition, the apostles refused to let the religious authorities squelch their proclamation of the Gospel. They were divinely compelled to tell others about the Savior. *And every day in the temple and at home they did not cease to teach and proclaim Jesus as the Messiah* (5:42).

SUGGESTIONS TO TEACHERS

We live in an age when individual freedom is considered the greatest value. And we are told that we should try to feel free from as many constraints as possible. The word "obedience" is used only for dogs and perhaps new recruits at boot camp. That's why this week's lesson about obeying God may not appeal to modern listeners. Though obedience to God does not take place easily or willingly, it is nonetheless possible. As we will learn, only the Spirit can move us to obey the Lord!

1. ESCAPE FROM JAIL. Acts 5:17-26 provides a touch of humor in the narrative of the early days of the church by describing the apostles' jailbreak and the consternation of the authorities. The point, however, is to stress that the Lord watches over His faithful followers. This may sometimes take the form of literally rescuing a Christian from the depths of a dungeon. At other times God may free a believer from the depths of despair. Have your students consider different types of "imprisonments" that may chain them. How has the Lord helped them to "escape" from these hampering situations?

2. OBEDIENT TO GOD. Despite arrest and mistreatment from the authorities, the apostles' obedience to God never faltered. It meant standing firm in the face of the terrifying threats of the powerful civil and religious authorities. Encourage the members of your class to discuss where it will be hardest for them in the coming week to obey God.

3. ADVICE FROM GAMALIEL. Gamaliel presented some sound advice about reacting to religious movements. Unless adherents in these groups endorse obviously dangerous doctrines or practices, it is often wiser to be tolerant rather than repressive. Sometimes only time will tell if they are merely the work of humans or if God is trying to say something through them. God's ways will always prevail!

4. INSISTENCE ON EVANGELIZING. Note that obedience to the Spirit came from regular, disciplined worship, both publicly and privately. In addition, teaching and witnessing were considered vital. Discuss how your students can become more disciplined in doing these things.

FOR ADULTS

■ TOPIC: Spirit-Empowered Obedience

■ QUESTIONS: 1. How do you think the apostles felt as they stood before the council? 2. Why did the apostles stress obedience to God over any human authority? 3. Who was Gamaliel, and what advice did he give to the Jewish council? 4. Do you think subtle attacks to the Christian faith are more dangerous or less dangerous than overt attacks? Why? 5. As your commitment to Christ is challenged, what things might you lose when you decide to obey God? What might you gain?

■ ILLUSTRATIONS:

Shallow Spirituality. Large majorities of Americans say they are religious and claim that spirituality is important. However, that does not seem to be translated into any form of Spirit-empowered obedience. Few show commitment to a single faith, a local congregation, or regular time of corporate worship. A MacArthur Foundation survey recently indicated that more than seven out ten Americans say they feel religious and consider spirituality to have a key role in their lives. But about half attend services either never or less than once a month.

Another study, this one done by the Barna Research Group, disclosed that nearly one-third of America's adults have not attended a worship service in the past six months other than for a special event. This same study found that 31 percent of Americans—a proportion representing between 60 to 65 million adults—could be classified as "unchurched" because they were not present at any Christian worship service during the past six months (other than a wedding or funeral or a holiday service such as Christmas Eve or Easter). Eighteen months earlier, researchers from the Barna Group found that 27 percent of adults could be called unchurched. The younger and more educated a person is, the study discovered, the less likely she or he would be attached to any congregation.

"Spirituality in the U.S. is a mile wide and an inch deep," reported David Kinnaman of the Barna Research Group. "Though there is an all-time high interest in spirituality," Kinnaman added, "people are beginning to develop a hybrid personal faith that integrates different perspectives from different religions that may even be contradictory. But that doesn't seem to bother them."

What a contrast this is to the Spirit-empowered obedience we see in the early Christians. They were clear about what they believed and the one they served.

Perseverance Pays Off. Barry Clifford and his dogged crew were certain in 1984 that they had located the remains of a pirate ship, the Whydah, off the coast of Cape Cod. Experts doubted their claims of finding the vessel, which had been commanded by "Black Sam" Bellamy. The ship went down off Marconi Beach during a storm in 1717 with a reputed fortune in loot.

Most persons dismissed Clifford and his fellow workers as either silly or stupid. Skeptics were convinced they would never find the real treasure ship. Even when Clifford and his crew brought up the ship's bell marked with the name of the Whydah, critics scoffed that he had had a fake bell made. The diver who worked with Clifford from the start said that he and the rest of their party "just stopped listening to it all." The diver also added, "We persevered!"

This meant the crew had to heed their conviction that they had located the wreckage of the Whydah. Their determination paid off. Not only was the ship's bell proved to be authentic but also rare. African gold jewelry, silver coins, cannons, flintlock pistols, and other artifacts worth $10 million so far have been recovered. Estimates run as high as $400 million for the treasure from the nearly 110,000 items that will be salvaged from the sunken wreck. Recognition finally came when the National Geographic Society honored the persevering Whydah salvagers with a special award ceremony in 1999.

This is the kind of perseverance that God calls believers to maintain in their faith. Through the power of the Spirit, they can prevail in their service for Christ.

Toss-Up Obedience. There's an old story about a man who drove to his country club one Sunday morning. Breathlessly, he rushed into the locker room to change into his golf shoes. When someone asked why he was late, the man replied, "Well, it was a toss-up between whether I'd go to church or play golf this morning." He paused reflectively, then added, "And I had to toss up fifteen times!" Is this what our obedience to Christ should be like?

■ TOPIC: Power Words

■ QUESTIONS: 1. Why were the members of the council upset at being blamed for Jesus' crucifixion? 2. Why did the apostles stress that the Spirit bore witness to the good news of salvation? 3. Why did the council have the apostles flogged? 4. How can Christians distinguish between a real challenge to their faith in Christ and a restriction that they just don't like? 5. In what ways, if at all, should we model our behavior after the apostles' reaction to the Sanhedrin?

■ **ILLUSTRATIONS:**

On a Mission. Peggy Wehmeyer may not be a national news anchor, but she is network television's only full-time religion reporter working for ABC (American Broadcasting Company). Claiming that her faith makes her a better reporter, she has scored some exclusive stories, such as interviewing the McCaugheys (the parents of Iowa's septuplets) and Rex Horne (President Clinton's pastor).

Wehmeyer acknowledges that no other primetime network has followed ABC's lead in creating a religion editor. The belief is that religion does not matter or that it is a hobby. But Wehmeyer believes that her mission is to bring an awareness of God to television news. Like the early Christians, she works tirelessly in her efforts to proclaim God's presence and actions in the world.

Missing the Decisive Moment. Every challenge to our witness represents a decisive moment that we dare not miss. The following account is an example of the consequences of a decisive moment in the history of the manufacture of watches, taken from *Great Preaching* by James A. Harnish:

> Prior to 1967, the Swiss controlled more than eighty percent of the wristwatch market. But that year, a new watch, powered by the quartz crystal, was introduced. It swept the market and today the Swiss produce less than five percent of the world's watches. Prior to 1967 there were more than 65,000 Swiss watchmakers. Today there are fewer than 15,000.
>
> Who do you suppose invented the first quartz wristwatch? You guessed it: a Swiss watchmaker. He took the idea to his supervisors who told him to forget it. It would never sell. It didn't have wheels or springs . . . all things watches were supposed to have. It didn't even tick. The Swiss rejected it. Texas Instruments from America and Seiko from Japan picked up the idea, and the rest is history.

Challenged Authority. A fight erupted on March 8, 1999, involving students from a high school in Pennsylvania. Police broke up the fight, and the students were ordered to disperse after two adolescents were arrested. Police claim that the students refused to leave the scene and taunted them. Students claim that the police created further confrontations and used pepper spray for no apparent reason.

One week later, 150 students staged a peaceful march to the police station, and asked that a civilian review board hear complaints about the community's police force. This demonstration and meeting were organized by the Student Forum and led by the student athletes.

These young people peacefully challenged the actions of the police. Peter and John, likewise, refused to bend to the injustice of an order to be silent. Instead, they continued to speak and witness for the Lord.

EMPOWERED TO SERVE

BACKGROUND SCRIPTURE: Acts 6:1—8:3
DEVOTIONAL READING: Micah 4:1-7

KEY VERSE: The word of God continued to spread; the number of the disciples increased greatly in Jerusalem, and a great many of the priests became obedient to the faith. Acts 6:7.

KING JAMES VERSION

ACTS 6:1 And in those days, when the number of the disciples was multiplied, there arose a murmuring of the Grecians against the Hebrews, because their widows were neglected in the daily ministration.

2 Then the twelve called the multitude of the disciples unto them, and said, It is not reason that we should leave the word of God, and serve tables.

3 Wherefore, brethren, look ye out among you seven men of honest report, full of the Holy Ghost and wisdom, whom we may appoint over this business.

4 But we will give ourselves continually to prayer, and to the ministry of the word.

5 And the saying pleased the whole multitude: and they chose Stephen, a man full of faith and of the Holy Ghost, and Philip, and Prochorus, and Nicanor, and Timon, and Parmenas, and Nicolas a proselyte of Antioch:

6 Whom they set before the apostles: and when they had prayed, they laid their hands on them.

7 And the word of God increased; and the number of the disciples multiplied in Jerusalem greatly; and a great company of the priests were obedient to the faith.

8 And Stephen, full of faith and power, did great wonders and miracles among the people. . . .

7:55 But he, being full of the Holy Ghost, looked up stedfastly into heaven, and saw the glory of God, and Jesus standing on the right hand of God,

56 And said, Behold, I see the heavens opened, and the Son of man standing on the right hand of God.

57 Then they cried out with a loud voice, and stopped their ears, and ran upon him with one accord,

58 And cast him out of the city, and stoned him: and the witnesses laid down their clothes at a young man's feet, whose name was Saul.

59 And they stoned Stephen, calling upon God, and saying, Lord Jesus, receive my spirit.

60 And he kneeled down, and cried with a loud voice, Lord, lay not this sin to their charge. And when he had said this, he fell asleep.

8:1 And Saul was consenting unto his death.

NEW REVISED STANDARD VERSION

ACTS 6:1 Now during those days, when the disciples were increasing in number, the Hellenists complained against the Hebrews because their widows were being neglected in the daily distribution of food. 2 And the twelve called together the whole community of the disciples and said, "It is not right that we should neglect the word of God in order to wait on tables. 3 Therefore, friends, select from among yourselves seven men of good standing, full of the Spirit and of wisdom, whom we may appoint to this task, 4 while we, for our part, will devote ourselves to prayer and to serving the word." 5 What they said pleased the whole community, and they chose Stephen, a man full of faith and the Holy Spirit, together with Philip, Prochorus, Nicanor, Timon, Parmenas, and Nicolaus, a proselyte of Antioch. 6 They had these men stand before the apostles, who prayed and laid their hands on them.

7 The word of God continued to spread; the number of the disciples increased greatly in Jerusalem, and a great many of the priests became obedient to the faith.

8 Stephen, full of grace and power, did great wonders and signs among the people. . . .

7:55 But filled with the Holy Spirit, he gazed into heaven and saw the glory of God and Jesus standing at the right hand of God. 56 "Look," he said, "I see the heavens opened and the Son of Man standing at the right hand of God!" 57 But they covered their ears, and with a loud shout all rushed together against him. 58 Then they dragged him out of the city and began to stone him; and the witnesses laid their coats at the feet of a young man named Saul. 59 While they were stoning Stephen, he prayed, "Lord Jesus, receive my spirit." 60 Then he knelt down and cried out in a loud voice, "Lord, do not hold this sin against them." When he had said this, he died. 8:1 And Saul approved of their killing him.

5

Monday, March 26	Acts 6:1-7	*Chosen to Serve*
Tuesday, March 27	Acts 6:8-15	*Stephen Arrested*
Wednesday, March 28	Acts 7:1-8	*Stephen Speaks of Abraham and Isaac*
Thursday, March 29	Acts 7:9-16	*Stephen Speaks of Joseph*
Friday, March 30	Acts 7:20-35	*Stephen Speaks of Moses*
Saturday, March 31	Acts 7:36-50	*Stephen Speaks of God's Blessings*
Sunday, April 1	Acts 7:51—8:1	*Stephen Martyred in Saul's Presence*

BACKGROUND

Though the Jerusalem congregation was entirely Jewish in its composition, there were two different groups that belonged to it. Native-born Jews were those from Palestine who spoke Aramaic, used the Hebrew Old Testament, and observed the Jewish traditions. The Hellenists were Jews who grew up outside the land of Israel, spoke Greek, used the Septuagint (an ancient Greek translation of the Old Testament), and observed Hellenistic customs.

Some think that the Hellenists refer to Greeks (non-Jews), but this is not likely for two reasons. First, the context of Acts 1—5 is the spread of the church among Jews in Judea. Second, the Gentiles being admitted into the church marked a new phase that isn't dealt with until chapters 10 and 11 of Acts. Third, the later conflict of the church regarding the admission of the Gentiles without circumcision (chap. 15) would have been pointless if the Gentiles were admitted into the church at it's inception.

Acts 6:1-6 indicates that the native-born Jews in the Jerusalem congregation considered the Greek-speaking Jews to be outsiders. The presence of animosity between the two groups suggests there was also distrust and tension over the care of the needy widows belonging to the Hellenists. Discrimination emerged when some were not given their rightful share of the food being distributed daily.

Despite the cultural and linguistic differences between these two groups of believers, God had brought them together to form the first local congregation of Christians. It was now up to the apostles to insure that equality was established. The walls of division had to come down. The Twelve thus moved quickly to commission seven believers to oversee the fair distribution of care among those in need. The leadership knew that if the congregation was going to continue growing, all traces of discrimination had to be eliminated.

NOTES ON THE PRINTED TEXT

As the number of believers rapidly increased, there were signs of discontent. Those who spoke Greek complained that those who spoke Hebrew were discriminating against their widows *in the daily distribution of food* (Acts 6:1). This was a serious problem that couldn't be ignored.

In the early church the death of a woman's husband could leave her in an abandoned and helpless state. And widowhood was viewed with reproach by many in Greco-Roman society. Thus, a widow without legal protection was often vulnerable to neglect or exploitation. If a woman's husband died when her children were adolescents, they were considered orphans. Sadly, it was far too common for greedy and unscrupulous agents to defraud a destitute widow and her children of whatever property they owned.

There were three primary ways a widow could provide for the financial needs of herself and her children. First, she could return to her parents' house; second, she could remarry, especially if she was young or wealthy; and third, she could remain unmarried and obtain some kind of employment. The last prospect was rather bleak, for it was difficult in ancient times for a widow to find suitable work that would meet the economic needs of herself and her family.

Recognizing the gravity of the situation, the apostles *called together the whole community of the disciples* (6:2). The Twelve stated that they wanted to spend their time in preaching and teaching God's Word, not in administering a food program. The apostles therefore asked the members of the Jerusalem congregation to *select from among yourselves seven men of good standing, full of the Spirit and of wisdom* (6:3). The Twelve would then put these well-respected believers in charge of the daily distribution of food. The apostles, in turn, would devote themselves *to prayer and to serving the word* (6:4).

The apostles' priorities were correct. The ministry of the Word should never be neglected because of administrative burdens. Instead, the work of the church should be spread among its members.

The plan was agreeable to the rest of the congregation, and they chose seven believers. Among them was Stephen, whom Luke said was *full of faith and the Holy Spirit* (6:5). Verse 8 adds that he was full of God's grace and power and that he did *great wonders and signs among the people.*

The seven believers were presented to the apostles, and they *prayed and laid hands on them* (6:6). Laying hands on someone was an ancient Jewish practice of setting a person apart for special service. The appointing of the seven believers over the daily distribution of food apparently helped to ease tensions within the Jerusalem congregation, for the Gospel continued to spread and more people were being converted to the faith, including a *great many of the priests* (6:7).

Stephen's success as a witness for Christ generated great anger and hatred from the religious authorities. He was eventually arrested on a trumped-up charge of blasphemy. False witnesses framed him before the Sanhedrin, citing Stephen's insistence that the temple and any sacrifices were unnecessary since the coming of Christ (6:8-15).

Stephen calmly offered his defense of the Gospel. Detailing Israel's history, he pointed out God's mercy, despite the people's rejection of His commands and His prophets. Stephen reminded the council that God did not dwell in a house. Growing bolder, Stephen accused the religious leaders of rebelling against the

Spirit, an opposition that caused them to reject and murder Jesus, the Messiah (7:1-53).

The council was furious (7:54). Stephen, though, was at peace. Knowing that death was imminent, he sensed the comfort of Christ close at hand. While filled with the Spirit, Stephen gazed into heaven and saw the glory of God and Jesus standing at the Father's right hand (7:55-56). The Sanhedrin then seized Stephen, dragged him outside Jerusalem, and stoned him to death. Amazingly, he forgave his executioners (one of whom was Saul of Tarsus) before he died (7:57—8:1).

SUGGESTIONS TO TEACHERS

There never has been a time when the church has not been beset with some conflict both from within and from without. Even in those glorious early days described in Acts, believers had to handle problems brought on in their dealings with each other as fellow Christians and with problems presented by the world around them. This week's lesson will offer guidance to your students as they try to serve with grace in tense and troublesome situations.

1. RESOLVING CONFLICTS. Use the complaints and tensions that arose in the Jerusalem congregation as a case study for resolving conflicts among believers today. The key then and now is reliance on the Spirit to lead all groups to seek ways of serving Christ as effectively as possible.

2. REFUTING CHARGES. Next consider Stephen's sermon and how he effectively answered the charges brought against him. Note also how he accused the religious authorities of rejecting Jesus, God's chosen one. Stephen's testimony led to his death. Encourage the members of your class to have the same courage to tell the world about Christ.

3. RECOGNIZING CHRIST. Stephen's final words showed that he knew he was in the presence of Jesus. And even as he was dying, Stephen's trust was unshaken. His death was not in vain, for one of those present was Saul. He eventually would be converted and become a great evangelist to the Gentiles.

4. REMAINING COMMITTED. The persecution that erupted against believers after Stephen's martyrdom seemed to spell disaster for the Christian cause. But God used this apparent setback to bring about even greater things. For instance, though believers were forced to flee from Jerusalem, God used this scattering to spread the Gospel far and wide. Though we don't like to experience discomfort, God can work through it to bring about His will. In fact, He often uses our afflictions to prepare us for a special task.

FOR ADULTS

■ **TOPIC:** Called to Serve and Forgive

■ **QUESTIONS:** 1. Why do you think the apostles delegated the task of choosing seven believers to oversee the daily distribution of food? 2. Why did the apostles want believers who would serve in the church to be full of the Spirit? 3. How might the resolution of the emerging conflict within the church have contributed to the rapid growth that followed? 4. When you are performing your Christian duties, what risks bother you the most? Why? 5. How do you deal with the risks involved in Christian service?

■ ILLUSTRATIONS:

Sacrificial Serving. Ernest Gordon was serving in the British Army when Singapore fell to the Japanese during the early days of World War II. After being taken prisoner, he and thousands of others were forced to construct the "Death Railway," which was made famous by the movie *The Bridge Over the River Kwai.*

Conditions among the captives were indescribably terrible. Thousands died of disease and malnutrition, or from brutal treatment by the guards. The prisoners in the camps seemed to become dehumanized, stealing from each other and suspicious of each other. A kind of buddy arrangement, called the "mucker system," evolved whereby two buddies teamed up to look after each other by "mucking" for the other. Nevertheless, the camp seethed with greed and anger.

Gordon recounted how one prisoner became critically ill and was carried to the hut known as "the hothouse" (a bamboo shelter where a sick prisoner was left unattended to die). After the victim had died of disease or starvation, the hut was burned and a new one quickly erected. To everyone's amazement, a week after entering the hothouse, that prisoner walked out. Tragically, however, his previously-healthy mucker grew so weak that he was carried to the hothouse. Shortly afterward, that man died.

Then it was learned that this mucker had, under the risk of being shot or bayoneted, sneaked out every day to the hothouse and shared his meager rice ration with his sick buddy, and each evening he would slip past the guards with his blanket to the hothouse to wrap his shivering mucker. But his acts of caring weakened him so severely that he became ill. This person's testimony so affected the others in the camp that the hardened prisoners stopped thinking only of their own survival. Instead, they started to show concern for each other.

Gradually, Gordon reported, the entire camp became different. A sense of Christian community developed, and worship began. Later, when the survivors were liberated at the close of the war, they even forgivingly and spontaneously spilled out of a train to give food, water, and medical attention to a group of sick and injured former enemy soldiers who had been abandoned by their own Japanese buddies. The Spirit impelled Gordon and his fellow muckers to show Christlike service and mercy to each other and even to their oppressors!

God's Grain. Ignatius of Antioch was a devoted Christian pastor in Asia Minor near the end of the first century A.D. He was hauled to Rome because he refused to worship the Emperor Trajan as the Lord God. Ignatius steadfastly insisted that only Jesus could be given that title. Ignatius was denounced as an "atheist" and called "unpatriotic," then told to recant his views about Jesus. Ignatius refused to back down or change his opinions. He was threatened with death, but still refused to be moved. He was then tied inside the bloody skins of freshly slaughtered-animals and dragged into an arena before thousands of spectators. Wild dogs that had not been fed for days were unleashed. Ignatius was torn apart by the ravenously hungry animals. His last words were, "I am God's grain!" The martyrdom of Ignatius, along with beautiful letters he wrote while a prisoner, spurred other believers to remain faithful to Christ despite the severe persecution they experienced from their enemies.

Archbishop's Answer. A young pastor came to the beloved William Temple, the former Archbishop of Canterbury, and complained how difficult it would be to serve in the new parish to which he was being assigned. Temple listened graciously. The young pastor continued to whine and object vigorously. "If I go there," he exclaimed with a voice dripping with self-pity, "it will kill me!" Temple wryly smiled and said, "Well now, you and I don't mind a little thing like that, do we?"

FOR YOUTH

■ TOPIC: Giving It All

■ QUESTIONS: 1. What might have been the outcome had the apostles chosen to ignore the problem festering in the Jerusalem congregation? 2. What was the value of the apostles laying their hands on the seven believers? 3. How do you think the people who knew Stephen best would have described him? 4. How did Stephen respond to the attacks of his enemies? 5. What has God called you to do in your church? How have you responded?

■ ILLUSTRATIONS:

Challenged Authority. The sixth graders at a middle school in the central part of the United States had finished a unit on drugs when they noticed a billboard being changed outside their school. The advertisement for a hemp-based shampoo featured a huge marijuana leaf.

Trained to "Say No" to drugs, the students considered their options before writing a letter to the advertising agency. They stated that though they did not expect the firm to censor their clients' advertisements, they nevertheless objected to the placement of the billboard so near to their school. School administrators expected little to happen from the sixth graders' challenge. However, one day later the advertisement was removed!

Here was a group of 20 sixth-graders who dared to object, and finally triumphed through their efforts. Like Stephen, they were willing to stand up for their convictions and challenge powerful interests.

Gave Time. At 14, Patrick wanted to coach baseball. He volunteered at the local Boys and Girls Club. Four years later, the senior high student was honored by the local United Way for his volunteer service. Patrick started a baseball clinic and then a tutoring program that now has over 40 student volunteers. He also started a fundraiser to obtain money for bicycle helmets when some bikes were donated. In addition, he wrote a proposal that obtained a $15,000 grant for a golf program he had created.

Patrick is one individual who serves the needs of others. He is willing to volunteer and work for a cause he believes in. Like Patrick and Stephen, you should do likewise.

Gave His Life. Steve Biko was born in Kingwilliamstown, South Africa, in 1946. As a young man, he founded the South African Students Organization and wrote for the cause until it was banned in 1973. He spoke out vehemently against apartheid (the strict segregation of blacks and whites), white domination, and the suppression of black people. He then founded the Black Consciousness Movement, a Christian organization that spoke out against injustice, exploitation, and the oppression of blacks while seeking the reconciliation of all people. He often quoted Colossians 3:11.

On September 6, 1977, Steve was stopped by South African Security Police at a roadblock near Grahamstown in the Eastern Cape Province. Along with a black youth worker, he was arrested and taken to Room 619 of the police station in Port Elizabeth. For hours, the two were handcuffed, shackled, and brutally beaten and interrogated. Biko suffered brain damage and lapsed into unconsciousness. His interrogators finally drove him in the back of an open truck over 750 miles to Pretoria to a hospital, where he died as a result of his beating and the delay of obtaining any medical care.

Biko gave his all—his very life—for the good of his people. Now included in the church's Calendar of Martyrs, he is recalled as a champion of black South Africans. Among the early Christians, Stephen was also a champion for his Lord and his faith.

WITNESSING BEYOND JERUSALEM

BACKGROUND SCRIPTURE: Acts 8:4-40
DEVOTIONAL READING: Micah 5:7-9

KEY VERSE: Those who were scattered went from place to place,
proclaiming the word. Acts 8:4.

KING JAMES VERSION

ACTS 8:4 Therefore they that were scattered abroad went every where preaching the word.

5 Then Philip went down to the city of Samaria, and preached Christ unto them.

6 And the people with one accord gave heed unto those things which Philip spake, hearing and seeing the miracles which he did.

7 For unclean spirits, crying with loud voice, came out of many that were possessed with them: and many taken with palsies, and that were lame, were healed.

8 And there was great joy in that city. . . .

26 And the angel of the Lord spake unto Philip, saying, Arise, and go toward the south unto the way that goeth down from Jerusalem unto Gaza, which is desert.

27 And he arose and went: and, behold, a man of Ethiopia, an eunuch of great authority under Candace queen of the Ethiopians, who had the charge of all her treasure, and had come to Jerusalem for to worship,

28 Was returning, and sitting in his chariot read Esaias the prophet.

29 Then the Spirit said unto Philip, Go near, and join thyself to this chariot.

30 And Philip ran thither to him, and heard him read the prophet Esaias, and said, Understandest thou what thou readest?

31 And he said, How can I, except some man should guide me? And he desired Philip that he would come up and sit with him.

32 The place of the scripture which he read was this, He was led as a sheep to the slaughter; and like a lamb dumb before his shearer, so opened he not his mouth:

33 In his humiliation his judgment was taken away: and who shall declare his generation? for his life is taken from the earth.

34 And the eunuch answered Philip, and said, I pray thee, of whom speaketh the prophet this? of himself, or of some other man?

35 Then Philip opened his mouth, and began at the same scripture, and preached unto him Jesus.

NEW REVISED STANDARD VERSION

ACTS 8:4 Now those who were scattered went from place to place, proclaiming the word. 5 Philip went down to the city of Samaria and proclaimed the Messiah to them. 6 The crowds with one accord listened eagerly to what was said by Philip, hearing and seeing the signs that he did, 7 for unclean spirits, crying with loud shrieks, came out of many who were possessed; and many others who were paralyzed or lame were cured. 8 So there was great joy in that city. . . .

26 Then an angel of the Lord said to Philip, "Get up and go toward the south to the road that goes down from Jerusalem to Gaza." (This is a wilderness road.) 27 So he got up and went. Now there was an Ethiopian eunuch, a court official of the Candace, queen of the Ethiopians, in charge of her entire treasury. He had come to Jerusalem to worship 28 and was returning home; seated in his chariot, he was reading the prophet Isaiah. 29 Then the Spirit said to Philip, "Go over to this chariot and join it." 30 So Philip ran up to it and heard him reading the prophet Isaiah. He asked, "Do you understand what you are reading?" 31 He replied, "How can I, unless someone guides me?" And he invited Philip to get in and sit beside him. 32 Now the passage of the scripture that he was reading was this:

"Like a sheep he was led to the slaughter,
    and like a lamb silent before its shearer,
        so he does not open his mouth.
33 In his humiliation justice was denied him.
    Who can describe his generation?
        For his life is taken away from the earth."
34 The eunuch asked Philip, "About whom, may I ask you, does the prophet say this, about himself or about someone else?" 35 Then Philip began to speak, and starting with this scripture, he proclaimed to him the good news about Jesus.

HOME BIBLE READINGS

BACKGROUND

We learn in this week's lesson that Philip proclaimed the Gospel to a man from Ethiopia. In ancient times Ethiopia was located in the region of Nubia, just south of Egypt, where the first waterfall of the Nile goes into the Sudan. The modern nation of Ethiopia is located further to the southeast.

Many Bible scholars equate Ethiopia with the land of Cush (Gen. 2:13; Isa. 11:11). Cush was an enemy of Egypt for centuries, gaining and losing independence, depending on the pharaoh. After the Assyrians conquered the Egyptians in 671 B.C., Ethiopia maintained a strong center of trade. Job saw Cush as a rich source of topaz and other minerals (Job 28:19). The most influential Ethiopian leader, Tirhakah, aided Hezekiah when Sennacherib invaded Judah in 701 B.C. (2 Kings 19:9; Isa. 37:9).

The capital, Napata, was abandoned around 300 B.C. The capital of Ethiopia then moved south to Meroe, where the kingdom continued on for another 600 years. Archaeological digs in Napata and Meroe have disclosed a number of pyramid tombs, as well as temples to the Egyptian god Amun.

During the New Testament era, several queens of Ethiopia bore the name Candace, which was probably a title, not a proper name. Modern Ethiopian Christians consider the eunuch of this week's text their country's first evangelist. In fact, many regard his conversion the beginning of the fulfillment of Psalm 68:31—*Let Ethiopia hasten to stretch out its hands to God.*

Surprisingly, the first coin ever minted with an uncontested Christian theme was not issued in Rome by Constantine in the early third century A.D. That honor, rather, belongs to the kingdom of Axum (now in modern Ethiopia). The Axumite king, Ezanas, converted to Christianity earlier and minted coins with a cross in the center of his coinage. How Christianity found its way to his kingdom is at the heart of this week's lesson.

NOTES ON THE PRINTED TEXT

The religious authorities in Jerusalem thought they were extinguishing the fledgling Christian movement. But their persecution turned out to be like stomping on blazing coals, scattering burning embers everywhere. The attempts at ending evangelistic efforts in Jerusalem not only spurred the early

Christians' dedication to continue sharing their faith but also sent displaced believers into outlying areas to evangelize (Acts 8:4).

Those who seemed to be most effective at witnessing beyond Jerusalem were from the group of Greek-speaking Jews who became believers. They were so filled with joy and zeal to tell others about God's great promises through Jesus that they proclaimed the good news to people that previously were ignored or avoided—like Samaritans.

In 8:5 we learn that *Philip went down to the city of Samaria and proclaimed the Messiah to them.* Jews saw Samaritans as ceremonially unclean half-breeds because they were descendants of Israelites who had intermarried with non-Israelites (2 Kings 17:24-41). Philip, though, saw the Samaritans as equals and people who needed to hear about God's love in Christ.

Philip's teaching had effect. Equally impressive were his healings and exorcisms (8:7-8). *The crowds with one accord listened eagerly to what was said by Philip, hearing and seeing the signs that he did* (8:6).

After helping to establish a Christian congregation in Samaria, Philip felt the nudge of the Spirit urging him south. Running through the desert south of Jerusalem was a well-traveled road, and it was also a main route toward Egypt. On the road was a eunuch returning from Jerusalem to his native Nubia. *Then an angel of the Lord said to Philip, "Get up and go toward the south to the road that goes down from Jerusalem to Gaza." (This is a wilderness road.)* (8:26).

The eunuch had come to Jerusalem to attend a religious festival and now was on his way back to his native land. By the eunuch's chariots and servants, it's clear he was an important governmental official. In fact, he was a sort of secretary of the treasury for *Candace, queen of the Ethiopians* (8:27).

Officials in the courts of ancient rulers were often eunuchs, that is, castrated men. Not being subject to the same drives as other men, eunuchs could even be trusted to oversee the king's harem. In some cases, however, the word *eunuch* seems to have been purely a governmental title, not necessarily applied to a castrated man.

Some commentators think the Ethiopian eunuch was of this type. They say this, for one thing, because the eunuch had been in Jerusalem for worship. Jewish law prohibited the participation of eunuchs in the Jewish assembly (Deut. 23:1). Furthermore, the Ethiopian (Nubian) was in charge of finances, not a harem.

When Philip saw the official sitting and reading the scroll of the prophet Isaiah (Acts 8:28), the Spirit told him to go and stand beside the Ethiopian's coach. *"Go over to this chariot and join it"* (8:29). By doing this, Philip would be able to help the man understand what he was reading.

As the Ethiopian rode along in his chariot, he read aloud to himself. (In ancient times reading aloud was a common practice.) Philip sensed the Spirit urging him closer to the chariot, where he heard the official reading from Isaiah 53:7 and 8 (quoted in Acts 8:32-33), a passage describing the suffering Servant of the Lord.

Looking for an avenue to begin his teaching and his testimony, Philip asked if the Ethiopian understood the prophet's meaning. *"Do you understand what you are reading?* (Acts 8:30). The official's reply gave Philip the opportunity he needed. *"How can I, unless someone guides me?"* (8:31). Demonstrating his willingness to be guided, the official invited Philip to climb into his chariot.

The Ethiopian said, *"About whom, may I ask you, does the prophet say this, about himself or about someone else?"* (8:34). While seated with the official, Philip shared the Gospel and led him to faith in Christ (8:35). Since the Ethiopian now believed in Jesus, he ordered his driver to stop his chariot, stepped into some nearby water, and allowed Philip to baptize him (8:36-38). Then, after the Spirit had miraculously transported Philip to Azotus, he traveled north to Caesarea and proclaimed the Gospel in various cities along the way (8:39-40).

SUGGESTIONS TO TEACHERS

Palm Sunday often means drama, pageantry, and special music for church people. But all the celebration over Jesus' kingly entrance into Jerusalem must not obscure the call to witness in the community. Yes, let's commemorate the Lord's triumphal entry; but let's also tell the world the good news of God's love and triumph through Jesus!

1. PHILIP AND THE SAMARITAN MISSION. The early disciples knew about Jesus' kingly entrance into Jerusalem. They also knew about His death on the cross and resurrection from the dead. Moreover, they were so touched by the Spirit that they sought to tell others, regardless of their background, of God's love through Christ. Often Christians today allow social differences to hinder their relationships with others. However, the command to spread the Gospel demands that we see all people as individuals for whom Christ died.

2. PETER AND SIMON THE MAGICIAN. Simon, a person who had formerly practiced sorcery and who had heard Philip preach the Gospel, believed and was baptized. The Jerusalem congregation dispatched Peter and John to Samaria, and God used them to impart the Spirit on the new converts. When Simon tried to purchase from Peter the power to impart the Spirit, the apostle rebuked him and urged him to repent of his wickedness. Through the ministry of Peter and John many more Samaritans heard the Gospel (Acts 8:9-25). Remind your students that the Spirit cannot be manipulated for personal use. Rather, He lives in us and enables us to serve Christ faithfully.

3. PHILIP AND THE ETHIOPIAN OFFICIAL. Philip was a fearless groundbreaker. In Samaria he had to overcome whatever religious disagreements and racial prejudice he might have had regarding the Samaritans in order to proclaim the Gospel to them. Later he had to go beyond the barriers of race and social class to tell the good of Jesus to the Ethiopian official. Philip was obedient to God and overcame social barriers in the process. Through Christ we too can overcome these barriers and share the Gospel with those who are different from us.

■ **TOPIC:** Called to Witness to All People

■ **QUESTIONS:** 1. What was the purpose of miracles, signs, and wonders in promoting the Gospel of Christ? 2. How was God at work in bringing about the conversion of so many Samaritans? 3. If you were Philip, how would you have felt while you were baptizing the Ethiopian? Why? 4. How does the presence of Christ dwelling within you help you overcome the fear of people who are socially different from you? 5. What social barriers hinder you from becoming a more effective witness for Christ? How do you plan to overcome them?

■ **ILLUSTRATIONS:**

"Live or Die, I Must Ride!" Francis Asbury was a young English lay preacher when John Wesley sent him to the American colonies in 1771. When Asbury arrived, he found that most preachers were settled in the cities on the east coast. "Most of my brethren," Asbury wrote, "seem unwilling to leave the cities, but I think I will show them the way."

The dedicated evangelist set out on foot and horseback and traveled through the lonely frontier to bring the good news of Christ to the scattered settlements where other preachers had not gone. Then, when the American Revolution broke out, those adhering to Wesley's group were suspected of loyalist sympathies to England. Though most Wesleyan preachers fled, Asbury stayed.

Asbury steadfastly continued his travels in the back country to spread the Gospel to isolated villages and farms. He became known as "the prophet of the long road." He never married or owned any property. He rode more than 275,000 miles, and preached at least once a day for more than 50 years.

Thanks to his determination to witness to all people and not just city folk, Asbury's group of Wesleyan followers grew from six preachers and 700 members in 1771 to 700 preachers and 200,000 members by the time he died. The Methodist church in the United States looks to this tireless circuit-riding pastor as its founder. His motto was "Live or die, I must ride!" And ride Francis Asbury did until the day of his death in 1816.

Ragbag Preacher. Edgar Helms was another Spirit-empowered believer who witnessed to people whom others overlooked. The son of a poor farmer, Helms wanted wealth and fame as a young man. Soon he was on his way to having a successful career as a newspaperman and politician. But the call of Christ led him to abandon his worldly ambitions. Instead, he decided to study for the ministry and then go overseas as a missionary. However, when he and his bride were ready to go to India, the severe economic turndown in the 1890s caused his church to be so short of funds that they had no money to send him overseas.

A high ranking church official told the disappointed couple that a more difficult mission field than India lay closer to home, and urged them to begin a ministry in the worst slum in Boston. Helms quickly discovered appalling poverty, ignorance, and filth among the people living in the crowded area. He established a chapel, developed a program to teach trades, and opened an employment agency.

When the depression of 1902–1905 caused terrible hardship among poor people, Helms recognized that pride prevented them from wanting handouts. He thus became determined to find a way to preserve the dignity of those whom he knew needed assistance. Though few anywhere in Boston could give cash, Helms realized that many could donate used clothing, household articles, and furniture. He persuaded wholesale coffee businesses to give him burlap sacks, and then he distributed these throughout Boston. He also began to collect used articles in the sacks.

At first Helms pushed a wheelbarrow. He then got a horse and wagon before finally acquiring an old truck to pick up his "Goodwill" burlap bags. He set his jobless slum dwellers to work sorting, repairing, and selling the articles collected, and he paid these workers enough to buy food and pay rent. He used the program also as a training program to prepare people for better jobs.

As economic conditions improved, Helms and his Morgan Chapel programs began expanding to train the handicapped. When World War I ended and many found themselves handicapped by war wounds, Helms and his ministries specialized in helping them to be trained to take jobs in industry.

Edgar Helms's ministry came to be known as Goodwill Industries, and continues doing outstanding work. By the time of Helms's death in 1942, his missionary efforts to the poor—starting with collecting rags, newspapers, used clothes, and castoff furniture—had grown into a multimillion dollar enterprise. Helms insisted that Christian witnessing meant reaching out to the poor and handicapped through organized goodwill efforts.

FOR YOUTH

■ **TOPIC:** Let Me Help You

■ **QUESTIONS:** 1. What anxieties and fears might Philip have had in preaching to the Samaritans? 2. Why was Philip a good choice to be the one to share the Gospel with the Ethiopian? 3. What does the account of the official suggest about the role that Bible study can play in conversion? 4. How do you think the conversion of the Ethiopian helped the spread of the Gospel? 5. What opportunities to witness for Christ do you see in your community?

■ **ILLUSTRATIONS:**

Outsiders. Samaritans and Gentiles were the outsiders that Philip and the early church encountered. These outsiders were hated by religious legalists. But the Spirit helped believers understand that no one was to be hated or considered an outsider.

Sadly, the United States has many so-called "outsiders" today. These people are the victims of hate crimes. Reported acts of violence against them have risen slightly each year. For instance, the Federal Bureau of Investigation (FBI) reported 8,759 incidents in 1996, which was up from 7,947 in 1995. These figures do not include the distribution of hate literature, public rallies organized by hate groups, offensive graffiti, lewd remarks, and racial slurs. Most of the incidents are against "people of color," followed by Jews, immigrants, and biracial people (to name a few groups).

The Holy Spirit is still at work nudging believers to break down social, racial, and economic barriers and accept all people. No one should be an outsider when it comes to proclaiming the Gospel!

No Untouchables. Mother Theresa of Calcutta is best remembered for her outreach to India's untouchables. No one was outside her interest. She ministered to everyone, male or female, young or old, regardless of caste or condition. This servant of the Lord embodied Christ's love for all. She actively demonstrated the early church's understanding that everyone counts!

Under the Gallows. Back in 1738, London's main prison was called Newgate. Charles Wesley (later to be the great Christian hymn writer) frequently went there, preaching to those prisoners sentenced to death. On one occasion Charles was even locked in overnight in order to pray with and comfort prisoners.

In his *Journal*, Wesley tells of a poor man who was condemned to die. Wesley told him of "one who came down from heaven to save the lost and him in particular." Wesley led this man to faith in Christ. After Wesley served this man Communion, he accompanied the man to the gallows. The assurance of salvation was etched on the new convert's face. Because of his new friend's faith, Wesley penned, "That hour under the gallows was the most blessed hour of my life!"

PROCLAIMING THE RISEN LORD

BACKGROUND SCRIPTURE: Luke 24:1-12; Acts 9:1-31
DEVOTIONAL READING: John 20:1, 11-18

KEY VERSE: "Why do you look for the living among the dead?
He is not here, but has risen." Luke 24:5b.

KING JAMES VERSION

LUKE 24:1 Now upon the first day of the week, very early in the morning, they came unto the sepulchre, bringing the spices which they had prepared, and certain others with them.

2 And they found the stone rolled away from the sepulchre.

3 And they entered in, and found not the body of the Lord Jesus.

4 And it came to pass, as they were much perplexed thereabout, behold, two men stood by them in shining garments:

5 And as they were afraid, and bowed down their faces to the earth, they said unto them, Why seek ye the living among the dead?

6 He is not here, but is risen: remember how he spake unto you when he was yet in Galilee,

7 Saying, The Son of man must be delivered into the hands of sinful men, and be crucified, and the third day rise again.

8 And they remembered his words,

9 And returned from the sepulchre, and told all these things unto the eleven, and to all the rest.

10 It was Mary Magdalene and Joanna, and Mary the mother of James, and other women that were with them, which told these things unto the apostles. . . .

ACTS 9:19 And when he had received meat, he was strengthened. Then was Saul certain days with the disciples which were at Damascus.

20 And straightway he preached Christ in the synagogues, that he is the Son of God.

26 And when Saul was come to Jerusalem, he assayed to join himself to the disciples: but they were all afraid of him, and believed not that he was a disciple.

27 But Barnabas took him, and brought him to the apostles, and declared unto them how he had seen the Lord in the way, and that he had spoken to him, and how he had preached boldly at Damascus in the name of Jesus.

28 And he was with them coming in and going out at Jerusalem.

31 Then had the churches rest throughout all Judæa and Galilee and Samaria, and were edified; and walking in the fear of the Lord, and in the comfort of the Holy Ghost, were multiplied.

NEW REVISED STANDARD VERSION

LUKE 24:1 But on the first day of the week, at early dawn, they came to the tomb, taking the spices that they had prepared. 2 They found the stone rolled away from the tomb, 3 but when they went in, they did not find the body. 4 While they were perplexed about this, suddenly two men in dazzling clothes stood beside them. 5 The women were terrified and bowed their faces to the ground, but the men said to them, "Why do you look for the living among the dead? He is not here, but has risen. 6 Remember how he told you, while he was still in Galilee, 7 that the Son of Man must be handed over to sinners, and be crucified, and on the third day rise again." 8 Then they remembered his words, 9 and returning from the tomb, they told all this to the eleven and to all the rest. 10 Now it was Mary Magdalene, Joanna, Mary the mother of James, and the other women with them who told this to the apostles.

ACTS 9:19 For several days he was with the disciples in Damascus, 20 and immediately he began to proclaim Jesus in the synagogues, saying, "He is the Son of God." . . .

26 When he had come to Jerusalem, he attempted to join the disciples; and they were all afraid of him, for they did not believe that he was a disciple. 27 But Barnabas took him, brought him to the apostles, and described for them how on the road he had seen the Lord, who had spoken to him, and how in Damascus he had spoken boldly in the name of Jesus. 28 So he went in and out among them in Jerusalem, speaking boldly in the name of the Lord. . . .

31 Meanwhile the church throughout Judea, Galilee, and Samaria had peace and was built up. Living in the fear of the Lord and in the comfort of the Holy Spirit, it increased in numbers.

7

Monday, April 9	Luke 24:1-10	*The Empty Tomb*
Tuesday, April 10	Acts 9:1-9	*The Conversion of Saul*
Wednesday, April 11	Acts 9:10-19a	*Ananias, a Reluctant Witness*
Thursday, April 12	Acts. 9:19b-25	*Saul Preaches and Leaves Damascus*
Friday, April 13	Acts. 9:26-31	*Saul in Jerusalem*
Saturday, April 14	Acts. 9:32-43	*Peter Heals Aeneas and Raises Tabitha*
Sunday, April 15	Psalm 63	*Have Faith! God Will Provide*

BACKGROUND

All four Gospels give an account of Jesus' resurrection (Matt. 28:1-10; Mark 16:1-18; Luke 24:1-12; John 20:1-29). Moreover, the rest of the New Testament speaks with a tremendous sense of confidence about the empty tomb and the triumph of Christ over death.

We shouldn't be surprised, for the Resurrection is the most amazing news the world has ever heard. It means there is a God after all. It also means that Jesus really is God's Son. And it means that Christ is alive, that we can know Him, and that we can be touched by His life and power. Believers need not fear death, for we are not destined for oblivion but rather to spend eternity with God.

There are at least four lines of evidence indicating that Jesus truly rose from the dead. First, every source we have indicates that Jesus truly died. He was publicly executed before large crowds, and His death was certified by both a centurion in charge (a military professional whose job it was to determine that death had taken place) and by the regional governor, Pilate, who sent to have the matter checked.

Second, Jesus was buried in a new tomb, one that had never been used (John 19:41). That means it was in perfect condition and would have been easy to locate. But when Jesus' friends arrived on the second morning after His death, His body was gone. All the accounts agree on this.

Third, Jesus appeared after His death to many witnesses. Each of the Gospels recounts Jesus' post-resurrection appearances to His fearful, doubting followers over a period of 40 days. These weren't hallucinations, for they happened to too many people, among them hardheaded fishermen, steadfast women, civil servants, and the ultimate skeptic, Thomas.

Fourth, countless people have encountered the living Jesus and been changed by Him. The Resurrection is not simply a matter of intellectual curiosity or theological argument, but of personal experience. Consider the women who visited the empty tomb at dawn on Easter Sunday. And how about the apostles who subsequently became ambassadors for Christ. And don't forget Paul, who once persecuted the church but then became an ardent spokesperson for the Gospel.

From the first century to today there have been innumerable people who have turned from being totally opposed or indifferent to Christianity to being utterly convinced that it is true. What changed them? They met the risen Lord!

In the early morning darkness, just as the sun was beginning to break over the horizon, Mary Magdalene, Joanna, Mary the mother of James, and some other women arrived at the tomb (Luke 24:10). They carried aloes and myrrh, which they had prepared to properly wrap Jesus' body. It was to be their final act of love. *But on the first day of the week, at early dawn, they came to the tomb, taking spices that they had prepared* (24:1).

The women had been preoccupied with how they were going to move the huge circular stone covering the entrance to the tomb (Mark 16:3). Upon entering the cave, they discovered that it was empty. There was no corpse to be found anywhere! *They found the stone rolled away from the tomb, but when they went in, they did not find the body* (Luke 24:2-3).

The now confused women became terrified by the appearance of two angels in bright clothing (24:4). Fear and awe caused the women to bow to the ground in a display of respect. The angels, however, announced that Jesus was alive! *"Why do you look for the living among the dead? He is not here, but has risen"* (24:5).

Continuing, the angels reminded the women of Jesus' earlier predictions of His arrest, crucifixion, and the resurrection. *"Remember how he told you, while he was in Galilee, that the Son of Man must be handed over to sinners, and be crucified, and on the third day rise again"* (24:6-7).

The women then recalled Jesus' statements (24:8). They then hurried back to Jerusalem to tell the disciples that Jesus had risen from the dead (24:9). That truth has become the foundation of the believers' faith.

The risen Lord's ability to radically transform a person's life is evident in Saul (later called Paul). Though he once strove to wipe out the church, his encounter with Christ while heading north from Jerusalem to Damascus forever changed Saul (Acts 9:1-18). Luke said the following concerning him: *For several days he was with the disciples in Damascus, and immediately he began to proclaim Jesus in the synagogues, saying, "He is the Son of God"* (9:19-20).

Saul's bold and powerful witness concerning the Savior led some religious legalists to plot Saul's murder. When the scheme was discovered, some disciples helped him escape to Jerusalem (9:21-25). Then, after Saul arrived in the holy city, *he attempted to join the disciples; and they were all afraid of him, for they did not believe that he was a disciple* (9:26).

Thankfully, a trusting believer named Barnabas was impressed enough with Saul to stake his reputation on the new convert. Barnabas took him to meet the leaders of the Jerusalem church and described how Saul had met the risen Savior. *But Barnabas took him, brought him to the apostles, and described for them how on the road he had seen the Lord, who had spoken to him, and how in Damascus he had spoken boldly in the name of Jesus* (9:27).

The apostles accepted the testimony of Barnabas. Saul then began an assault on the views held by the Hellenistic Jews of Jerusalem. He debated them, showing that Jesus is the Messiah. *So he went in and out among them in Jerusalem, speaking boldly in the name of the Lord* (9:28).

When the opposition plotted to murder Saul, he was smuggled to Caesarea and then to Tarsus, his hometown. Meanwhile, during the peaceful period that followed, the church continued to grow both spiritually and numerically. *Meanwhile, the church throughout Judea, Galilee, and Samaria had peace and was built up. Living in the fear of the Lord and in the comfort of the Holy Spirit, it increased in numbers* (9:31).

SUGGESTIONS TO TEACHERS

The newspapers and television commercials have drenched us with photos of baby chicks and announcements of egg hunts. And many people seem to celebrate Easter by wearing a pair of cute bunny ears and munching giant chocolate eggs! Your task in this week's lesson is to refocus the attention of your students on the good news of the risen Lord.

1. UNSUSPECTING MOURNERS. Begin the teaching time by having your students consider the visit of the women to the tomb. Point out that they anticipated finding Jesus' corpse. Otherwise why would they have come to prepare the body for permanent interment? But they learned that God had raised Jesus from the dead. Be sure to stress that the Resurrection was not a hoax or hallucination, but rather a genuine historical event.

2. UNEXPECTED ENCOUNTER. Next have the members of your class consider Saul's encounter with the risen Lord. The evidence indicates that only the Savior could have turned around this implacable foe of early Christians. Note that Jesus sometimes meets us in ways and at times we may not expect.

3. UNRECOGNIZED CHRIST. At first Saul did not realize that Jesus was confronting him. The unsaved are so entrenched in sin and unbelief that it takes the power and presence of God to make them realize their need for Christ.

4. UNHESITATING BROTHER. Imagine how Ananias must have felt when Saul was brought to his house. Have the students comment on ways Ananias might have responded. Instead of rejecting this former persecutor or reluctantly offering Saul hospitality, Ananias graciously welcomed Saul as a fellow believer. Only the living Jesus could have made this response possible!

5. UNMISTAKABLE CHANGE. Saul the former persecutor of the church soon became Paul the evangelist. Such a dramatic turnabout can be explained only by the fact that the risen Lord had dramatically transformed this enemy into a friend and advocate of the church. Do your students realize how much God wants to transform them? What changes has Christ brought about in the lives of each person in your class? Encourage them to list these, and also those they would like the Savior to bring about in the days ahead.

6. UNAFRAID DISCIPLE. Most of the disciples in Jerusalem were afraid to welcome Saul as a believer because of his fierce persecution of the church before his conversion. Barnabas was one of the few who was willing to affirm and accept this new believer. Clearly, Barnabas was most interested in having the good news of the risen Lord proclaimed. Likewise, our primary task is to present the resurrected Christ, not prejudge other believers.

FOR ADULTS

■ **TOPIC:** Called to Proclaim the Risen Lord
■ **QUESTIONS:** 1. Why did the women come to the tomb so early in the day? 2. Why were the disciples so reluctant at first to believe that Jesus had risen from the dead? 3. What risks did Barnabas take when he affirmed Saul to the apostles? 4. What could be done to get more Christians involved in witnessing for Christ? 5. How has the risen Christ shown His power in your life and in your church?

■ **ILLUSTRATIONS:**

A Decision to Stay. Courtney discovered the campus life at her large state university had not proved to be as much fun she had expected. Most of her dorm mates drank heavily and several were weekend binge drinkers. A couple of girls on her floor did drugs. And several were sexually immoral.

Courtney found herself struggling to maintain the values she had received from her parents and her church. She privately had questions about the Bible and doubts about the person of Christ. Previously Courtney's faith had not meant much to her. But in the crucible of dorm life, this sophomore found herself torn between going along with the pleasure-seeking values of her peers and the traditional ideas of her upbringing. The inner tug-of-war became increasingly difficult to endure.

One evening, while lying in bed and pondering her situation, Courtney found Galatians 2:20 coming to mind: *It is no longer I who live, but it is Christ who lives in me.* The young woman was surprised that these words presented themselves to her, for she had not looked at a Bible or thought about Jesus much since leaving home. But the verse seemed to bring her a sense of calm and hope.

Over the next few days, Courtney found herself repeating the verse. Strangely, she became aware that the Lord seemed to be accompanying her. His Presence, to her surprise, seemed to confer stamina and stability to her pressure-filled daily life. Eventually, Courtney realized that the Savior was actually with her in her trials.

Courtney sought out the university chaplain and discovered a supportive community of friendly fellow Christians. At first, she was ready to move out of her dorm and find a residence with women who shared her faith in the resurrected Jesus. But as Courtney engaged in Bible study and discussion with her Christian friends, she sensed that the Lord wanted her to remain in her dorm as a witness for Him.

Courtney decided to stay in her old room, and her quiet testimony as a Christian won the respect of many of her peers. Several, in fact, privately came to her asking about her faith. When this happened, she would smile and share the Gospel!

Something Better Is Coming. The woman had been diagnosed with a rapidly spreading form of cancer and told she had three months to live. Shortly before she died, she contacted her pastor and discussed with him the details of her funeral service, including the Scripture passages, hymns, and other arrangements. The woman mentioned that she would like to have her favorite Bible placed in her casket. The pastor nodded and then stood to leave when she interrupted. "There is one more very important matter," she said. "I want to be laid out and buried with a fork in my right hand."

The minister looked at her strangely. "A fork?" "Yes," the woman replied. "That seems strange to you, doesn't it?" The clergyman nodded and said, "Well, I admit it does seem a bit odd. And I'm puzzled. I haven't had a request like that ever before. But why the fork?"

The woman replied, "I've been attending church suppers and gatherings for years where food has been served. And my favorite part was always when someone clearing away the plates after the main course would lean over and say, 'Keep your fork!' I liked that best because I knew something better was coming. When they told me to keep my fork, I could be certain that a great joy was on its way for me. It wouldn't be just plain jello or a bland pudding. It would be a sumptuous piece of pie or a big slice of cake! Something with real substance! Therefore, I want you to tell the folks who ask about my holding that fork that something better is coming."

The pastor's eyes filled with tears as he and the woman prayed. He sensed that she had a better understanding of the resurrection hope than he did.

The woman passed away soon after their meeting. As people passed by her open casket, they noticed the Bible resting beside her body and the fork placed in her right hand. Many whispered, "What's with the fork?" During the funeral service the pastor told about the woman's request for the fork. Like the pastor, those present could not help but think from then on whenever they reached for the fork at a church potluck meal that something better is coming!

FOR YOUTH

■ TOPIC: A New Beginning

■ QUESTIONS: 1. How did the women react to the empty tomb and to the angels? 2. Why was it initially hard for Ananias and the Jerusalem church to accept Saul's conversion as genuine? 3. Why was Saul so powerful in his preaching, and why did his preaching arouse death plots against him? 4. What has been your most memorable experience in witnessing for Christ?

Why was it so memorable? 5. What are some ways your church can help you fulfill the Great Commission?

■ **ILLUSTRATIONS:**

Lives Again. Her remains were excavated by the Association for the Preservation of Virginia Antiquities, the group that owns the Jamestown site. She was discovered in the fall of 1998 by Jamie May as part of an on-going archaeological dig at the historical site.

This first lady was Mistress Forrest, the wife of Thomas Forrest. She had come to Jamestown in October 1608 from England. She was accompanied by her maid, Anne Burras. Mistress Forrest died shortly after arriving and was buried naked in an elaborate pinewood coffin. (In those days clothing was considered too valuable to bury with the dead.)

The remains of Mistress Forrest were taken to the Smithsonian Institution for careful examination. Painstaking analysis determined her diet to have been wheat rather than corn. It was also discovered that she was a Caucasian, four feet eight inches tall, and about 35 years old (quite old for that time!). Even her facial features were reconstructed using modern technology. But despite this, Mistress Forrest remains a lifeless mass.

Centuries earlier, others trooped to a burial site to look at the remains of someone who had meant so much to them. His life and words had been indelibly inscribed into their lives. However, instead of gazing at a corpse, they met the risen Lord. They discovered that He lives forevermore!

Put Things Right. On August 10, 1944, John McConnan was an aviator on a B-24 Liberator, guiding the plane back from a bombing raid over the German-held oil fields in Ploesti, Romania. The plane was hit by antiaircraft fire that severed the tail. Four men parachuted out and were captured by the Germans. McConnan and five others rode the plane down and were killed in what is today Albania. When the war ended and the Iron Curtain descended, there was no word of McConnan's body. This bothered James McConnan, John's younger brother.

When the Iron Curtain was lifted, James contacted Albanian journalists and enlisted help in searching for his brother's remains. James finally learned that the B-24 had crashed into a farmhouse and killed the entire family in Goraj, Albania. Villagers had buried two of the crewmen in an unmarked grave. Responding to James' request, members of the U.S. Army's Memorial Affairs Activity in Europe spoke with villagers, who directed them to the graves in 1995.

In April of 1998, James McConnan traveled to Albania to meet with men from the U.S. Army's Central Identification Laboratory. The group recovered the remains of the two servicemen. On March 5, 1999, the remains were positively identified as those of John McConnan and Wayne O. Shaffner. The remains were to be returned to the families for burial.

John McConnan was reburied on May 15, 1999, because a brother refused to rest until the fallen aviator was given a decent burial. James admitted, "It doesn't solve any problems and it doesn't make anything really different, but it puts it right."

Almost two millennia ago some women also wanted to put things right. They went out knowing that their simple embalming chores would not change recent events, but at least it would give their friend a decent burial. However, early that Sunday morning they discovered that Jesus was alive! No longer would He be just a memory. Now He was present among them!

Waiting for Someone to Come. Marilyn Laszlo serves as a Bible translator in the jungles of Papua New Guinea. In the village of Hauna she teaches the people to read and write their own language and has aided in the formation of a strong church.

One day, a canoe loaded with 15 people from a distant village arrived to receive medical help. They stayed for a week and attended services where they heard the Gospel for the first time. Before they returned home, the visitors asked, "Could you come to our village and give us God's Word so that we might know about God, too?"

Several weeks later, some Christians set out for the village. They arrived to find a new building, very different from their houses, standing in the center of the village. When the missionaries asked about the structure, they were told, "That's God's house! That's our church!"

The missionaries were puzzled, knowing there had not been any Christian work in that part of the country. "What's the building for?" they asked. "Well, we saw that church in your village, and our people decided to build a church, too. Now we are waiting for someone to tell us about God in our language."

Today there are over 2,000 groups like this one waiting to hear the Word of God in their language. They're waiting for someone like you to respond.

GENTILES RECEIVE THE SPIRIT

BACKGROUND SCRIPTURE: Acts 10:1—11:18
DEVOTIONAL READING: Galatians 3:11-14

KEY VERSE: "God shows no partiality, but in every nation anyone
who fears him and does what is right is acceptable to him." Acts 10:34b-35.

KING JAMES VERSION

ACTS 10:30 And Cornelius said, Four days ago I was fasting until this hour; and at the ninth hour I prayed in my house, and, behold, a man stood before me in bright clothing,

31 And said, Cornelius, thy prayer is heard, and thine alms are had in remembrance in the sight of God.

32 Send therefore to Joppa, and call hither Simon, whose surname is Peter; he is lodged in the house of one Simon a tanner by the sea side: who, when he cometh, shall speak unto thee.

33 Immediately therefore I sent to thee; and thou hast well done that thou art come. Now therefore are we all here present before God, to hear all things that are commanded thee of God.

34 Then Peter opened his mouth, and said, Of a truth I perceive that God is no respecter of persons:

35 But in every nation he that feareth him, and worketh righteousness, is accepted with him.

36 The word which God sent unto the children of Israel, preaching peace by Jesus Christ: (he is Lord of all:)

37 That word, I say, ye know, which was published throughout all Judæa, and began from Galilee, after the baptism which John preached;

38 How God anointed Jesus of Nazareth with the Holy Ghost and with power: who went about doing good, and healing all that were oppressed of the devil; for God was with him.

39 And we are witnesses of all things which he did both in the land of the Jews, and in Jerusalem. . . .

44 While Peter yet spake these words, the Holy Ghost fell on all them which heard the word.

45 And they of the circumcision which believed were astonished, as many as came with Peter, because that on the Gentiles also was poured out the gift of the Holy Ghost.

46 For they heard them speak with tongues, and magnify God. Then answered Peter,

47 Can any man forbid water, that these should not be baptized, which have received the Holy Ghost as well as we?

48 And he commanded them to be baptized in the name of the Lord. Then prayed they him to tarry certain days.

NEW REVISED STANDARD VERSION

ACTS 10:30 Cornelius replied, "Four days ago at this very hour, at three o'clock, I was praying in my house when suddenly a man in dazzling clothes stood before me. 31 He said, 'Cornelius, your prayer has been heard and your alms have been remembered before God. 32 Send therefore to Joppa and ask for Simon, who is called Peter; he is staying in the home of Simon, a tanner, by the sea.' 33 Therefore I sent for you immediately, and you have been kind enough to come. So now all of us are here in the presence of God to listen to all that the Lord has commanded you to say."

34 Then Peter began to speak to them: "I truly understand that God shows no partiality, 35 but in every nation anyone who fears him and does what is right is acceptable to him. 36 You know the message he sent to the people of Israel, preaching peace by Jesus Christ—he is Lord of all. 37 That message spread throughout Judea, beginning in Galilee after the baptism that John announced: 38 how God anointed Jesus of Nazareth with the Holy Spirit and with power; how he went about doing good and healing all who were oppressed by the devil, for God was with him. 39 We are witnesses to all that he did both in Judea and in Jerusalem. . . ."

44 While Peter was still speaking, the Holy Spirit fell upon all who heard the word. 45 The circumcised believers who had come with Peter were astounded that the gift of the Holy Spirit had been poured out even on the Gentiles, 46 for they heard them speaking in tongues and extolling God. Then Peter said, 47 "Can anyone withhold the water for baptizing these people who have received the Holy Spirit just as we have?" 48 So he ordered them to be baptized in the name of Jesus Christ. Then they invited him to stay for several days.

Monday, April 16	Acts 10:1-8	*Cornelius Sends for Peter*
Tuesday, April 17	Acts 10:9-16	*Peter's Vision*
Wednesday, April 18	Acts 10:17-22	*The Men at the Gate*
Thursday, April 19	Acts 10:23-33	*Peter Goes to Caesarea*
Friday, April 20	Acts 10:34-43	*Gentiles Hear the Good News*
Saturday, April 21	Acts 10:44-48	*Gentiles Receive the Holy Spirit*
Sunday, April 22	Acts 11:1-18	*Peter's Report in Jerusalem*

BACKGROUND

Cornelius was a centurion in the Roman military. A centurion was an offi-cer in charge of 100 soldiers. Sixty centurions were in a Roman legion, which was divided into 10 regiments or cohorts. Each cohort of 600 men had six centurions leading it. During the time of Cornelius, five cohorts were sta-tioned in Caesarea and one in Jerusalem.

Centurions were the equivalent of today's U.S. army sergeant major. Centurion was the highest rank that an ordinary enlisted soldier could attain. Promotion to this position was dependent upon battle experience and military savvy. Since cen-turions were given a great deal of autonomy on the battlefield, they had to think well on their feet.

The position of centurions was prestigious, and they were generally paid quite well. If his superiors thought well of him, a centurion could serve throughout the Roman Empire. And if a soldier reached the level of centurion, he generally stayed in that position for life.

The first Christians, who were Jews, had been carefully taught to hate and fear Gentiles. This week's lesson examines Peter's visit to Cornelius, a Roman centu-rion, and how the Spirit helped the apostle triumph over his prejudice and lead Cornelius to faith in his Jewish Messiah.

NOTES ON THE PRINTED TEXT

The earliest disciples were Jews, and they found it difficult to break with their ancient tradition of not associating with Gentiles. Gentiles occasion-ally converted to Judaism. But generally legalistic Jews dismissed Gentiles as pagans who were to be avoided. Early Christians in Judea—including Peter—found it difficult to shake their prejudices toward Gentiles. It took the work of the Spirit to overcome such personal bias.

In Caesarea [sess-uh-REE-uh] an angel appeared to Cornelius, a Roman centu-rion who worshiped the true God. The angel instructed Cornelius to send men to Joppa for Peter, and the noncommissioned military officer did as instructed. The day after Cornelius's vision, Peter too had a vision. Three times he saw a sheet con-taining unclean as well as clean animals. And three times a voice told Peter to kill and eat the animals because God had made them clean (Acts 10:1-16).

Peter welcomed Cornelius's servants and returned with them to Caesarea (10:17-28). In 1993, excavators from Corona, California, unearthed a wonderfully preserved mosaic floor that consisted of grape vines growing from vases in the corners, and these encircled birds, animals, and several human figures, creating the effect of a pattern of medallions. It was part of a private residence in Caesarea. Perhaps this is what the house of Cornelius looked like when Peter visited it.

Peter pointedly asked Cornelius why the soldier wanted him to come to Caesarea (10:29). In response, Cornelius said, *"Four days ago at this very hour, at three o'clock, I was praying in my house when suddenly a man in dazzling clothes stood before me"* (10:30). The heavenly messenger reassured the startled centurion that God had seen his faithfulness and generosity and had heard his prayer to know the Lord. *"Cornelius, your prayer has been heard and your alms have been remembered before God"* (10:31).

The angel directed Cornelius to dispatch messengers to find Peter and bring him back. The apostle was at the old seaport of Joppa (where Jonah had once disembarked). Cornelius complied and had Peter escorted. Given that the trip from Joppa to Caesarea was about 80 miles and normally took four days to make, it was expedient to act quickly. *"Send therefore to Joppa and ask for Simon, who is called Peter; he is staying in the home of Simon, a tanner, by the sea"* (10:32).

Peter's lodging in the home of Simon is noteworthy. Since tanners dealt with dead animals, this made Simon—and anyone in his house—ceremonially unclean. Strict Jews would never have associated with a tanner, but perhaps Peter had become sufficiently enlightened by the Spirit to break with some of the legalistic traditions of his past.

By the time Peter had arrived in Caesarea (along with six Jewish Christians from Joppa), Cornelius had gathered together all his family and friends to hear the apostle. *"Therefore I sent for you immediately, and you have been kind enough to come. So now all of us are here in the presence of God to listen to all that the Lord has commanded you to say"* (10:33).

Peter acknowledged a new understanding of the way God works. The apostle admitted that God is interested in Gentiles as well as Jews, that He does not show favoritism, and that He accepts people from every nation who honor Him as God (10:34-35). It's clear that Cornelius fit this description.

The apostle reminded his audience that Jesus' mission of peace—that is, reconciliation with God—was first given to the Israelites. Now that Christ had risen from the dead, His peace extended to Gentiles as well as Jews. That's why Peter referred to Jesus as *Lord of all* (10:36).

Peter stated that the Gospel was first proclaimed to the inhabitants living in Jerusalem and Judea. The apostle then took his audience back to the beginning of Jesus' earthly ministry. After John had baptized Jesus, He began to minister in Galilee (10:37). All that Jesus did was sanctioned by the Father and met with His approval, for He had given Jesus the Spirit and supernatural power. Jesus *"went about doing good and healing all who were oppressed by the devil, for God was with him"* (10:38).

Peter declared, *"We are witnesses to all that he did both in Judea and in Jerusalem"* (10:39). For instance, the apostle noted that though the authorities had crucified Jesus, God raised Him from the dead and allowed Him to appear to His followers, namely, those who had been with Him after His resurrection (10:39-41). God had directed Jesus' disciples to proclaim the good news of salvation so that all who trusted in Him would have their sins forgiven (10:42-43).

Even as Peter was saying these things, *the Holy Spirit fell upon all who heard the word* (10:44). The Jewish Christians who had come with Peter were amazed that God had poured out His Spirit on believing Gentiles (10:45-46). There could be no doubt that God had given *even to Gentiles the repentance that leads to life* (11:18).

SUGGESTIONS TO TEACHERS

Like certain exclusive country clubs, some churches are determined to keep membership limited to "those who are our kind of people." Most Christian churches have gone on record as welcoming all persons, but few congregations include many of a different racial, ethnic, or national origin. This week's lesson centers on how the early church was prompted to welcome Gentiles. We are reminded that the Spirit wants us to be inclusive of all.

1. THE SPIRIT INTERCEDES WITH CORNELIUS. Cornelius, the Roman centurion, was a devout Gentile who feared God (Acts 10:1-2). Nevertheless, he was a stranger to *the covenants of promise* (Eph. 2:12). In fact, he lacked one thing, namely, a knowledge of Jesus as Messiah. God answered the prayers of Cornelius when the Spirit brought Peter into the centurion's life. Let your students know that many outside the church long and even pray for a deeper knowledge of God. Encourage the class members to let the Spirit use them to bring the Gospel to those in their community who need to hear it.

2. THE SPIRIT INTERVENES WITH PETER. At first Peter had no intention of fellowshipping with a Gentile. But the Spirit intervened and changed Peter's outlook (Acts 11:16-17). How has the Spirit worked in the lives of your students to help them overcome any personal prejudices that may be limiting their Christian witness?

3. THE SPIRIT INTERPRETS FOR SKEPTICS. The Spirit gets all the credit for getting the early church to welcome outsiders. To the world at that time, this inclusive attitude may have seemed radical. In our world with fighting and murders between ethnic and religious groups, some conclude that it's futile to think people can welcome anyone who is different. Encourage your students to pray for God's peace and love to prevail in their community and around the world.

4. THE SPIRIT INTERPOSES WITH CRITICS. Note that initially the Jewish believers back in Jerusalem could not comprehend the extraordinary work of God among the Gentiles. They criticized Peter, who was forced to defend his actions and show that the gift of the Spirit to Gentile believers was God's decision, not his (Acts 11:1-18). Just as God used Peter, so too He can use the witness of your students to make His will and ways known to others.

<table>
<tr><td rowspan="2">FOR ADULTS</td><td>■ TOPIC: Called to Be Inclusive</td></tr>
<tr><td>■ QUESTIONS: 1. How do Cornelius's words to Peter show that the</td></tr>
</table>

■ **TOPIC:** Called to Be Inclusive
■ **QUESTIONS:** 1. How do Cornelius's words to Peter show that the centurion had a heart that was open to God? 2. What great change in God's dealings with humanity does Acts 10:34-35 show? 3. How did the coming of the Spirit in Cornelius's home show that God did not intend the Gentiles to be second-class church members? 4. Why is racial prejudice a powerful and long-lasting influence on social relationships? 5. In what sense might we be tempted to call "impure" those whom God has made clean?

■ **ILLUSTRATIONS:**

The Detrimental Effect of Prejudice. During his student days, Indian nationalist leader Mahatma Gandhi was genuinely interested in the Bible. He admitted being deeply touched by reading the Gospels and seriously considered becoming a Christian. He sensed that this religion offered a real solution to the caste system that divided the people of his country.

One Sunday Gandhi visited a nearby church. He wanted to see the minister and ask him for instruction on how to be saved. When Gandhi entered the sanctuary, however, the ushers refused to give him a seat. They suggested that he go and worship with his own people. Gandhi left that church and never came back. He remembered saying to himself, "If Christians have caste differences also, I might as well remain a Hindu."

When we allow personal prejudices to exist in our lives, it will limit our Christian witness. With God's help we can abandon our prejudices of others who seem different from us.

Welcoming Our New Neighbors? Immigration is changing the complexion of America. Since the early 1980s, more than 13 million newcomers have settled here—a number roughly equal to the population of New England. In many ways, this new wave of immigrants is creating two Americas: one that is young, urban, and multicultural, and another that is elderly, suburban or rural, and almost all white. How are we in the church responding to this influx of new neighbors? How welcoming are Caucasian Christians to the non-white, non-English speaking among us?

An Inclusive Church. When Henry Coffin became pastor of the Madison Avenue Presbyterian Church in New York City in 1905, he was chagrined to find two separate congregations under one roof. There was a small chapel for use by lower-class families for worship. These were denied access to the main sanctuary, a common practice in the city at that time.

Coffin got the church officers to combine all families into one worshiping congregation and stopped the longstanding practice of pew rents. He saw to it that the doors of the church were no longer locked between Sundays. He welcomed health and welfare groups to meet at the Madison Avenue Church. Other congregations took their cue from Henry Coffin, and unlocked their doors to the community. And Madison Avenue Church's membership grew from about 500 members in 1905 to over 2,200 by the time Coffin left.

FOR YOUTH

■ **TOPIC:** Everyone Counts
■ **QUESTIONS:** 1. In what ways did both Cornelius and Peter obey God? 2. Why did Peter's personal testimony make his message more powerful? 3. If you had been a member of Peter's group, how would you have answered those who argued against the inclusion of Gentiles? 4. What walls have come down in your relationships as a result of knowing Jesus? What walls still need to come down? 5. What can your church do to help newcomers feel welcome?

■ **ILLUSTRATIONS:**

All Count in the Game. Though he was never credited for it, former manager and Hall of Famer, Leo Durocher, played a key role in Jackie Robinson's historic breaking of baseball's color line with the Brooklyn Dodgers after World War II. In 1947, the Dodgers went to Panama for several exhibition games. A number of the players were angry that Robinson, an African American, was debuting at the major league level. They drew up a petition stating that they would walk out if Robinson played.

When Durocher heard about the petition, he had all the players awakened in the middle of the night and assembled in the hotel kitchen. Without mincing words and using typical Durocher terminology, the manager told the team what he thought about their petition and their prejudices. He stated that he admired Robinson, and said he thought Robinson would make the Dodgers a better team. The petition was never mentioned again!

Durocher was one person who stood up for integrated sports. He should be respected and recognized for the courageous and unpopular stand he took. Peter, too, learned that everyone counts when it comes to the proclamation of the Gospel and that everyone should be given an opportunity to believe in Christ.

Elitism. On July 19, 1998, owners of several of Europe's top soccer clubs met in London to form their own super league in the 2000–2001 season. The meeting of powerhouse teams was so secret that the clubs would not admit that a meeting ever took place. The clubs, who are the richest, were unhappy with the Premier League (the group that oversees the 20-club league) and would prefer playing only each other on a regular basis rather than other teams.

These elite groups wanted to exclude others from playing because they supposedly were not as good at the game. The same feelings of elitism existed in the early church, too. And it took the Spirit of God to break such prejudice.

Last Bastions. Steven Spielberg was the director of *Schindler's List*, the Oscar-winning movie about the Holocaust. According to the June 29, 1994, edition of the *Portland Press Herald*, Spielberg said the following in a hearing before the U.S. Senate:

> Hatred exists, not because people have never seen or heard of a Jew, or a Latino, or an African American, or an Asian, or a Native American . . . it exists because people learn to hate.

Only God can set us free from whatever prejudices we have. Let us lean on Him for the strength to overcome our generalized fears and adverse feelings toward others.

THE CHURCH IN ANTIOCH

BACKGROUND SCRIPTURE: Acts 11:19-30; 13:1-3
DEVOTIONAL READING: Ephesians 3:7-12

KEY VERSE: While they were worshiping the Lord and fasting, the Holy Spirit said, "Set apart for me Barnabas and Saul for the work to which I have called them." Acts 13:2.

KING JAMES VERSION

ACTS 11:19 Now they which were scattered abroad upon the persecution that arose about Stephen travelled as far as Phenice, and Cyprus, and Antioch, preaching the word to none but unto the Jews only.

20 And some of them were men of Cyprus and Cyrene, which, when they were come to Antioch, spake unto the Grecians, preaching the Lord Jesus.

21 And the hand of the Lord was with them: and a great number believed, and turned unto the Lord.

22 Then tidings of these things came unto the ears of the church which was in Jerusalem: and they sent forth Barnabas, that he should go as far as Antioch.

23 Who, when he came, and had seen the grace of God, was glad, and exhorted them all, that with purpose of heart they would cleave unto the Lord.

24 For he was a good man, and full of the Holy Ghost and of faith: and much people was added unto the Lord.

25 Then departed Barnabas to Tarsus, for to seek Saul:

26 And when he had found him, he brought him unto Antioch. And it came to pass, that a whole year they assembled themselves with the church, and taught much people. And the disciples were called Christians first in Antioch.

27 And in these days came prophets from Jerusalem unto Antioch.

28 And there stood up one of them named Agabus, and signified by the Spirit that there should be great dearth throughout all the world: which came to pass in the days of Claudius Caesar.

29 Then the disciples, every man according to his ability, determined to send relief unto the brethren which dwelt in Judæa:

30 Which also they did, and sent it to the elders by the hands of Barnabas and Saul.

13:1 Now there were in the church that was at Antioch certain prophets and teachers; as Barnabas, and Simeon that was called Niger, and Lucius of Cyrene, and Manaen, which had been brought up with Herod the tetrarch, and Saul.

2 As they ministered to the Lord, and fasted, the Holy Ghost said, Separate me Barnabas and Saul for the work whereunto I have called them.

3 And when they had fasted and prayed, and laid their hands on them, they sent them away.

NEW REVISED STANDARD VERSION

ACTS 11:19 Now those who were scattered because of the persecution that took place over Stephen traveled as far as Phoenicia, Cyprus, and Antioch, and they spoke the word to no one except Jews. 20 But among them were some men of Cyprus and Cyrene who, on coming to Antioch, spoke to the Hellenists also, proclaiming the Lord Jesus. 21 The hand of the Lord was with them, and a great number became believers and turned to the Lord. 22 News of this came to the ears of the church in Jerusalem, and they sent Barnabas to Antioch. 23 When he came and saw the grace of God, he rejoiced, and he exhorted them all to remain faithful to the Lord with steadfast devotion; 24 for he was a good man, full of the Holy Spirit and of faith. And a great many people were brought to the Lord. 25 Then Barnabas went to Tarsus to look for Saul, 26 and when he had found him, he brought him to Antioch. So it was that for an entire year they met with the church and taught a great many people, and it was in Antioch that the disciples were first called "Christians."

27 At that time prophets came down from Jerusalem to Antioch. 28 One of them named Agabus stood up and predicted by the Spirit that there would be a severe famine over all the world; and this took place during the reign of Claudius. 29 The disciples determined that according to their ability, each would send relief to the believers living in Judea; 30 this they did, sending it to the elders by Barnabas and Saul. . . .

13:1 Now in the church at Antioch there were prophets and teachers: Barnabas, Simeon who was called Niger, Lucius of Cyrene, Manaen a member of the court of Herod the ruler, and Saul. 2 While they were worshiping the Lord and fasting, the Holy Spirit said, "Set apart for me Barnabas and Saul for the work to which I have called them." 3 Then after fasting and praying they laid their hands on them and sent them off.

BACKGROUND

After the stoning of Stephen, many Christians from the early church in Jerusalem fled for their lives. A number of them were Greek-speaking Jews, and they went telling the good news throughout the surrounding region, eventually reaching Antioch of Syria. As a result, in the course of the next few decades, the center of evangelistic activity shifted from Jerusalem to Antioch. In fact, as we will learn in this week's lesson, the city became the hub for much of the Spirit's most creative work.

Antioch at that time was one of the three largest metropolitan areas of the Roman Empire. And, as a rival to Rome and Alexandria, Antioch was one of the world's chief commercial centers. The city was also renowned for its wealth and culture. Its citizens were regarded as worldly and sophisticated.

In the midst of this great city, the Spirit seemed to bring together a community of dedicated believers who used their gifts and intelligence to serve Christ. This enabled the congregation at Antioch to be resourceful and vigorous in reaching out to others with the Gospel. All three of Paul's missionary journeys started in Syrian Antioch. In fact, the city was the home of Paul and Barnabas during their evangelistic partnership.

NOTES ON THE PRINTED TEXT

Like shock waves moving out in concentric circles from an earthquake's epicenter, the Gospel continued to spread beyond Jerusalem. It proceeded up the Mediterranean coastline through what is today Lebanon and into Turkey and westward toward Cyprus. *Now those who were scattered because of the persecution that took place over Stephen traveled as far as Phoenicia, Cyprus, and Antioch, and they spoke the word to no one except Jews* (Acts 11:19).

Antioch (now modern day Antakia, Turkey) was the third most important city of the Roman Empire and the capitol of the Roman province of Syria. Antioch was situated on major land and sea trade routes, and it was a wealthy and cultured city with temples, theaters, palaces, villas, a circus, and a forum. Antioch also boasted the world-renowned groves of Daphne and a sanctuary dedicated to Apollo. It had a huge Jewish population that made it especially attractive to believers proclaiming the Gospel far and wide.

At first the good news was shared only with Jews. But some believers who went to Antioch from Cyprus (an island only 62 miles away) and Cyrene (a North African port city) began preaching to Hellenists about the Savior. *But among them were some men of Cyprus and Cyrene who, on coming to Antioch, spoke to the Hellenists also, proclaiming the Lord Jesus* (11:20). These evangelistic efforts brought amazing results, and the church grew significantly. *The hand of the Lord was with them, and a great number became believers and turned to the Lord* (11:21).

The growth in new converts, while a cause for celebration, was also one of concern. The Jerusalem leaders, being cautious by nature, were initially leery when they heard about what was taking place in Antioch. (After all, the city had a bad moral tone because of the lewd rites associated with the temple of Apollo.) They sent Barnabas to investigate the genuineness of the new members' conversion. At 375 miles, all done on foot and covering roughly 20 miles per day, this would have been a rigorous trip. *News of this came to the ears of the church in Jerusalem, and they sent Barnabas to Antioch* (11:22).

The work and power of the Holy Spirit impressed Barnabas immensely, and he praised God. Not content to sit and idly watch others do the hard work of ministry, Barnabas aided in the evangelistic effort. Consequently, more and more Gentiles committed their lives to Christ. *When he came and saw the grace of God, he rejoiced, and he exhorted them all to remain faithful to the Lord with steadfast devotion; for he was a good man, full of the Holy Spirit and of faith. And a great many people were brought to the Lord* (11:23-24).

Barnabas was astute enough to realize that additional help was needed for the growing congregation. That's when he remembered Saul (Paul). After Barnabas brought Saul to Antioch, the two worked for a year ministering to the rapidly growing church. It was here that the name "Christian" was first given to believers. Originally, it was a sarcastic label full of ridicule and scorn, but eventually it became a title of distinction. *Then Barnabas went to Tarsus to look for Saul, and when he had found him, he brought him to Antioch. So it was that for an entire year they met with the church and taught a great many people, and it was in Antioch that the disciples were first called "Christians."* (11:25-26).

The believers' commitment to Christ was evidenced by their actions. Prophets arrived from Jerusalem and one of them, Agabus, warned that a famine was coming (11:27-28). The reign of Emperor Claudius endured several severe famines that produced misery and hunger. Food became scarce and expensive. The church of Antioch set about to raise a relief fund for the hungry believers in Jerusalem. Barnabas and Saul then hand-delivered their donations. *The disciples determined that according to their ability, each would send relief to the believers living in Judea; this they did, sending it to the elders by Barnabas and Saul* (11:29-30).

After Barnabas and Saul completed their mission in Jerusalem, they returned to Syrian Antioch and brought with them John Mark, Barnabas's cousin (Col.

4:10). Barnabas and Saul continued to provide capable and vibrant leadership for the church at Antioch, along with three other men, one of whom had ties to Herod's court (Acts 13:1). (The church's evangelism program had reached into government circles! Also, the two leaders were from Africa.)

The disciplined group worshiped, prayed, and fasted together, and they tried to discern God's will. The Spirit disclosed to the believers that they were to ordain and commission Barnabas and Saul to go on an evangelistic journey. *While they were worshiping the Lord and fasting, the Holy Spirit said, "Set apart for me Barnabas and Saul for the work to which I have called them"* (13:2).

After the leaders of the congregation engaged in more fasting and praying, they dedicated Barnabas and Saul for the work awaiting them by laying hands on them (an ancient Jewish practice). Then the congregation *sent them off* (13:3).

SUGGESTIONS TO TEACHERS

Where will your congregation be in 10 years? Is it merely trying to survive? Do outsiders see it as a vibrant community of energetic Christians? Do your fellow members merely regard their task as a holding operation, especially in the midst of all the change taking place in the world? Do you hear some saying, "We'll try to keep plodding along as before"? If your answer to any of these questions is *yes,* then this week's lesson describing the church in Syrian Antioch may be the jump-start by the Spirit your congregation needs!

1. NEW LEADERS. Begin by noting the list of those heading the ministry of the Syrian Antioch congregation. Most of them were from places other than Judea. The old guard of believers in Jerusalem gradually faded into the background. The Spirit was calling forth a new group of multicultural Christians to proclaim the Gospel far and wide. And the church was willing to acknowledge these new leaders. How may such a humble and flexible attitude allow the Spirit to raise up new leaders in your church?

2. NEW NAME. The name "Christian" was first used in Syrian Antioch. When it was initially thrown at believers, it was meant as a term of contempt. Fellow citizens in Antioch were famous for deriding others with nicknames meant to poke fun and belittle. But believers in Antioch accepted what was meant as a put-down. The word "Christian" originally meant a mini-Christ, and eventually church people everywhere proudly bore the name. Ask whether the members of your class regard themselves as followers of Christ in this way. Do others see Jesus in action through the lives of your students?

3. NEW CENTER. Syrian Antioch eventually supplanted Jerusalem as the hub of activity for the spread of the Gospel. This meant that some had to learn to let go of old ways and old attitudes. What changes in your church is the Spirit trying to bring about? Which are the hardest to accept? Why? What can your students do to help the transition go more smoothly?

4. NEW MISSION. The church in Syrian Antioch sent relief aid to suffering fellow Christians, including those in Jerusalem. In addition to sending aid, the believers in Antioch also sent capable helpers (for example, Barnabas and Saul). The Spirit had given the church the desire and ability to meet a variety of human needs in the name of Christ. Even today a congregation that is spiritually alive remains sensitive to the needs of the hungry and destitute.

5. NEW TRIALS. Fresh persecution tested the faith of the fledgling congregations in Syrian Antioch and Jerusalem. The account of Peter's dramatic release from prison reminds us that believers may expect opposition and hardship, but also know that the Spirit stands with those who suffer for Christ (Acts 12:1-17).

6. NEW FORMS. The church in Syrian Antioch broke new ground by designating *prophets and teachers* (Acts 13:1) as the titles for the principal leaders in the congregation. Take time to discuss what these two titles suggest for the church today. Are there persons who are capable spokespersons for the Lord in your congregation? And who are the real teachers? How may your students assist the Spirit to raise up such believers for Christian service?

FOR ADULTS	■ **TOPIC:** Reaching Out to Others ■ **QUESTIONS:** 1. How did the persecution of the Christians in Jerusalem contribute to the spread of the Gospel?

2. How was the hand of God evident in the evangelistic efforts of the early Christians? 3. In what ways do you think the character of Barnabas helped the Antioch church? 4. If you had been a member of the Antioch church, how would you have reacted to Agabus's prophecy? Why? 5. What can churches do to build relationships with congregations of other ethnic groups?

■ **ILLUSTRATIONS:**

Apostle to Cannibals. Today tourists enjoy the hospitality of the friendly people in the South Seas nation of Vanuatu. Formerly known as the New Hebrides, and situated between Australia and Fiji, Vanuatu gained its independence in 1980. Christian churches led by native-born pastors are in evidence everywhere. The gentle inhabitants of the islands making up the nation welcome visitors. But few people coming to these islands realize that only a century and a half ago, the ancestors of the pleasant, friendly inhabitants in Vanuatu today were fierce cannibals. The dramatic change is largely due to a believer named John G. Paton.

Paton was born in Scotland in 1824. Despite being raised in a poor home and having little formal education, John answered Christ's call to serve as a missionary. Paton, his bride, and two associates sailed to the New Hebrides in 1858. They quickly discovered how difficult the living conditions were and how fierce the opposition proved to be.

In 1859, Paton's wife gave birth to their child, a baby boy whom they named

Peter, but Mrs. Paton became ill and died. A week later, little Peter also died. Paton had to dig the graves himself for his wife and baby. Despite these tragic losses, John continued to persevere. He sought to reach out to natives who fought viciously among themselves, cooked and ate their victims, robbed each other, and lived in superstition.

Paton's life was threatened repeatedly. In 1862, he was driven from the island of Tanna, where he had built a small chapel and school, fleeing with only the clothes on his back, his Bible, and the notes for a translation of parts of the Bible into Tannese. Rather than quit, Paton started over again on the neighboring island of Aniwa. And despite continuing privations and dangers, he eventually developed a training institute, a church, an orphanage, and hospitals. People finally began to respond to this kindly Scot's missionary message.

When a chief became a Christian, the scene changed for the better. Chief Namakei publicly testified that the Christian missionaries had brought good news, stating, "Something here in my heart tells me that the Lord God does exist—whom we never heard about until these missionaries came." This chief's witness helped to break the hold of violence and superstition in the islands. Without coercion, the entire population of the New Hebrides gradually became Christians! Paton finally retired, and passed away in Australia in 1907, knowing that he had succeeded in reaching a population of Pacific islanders for the Lord.

Wake-up Call. In *Survival or Revival: Ten Keys to Church Vitality* (Westminster John Knox Press, 1998), Carnegie S. Calian wrote the following:

> Will churches merely survive or will they come alive in the twenty-first century? This is the real question facing most churches; the many publicized issues only cloud the picture. How do we work for congregational vitality as we enter the next century? What commitments are we willing to initiate and sustain toward this goal? Is there a singular vision for congregational vitality? We have tall challenges before us if our churches are to be transformed into vital congregations. The choice is ours: Do we wish merely to survive or do we want to come alive in the twenty-first century? The wake-up call beckons.

FOR YOUTH

■ TOPIC: Build Up the Body
■ QUESTIONS: 1. How much courage do you think it took for some Christians to reach out to pagan Gentiles with the Gospel? 2. Why did the leaders in the Jerusalem church think it was necessary to send Barnabas to Syrian Antioch? 3. What attributes do you think Barnabas spotted in Saul that convinced him that Saul would be a good partner? 4. Do you think it is rare today for one church to give financial resources to another? If so, why? 5. In what ways can people in your church support missionaries and evangelists?

■ ILLUSTRATIONS:

Lost Vitality. Bellefield Tower sits at the corner of Fifth and Bellefield Avenues in Pittsburgh. Originally it was the bell tower and spire of a local church that was constructed in 1889.

Through the years the church flourished. However, by the 1960's the church, like many inner city congregations, experienced a membership loss as parishioners fled to the suburbs. As membership declined, so did the vitality of the church. The median age rose. Finally, because the congregation could not afford to maintain itself, it closed. On April 14, 1985, the final service was held in the sanctuary. The site was then sold to National Development, a company that constructed an office complex on the property. However, the tower was left as a decoration.

Contrast the loss of this church's vitality with the enormous energy of the congregation in Antioch. It was eager to reach out and participate in ministry. It sent missionaries and money. And it proved to be a vibrant and alive fellowship.

Felt the Urgency. From 1970 to 1995, the proportion of hungry people worldwide dropped from one-third to one-fifth. The findings were made in a report by Bread for the World Institute, a nonprofit Christian organization.

The report noted that the planet has been able to respond to potential famine and increased government spending. However, world leaders still do little to feed the poor, even in the United States. As a result, hunger still remains a chronic problem. For instance, over 841 million people are malnourished in South Asia and Africa. The report stated that it would take a modest effort to end hunger and malnutrition by 2015. Bread for the World urged a recapture of the "religious urgency" to end famine around the globe.

The early church had a genuine desire to feed the hungry and malnourished. For example, Barnabas and Saul carried the Antioch church's offering to Jerusalem in order that no believer there should suffer hunger any longer.

Promoting Unity through Caring. Lee Iacocca once asked legendary football coach Vince Lombardi what it took to make a winning team. He answered, "If you're going to play together as a team, you've got to care for one another. You've got to love each other. Each player has to be thinking about the next guy and saying to himself: 'If I don't block that man, Paul is going to get his legs broken. I have to do my job well in order that he can do his.'"

In a Christ-centered church each believer cares for one another. They do so regardless of who they are or where they're from. This attitude promotes a unity within the body that transcends racial, ethnic, and cultural differences.

MISSION TO GENTILES

BACKGROUND SCRIPTURE: Acts 13:4—14:28

DEVOTIONAL READING: Psalm 96

KEY VERSE: "I have set you to be a light for the Gentiles, so that you may bring salvation to the ends of the earth. Acts 13:47.

KING JAMES VERSION

ACTS 13:14 But when they departed from Perga, they came to Antioch in Pisidia, and went into the synagogue on the sabbath day, and sat down.

15 And after the reading of the law and the prophets the rulers of the synagogue sent unto them, saying, Ye men and brethren, if ye have any word of exhortation for the people, say on. . . .

42 And when the Jews were gone out of the synagogue, the Gentiles besought that these words might be preached to them the next sabbath.

43 Now when the congregation was broken up, many of the Jews and religious proselytes followed Paul and Barnabas: who, speaking to them, persuaded them to continue in the grace of God.

44 And the next sabbath day came almost the whole city together to hear the word of God.

45 But when the Jews saw the multitudes, they were filled with envy, and spake against those things which were spoken by Paul, contradicting and blaspheming.

46 Then Paul and Barnabas waxed bold, and said, It was necessary that the word of God should first have been spoken to you: but seeing ye put it from you, and judge yourselves unworthy of everlasting life, lo, we turn to the Gentiles.

47 For so hath the Lord commanded us, saying, I have set thee to be a light of the Gentiles, that thou shouldest be for salvation unto the ends of the earth.

48 And when the Gentiles heard this, they were glad, and glorified the word of the Lord: and as many as were ordained to eternal life believed.

49 And the word of the Lord was published throughout all the region.

50 But the Jews stirred up the devout and honourable women, and the chief men of the city, and raised persecution against Paul and Barnabas, and expelled them out of their coasts.

51 But they shook off the dust of their feet against them, and came unto Iconium.

52 And the disciples were filled with joy, and with the Holy Ghost.

NEW REVISED STANDARD VERSION

ACTS 13:14 But they went on from Perga and came to Antioch in Pisidia. And on the sabbath day they went into the synagogue and sat down. 15 After the reading of the law and the prophets, the officials of the synagogue sent them a message, saying, "Brothers, if you have any word of exhortation for the people, give it." . . .

42 As Paul and Barnabas were going out, the people urged them to speak about these things again the next sabbath. 43 When the meeting of the synagogue broke up, many Jews and devout converts to Judaism followed Paul and Barnabas, who spoke to them and urged them to continue in the grace of God.

44 The next sabbath almost the whole city gathered to hear the word of the Lord. 45 But when the Jews saw the crowds, they were filled with jealousy; and blaspheming, they contradicted what was spoken by Paul. 46 Then both Paul and Barnabas spoke out boldly, saying, "It was necessary that the word of God should be spoken first to you. Since you reject it and judge yourselves to be unworthy of eternal life, we are now turning to the Gentiles. 47 For so the Lord has commanded us, saying,

'I have set you to be a light for the Gentiles,
so that you may bring salvation to the ends of
the earth.'"

48 When the Gentiles heard this, they were glad and praised the word of the Lord; and as many as had been destined for eternal life became believers. 49 Thus the word of the Lord spread throughout the region. 50 But the Jews incited the devout women of high standing and the leading men of the city, and stirred up persecution against Paul and Barnabas, and drove them out of their region. 51 So they shook the dust off their feet in protest against them, and went to Iconium. 52 And the disciples were filled with joy and with the Holy Spirit.

10

BACKGROUND

The church in Syrian Antioch poured forth exciting new forms of witnessing and serving. The Spirit-led members of that young congregation seemed unhampered by past traditions and were willing to embark on untried paths. Among other new ventures, the Antioch Christians decided to dispatch two of their number, Barnabas and Saul, on an evangelistic tour of Cyprus.

Cyprus was an island easily reached from Syrian Antioch in ancient times. Cyprus was also the home of Barnabas. We don't know whether Barnabas had heard about Jesus and been baptized earlier while on Cyprus or later after leaving for the mainland. But it's clear that Barnabas felt a concern to bring the good news of Christ to his friends and relatives back home.

Saul's dramatic conversion, which occurred while he was heading to Damascus to persecute Christians, had proven to be genuine. After initial reluctance by some believers to accept him, he had gained respect for his tireless efforts to introduce the Gospel to everyone he met. He was in his hometown of Tarsus when Barnabas sought him out and brought him to Syrian Antioch.

After being set apart by the church through the laying on of hands, and having been commissioned by the church as traveling evangelists, Barnabas and Saul sailed to Cyprus. It was the start of the momentous missionary journeys described in Acts. They boldly preached first in synagogues to offer Jews the good news of the Messiah. When pushed out, the missionaries next preached on street corners and in marketplaces, inviting Gentiles to receive the Savior by faith. Despite opposition, beatings, imprisonment, and other afflictions, this pair of early missionaries fearlessly carried God's Word to the cities in Cyprus and across into what is now known as Asia Minor.

NOTES ON THE PRINTED TEXT

Paul, Barnabas, and Mark traveled from Syrian Antioch to the port city of Seleucia and from there to Cyprus. After they evangelized their way across the island to the city of Paphos, Paul and Barnabas sailed to Perga. But Mark quit and returned to Jerusalem (Acts 13:1-13).

Meanwhile the two missionaries hiked almost 150 miles to Antioch in Pisidia (now Yalvac in modern Turkey). The trip would have been grueling, moving from the coastlands across a towering mountain range that rises 7,000 feet. The rocky terrain would have been snow covered, making progress slow. Certainly the two covered less than the daily average of 20 miles. Floods, hail, cold, rockslides, wild animals, and thieves would have made the trip even more hazardous.

The missionaries *went on from Perga and came to Antioch in Pisidia* (13:14). This city was a Roman civil and military administrative center built almost midway on the main trading route between Ephesus and Cilicia. It also had a large Jewish population. Paul and Barnabas sought out these people. *And on the sabbath day they went into the synagogue and sat down.*

The service normally included readings from the law and the prophets, after which visitors were invited to speak. *After the reading of the law and the prophets, the officials of the synagogue sent them a message, saying, "Brothers, if you have any word of exhortation for the people, give it"* (13:15).

Paul reviewed Israel's history from God's choice of the Hebrew people up until Jesus' death and resurrection. The apostle also commented on the Exodus and gave a brief overview of the history of Israel's kings. Most importantly, Paul emphasized the forgiveness of sins that is available to all people through faith in the Messiah (13:16-41).

As the missionaries left the synagogue, enthusiastic worshipers asked them to speak at the next service. *As Paul and Barnabas were going out, the people urged them to speak about these things again the next sabbath* (13:42). As the two exited, surrounded by thrilled listeners, they urged the people to live God-centered lives. *When the meeting of the synagogue broke up, many Jews and devout converts to Judaism followed Paul and Barnabas, who spoke to them and urged them to continue in the grace of God* (13:43).

During the week between the two services, Paul's sermon was frequently discussed. The next Sabbath the synagogue was packed, much to the disgust of the religious leaders. They were upset that Paul had declared that the Gentiles were also accepted by God. *But when the Jews saw the crowds, they were filled with jealousy; and blaspheming, they contradicted what was spoken by Paul* (13:45)

If the legalists refused to accept the Gospel, then Paul and Barnabas would share it elsewhere, even if it meant taking it to those long considered to be outside the scope of God's love. *"It was necessary that the word of God should be spoken first to you. Since you reject it and judge yourselves to be unworthy of eternal life, we are now turning to the Gentiles"* (13:46).

Paul, quoting from Isaiah 49:6, reminded the congregation that God had always been interested in bringing Gentiles to a knowledge of the truth. And the Lord originally intended His people to shine the light of salvation to the ends of the earth. *"For so the Lord has commanded . . . 'I have set you to be a light for the Gentiles, so that you may bring salvation to the ends of the earth'"* (Acts 13:47).

The preaching of Paul and Barnabas continued to bring new people to Christ. *When the Gentiles heard this, they were glad and praised the word of the Lord;*

and as many as had been destined for eternal life became believers (13:48). However, their preaching also produced a backlash. Suspicion and jealousy led to political maneuvering, and the two were forced out of the district. *But the Jews incited the devout women of high standing and the leading men of the city, and stirred up persecution against Paul and Barnabas, and drove them out of their region* (13:50).

Often Jews would shake the dust off their feet when leaving a Gentile town on the way back to their own land. This symbolized cleansing themselves from the contamination of those who did not worship God. For Paul and Barnabas to do this to religious legalists demonstrated that those who rejected the Gospel were not truly part of the community of faith and were no better than Gentile unbelievers. Paul and Barnabas were not to blame for the good news being rejected, for they had faithfully presented it. They reflected this unwavering commitment by going on to Iconium (13:51). Meanwhile, *the disciples were filled with joy and with the Holy Spirit.*

SUGGESTIONS TO TEACHERS

You've undoubtedly heard someone say, "I don't believe in missions. Why bother to send missionaries? There's plenty to do here at home!" Thankfully, the Christians in Syrian Antioch didn't feel that way. And this wasn't the attitude of countless forgotten missionaries who have brought the light of Christ to the world down through the centuries. Even today the Spirit impels us to share the glad tidings everywhere!

1. PROMISING POSSIBILITIES. Begin by pointing out to your students how Paul and Barnabas traveled to new areas and tried new methods in their evangelistic endeavors. They even broke with tradition by welcoming non-Jews into the community of faith. Formerly, only an occasional Gentile was welcomed, but now these missionaries established congregations made up principally of former pagans. What daring new approaches to telling others about Christ could the Spirit be suggesting the members of your class to try?

2. PREACHING PATTERN. The usual way Paul and Barnabas spread the Gospel was to preach first in the local synagogue. They looked upon the Jewish community as a possible seedbed for planting the truth of the Gospel. As time permits, have your students look at the sermon Paul proclaimed in Antioch of Pisidia (Acts 13:16-41). (This city, located in Asia Minor, was different from the Antioch of Syria). Ask the class members to pick out the main points Paul stressed in his message. In what ways are his statements still valid today?

3. PERSISTENT PERSECUTION. The brave pair of missionaries suffered severely for their efforts to tell others about Christ. Ask your students to note some of the times that Paul and his associates were rejected and jailed. The class members will see that spreading the Gospel cost the missionaries safety and comfort. What challenges do your students encounter to their faith? How have they learned to handle these challenges? Note that God calls us to make Christ known to others, regardless of the personal cost.

4. PROPER PRAISE. After returning to Syrian Antioch, Paul and Barnabas related how successful they had been in establishing a cluster of Christian congregations in the heart of Asia Minor (Acts 14:26). Note how they properly ascribed their success to the Lord: *They . . . related all that God had done with them* (14:27). Humility is a sign of a true follower of Christ! Encourage your students to give God the credit for their successes in ministry.

FOR ADULTS

■ **TOPIC:** Opening New Doors

■ **QUESTIONS:** 1. Why did Paul, rather than Barnabas, take the lead in preaching the Gospel to the people in the synagogue in Pisidian Antioch? 2. What truths had Paul presented in his sermon that grabbed the interest of his listeners? 3. How did Paul and Barnabas deal with the rejection they experienced in Pisidian Antioch? 4. Why are many people not content just to reject the Gospel message, but also oppose it? 5. Should modern Christians ever do anything equivalent to shaking the dust off their feet? If so, when and under what circumstances?

■ **ILLUSTRATIONS:**

A Reason for Rejoicing. Are most people happy? Dennis Wholey, author of *Are You Happy?* reports that according to expert opinion, perhaps only 20 percent of Americans are happy. Those experts would probably agree with the wry definition of happiness offered by psychiatrist Thomas Szaz, who said, "Happiness is an imaginary condition, formerly attributed by the living to the dead, now usually attributed by adults to children and by children to adults."

The good news that Christ has come dispels any reason for being unhappy. Only Christ can fill dissatisfied people with contentment and give meaning to those who think their lives no longer have any purpose. Let us not only recall the fact that the Messiah has come, but also rejoice in this wonderful truth!

Opening the Door to Peace. The football rivalry between two high schools in the western part of the United States goes back over 100 years. Gradually, over the years, the competition had escalated into violence during the games and fights between groups of youths from the two schools. At this point a local congregation decided to open a door for reconciliation between the two rivals.

Beginning in 1993, the church has hosted a "Sportsmanship Breakfast" for varsity football players from the two high schools a few days before the big game. Volunteers get up at 4:30 A.M. to turn on the ovens and start mixing juice. Soon after, they're cooking the sausages, and by 6 o'clock they're pouring the batter for the pancakes. Over 100 athletes from the rival schools gather. Seats at the tables are assigned so that each player or coach from one school sits next to someone from the other school. The athletic directors, principals, and superintendents from the two schools serve the food.

Sharing the meal has helped create a healthier kind of relationship in which good fellowship and ethical behavior is emphasized. This "Sportsmanship Breakfast" has also opened the door for genuine friendships in both schools. Such cooperation should also exist among believers in different churches.

The Still Point. Life is filled with change for each person. How does one survive the constant pressures and challenges? The poet T. S. Eliot called Christ "the still point in a turning world." As the world of every person turns with bewildering speed and in frightening directions, we may think that hopeless confusion is all there is in existence. When Jesus is acknowledged as "the still point" in one's churning, turbulent world, there is an unshakable sense of stability. Let us invite others also to experience the same thing!

■ TOPIC: Keep the Faith

■ QUESTIONS: 1. What was the advantage of Paul and Barnabas beginning their evangelistic efforts in the synagogue in Pisidian Antioch? 2. How did the people initially respond to the missionaries' proclamation of the Gospel? 3. How did the attitude of some people drastically change? Why did this happen? 4. Why did the missionaries decide to focus their evangelistic efforts on the Gentiles? 5. Why is it important for a church to be involved in taking the Gospel to other people?

■ ILLUSTRATIONS:

Jealousy's Product. Emily Dickinson, the great American poet, was a virtual recluse as a result of a brief unhappy love affair in 1853. By 1862, she had withdrawn from the world and lived in seclusion, rarely leaving her Amherst home except near dusk to look after her plants. She saw only her sisters and a few close friends. Strangely, during her lifetime, she allowed only three or four of her poems to be published, even though she wrote over 1,700, most in secret.

At Emily's death on May 16, 1886, her sister, Sue, discovered her works but was uninterested in them. Emily's other sister, Lavinia, gave the poems to a Mrs. Todd, who saw their potential. When published, they were an unparalleled success, which made the two sisters bitter and jealous over the proceeds. The two died quarreling with one another over how much each supposedly should have received in royalties.

Tragically, success often breeds resentment in people. This was true in Antioch of Pisidia. The success of Paul and Barnabas led to their eventual expulsion by the religious legalists, who resented the attention the missionaries got from others.

Tempted to Give Up? The tragic story of the heavy cruiser, USS Indianapolis, was recounted in the film *Jaws*. For most younger Americans, this was the only hearing of the terrible story.

The cruiser had completed a rapid unescorted run from San Francisco to Tinian to deliver the uranium core of the atomic bomb. The cruiser then headed for Leyte. On the night of July 29–30, 1945, the ship was struck on the starboard side by two torpedoes from a Japanese submarine. Within 12 minutes, the ship capsized and sank without being able to dispatch a distress signal.

Of the 1,196 sailors aboard, approximately 800 were able to scramble into the water. However, only 316 survived until Thursday, August 2, when a Navy escort destroyer rescued them. The heat, lack of drinking water, and sharks claimed some. Others, though, simply lost hope of any rescue and gave up. In other words, they lost their will to live.

Perhaps you know some people who have given up. Life for them may seem to be one vast ocean of despair and disappointment. Or perhaps the "torpedoes" of trouble and temptation have nearly finished them off. Regardless of the situation, they should be encouraged to consider the lives of Paul and Barnabas. Their evangelistic efforts were repeatedly torpedoed by enemies. Did they give up? No! Instead, they continued to trust in and serve Christ. Their example is worth serious consideration.

Spokespersons of Promise. Who had the toughest job in the ranks of Washington's Continental Army? It might surprise you to learn that it was the chaplains. They were expected to maintain the high moral ground against profanity, drunkenness, and neglect of Sunday worship while contending with disrespect. They were also to help officers write speeches and keep the hopes and ideals of the war alive while maintaining discipline and sharing with the soldiers inadequate provisions, pay, and leadership. Despite all this adversity, the chaplains were the spokespersons of promise.

Paul and Barnabas, too, were spokespersons of promise. Despite adversity, hostility, threats, and pressures, they faithfully shared the message of God's love with others.

THE JERUSALEM CONFERENCE

BACKGROUND SCRIPTURE: Acts 15:1-35
DEVOTIONAL READING: Romans 3:21-26

KEY VERSE: "We should not trouble those Gentiles who are turning to God." Acts 15:19.

KING JAMES VERSION

ACTS 15:1 And certain men which came down from Judæa taught the brethren, and said, Except ye be circumcised after the manner of Moses, ye cannot be saved.

2 When therefore Paul and Barnabas had no small dissension and disputation with them, they determined that Paul and Barnabas, and certain other of them, should go up to Jerusalem unto the apostles and elders about this question. . . .

6 And the apostles and elders came together for to consider of this matter.

7 And when there had been much disputing, Peter rose up, and said unto them, Men and brethren, ye know how that a good while ago God made choice among us, that the Gentiles by my mouth should hear the word of the gospel, and believe.

8 And God, which knoweth the hearts, bare them witness, giving them the Holy Ghost, even as he did unto us;

9 And put no difference between us and them, purifying their hearts by faith.

10 Now therefore why tempt ye God, to put a yoke upon the neck of the disciples, which neither our fathers nor we were able to bear?

11 But we believe that through the grace of the LORD Jesus Christ we shall be saved, even as they.

12 Then all the multitude kept silence, and gave audience to Barnabas and Paul, declaring what miracles and wonders God had wrought among the Gentiles by them.

13 And after they had held their peace, James answered, saying, Men and brethren, hearken unto me:

14 Simeon hath declared how God at the first did visit the Gentiles, to take out of them a people for his name.

15 And to this agree the words of the prophets. . . .

19 Wherefore my sentence is, that we trouble not them, which from among the Gentiles are turned to God:

20 But that we write unto them, that they abstain from pollutions of idols, and from fornication, and from things strangled, and from blood.

NEW REVISED STANDARD VERSION

ACTS 15:1 Then certain individuals came down from Judea and were teaching the brothers, "Unless you are circumcised according to the custom of Moses, you cannot be saved." 2 And after Paul and Barnabas had no small dissension and debate with them, Paul and Barnabas and some of the others were appointed to go up to Jerusalem to discuss this question with the apostles and the elders. . . .

6 The apostles and the elders met together to consider this matter. 7 After there had been much debate, Peter stood up and said to them, "My brothers, you know that in the early days God made a choice among you, that I should be the one through whom the Gentiles would hear the message of the good news and become believers. 8 And God, who knows the human heart, testified to them by giving them the Holy Spirit, just as he did to us; 9 and in cleansing their hearts by faith he has made no distinction between them and us. 10 Now therefore why are you putting God to the test by placing on the neck of the disciples a yoke that neither our ancestors nor we have been able to bear? 11 On the contrary, we believe that we will be saved through the grace of the Lord Jesus, just as they will."

12 The whole assembly kept silence, and listened to Barnabas and Paul as they told of all the signs and wonders that God had done through them among the Gentiles. 13 After they finished speaking, James replied, "My brothers, listen to me. 14 Simeon has related how God first looked favorably on the Gentiles, to take from among them a people for his name. 15 This agrees with the words of the prophets. . . . 19 Therefore I have reached the decision that we should not trouble those Gentiles who are turning to God, 20 but we should write to them to abstain only from things polluted by idols and from fornication and from whatever has been strangled and from blood."

Home Bible Readings

Background

After leaving Pisidian [pih-SID-ih-uhn] Antioch, the missionaries traveled to Iconium [eye-KOH-nee-uhm] in the central province of Galatia, proclaimed the Gospel in the local synagogue, and led many Jews and Gentiles to faith. Despite opposition from some unbelievers, Paul and Barnabas remained a considerable amount of time and confirmed their witness through the performance of miracles. When the missionaries learned that some antagonists were plotting to stone them, they fled east to Lystra [LISS-truh] and Derbe [DURR-bee], which were in the district of Lycaonia [lick-ay-OH-nee-uh]. There they heralded the Gospel (Acts 14:1-20).

While in Lystra, Paul healed a man who had been crippled from birth. When the crowd saw what the apostle had done, they declared him to be Hermes [HURR-meez] and Barnabas to be Zeus. When the local priest as well as the crowd attempted to offer sacrifices to the missionaries, the two implored the people not to do it. Then some unbelieving Jews came from Pisidian Antioch and Iconium and convinced the crowd to stone Paul, whom they then dragged out of the city, supposing that he had died. But Paul was able to get up and return to the city; then the next day the missionaries left for Derbe (14:8-20).

After proclaiming the Gospel in Derbe and leading many people to Christ, the missionaries revisited Lystra, Iconium, and Antioch. In addition to encouraging the disciples to remain faithful to the Lord, Paul and Barnabas appointed elders over each newly established congregation. The missionaries next returned to Perga [PURR-guh], evangelized there, and then went to Attalia [at-uh-LIGH-uh], which was a seaport on the coast of Pamphylia [pam-FILL-ee-uh]. Paul and Barnabas boarded a ship, returned to Syrian Antioch, and reported all that God had accomplished through them on their recent trip. For about the next year, the two remained in the city and served the needs of the congregation there (14:21-28).

Notes on the Printed Text

The entrance of so many Gentiles into the church brought joy to some and concern to others, particularly many Jewish believers in Judea. Thus some of the dissatisfied Jewish Christians decided to take action. These teachers (now called Judaizers) went to Syrian Antioch, the center of outreach to the

Gentiles. They intended to bring the uncircumcised Gentiles into the full experience of salvation. They declared, *"Unless you are circumcised according to the custom of Moses, you cannot be saved"* (Acts 15:1).

The rules of the flesh were those that legalists wanted to impose on Gentiles in order to make them Jewish by religion. Some presumed the prophecy about Gentiles being blessed through Abraham's seed (Gen. 12:3) meant that non-Jews would become Jews. After all, the Jews were God's chosen people.

The same logic persisted in the early church. Gentiles were accepted as long as they became Jewish believers. They had to come to the church by way of the law, and especially by circumcision. Circumcision of male children was usually done eight days after the child had been born. It served as a sign that the individual belonged to the God of Israel and the community of His people (17:9-14).

God was not bound by the logic of the religious legalists. His plan was to accept for salvation everyone who believes in His Son regardless of whether they obeyed all the Jewish laws and customs. Paul and Barnabas understood this, and that's why they *had no small dissension and debate with [the legalists]* (Acts 15:2).

Unable to resolve the differences on their own, the Christians of Syrian Antioch decided to send a delegation, including Paul and Barnabas, to Jerusalem. The church wanted to know what the apostles and elders there might say about the matter. When the group arrived in Jerusalem, the leadership of the congregation welcomed them, and the group reported all that God had done through them. Meanwhile, some believing Pharisees insisted that the Gentiles had to convert to Judaism to be saved (15:3-5).

This was a serious issue that threatened to divide the unity of believing Jews and Gentiles. That's why *the apostles and elders met together to consider this matter* (15:6). After a considerable amount of discussion over the issue, Peter related how God had used him to open the door of the church to the Gentiles (15:6-7). The apostle also noted that the Lord made no distinction in His bestowal of the Spirit on both believing Jews and Gentiles (15:8-9).

Peter moreover asserted that grace alone, apart from observing the Mosaic law, was the basis for any person's salvation. The apostle continued, *"Now therefore why are you putting God to the test by placing on the neck of the disciples a yoke that neither our ancestors nor we have been able to bear? On the contrary, we believe that we will be saved through the grace of the Lord Jesus, just as they will"* (15:10-11).

Barnabas and Paul next described what God had done through them among the Gentiles (15:12). Then James (the brother of Jesus and the current leader in the Jerusalem church) affirmed what Peter had said and noted that the conversion of the Gentiles was prophesied in Scripture (15:13). *"Simeon has related how God first looked favorably on the Gentiles, to take from among them a people for his name. This agrees with the words of the prophets"* (15:14-15).

James wanted his colleagues to know that his decision rested primarily on the truth of God's Word, not on the experience of believers. James also realized that the teaching of the Bible on the matter of grace versus works would have carried the greatest measure of influence among the religious legalists. They would have to acknowledge that the Hebrew Scriptures, which they valued so much, affirmed the truths that had been declared by James and Peter.

James recommended that the Gentile believers not be required to convert to Judaism but that they remain sensitive to the convictions of their fellow believing Jews about certain practices (15:19). *"We should write to them to abstain only from things polluted by idols and from fornication and from whatever has been strangled and from blood"* (15:20).

The Jerusalem council accepted this decision and sent their own delegation with Paul and Barnabas back to Syrian Antioch. (Their decision ensured that the church could grow unhindered by the cultural differences between Jews and Gentiles.) The council also gave the travelers a letter conveying the instructions of James. In Antioch the believers welcomed and were encouraged by the delegation and the letter (15:22-31).

SUGGESTIONS TO TEACHERS

It appears that many people in our society, both inside and outside the church, have decided that commitment is not in their best interest. People view commitment negatively because they think it limits their ability to feel independent and free, to experience new things, to change their minds on the spur of the moment, and to focus on self-gratification rather than helping others.

This low level of commitment becomes disturbing when Christians treat vital Bible doctrines and a God-honoring lifestyle as unimportant. Keeping one's options open may have significant value, but Christians must beware of casting aside important biblical truths, such as eternal salvation through faith in Christ's atoning work on the cross. In fact, it was a lack of commitment to this foundational truth that prompted the Jerusalem conference.

1. GRACE VERSUS WORKS. Throughout church history, people have distorted the Bible's teaching on salvation. In fact, it became so bad in the fifteenth century that people even tried to buy God's grace. But the good news is that Jesus died on the cross to redeem us from our sins. When we trust in Him, we are delivered from God's wrath. This is a precious message, and we must never allow its integrity to be compromised. As you teach the lesson, be sure to emphasize this truth to your students.

2. VIGOROUS DEBATE. Certainly none of God's servants has ever held the Gospel more faithfully than Paul. In his years of seeking to be justified in the sight of God through observance of the law, Paul had found no salvation; but when he trusted in Christ, he received forgiveness and assurance of eternal life. That's why Paul became such an ardent preacher of the Gospel, stressing its great power to change people's lives. And that's why he (along with Barnabas) refused to back down when legalists asserted that what Jesus did was not totally sufficient and that believers must do something more to be saved.

3. SALVATION BY GRACE. Among secular educators there is a strong tendency to propose that intellectuals should be broadminded toward varying viewpoints. The adults in your class have probably been exposed to this philosophy. Be sure to stress that the Gospel of Christ is not open to debate or compromise. Only God's undeserved mercy, not our human efforts, delivers us from the bondage of sin.

4. A VOTE FOR GRACE. Not even the legalists would have doubted the commitment of James to keep the Mosaic law. If such a staunch supporter of the law declared that the observance of it was not a precondition for Gentiles being saved, how could the legalists insist otherwise? They could see that it would have been futile for them to dissent from the majority view, which favored grace.

5. MINIMIZING TENSION. James knew that it was important for believing Jews and Gentiles to maintain harmonious relations. Also, there were certain practices among the Gentiles that were offensive to pious Jews. So that there would be a minimum of tension between the Gentile and Jewish Christian communities, James recommended that the Gentile believers refrain from the practices mentioned in Acts 15:20 and 29. Today what can believers who are from different cultures do to maintain harmonious relations?

FOR ADULTS

■ **TOPIC:** Defending the Truth

■ **QUESTIONS:** 1. Why were the religious legalists eager for the Gentile converts to observe the Mosaic laws? 2. What was there about Peter that made his speech effective? 3. How might the reputation of James as a rigorous keeper of the law have made his decision more forceful and accepted? 4. What are some of the false teachings about salvation you have heard? 5. How does your church prepare its members to reply to current false teachings about salvation?

■ **ILLUSTRATIONS:**

Friendly Adversaries. John Adams and Thomas Jefferson were bitter political adversaries. Each strenuously defended his opinions, and they seldom agreed with each other. Yet their rivalry never caused them to vilify each other. Despite the sharp differences between them during their entire political careers, they respected each other and worked for the greater good of the United States. They maintained a personal friendship to the day they both died, July 4, 1826, which was the fiftieth anniversary of the signing of the Declaration of Independence.

"It is known to those who ever heard me speak of Mr. Adams that I have ever done him justice myself, and defended him when assailed by others, with the single exception of his political opinions," Jefferson told one of their mutual friends in 1811. Writing to Adams in 1823, Jefferson stated the following:

> The circumstances of the times in which we happened to live, and the partiality of our friends at a particular period, placed us in a state of apparent opposition, which some might suppose to be personal also; and there might not be wanting those who wish'd to make it so, by filling our ears with malignant falsehoods, by dressing up hideous phantoms of their own creation, . . . endeavoring to instill into our minds things concerning each other the most destitute truth. Beseeching you not to suffer your mind to be disquieted by this wicked attempt to poison its peace, . . . I add sincere assurances of my unabated and constant attachment, friendship, and respect.

Here is a case study worthy of examination by every believer. God wants us to maintain harmonious relations with one another for the cause of Christ.

Extreme Legalism. Some years ago, a news report told how a bus driver put regulations ahead of compassion. It seems that this driver discovered an 80-year-old woman with a crutch carrying a small puppy on his bus. He refused to listen to her explanation that she was returning home from her birthday party with the gift of the puppy she had been given. The bus company had a rule—*no pets were allowed on buses*. The driver insisted on trying to dump the woman at a truck stop 80 miles from her home at 3 o'clock in the morning. When she protested, he called the police, and watched with gleeful satisfaction as burly sheriff's deputies hauled the elderly woman away from the bus.

Thankfully, the law enforcement people had compassion and common sense. They realized that the woman had difficulty hearing and seeing as well as walking. After buying her coffee and a sandwich, they arranged with four other fellow police departments to take the frightened woman to her home. When the bus company heard about the incident, they sent a letter of apology and a refund ticket to the woman. They also fired the driver.

Rules have their place, but the rule of compassion and grace should always take precedence. Thankfully, the majority at the Jerusalem conference had their wits about them, rejecting extreme legalism for God's grace.

The Need for Grace. In his book *Healing Grace*, David Seamands included this story:

> In 1916 Emperor Franz-Josef I of Austria died. To the accompaniment of a military band's somber dirges and by the light of torches, a processional of important people descended the stairs of the Capuchin monastery in Vienna. At the bottom was a great iron door leading to a burial chamber. Behind the door was the cardinal-archbishop of Vienna.
>
> Following the prescribed ceremony, the officer in charge cried,

"Open!" The cardinal responded, "Who goes there?" The officer then began to recite the emperor's thirty-seven impressive titles. The cardinal answered, "We know him not. Who goes there?" This time when the officer replied by using an abbreviated and less flamboyant title, the cardinal again said, "We know him not. Who goes there?" The officer tried a third time, stripping the emperor of all but the humblest of titles: "We bear the body of Franz-Josef, our brother, a sinner like us all." At that the doors swung open, and the corpse was allowed to be brought in.

In death all are reduced to the same level. Neither good works, fame, nor wealth can open the way of salvation. Only God's grace can do so, and it is given to those who will humbly acknowledge their need.

FOR YOUTH

■ TOPIC: Talk It Out

■ QUESTIONS: 1. Why did Paul and Barnabas react so strongly to the teaching of the Judaizers? 2. What do you think was Peter's strongest argument against imposing circumcision on Gentile converts? Why? 3. Why did James provide a confirmation from Scripture of his decision? 4. Why do some people accept false teachings about salvation? 5. Why is the knowledge of Scripture ultimately the best defense against such false teachings?

■ **ILLUSTRATIONS:**

The Reality of Grace. During a Sunday morning worship service, Pastor Greg Asimakoupoulous shared with his congregation that Nome, Alaska, on the edge of the Bering Sea, is like many villages of the Arctic. The ground on which the community sits is frozen, sponge-like tundra. Burying the dead is a real challenge. Sanitation landfills are unheard of. Garbage trucks do not haul off the kind of refuse people leave curbside in the "lower 48." Instead a typical front yard displays broken washing machines, junked cars, old toilets, scrap wood, and piles of non-degradable refuse.

Tourists who visit Nome in the summer are amazed at the debris and shake their heads. "How could anyone live like that?" they wonder. What those visitors don't realize is that for nine months of the year Nome sits under a blanket of snow that covers the garbage. During those months, the little town is a quaint winter wonderland of pure white landscapes.

The reality of grace is that the garbage of our lives has been covered by a blanket of forgiveness. The prophet Isaiah declared that the blight of our sin, once red as crimson, is now white as freshly fallen snow (Isa. 1:18). And unlike the situation in Nome, our sin is covered forever!

Tragically Wrong. An anesthesiologist was administering a controlled mixture of oxygen and gas to a patient in a New York hospital. When one of the tanks was empty, the doctor began using a new one clearly marked "Oxygen." Almost immediately the patient died. The coroner's autopsy revealed carbon dioxide poisoning. Upon investigation the second tank was found to contain pure carbon dioxide and had been mislabeled.

Thankfully, such errors are rare. But in the spiritual realm they occur all the time. Regarding salvation many people say, "As long as I sincerely try to be a good person, I'll come out all right in the end." No matter how correct such notions may seem, they are tragically wrong. The only way a person can be saved is by trusting in Christ for eternal life.

A Gift for Private Ryan. In the Winter 1999 issue of *Leadership* journal, Michael Lester commented on Steven Spielberg's movie, *Saving Private Ryan*. The movie tells the story of an Army captain named John Miller (played by Tom Hanks) who in the aftermath of the World War II D-day invasion at Normandy Beach is ordered to find a solitary private among thousands of deployed soldiers. He must return Private James F. Ryan home to his mother, whose other three sons have just been killed in action.

Captain Miller and the small group of men assigned to him successfully locate Ryan, but then are forced to defend a strategic bridge against enemy tanks and troops. Captain Miller is fatally wounded. In his dying moments, he reaches out to Private Ryan, and with great emotion says, "Earn this! Earn this!"

Many years later as an old man, James Ryan stands in a veteran's cemetery tearfully looking at the tombstone of the man who saved his life. He wonders aloud if he has indeed earned the great gift he received.

Two thousand years ago Jesus Christ died on the Cross that we might live forever. In His final words He did not suggest that we could ever earn such a gift. Instead, He cried triumphantly, *"It is finished"* (John 19:30).

REACHING INTO MACEDONIA

BACKGROUND SCRIPTURE: Acts 16:6-40
DEVOTIONAL READING: Philippians 1:3-11

KEY VERSE: "Come over to Macedonia and help us." Acts 16:9b.

KING JAMES VERSION

ACTS 16:9 And a vision appeared to Paul in the night; There stood a man of Macedonia, and prayed him, saying, Come over into Macedonia, and help us.

10 And after he had seen the vision, immediately we endeavoured to go into Macedonia, assuredly gathering that the Lord had called us for to preach the gospel unto them.

11 Therefore loosing from Troas, we came with a straight course to Samothracia, and the next day to Neapolis;

12 And from thence to Philippi, which is the chief city of that part of Macedonia, and a colony: and we were in that city abiding certain days.

13 And on the sabbath we went out of the city by a river side, where prayer was wont to be made; and we sat down, and spake unto the women which resorted thither.

14 And a certain woman named Lydia, a seller of purple, of the city of Thyatira, which worshipped God, heard us: whose heart the Lord opened, that she attended unto the things which were spoken of Paul.

15 And when she was baptized, and her household, she besought us, saying, If ye have judged me to be faithful to the Lord, come into my house, and abide there. And she constrained us. . . .

27 And the keeper of the prison awaking out of his sleep, and seeing the prison doors open, he drew out his sword, and would have killed himself, supposing that the prisoners had been fled.

28 But Paul cried with a loud voice, saying, Do thyself no harm: for we are all here.

29 Then he called for a light, and sprang in, and came trembling, and fell down before Paul and Silas,

30 And brought them out, and said, Sirs, what must I do to be saved?

31 And they said, Believe on the Lord Jesus Christ, and thou shalt be saved, and thy house.

32 And they spake unto him the word of the Lord, and to all that were in his house.

33 And he took them the same hour of the night, and washed their stripes; and was baptized, he and all his, straightway.

NEW REVISED STANDARD VERSION

ACTS 16:9 During the night Paul had a vision: there stood a man of Macedonia pleading with him and saying, "Come over to Macedonia and help us." 10 When he had seen the vision, we immediately tried to cross over to Macedonia, being convinced that God had called us to proclaim the good news to them.

11 We set sail from Troas and took a straight course to Samothrace, the following day to Neapolis, 12 and from there to Philippi, which is a leading city of the district of Macedonia and a Roman colony. We remained in this city for some days. 13 On the sabbath day we went outside the gate by the river, where we supposed there was a place of prayer; and we sat down and spoke to the women who had gathered there. 14 A certain woman named Lydia, a worshiper of God, was listening to us; she was from the city of Thyatira and a dealer in purple cloth. The Lord opened her heart to listen eagerly to what was said by Paul. 15 When she and her household were baptized, she urged us, saying, "If you have judged me to be faithful to the Lord, come and stay at my home." And she prevailed upon us. . . .

27 When the jailer woke up and saw the prison doors wide open, he drew his sword and was about to kill himself, since he supposed that the prisoners had escaped. 28 But Paul shouted in a loud voice, "Do not harm yourself, for we are all here." 29 The jailer called for lights, and rushing in, he fell down trembling before Paul and Silas. 30 Then he brought them outside and said, "Sirs, what must I do to be saved?" 31 They answered, "Believe on the Lord Jesus, and you will be saved, you and your household." 32 They spoke the word of the Lord to him and to all who were in his house. 33 At the same hour of the night he took them and washed their wounds; then he and his entire family were baptized without delay.

12

BACKGROUND

You have probably noticed that Paul has had more and more of a central place in the Book of Acts. In contrast, the leaders in the Jerusalem church have been featured less and less. From Acts 16 to the end of the book, the narrative focuses on Paul and his missionary journeys. Luke, the writer, however, did not intend to produce a biography of the great apostle to the Gentiles. Rather, Luke's aim was to show how the good news of God spread from Jerusalem to Rome, the capitol of the empire.

This week's lesson describes the momentous step Paul and his associates took when they crossed from Asia Minor into Europe. From then on, people would see Christianity as being worldwide in focus. This fit Luke's purpose, for he wanted his readers to know that Jesus came to provide salvation for all persons everywhere.

NOTES ON THE PRINTED TEXT

On his second missionary journey, Paul discovered that his initial itinerary (Asia Minor) had been altered by the Spirit. And the apostle's next plan (Bithynia) was also blocked by the Spirit. As Paul, Silas, and Timothy sat in Troas, they perhaps wondered where God wanted them next to evangelize. *During the night Paul had a vision: there stood a man of Macedonia pleading with him and saying, "Come over to Macedonia and help us"* (Acts 16:9).

In response to this vision, Paul planned to sail to Philippi [FIH-lih-pie], which was a Roman colony and a leading city in the eastern portion of Macedonia [mass-uh-DOE-nee-uh] (16:10-12). Philippi was situated on the edge of the most fertile plain in Macedonia, near the gold mines of Mount Pangaeus. The beautiful Graeco [GREH-koh]-Roman city had a mixed population, with a small Jewish contingent, but no synagogue.

Paul and his associates went outside Philippi to a nearby river. Archaeologists excavating at the city have unearthed the foundations of a great arched gateway of the main Roman road at the northwest border of the city. Within one mile to the west of this spot flows the Gangites River. Within this general area, the Gospel was first shared in Europe, and the first listeners were women. *On the sabbath day we went outside the gate by the river, where we supposed there was a place of prayer; and we sat down and spoke to the women who had gathered there* (16.13).

Within that group was a wealthy business woman named Lydia from Thyatira [thigh-uh-TIE-ruh] who sold *purple cloth* (16:14). She listened intently to the Gospel and put her trust in Christ. Both she and her family were baptized in the Gangites River. Then Lydia opened up her home as a base of operations for Paul and his associates. *She urged us, saying, "If you have judged me to be faithful to the Lord, come and stay at my home." And she prevailed upon us* (16:15).

The next convert was a slave girl who fell into trances. Tragically, the girl's condition was exploited by her owners for their profit. As she followed Paul, she screamed that he and his associates were servants of the Lord. Paul freed the girl of her oppression by exorcising the demon. This so enraged the owners that they dragged Paul and Silas into the marketplace before the authorities (16:16-19).

Archaeologists excavating Philippi's marketplace have found a platform at the north end of the open square. Perhaps the town leaders sat there. Paul and Silas were stripped, beaten with rods, thrown into jail, and placed into stocks, which forced their legs apart and would have caused severe pain (16:20-24).

Far from being dispirited and having their morale broken, the two missionaries prayed and sang in jail. Suddenly, there was a severe earthquake, and the prison was shaken to its foundations. All the doors flew open, and the chains of every prisoner fell off (16:25-26). The jailer panicked, believing the prisoners had escaped. Since they were his responsibility, the loss would cost him his life. He thus *drew his sword and was about to kill himself* (16:27).

From the shaken ruins of the prison, Paul yelled, *"Do not harm yourself, for we are all here"* (16:28). The startled jailer called for lights, ran to the dungeon, and fell down before Paul and Silas (16:29). After bringing the two missionaries out, he asked them, *"Sirs, what must I do to be saved?"* (16:30).

The answer the jailer received remains applicable to this day. *"Believe on the Lord Jesus, and you will be saved, you and your household"* (16:31). Paul and Silas explained the Gospel to the jailer and his family, and they received the truth wholeheartedly (16:32).

The jailer, now a follower of Christ, washed the wounds of the missionaries. Then the jailer and his family were immediately baptized (16:33). Next, the jailer brought Paul and Silas into his house and set a meal before them. The jailer *and his entire household rejoiced that he had become a believer in God* (16:34).

SUGGESTIONS TO TEACHERS

Paul answered the call, *"Come over to Macedonia and help us"* (Acts 16:9). Your aim in this week's lesson is to encourage your students not to allow the obstacles they encounter to deter them from speaking the Gospel. You will also want to stress that serving Christ includes responding to the needs of others.

1. CAUSING A CHANGE IN PLANS. Point out that originally Paul and his associates had intended to evangelize in Bithynia. But then the Spirit redirected them to the coast of Asia Minor. Yes, God had overridden the original plans of the missionaries. But as a result, the Lord opened the way for the Gospel to spread to Europe. Use this example to talk about handling times when our human plans seem to be checked by God. Stress that the Lord has a purpose in the detour they sometimes might encounter.

2. CALLING FROM A EUROPEAN. We don't know the identity of the man from Macedonia, but his plea prompted Paul to respond immediately. The vision the apostle experienced was not a spooky nightmare but rather a revelation from God. What is God leading the members of your class to do for Him? Also, what is He calling your church to do in the community where it is located?

3. CONVENING AT THE RIVERSIDE. Devote some time to discuss how the Gospel made inroads into Philippi. As a result of the conversion of Lydia and others, a strong church was established.

4. COMMUNICATING IN A PRISON. Paul and Silas found themselves imprisoned in Philippi. Despite this deplorable situation, they remained confident in their outlook. For instance, though the missionaries had been severely beaten, they prayed and sang hymns to God. What a remarkable testimony! Christians are able to raise a doxology to the Lord even in the worst of circumstances.

5. COMFORTING A TRAUMATIZED JAILER. The Philippian jailer would have killed himself if it had not been for the timely intervention of Paul. Then he and Silas seized the opportunity to proclaim Christ to the jailer. The Lord used the bold witness of the two missionaries to bring about the conversion of the jailer and his family. Like Paul and Silas, God wants us to use every opportunity we have to proclaim Christ.

6. CREATING CREDIBILITY. When the town authorities wanted to release Paul and Silas quietly, the pair did not take off immediately, but instead insisted on a public apology (Acts 16:35-39). This was for the sake of the new converts in Philippi. From this we see that Paul was ever mindful of others. His example is worthy of our thoughtful consideration.

FOR ADULTS

■ TOPIC: Responding to Need

■ QUESTIONS: 1. What kind of help do you think the man in Paul's vision wanted? 2. What do Paul's actions by the river say about his character? 3. Why would Lydia want Paul and his companions to stay in her home? 4. What reasons did Paul and Silas have for rejoicing while in the jailer's home? 5. What are some current obstacles Christians may face when presenting the Gospel in our society? How can these obstacles be overcome?

■ **ILLUSTRATIONS:**

Caring in Cohasset. In February 1799, a sailing ship from Denmark was bound for Boston with a load of hemp for rope. A violent Atlantic winter storm, however, forced the ship on to the treacherous shoals off Brush Island, near Cohasset,

Massachusetts, and broke up the vessel. The 22 Danish crewmembers and their captain managed to save themselves by clinging to the broken mast. Finally, they were washed ashore on the island, where they survived a bitterly cold night. In the morning, seafarers from Cohasset rescued them. The entire community responded to the plight of the shipwrecked Danes, and offered shelter, food, and warm clothing.

Then the people of Cohasset took carts to the beach and salvaged the hemp that had washed ashore. They cleaned the sand and seaweed from the bales. Then they sold the hemp at a public auction for over $12,000. The Cohasset folk then used this money to purchase another ship so that the captain and his crew could return to Denmark. The king of Denmark was so appreciative that he presented the people of Cohasset a set of silver communion ware for their church, most of which is still used to this day in the old local congregation.

But the most amazing part of the story is that none of the shipwrecked Danes understood English and none of the residents in Cohasset spoke Danish. Yet the Christians in the town responded to the need presented that cold February over 200 years ago. Their love for others in Christ's name made them guarantee the comfort of the needy in their midst.

Needs in Our Country. In late 1998, a U.N. study found that even in the world's wealthiest nations, poverty is spreading and many people are being denied the basic rewards of affluence: getting a job, learning to read, and living longer. Poor people living in leading industrialized nations like the United States and Great Britain suffer from "multiple deprivation" of their basic human needs, the Human Development Report said.

Researchers with the U.N. Development Program examined income, education, life expectancy, and health care in assessing the quality of life in 174 countries. Among their findings: 16.5 percent of Americans live in poverty despite the fact that the United States leads the world in per-capita consumption. Worldwide, the richest nations are home to more than 100 million people who live in poverty, according to the report.

We who are Christians must face our Lord, who asks what we are doing to respond to these needs.

Overcoming Obstacles. In 1921 an attack of infantile paralysis left Franklin D. Roosevelt crippled from the waist down. The experts at the time thought this would end his promising political career. Roosevelt, however, would not permit his illness to hinder him from pursuing his political goals. With determination he learned how to walk with artificial supports and a cane. By 1928 Roosevelt had made a successful comeback, becoming governor of New York. And in 1932 he was elected president of the United States, an office which he held until his death in 1945.

Many obstacles we encounter can deter us from spreading the Gospel. With God's help, however, we can overcome these problems and be victorious in our efforts to proclaim the good news of Christ to others.

<table>
<tr><td>

FOR YOUTH

</td><td>

■ TOPIC: Spread the News

■ QUESTIONS: 1. How do you think Paul and his associates might have felt as the Spirit redirected their path? 2. How did the mis-

</td></tr>
</table>

sionaries respond to the Spirit's leading? 3. How did Paul and Silas reflect the character of Christ while they were shackled in the Philippian prison? 4. What has caused you to share the Gospel with a particular person? 5. How is your church equipping you for the task of spreading the Gospel?

■ ILLUSTRATIONS:

Children's Crusade. A group of fifth graders at a community school in Colorado listened as their teacher read a newspaper story about the African country of Sudan and how thousands of people were being sold as slaves. Earlier in the school year, the teacher had told the class about the history of slavery and emancipation in the United States. On hearing that slavery still exists today, the teacher's students became upset. At first they could not believe that women and children their own age were being chained and sold. Then the kids in the school decided they wanted to do something about the terrible situation in Sudan.

At their teacher's suggestion, the members of the class wrote letters to various well-known persons they thought could help. One girl even penned a letter to her state senator, stating, "We would like to know if you could contact the United States Government and let them know what is going on, so they can take action and put a stop to slavery!"

The students weren't discouraged when they received few responses from the notables. So the youngsters explored the issue on the Internet. They eventually found the website of a European-based human-rights group that specializes in buying back victims of religious oppression held in bondage. The children discovered that for $50 to $100, they could purchase the freedom of a Sudanese slave through this human-rights group.

The class members kept careful records and case histories of over 4,000 persons, mostly members of the Dinka tribe in Sudan, who have been rescued by their efforts. The class launched a fund-raising drive, using the dimes and quarters from their allowances and proceeds from lemonade and T-shirt sales, to purchase the freedom of as many slaves as possible.

Then one of those who'd received one of the students' earlier letters, Sumner Redstone, Chairman of Viacom, put the class on his Nickelodeon Channel. Suddenly donations poured in from many places. Over $50,000 was raised that first year! A new class of fifth graders entered the teacher's classroom the following year, 1998, and the efforts to respond to the need have continued since that first group of fifth graders decided to act.

New Direction. In India, Eva was 12 when she sensed God's claim on her life at a Youth for Christ rally. Admitting that neither her faith remained strong nor her sense of call focused, she later wavered. She eventually married Richard. The two, however, refused to participate in bribery, the accepted political way of doing business in India. The constant pressure and humiliation broke Eva's health and she almost died.

Through her involvement in political causes, Eva sensed a call to help women, but she had no definite direction. One day, a pastor called her and asked for her help in caring for a teenage girl whom he had rescued from forced prostitution. Eva and her family took the girl into their home and watched her transformation. Soon other girls followed. Their home became a rehabilitation center.

Police and prison officials began making referrals. Counseling was initiated. Medical treatment was given as well as educational lessons and practical lessons in sewing, tailoring, and handicrafts. Eva began to sense the Spirit's nudge in a new direction, away from politics. Years later she could see that through the call of a pastor, who was her "Man from Macedonia" (so to speak), came the Comforter Ministries of India.

Like Eva, each of you will encounter your own person "from Macedonia," and God can use this experience to nudge you into new areas of humble Christian service. The Lord wants to use your talents for His glory and humankind's benefit!

Being an Obstacle Overcomer. One day a little boy with a small shovel tried to clear a pathway through deep, new-fallen snow in front of his house. A man paused to observe the child's enormous task. "Little boy," he inquired, "how can someone as small as you expect to finish a task as big as this?" The boy looked up and replied confidently, "Little by little, that's how!" And he continued shoveling.

Henry G. Bosch wrote, "Day by day perform your mission; with Christ's help keep at your tasks. Be encouraged by His presence, for faithfulness is all He asks." The task of spreading the Gospel may seem daunting to us, especially if we have encountered a number of seemingly insurmountable obstacles. As we rely on God, however, He can give us one small victory after another. With His help, we can eventually work through the obstacles to evangelism.

SERVING WITH HUMILITY

BACKGROUND SCRIPTURE: Acts 20:13-38
DEVOTIONAL READING: 1 Corinthians 15:1-11

KEY VERSE: I do not count my life of any value to myself, if only I may finish my course and the ministry that I received from the Lord Jesus, to testify to the good news of God's grace. Acts 20:24.

KING JAMES VERSION

ACTS 20:18 Ye know, from the first day that I came into Asia, after what manner I have been with you at all seasons,

19 Serving the Lord with all humility of mind, and with many tears, and temptations, which befell me by the lying in wait of the Jews:

20 And how I kept back nothing that was profitable unto you, but have shewed you, and have taught you publickly, and from house to house,

21 Testifying both to the Jews, and also to the Greeks, repentance toward God, and faith toward our Lord Jesus Christ.

22 And now, behold, I go bound in the spirit unto Jerusalem, not knowing the things that shall befall me there:

23 Save that the Holy Ghost witnesseth in every city, saying that bonds and afflictions abide me.

24 But none of these things move me, neither count I my life dear unto myself, so that I might finish my course with joy, and the ministry, which I have received of the Lord Jesus, to testify the gospel of the grace of God.

25 And now, behold, I know that ye all, among whom I have gone preaching the kingdom of God, shall see my face no more.

26 Wherefore I take you to record this day, that I am pure from the blood of all men.

27 For I have not shunned to declare unto you all the counsel of God.

28 Take heed therefore unto yourselves, and to all the flock, over the which the Holy Ghost hath made you overseers, to feed the church of God, which he hath purchased with his own blood.

29 For I know this, that after my departing shall grievous wolves enter in among you, not sparing the flock.

30 Also of your own selves shall men arise, speaking perverse things, to draw away disciples after them.

31 Therefore watch, and remember, that by the space of three years I ceased not to warn every one night and day with tears.

32 And now, brethren, I commend you to God, and to the word of his grace, which is able to build you up, and to give you an inheritance among all them which are sanctified.

NEW REVISED STANDARD VERSION

ACTS 20:18 "You yourselves know how I lived among you the entire time from the first day that I set foot in Asia, 19 serving the Lord with all humility and with tears, enduring the trials that came to me through the plots of the Jews. 20 I did not shrink from doing anything helpful, proclaiming the message to you and teaching you publicly and from house to house, 21 as I testified to both Jews and Greeks about repentance toward God and faith toward our Lord Jesus. 22 And now, as a captive to the Spirit, I am on my way to Jerusalem, not knowing what will happen to me there, 23 except that the Holy Spirit testifies to me in every city that imprisonment and persecutions are waiting for me. 24 But I do not count my life of any value to myself, if only I may finish my course and the ministry that I received from the Lord Jesus, to testify to the good news of God's grace.

25 "And now I know that none of you, among whom I have gone about proclaiming the kingdom, will ever see my face again. 26 Therefore I declare to you this day that I am not responsible for the blood of any of you, 27 for I did not shrink from declaring to you the whole purpose of God. 28 Keep watch over yourselves and over all the flock, of which the Holy Spirit has made you overseers, to shepherd the church of God that he obtained with the blood of his own Son. 29 I know that after I have gone, savage wolves will come in among you, not sparing the flock. 30 Some even from your own group will come distorting the truth in order to entice the disciples to follow them. 31 Therefore be alert, remembering that for three years I did not cease night or day to warn everyone with tears. 32 And now I commend you to God and to the message of his grace, a message that is able to build you up and to give you the inheritance among all who are sanctified.

13

Monday, May 21	Acts 17:16-34	Paul in Athens
Tuesday, May 22	Acts 18:1-11	Paul in Corinth
Wednesday, May 23	Acts 19:1-10	Paul in Ephesus
Thursday, May 24	Acts 20:1-6	Paul in Macedonia and Greece
Friday, May 25	Acts 20:7-16	Paul in Troas and Miletus
Saturday, May 26	Acts 20:17-24	Paul Speaks to the Ephesian Elders
Sunday, May 27	Acts 20:25-38	Paul's Summary and Farewell

BACKGROUND

Paul learned that fellow Christians in Judea were suffering from financial poverty. With typical resolve, the apostle arranged to collect funds from newly established congregations in Greece and Asia Minor to take back to Jerusalem. This special relief offering would show how much the Gentile converts loved and appreciated their fellow believers in Jerusalem (Rom. 15:25-28).

Perhaps Paul suspected that some believers back in Judea continued to feel uneasy about the sincerity of these former pagans in distant Greek-speaking cities. The collection for the Jerusalem Christians would surely witness to the unity of Jesus' followers, regardless of their language, location, or background.

Paul also knew that he had enemies. Rumors had reached him that a group of unbelievers were plotting to harm him (15:30-31). When Paul announced that he personally intended to take the relief fund to Jerusalem, accompanied by representatives from the Gentile churches, friends warned him of the danger that awaited him (Acts 20:22-24; 21:10-14). Perhaps Paul thought he could defuse some of the animosity that people felt toward him by worshiping in Jerusalem. He also perhaps felt that he could show he had not renounced his Jewish roots, especially the law of Moses and the ancient customs of the Jewish people (21:20-26).

Luke described the foreboding that Paul and others felt as he made his way back to Judea. The parallels between Jesus going to the cross in Jerusalem and Paul traveling to Jerusalem are apparent. The closer Paul came to Judea, the greater the sense of danger that must have been felt. Paul, realizing that he might not survive, was not afraid or morbid. Instead, with his faith firmly anchored in the living Christ, the apostle resolutely set his sights on Jerusalem.

NOTES ON THE PRINTED TEXT

After spending some time in Ephesus, Paul decided to leave the city and travel to Macedonia. The apostle visited a number of congregations and encouraged the believers before making his way to Greece. When Paul discovered a plot against his life, he changed his travel plans and returned to the province of Asia by way of Macedonia. An official delegation from various Gentile congregations accompanied the apostle as he made the return trip to Jerusalem (Acts 20:4-6).

During a lengthy message that Paul gave in an upstairs room, a young man named Eutychus [YOU-tih-kuss] dozed off, fell out of a third story window, and died. But Paul restored him to life. After the disciples brought the young man back into the house, the group fellowshipped some more with Paul before he left (20:11-12).

Paul and his associates eventually made their way to Miletus [my-LEET-us], which was 30 miles south of Ephesus. The apostle wanted to avoid visiting Ephesus [F-uh-suss] because he was hurrying to reach Jerusalem by the day of Pentecost. While in Miletus, Paul requested that the Ephesian elders come to him (20:13-17).

After the church leaders had arrived, Paul began his speech by noting his past faithfulness in ministry. His listeners could affirm that from the day he set foot in the Roman province of Asia, he had served the Lord with humility. In fact, the apostle did so with tears. *"You yourselves know how I [served] the Lord with all humility and with tears"* (20:18-19).

Paul had to endure many afflictions that came from the plots of religious antagonists. Though others may have wanted to quit, the apostle refused to do so. He never shirked his responsibility of telling the truth, either publicly or privately. *"I did not shrink from doing anything helpful, proclaiming the message to you and teaching you publicly and from house to house"* (20:20).

Regardless of whether Paul was preaching to Jews or Gentiles, he proclaimed a consistent message. He wanted all people to realize the necessity of turning away from sin and turning to God in faith through Christ. *"I testified to both Jews and Greeks about repentance toward God and faith toward our Lord Jesus"* (20:21).

Paul next focused on his determination to make the trip to Jerusalem. It was almost as if the Spirit was irresistibly drawing the apostle there. Though Paul wasn't sure exactly what he would experience, the Spirit did reveal that he would encounter some form of imprisonment and affliction. *"And now . . . I am on my way to Jerusalem, not knowing what will happen to me there, except that . . . imprisonment and persecutions are waiting for me"* (20:22-23).

Paul did not allow the possibility of suffering to stop him from serving Christ. In fact, the apostle declared to the Ephesian elders that his life counted most when he used it for doing the work that God had given him. Paul was specifically referring to the task of proclaiming to others the good news of God's kindness and love through Christ. *"I do not count my life of any value to myself, if only I may finish my course and the ministry that I received from the Lord Jesus, to testify to the good news of God's grace"* (20:24).

Paul's determination and faithfulness were especially evident among the believers in Ephesus. He noted that he had consistently proclaimed the kingdom of God to them. Now the apostle sensed that he might not ever see again his fellow believers in Ephesus (20:25). In light of this sobering thought, Paul asserted that *"I am not responsible for the blood of any of you"* (20:26). The reason is that the apostle never shrank from declaring to them *"the whole purpose of God"* (20:27).

As Paul looked to future, he gave a number of parting exhortations to the Ephesian elders. He told them to feed and shepherd God's flock, over whom the Holy Spirit had appointed them as church leaders. This was a solemn responsibility, for the congregation was *"the church of God that he obtained with the blood of his own Son"* (20:28).

Paul next urged his listeners to beware of dangers that lay ahead. The apostle was certain that after he left, religious frauds would infiltrate the flock, attack unsuspecting believers like crazed wolves, and not spare any of their victims. *"I know that after I have gone, savage wolves will come in among you, not sparing the flock"* (20:29).

Paul also warned the Ephesian elders of attacks from within their fellowship. The apostle noted that even some of their members would pervert the truth in order to seduce some naive believers to follow them. *"Some even from your own group will come distorting the truth in order to entice the disciples to follow them"* (20:30).

In light of these dangers, Paul's exhortation to be on the alert was timely. This is how he conducted his ministry while in Ephesus. He constantly watched over the flock and cared for them night and day, sometimes *"with tears"* (20:31).

Paul then declared that he was entrusting his Christian friends to God and the saving message of grace. The apostle was confident that God's Word could spiritually build them up and prepare them for the eternal inheritance that awaited all who were sanctified, or set apart, for Him (20:32).

Paul stated that he had not been motivated by greed, but rather supported himself as he ministered among them. His generous, self-sacrificing disposition reflected the teaching of Christ. After a time of prayer and well-wishes, the elders accompanied Paul to the ship that would take him to Palestine (20:32-38).

SUGGESTIONS TO TEACHERS

We have traced the dynamic spread of the Gospel from the earliest days after the Resurrection to its firm establishment throughout the Roman world. We conclude this teaching series from Acts with Paul's farewell speech to the Ephesian elders. This week's lesson emphasizes the importance of serving God with faith, humility, and confidence even in the midst of difficulties.

1. INTIMATIONS OF ARREST AND DEATH. Though the future did not look promising for Paul, his trust in Christ was unshakable. Remind your students that the future for some believers is difficult due to illness, loss, suffering, and death. Be sure to stress that that our lives ultimately are in God's hands. This is the basis for serving Him with faith, humility, and confidence.

2. INSTRUCTIONS TO CHURCH LEADERS. Always down-to-earth in his advice, Paul gave wise words to church leaders for all generations.

3. IMPLICATION OF DISCORD AND HARDSHIP. Paul never held out false hope but rather was consistently realistic. He taught that sin is real and evil is rampant. Paul particularly wanted his hearers to be wary of religious frauds who would undermine the work of the Spirit in a congregation.

4. AN EXAMPLE IN WORD AND DEED. Paul used his own life as an example of how Christians are called to serve. The apostle recounted how unsparing he had been in his efforts to spread the Gospel, and thereby challenges us to do likewise. He had not served out of greed or personal gain. Rather, his own life revealed his concern for helping the weak and showing generosity to the poor.

5. INVOCATION OF THE SPIRIT. Paul ended his speech by praying with his hearers. This would be a good place to have your students discuss the place and power of prayer in the lives of believers.

FOR ADULTS

■ TOPIC: Service with Faith and Confidence

■ QUESTIONS: 1. In what way did Paul live among the believers at Ephesus during his time of ministry there? 2. What threats did Paul face from religious antagonists? 3. Why did Paul feel impelled to go to Jerusalem? 4. Why did Paul exhort the Ephesian elders to keep watch over the flock of believers? 5. How can God's grace make a difference in your life and ministry?

■ **ILLUSTRATIONS:**

Exit Lines. Paul, the great missionary, served Christ faithfully until he died. Though imprisoned and condemned to be executed, he maintained a commitment to the Lord to the last. Among his most memorable words were those recorded in 2 Timothy 4:7: *I have fought the good fight, I have finished the race, I have kept the faith.*

Compare these sentiments with the final utterances of others who seemed to lack what Paul knew. For instance, Sir Winston Churchill's last words to his family were, "I am bored with it all." P. T. Barnum, the great showman, on his deathbed gasped, "How much were the circus receipts today at Madison Garden?" Writer O. Henry (William Sydney Porter) whispered before he died, "Turn up the lights. I don't want to go home in the dark." John Wilkes Booth's last words were, "Useless! Useless!" Lady Mary Wortley Montague sighed as she slipped away, "It's all been very interesting." Before expiring, Britain's Chief Justice Gordon Hewart muttered, "Drats! There's that cuckoo again." Actress Tallulah Bankhead parted this world with one word, "Bourbon." And author Oscar Wilde's final words were, "Either that wallpaper goes, or I do."

What would you hope your exit line will be as you complete your earthly life?

Humble Service. Chris Legree and Ervin Roberson are two African American former college athletes. Both men were given scholarships to go to college. They determined to use sports as a way to bring change for minority youngsters in New York City. That's why they brought Pop Warner Little Scholars football to a dusty patch of field underneath the Number 3 train tracks. Since organizing their team, the Mo' Better Jaguars, in 1995, the pair of dedicated volunteers and their 13 fellow coaches have made state history by winning the Empire State Classic Football Championship.

But Legree and Roberson get their greatest satisfaction not from victories and trophies, but from helping youngsters from the bleak streets and projects to study hard in school and avoid the wrong crowds. "We are black men out here teaching black boys how to be black men," they and the other coaches say. For many inner city 11 to 14-year-old boys (where over half grow up in single (female) parent households), the commitment of these 15 coaches is the only bond with a caring, concerned African American man they have.

Furthermore, few youngsters in that neighborhood can afford sports equipment or find playing fields for organized football. Legree, an electrical engineer, and Roberson, an architect, have managed to scrounge the $40,000 to fund the program for the 120 boys each year. They also engage a licensed teacher to work three hours before every practice to help with homework, and insist that each player enter a tutoring program if he is having trouble in any subject. A recent source of support has come from a group of eight women called the Team Mothers. Thanks to the faith and confidence of Chris Legree and Ervin Roberson, responsible youths are growing up on a dusty field.

Orkney Wisdom. George Mackay Brown, the poet from Scotland's Orkney Islands, summed up the wisdom every Christian should have by the end of one's life. Writing at the conclusion of his autobiography, *For the Islands I Sing*, he wrote, "To lose one's own will in the will of God should be the true occupation of every person's time on earth. Only a few of us—the saints—are capable of that simplicity."

FOR YOUTH

■ **TOPIC:** Never Give Up

■ **QUESTIONS:** 1. What characterized Paul's service among the Ephesian believers? 2. What was the heart of the message Paul proclaimed in Ephesus? 3. Why did Paul suspect he might not ever see the Ephesian believers again? 4. What threats faced the believers in the Ephesian church? 5. How can God's grace enable you to remain faithful to Him despite trials you might face?

■ **ILLUSTRATIONS:**

No Hope. He had spent six days walking with little food and water. He arrived with only what he was wearing. Standing in a huge refugee center in Klukes,

Albania, the unnamed 16-year-old boy wondered aloud to a visiting reporter if maybe he would have been better off dead. Some of his family had been killed by enemy death squads. The lad had been separated from his family upon arrival when his mother and younger siblings had been admitted ahead of him. Now, the teenager had spent hours searching for them in the worst camp imaginable. He had also now become separated from his father. Alone, without food, water, and family, the youngster saw absolutely no hope for the future in this war-torn portion of the world.

Even when the situation seemed the bleakest for Paul, he had hope in God. The apostle knew that his Savior would see him through any circumstance that life might present.

Advice. Winston Churchill was England's Prime Minister during World War II. During the darkest days of the war, he delivered some of the most challenging and memorable speeches, and these echoed his confidence in the Allied cause. Before the United States entered the war, he spoke to the students of Harrow School, stating, "Never give in! Never give in! Never, Never, Never, Never—in nothing great or small, large or petty—never give in except to convictions of honour and good sense."

Churchill's advice was echoed centuries earlier by the sold-out evangelist, Paul. He urged his friends and church leaders to never give up. The basis of the apostle's advice was the certainty that God was firmly in control of everything!

Willingly Risked Lives. On a late Monday night, March 15, 1999, Amtrack's *City of New Orleans* crashed into a flatbed truck loaded with steel beams near Bourbonnais, Illinois, about 50 miles south of Chicago. The impact knocked the train off of the tracks, killing 13 people and injuring 116 others of the 217 people aboard. As the momentum crushed the front two cars of the train and carried them on to the tops of the two locomotives, a fuel tank ruptured and started a fire in the already heavily damaged sleeping car, in which most of the deaths occurred.

Aboard were some students from a Mississippi college who had been vacationing over spring break on a Canadian ski trip. Risking their own lives, they helped people from the wreckage and were later hailed as heroes. Even when confronted with a life and death situation, these youth remained undaunted in wanting to help others. Paul, like those students, never gave up but rather served the Lord, even when confronted by the possibility of death.

DIVISION AND DECLINE

REHOBOAM: AN UNWISE DECISION

BACKGROUND SCRIPTURE: 1 Kings 12; 2 Chronicles 10:1—11:12
DEVOTIONAL READING: Matthew 11:27-30

KEY VERSE: "If you will be a servant to this people today and serve them, and speak good words to them when you answer them, then they will be your servants forever." 1 Kings 12:7.

KING JAMES VERSION

1 KINGS 12:3 That they sent and called him. And Jeroboam and all the congregation of Israel came, and spake unto Rehoboam, saying,

4 Thy father made our yoke grievous: now therefore make thou the grievous service of thy father, and his heavy yoke which he put upon us, lighter, and we will serve thee. . . .

6 And king Rehoboam consulted with the old men, that stood before Solomon his father while he yet lived, and said, How do ye advise that I may answer this people?

7 And they spake unto him, saying, If thou wilt be a servant unto this people this day, and wilt serve them, and answer them, and speak good words to them, then they will be thy servants for ever.

8 But he forsook the counsel of the old men, which they had given him, and consulted with the young men that were grown up with him, and which stood before him:

9 And he said unto them, What counsel give ye that we may answer this people, who have spoken to me, saying, Make the yoke which thy father did put upon us lighter?

10 And the young men that were grown up with him spake unto him, saying, Thus shalt thou speak unto this people that spake unto thee, saying, Thy father made our yoke heavy, but make thou it lighter unto us; thus shalt thou say unto them, My little finger shall be thicker than my father's loins.

11 And now whereas my father did lade you with a heavy yoke, I will add to your yoke: my father hath chastised you with whips, but I will chastise you with scorpions.

NEW REVISED STANDARD VERSION

1 KINGS 12:3 And they sent and called him; and Jeroboam and all the assembly of Israel came and said to Rehoboam, 4 "Your father made our yoke heavy. Now therefore lighten the hard service of your father and his heavy yoke that he placed on us, and we will serve you." . . .

6 Then King Rehoboam took counsel with the older men who had attended his father Solomon while he was still alive, saying, "How do you advise me to answer this people?" 7 They answered him, "If you will be a servant to this people today and serve them, and speak good words to them when you answer them, then they will be your servants forever." 8 But he disregarded the advice that the older men gave him, and consulted with the young men who had grown up with him and now attended him. 9 He said to them, "What do you advise that we answer this people who have said to me, 'Lighten the yoke that your father put on us'?" 10 The young men who had grown up with him said to him, "Thus you should say to this people who spoke to you, 'Your father made our yoke heavy, but you must lighten it for us'; thus you should say to them, 'My little finger is thicker than my father's loins. 11 Now, whereas my father laid on you a heavy yoke, I will add to your yoke. My father disciplined you with whips, but I will discipline you with scorpions.' "

HOME BIBLE READINGS

BACKGROUND

At its height of power, the empire of David and Solomon encompassed all of Palestine. Governing and guarding it required a huge number of officials and troops. This swarm of staff and soldiers had to be paid and posted throughout the realm. This required increasingly heavier taxes. It also demanded extensive—and expensive—building programs. To meet the staffing needs, Solomon finally resorted to pressing non-Israelite people into forced labor gangs and drafting Israelite citizens to serve as soldiers and officials for the nation (1 Kings 9:15-22).

By the time Solomon died, many of the people were agitating for some relief from the tax burdens and the labor drafts. An ambitious young official named Jeroboam had stirred up a minor revolt even before Solomon's death. When Solomon finally passed away and the crown went to his son Rehoboam, the unrest among the 10 northern tribes was deep and intense (11:26-40).

Instead of heeding the sensible advice of his father's senior advisors, Rehoboam brashly chose to listen to his hotheaded young cronies. To those pleading for him to ease the heavy load, he recklessly answered that he would make conditions even harsher (12:4, 14).

Because Rehoboam refused to heed the request of the people, the 10 northern tribes broke away and declared their independence. The newly formed northern kingdom of Israel then made Jeroboam its king. Rehoboam was left with the diminished southern kingdom of Judah. For the next two centuries, Israel, the northern kingdom, and Judah, the southern kingdom, went their separate ways, always suspicious and often hostile of each another (12:16-20).

NOTES ON THE PRINTED TEXT

Rehoboam agreed to journey north to Shechem for a face-to-face meeting with the leaders of the 12 tribes of Israel. (Shechem was a prominent site of ancient Israel located 35 miles north of Jerusalem.) The demands of the 10 northern tribes were presented (1 Kings 12:1-3). *"Your father made our yoke heavy. Now therefore lighten the hard service of your father and his heavy yoke that he placed on us, and we will serve you"* (12:4).

Solomon had organized a conscripted labor force to do his bidding. Taxes had skyrocketed to pay for the king's ambitious building projects and lavish lifestyle. It's no wonder that resentment over Solomon's preferential treatment of Judah seethed among the members of the 10 northern tribes (9:15-22).

In response to the people's request, Rehoboam stalled for time by asking for and receiving three days to consider the matter further (12:5). Rehoboam's cabinet consisted of two groups. The older group had counseled Solomon, and the heir apparent first sought their advice. Thus, King Rehoboam took counsel with the older men who had attended his father Solomon while he was still alive, saying, *"How do you advise me to answer this people?"* (12:6).

The elders urged conciliation. They wisely sensed that the unity and strength of the nation were worth agreeing to the demands of the 10 northern tribes. They answered him, *"If you will be a servant to this people today and serve them, and speak good words to them when you answer them, then they will be your servants forever"* (12:7).

Being arrogant, immature, and brash, Rehoboam bristled at the thought of entertaining such a plan. He thus disregarded the advice of the older advisers. Instead, he sought the help of some younger officials who had grown up with him. *But he disregarded the advice that the older men gave him and consulted with the young men who had grown up with him and now attended him* (12:8).

The younger men advocated a tough no-nonsense approach (12:9). They said Rehoboam's little finger was larger than his father's *"loins"* (12:10). This may have been a reference to Solomon's hips, which were basically the broadest part of a person's body. In other words, the new king was encouraged to boast of the superior power he wielded.

The younger officials said that the people in the 10 northern tribes had too much time to think and whine, so their workload should be increased. Rehoboam was encouraged to tip the end of the lashes with scorpions (namely, little bags stuffed with sand or lead) to show the complainers who was in charge. *"Now, whereas my father laid on you a heavy yoke, I will add to your yoke. My father disciplined you with whips, but I will discipline you with scorpions"* (12:11).

Three days later all the groups reassembled (12:12). To the surprise and disappointment of the leaders of the 10 northern tribes, Rehoboam delivered his decision. *The king answered the people harshly. He disregarded the advice that the older men had given him and spoke to them according to the advice of the young men* (12:13).

Rehoboam's decision shattered any hope of further unity (12:14). Angered at the king's hard-line approach, the 10 northern tribes voiced their decision for independence. They would break away and form their own nation. *It was a turn of affairs brought about by the LORD* (12:15). When all Israel saw that the king would not listen to them, the people answered the king, *"What share do we have in David? We have no inheritance in the son of Jesse. To your tents, O Israel! Look now to your own house, O David"* (12:16).

SUGGESTIONS TO TEACHERS

Every day we are bombarded with hundreds of messages advising us what to buy, how to be successful, where to have fun, where to go for answers to our problems, and why a certain lifestyle should be pursued. Whether in the form of advertisements, editorials, television programs, magazine articles, sermons, seminars, or conversations with friends, we find ourselves pushed to follow certain courses of conduct. How do we choose wisely among a variety of options?

In this week's lesson we will learn about a young monarch who listened to the wrong advice and made foolish choices. The insights we glean from King Rehoboam's decisions can help us in our daily living as Christians.

1. HUMBLE APPEAL. The leaders of the 10 northern tribes asked Rehoboam to lighten the burdens that were causing hardship for them. This should remind us to heed the voices of the poor and oppressed. The biblical message consistently is to remember those who are in dire situations. Thus, decisions should always be made in the light of the needs of the suffering and forgotten.

2. HELPFUL ADVICE. Rehoboam's wise advisers urged him to ease the burdens on the people in the 10 northern tribes, but the brash king chose to heed the council of his immature friends. Sometimes our friends will tell us only what we want to hear. And peer pressure can exert a powerful influence on us to act impulsively and foolishly. That's why when we have to make difficult decisions, we should seek out people who have wisdom and maturity. This increases the likelihood we will obtain advice that is unbiased and more in line with God's will.

3. HAUGHTY ATTITUDE. Rehoboam brashly assumed he was right, and was determined to have his way. His self-righteousness and stubbornness caused the kingdom he inherited from his father Solomon to split in two. From this we see that humility and consideration of others is always needed.

4. HEARTLESS ANSWER. Rehoboam's response to the leaders of the 10 northern tribes not only lacked tact and common sense, but also lacked thought and compassion. Speaking in love takes a special kind of grace. Talk with your students about how we in our society should learn to speak to each other with greater civility. The "in your face" kind of words evident in some talk shows and conversations betray a heartlessness that can tear apart relationships.

5. HARSH AFTEREFFECTS. Rehoboam's foolish choices had tragic results. The nation split, and hostilities persisted between the northern and southern kingdoms for years to come. Our choices usually have ramifications for us and others that that we rarely (but often should) consider.

6. HARMFUL APOSTASY. Part of the destructive fallout resulting from Rehoboam's foolish choice was Jeroboam's insistence on setting up a rival religion to the one found in Jerusalem. The new king of the 10 northern tribes was determined to lure his people away from traditional ceremonies in the Jerusalem temple that centered on the Lord (1 Kings 12:25-33).

■ **TOPIC:** Choose Wisely

■ **QUESTIONS:** 1. Why do you think Rehoboam sought counsel instead of deciding on his own? 2. Why do you think Rehoboam rejected the counsel of the elders? 3. What price did Rehoboam pay for ignoring his people's needs? 4. Have you ever seen church leaders abuse their authority because they wanted to control people? What were the consequences of that abuse? 5. Whom do you have authority over? How do you serve them?

■ **ILLUSTRATIONS:**

Wise Choice. Jay guarded a painful secret for years as he built his machine and tool company into a business bringing in over five million dollars a year. His secret was that he could not read. Jay found difficulty in learning to read in the elementary grades and was called stupid by more than one teacher. This caused Jay to cower in the back of classrooms and do whatever he could to hide his inability. Jay concluded that reading would always be impossible for him. Amazingly, he was able to pass through the public school system without ever mastering the basics of reading.

After graduating from high school in the early 1960s, Jay started a small machine shop with his savings of $200. The business grew, and today Jay has 50 employees. Over the years, he hid his inability to read by pretending to be too busy to review materials on his desk and delegating tasks to key managers or sorting through paperwork at night with his wife.

Finally, Jay chose to stop hiding and pretending. He chose to learn to read at the age of 56. In 1998, he found a tutor who instructed him for an hour each day. He told his friends and his employees, hoping his story would encourage others to learn to read. In 1999, the U. S. Chamber of Commerce honored Jay as one of six recipients of the National Blue Chip Enterprise Initiative Award. His wise choice ended years of torment for him.

Foolish Choice. Years ago a report circulated in Tennessee about two steamboats leaving Memphis at the same time. As the two vessels chugged side by side down the Mississippi River toward New Orleans, crewmen on one boat began to exchange jibes about the slow speed of the other boat. Soon a rivalry developed in which each vessel wanted to prove which one was the fastest. The two boats fired up their boilers and entered into a race. Soon they were churning down the river at a furious pace.

Unexpectedly, one boat began to run low on coal and began to fall behind. By this time, the captain and crew were so absorbed on competing with the other riverboat that they began to heave some of the cargo into the boilers to keep up steam. The cargo burned well, which enabled the boat to surge ahead and win the race. But by the time the vessel steamed into New Orleans, the crew had burned all the cargo they were being paid to transport!

Sometimes our choices turn out that way. We become so preoccupied on selfish concerns that we allow ourselves to make foolish decisions. It's only when we remember that our journey in life is to serve and honor God that we will make wise choices.

Besieged by Choices. We who live in the United States are besieged by an estimated 600 to 1,200 choices each day through advertising. For instance, when we visit a mall or a supermarket, we are confronted by dozens of commercial messages. And it isn't going to change.

Beginning in 1998, the advertising industry grew domestically to become a $200 billion-a-year business. Five blimps float over the Super Bowl, in addition to the once-extraordinary Goodyear blimp. Direct-mail videos and CD-ROMS began to promote political candidates in 1992, and are now used to entice people to buy everything from insurance policies to fitness programs. Movie advertisements appear at ATMs, and fast sound bites and video clips play while people wait for their money. Some gasoline stations have fitted gas-pump islands with video screens that run a stream of advertisements.

In such an environment, how do we choose wisely? The key is to give Jesus foremost priority in our lives.

■ **TOPIC:** Reject Bad Advice
■ **QUESTIONS:** 1. Why was the counsel of the elders wise advice? 2. What does the counsel of Rehoboam's friends say about his character? 3. What might Rehoboam have done to heal the rift between Judah and the other tribes of Israel? 4. In what ways might leaders in the church abuse their authority? 5. Why are the best Christian leaders those who serve their people well?

■ **ILLUSTRATIONS:**

Fatal Choice. Sue and a friend were playing in a large hole that had been created the day before when high winds had felled a huge tree in the woods behind Sue's home. Not long after the two had climbed into the hole, Sue's father repeatedly told his daughter and her friend to climb out. Finally, Sue's friend got out of the near crater size depression.

While Sue's father and his friend cut the tree up with their chain saws, she stubbornly stayed in the hole, failing to heed her father's command. As her father cut through the large tree trunk, the stump, which was still attached to its roots and now free of the tremendous weight of the rest of the tree, suddenly snapped back upright to its spot in the hole. Sue died instantly.

The little girl's failure to listen to her father's wise directive proved to be fatal. Likewise, Rehoboam's failure to listen to the wise advice of his older counselors proved to be fatal for his kingdom. Listening to unwise advice can be equally fatal to you, too!

Regrets. Steve had saved his money carefully for over one and a half years. Each paycheck that he earned from his busboy duties was banked with the hopes of buying a car during his senior year of high school.

When the time came, Steve went with his mother to look at some used cars. The dealer, who was a family friend, suggested that Steve buy a particular brand. The dealer pointed out that the car came with a warranty, had low mileage, and had been regularly maintained by the owner, who was a good customer of the dealer. It truly was a wonderful buy, especially considering what Steve could afford. Though the car was plain looking, the dealer said that it was dependable and would not give Steve any trouble.

Steve, however, liked a much sportier car on the same lot. It was a flashy red convertible with over 100,000 miles on it. The dealer advised against buying the car, for it carried no warranty. The dealer also said that he didn't know anything about the owner or how the car had been maintained. Moreover, the dealer noted that insuring the car would be very expensive for Steve.

But Steve ignored the dealer's wise advice and bought the more sporty car. Within six weeks, his "dream machine" had broken down. After a second break-down, Steve discovered that the car needed a new transmission and would likely also require a new engine. Both would mean that he would have to spend a large amount of money.

Tragically, Steve rejected wise advice and made a foolish decision. He lived to regret his choice. Rehoboam also rejected sound advice and lived to regret his decision.

ELIJAH: A PROPHET APPEARS

BACKGROUND SCRIPTURE: 1 Kings 17
DEVOTIONAL READING: Job 36:5-11

KEY VERSE: The jar of meal was not emptied, neither did the jug of oil fail, according to the word of the LORD that he spoke by Elijah. 1 Kings 17:16.

KING JAMES VERSION

1 KINGS 17:1 And Elijah the Tishbite, who was of the inhabitants of Gilead, said unto Ahab, As the LORD God of Israel liveth, before whom I stand, there shall not be dew nor rain these years, but according to my word.

2 And the word of the LORD came unto him, saying,

3 Get thee hence, and turn thee eastward, and hide thyself by the brook Cherith, that is before Jordan.

4 And it shall be, that thou shalt drink of the brook; and I have commanded the ravens to feed thee there.

5 So he went and did according unto the word of the LORD: for he went and dwelt by the brook Cherith, that is before Jordan. . . .

8 And the word of the LORD came unto him, saying,

9 Arise, get thee to Zarephath, which belongeth to Zidon, and dwell there: behold, I have commanded a widow woman there to sustain thee.

10 So he arose and went to Zarephath. And when he came to the gate of the city, behold, the widow woman was there gathering of sticks: and he called to her, and said, Fetch me, I pray thee, a little water in a vessel, that I may drink.

11 And as she was going to fetch it, he called to her, and said, Bring me, I pray thee, a morsel of bread in thine hand.

12 And she said, As the LORD thy God liveth, I have not a cake, but an handful of meal in a barrel, and a little oil in a cruse: and, behold, I am gathering two sticks, that I may go in and dress it for me and my son, that we may eat it, and die.

13 And Elijah said unto her, Fear not; go and do as thou hast said: but make me thereof a little cake first, and bring it unto me, and after make for thee and for thy son.

14 For thus saith the LORD God of Israel, The barrel of meal shall not waste, neither shall the cruse of oil fail, until the day that the LORD sendeth rain upon the earth.

15 And she went and did according to the saying of Elijah: and she, and he, and her house, did eat many days.

16 And the barrel of meal wasted not, neither did the cruse of oil fail, according to the word of the LORD, which he spake by Elijah.

NEW REVISED STANDARD VERSION

1 KINGS 17:1 Now Elijah the Tishbite, of Tishbe in Gilead, said to Ahab, "As the LORD the God of Israel lives, before whom I stand, there shall be neither dew nor rain these years, except by my word." 2 The word of the LORD came to him, saying, 3 "Go from here and turn eastward, and hide yourself by the Wadi Cherith, which is east of the Jordan. 4 You shall drink from the wadi, and I have commanded the ravens to feed you there." 5 So he went and did according to the word of the LORD; he went and lived by the Wadi Cherith, which is east of the Jordan.

8 Then the word of the LORD came to him, saying, 9 "Go now to Zarephath, which belongs to Sidon, and live there; for I have commanded a widow there to feed you." 10 So he set out and went to Zarephath. When he came to the gate of the town, a widow was there gathering sticks; he called to her and said, "Bring me a little water in a vessel, so that I may drink." 11 As she was going to bring it, he called to her and said, "Bring me a morsel of bread in your hand." 12 But she said, "As the LORD your God lives, I have nothing baked, only a handful of meal in a jar, and a little oil in a jug; I am now gathering a couple of sticks, so that I may go home and prepare it for myself and my son, that we may eat it, and die." 13 Elijah said to her, "Do not be afraid; go and do as you have said; but first make me a little cake of it and bring it to me, and afterwards make something for yourself and your son. 14 For thus says the LORD the God of Israel: The jar of meal will not be emptied and the jug of oil will not fail until the day that the LORD sends rain on the earth." 15 She went and did as Elijah said, so that she as well as he and her household ate for many days. 16 The jar of meal was not emptied, neither did the jug of oil fail, according to the word of the LORD that he spoke by Elijah.

HOME BIBLE READINGS

Monday, June 4	1 Kings 16:21-28	*Omri Reigns over Israel*
Tuesday, June 5	1 Kings 16:29-34	*Ahab Reigns over Israel*
Wednesday, June 6	1 Kings 17:1-7	*Elijah Predicts a Drought in Israel*
Thursday, June 7	James 5:13-18	*The Prayer of Faith*
Friday, June 8	1 Kings 17:8-16	*The Widow of Zarephath*
Saturday, June 9	1 Kings 17:17-24	*Elijah Revives the Widow's Son*
Sunday, June 10	Job 36:5-11	*God's Goodness*

BACKGROUND

The policies of Jeroboam and his successors were to keep Israel from Judah. One primary way to do this was to replace devotion to the Lord at the temple in Jerusalem with counterfeit shrines at Bethel and Dan (1 Kings 12:26-30). Bethel was located about 12 miles north of Jerusalem, while Dan was located much farther north near Mount Hermon.

By the time of King Ahab (874–853 B.C.), pagan ways of worship were widespread throughout the northern kingdom. Ahab's marriage to Jezebel, the daughter of the king of Tyre, brought in hundreds of pagan priests. And the worship of fertility deities, accompanied by lewd sexual practices that were led by foreign religious leaders (backed by Jezebel with Ahab's approval), further eroded whatever faith had once existed in the Lord (16:30-33).

Despite these moral excesses, God did not leave the northern kingdom without a witness. He raised up a handful of fearless spokespersons, one of whom was the prophet Elijah. He hailed from the city of Tishbe in Gilead (17:1).

Elijah and his colleagues often found themselves in opposition to Ahab and Jezebel. God's true prophets paid a fearsome price (18:4). And Elijah's encounters with Ahab usually ended with the king becoming angry and threatening (18:17). In fact, Elijah was sometimes forced to flee for his life (19:1-3).

In this week's lesson we learn that Elijah warned Ahab of a severe drought that would come on the land. This calamity would be God's hand of chastisement on the king and his people for their wickedness.

Sometime later Elijah ended up in Zarephath, a town on the Mediterranean coast just south of Sidon. Elijah found refuge in the house of a poor widow. Though she had only a small amount of food for her son and herself, she trusted Elijah's assurances that God would provide for them. Centuries later, in Jesus' sermon in His hometown synagogue, He held up this woman as an example of a Gentile who was pointed out by God because of her faith and obedience (Luke 4:25-26).

NOTES ON THE PRINTED TEXT

King Ahab married a tough-minded, strong-willed, and ruthless woman named Jezebel. She was determined to spread the worship of Baal (a Canaanite fertility god) throughout Israel (1 Kings 16:31-33). The cult soon became the official religion within the royal court, and hundreds of pagan priests lived and dined in the royal precincts.

Opposition arose, however. From the region of Galilee came an austere spokesperson for God. The prophet's name was Elijah, and God sent him to thunder His message of judgment to the leaders and people of Samaria (the capital of the northern kingdom). The clothing Elijah wore undoubtedly contrasted sharply with what the wicked rich in Samaria wore.

Perhaps after being ushered into Ahab's palace, Elijah skipped any formal greeting. Instead, the prophet condemned the king for his nation's unfaithfulness and promised impending calamity. The northern kingdom would suffer a severe drought for several years. Starvation would result, proving that the Lord, not Baal, controlled the weather (17:1).

Perhaps before Ahab had any time to respond, Elijah left the palace. God instructed His spokesperson to recross the Jordan and camp at an isolated brook (17:2). There, God would provide Elijah with food and water. *"Go from here and turn eastward, and hide yourself by the Wadi Cherith, which is east of the Jordan. You shall drink from the wadi, and I have commanded the ravens to feed you there"* (17:3-4).

Despite the odd nature of God's command, Elijah did not hesitate to obey (17:5). There, as the drought unfolded, the ravens brought the prophet bread and meat (17:6). The severity of the drought was seen in the fact that Elijah ate meat. Normally in ancient times people ate meat sparingly. However, many animals were dying as a result of the drought, and so meat was much more abundant.

As the severe shortage of water continued, the brook dried up (17:7). The Lord next ordered Elijah to travel to Zarephath, which was a Phoenician coastal city situated between Tyre and Sidon. There a Gentile widow would provide for the prophet (17:8). *"Go now to Zarephath, which belongs to Sidon, and live there; for I have commanded a widow there to feed you"* (17:9).

Elijah thus traveled west, recrossing the Jordan River and the northern kingdom of Israel. The prophet then traveled through Phoenicia to Zarephath. When Elijah came near the gate of the town, he spotted a poor woman who was gathering sticks to fuel a fire. Elijah asked her for water, and as an afterthought, something to eat. *"Bring me a little water in a vessel, so that I may drink." As she was going to bring it, he called to her and said, "Bring me a morsel of bread in your hand"* (17:10-11).

Upon hearing these requests, the desperate widow and mother pleaded that she was unable to be so hospitable. So destitute was the family, that she was preparing a final meal for herself and her son. She had intended to use the last portion of her precious ingredients to cook a mouthful of bread. *"As the LORD your God lives, . . . I am now gathering a couple of sticks, so that I may go home and prepare it for myself and my son, that we may eat it, and die"* (17:12).

The prophet, however, insisted that the widow first had to feed him. Then she and her son could eat. Through this test of faith, Elijah was pointing the widow directly to the Lord as the one who could sustain her. *"Do not be afraid; go and do as you have said; but first make me a little cake of it and bring it to me, and afterwards make something for yourself and your son. For thus says the LORD the God of Israel: The jar of meal will not be emptied and the jug of oil will not fail until the day that the LORD sends rain on the earth"* (17:13-14).

The widow responded in faith by doing exactly what Elijah had said. The Lord honored the widow's faith by enabling her, her son, and the prophet to eat from her supply of food for many days (17:15). In fact, regardless of how much the widow used, there was always enough left in the containers (17:16).

SUGGESTIONS TO TEACHERS

Begin the teaching time by asking your students what comes to mind when they hear the word "prophet." You may be surprised to learn that some don't understand what the Bible means by "prophet." Be sure to explain that a prophet was someone who spoke for God. Then note that this week's lesson concerns Elijah, one of the greatest prophets in the Old Testament.

1. PREDICTION. True prophets never resorted to sorcery or divination to foretell the future. Like Elijah, they were astute observers of the human scene. Because they were wise in God's ways, He gave them insights into the deplorable conditions plaguing their society. They especially knew that we live in an ethical universe in which disobeying God brings undesirable consequences. For instance, Elijah realized that a severe famine would come on the northern kingdom of Israel because the rulers and people had rebelled against God. The prophets also received direct revelations from God.

2. PROTECTION. True prophets in the Old Testament rarely had it easy. They were disliked and often treated harshly. Consider Elijah. He had to flee for his life on more than one occasion (1 Kings 19:3). But even when persecuted, Elijah knew that he was blessed with God's presence (19:4-18). Remind the members of your class that even when life seems unbearable, God is always with them.

3. PERCEPTION. After traveling to the pagan city of Zarephath, Elijah assured a Gentile widow that God would provide enough to keep her, her son, and Elijah alive. The widow fulfilled the prophet's request for food even though she initially had only enough to make one more meal for herself and her son. The widow demonstrated her faith by sharing what little she had. Jesus, in His synagogue sermon in His hometown, held up this woman's trust in and obedience to God's promise as being exemplary (Luke 4:25-26). Stress to your students that God is also worthy of their trust.

4. PROVISION. The Lord showed the Gentile widow that He is all-powerful and reliable. For instance, He miraculously ensured that enough flour and oil were available during the lean times to sustain the widow, her son, and her guest, Elijah. At this point invite your students to share some personal experiences they've had in which they learned firsthand about God's dependability. Then note that sometimes it's a struggle to remember to trust God enough to share with others, especially outsiders.

5. PRONOUNCEMENT. Elijah restored the widow's son to life after the boy had died (1 Kings 17:17-24). This reminds us that God is the Lord of life and death. Even in the spiritual realm, He can bring new life to those who are spiritually dead (Eph. 2:1-10). And God has given us His Spirit to declare this good news to a death-obsessed culture. Perhaps through our testimony, God might lead someone to say (as the widow did to Elijah), *"The word of the LORD in your mouth is truth"* (1 Kings 17:23).

FOR ADULTS

■ **TOPIC:** Follow Instructions

■ **QUESTIONS:** 1. What was the heart of Elijah's declaration to Ahab? 2. Why do you think God commanded Elijah to go the *"Wadi Cherith"* (1 Kings 17:3)? 3. How was God testing the widow's faith when Elijah asked her for a morsel of bread? 4. How did God demonstrate His faithfulness to the widow? 5. What are some ways that God has demonstrated His faithfulness to you?

■ **ILLUSTRATIONS:**

Trumpeter's Triumph. Dave Douglas, the acclaimed trumpeter, was on a performing tour of Italy with a band led by clarinetist Don Byron. One stop included Florence. On the day of the concert, Douglas visited the Santa Maria del Fiore Cathedral in the center of the city and learned the account of its construction.

It seems that in the thirteenth century, the Florentine builders wanted to create a cathedral more impressive than those in Pisa or Siena. But when they got to the dome, they found they lacked the engineering skill to construct the great rounded top. The cathedral stood without a dome for over a century. Finally, an architect named Filippo Brunelleschi solved the problem by turning to the Pantheon in Rome and studying its construction.

"This story really touched me," Douglas said. "Brunelleschi figured out how to do it by studying the past." Douglas began to direct his energies to studying the past masters of music, and he discovered new creativity and insights into playing.

The prophet Elijah similarly called God's people to look to their past and remember the covenant God had called them to enter into with Him. Following the past instructions of the Lord would bring them a new perspective on life. Likewise, our awareness of what God has done for us in the past can give us new hope for the present and renewed assurance concerning the future.

A Lot on the Ball. Tim Forneris was a 22-year-old part-time groundskeeper for the Saint Louis Cardinals in the summer of 1998. He retrieved Mark McGwire's sixty-second homerun ball, and became famous for turning the ball over to McGwire instead of holding on to it. Forneris could have sold the ball for an estimated $1 million. Many scoffed at Forneris, calling him an impulsive fool. But in a letter to *Time* magazine (dated March 22, 1999), Forneris wrote the following:

> I had thought over what I would do if I got a homerun ball, and discussed it with family and friends. What did influence my actions were my family and my friends. I have always been taught to respect others and their accomplishments. I have always valued all people's achievements, big and small. In my opinion, Mr. McGwire deserved not only the homerun record for his work but also this ball. Life is about more than just money. It is about family, friends, and the experiences you have with them. I believe some possessions are priceless. To put an economic value on Mr. McGwire's hard work and dedication is absurd. Being the person who received this ball was a great blessing to me. And being able to return it to Mr. McGwire was a real honor and thrill. I still would not trade that experience for a million dollars.

The incident involving Forneris reminds us of how important it is to keep our priorities straight in life, beginning with following God's instructions.

Taking a Great Risk. During World War II, after the Germans had forced the surrender of the French troops, the enemy compelled many captured soldiers to work in German factories. One group of prisoners quickly discovered that they were being made to help produce bombs in a munitions plant. That's when they remembered who they were and what their priorities should be.

Though reduced to the status of slave laborers, these prisoners tried to serve France in whatever ways they could. They worked on the production line, and saw the bombs they had helped make sent off to be dropped on their fellow citizens and their allies. But these brave workers had carefully and deliberately fixed the detonating mechanism on each bomb in such a way that it would not set off an explosion. For some time, the Nazi Luftwaffe dropped these deadly looking bombs before they discovered what these workers had done. Investigators found small slips of paper in the dummy bombs that said, "We're doing the best we can with what we've got, where we are, and in every opportunity we get."

Perhaps a similar message to us as Christ's people would be this: "Be faithful to the Lord by doing the best you can with what you have, where you are, and in every opportunity you get!"

FOR YOUTH

■ TOPIC: Trust Enough to Risk
■ QUESTIONS: 1. Why was Elijah so blunt in his remarks to Ahab?
2. How did God provide for Elijah when he was at the *"Wadi*

Cherith" (1 Kings 17:2)? 3. Why did the woman balk at Elijah's request for a morsel of bread? 4. How do you think the widow felt as she saw the miraculous way the Lord provided for her, her son, and Elijah? 5. Why should we continue trusting and obeying God even when life seems unbearable?

■ **ILLUSTRATIONS:**

Hospitable High Schoolers. In the spring of 1999, the senior class at a high school on the east coast of the United States was anticipating time at the beach. The class had held fundraisers all year to finance the trip. The annual event was a rite of passage after graduation and eagerly looked forward to by the seniors.

At one of the senior meetings, the issue of the Kosovo refugees was raised. The desperate conditions in the refugee camps had been carefully documented on television. Despair existed along with hunger, thirst, and cold. After a spirited debate, the senior class voted to donate all its money to the refugees.

Here is a group of young people who understand the meaning of hospitality. They wanted to share food and shelter with those who had experienced hardship.

Vocal Prayers. On May 10, 1999, Moore, Oklahoma, was rocked by more than 40 tornadoes over a 20-hour span. One giant, which originated near Chickasha, became historic, measuring one mile in width. The Doppler radar from the University of Oklahoma clocked peak winds at a speed of 318 mph, the strongest winds ever recorded on earth. The tornado leveled a huge gash through the northwestern corner of Oklahoma City and its suburbs.

As the funnel moved, a terrified resident prayed aloud, "God save us! God save us! God save us! O God!" Undoubtedly, the prayers of the Israelites were similar as a devastating drought and famine slashed through the land. God used Elijah to help them see that their faith was to be in the Lord, not the idols of Canaan.

Trust. Perhaps the best-remembered child in the twentieth century was Anne Frank. Born in Frankfurt, Germany, on June 12, 1929, she died of typhus in the Bergen-Belsen concentration camp during World War II. However, Frank's diary (which she received as a birthday present just weeks before the family went into hiding) details the events of two years of living in a secret attic room with her Jewish family. Most school districts require the reading of *Anne Frank: The Diary of a Young Girl.*

Anne's father, however, initially edited her work. The father removed things that he thought were too hurtful or damaging to Anne, such as her descriptions of her parent's loveless arranged marriage, or her curiosity about physical intimacy, or her doubts and questions about her faith and religion.

Ahab also had trouble believing and trusting in God's care. The king had to discover that the Lord was firmly in control of events and could be trusted.

ISRAEL: CALLED TO DECIDE

BACKGROUND SCRIPTURE: 1 Kings 18
DEVOTIONAL READING: Joshua 24:14-18

3

KEY VERSE: Elijah then came near to all the people, and said, "How long will you go limping with two different opinions? If the LORD is God, follow him; but if Baal, then follow him." The people did not answer him a word. 1 Kings 18:21.

KING JAMES VERSION

1 KINGS 18:20 So Ahab sent unto all the children of Israel, and gathered the prophets together unto mount Carmel.

21 And Elijah came unto all the people, and said, How long halt ye between two opinions? if the LORD be God, follow him: but if Baal, then follow him. And the people answered him not a word. . . .

30 And Elijah said unto all the people, Come near unto me. And all the people came near unto him. And he repaired the altar of the LORD that was broken down.

31 And Elijah took twelve stones, according to the number of the tribes of the sons of Jacob, unto whom the word of the LORD came, saying, Israel shall be thy name:

32 And with the stones he built an altar in the name of the LORD: and he made a trench about the altar, as great as would contain two measures of seed.

33 And he put the wood in order, and cut the bullock in pieces, and laid him on the wood, and said, Fill four barrels with water, and pour it on the burnt sacrifice, and on the wood.

34 And he said, Do it the second time. And they did it the second time. And he said, Do it the third time. And they did it the third time.

35 And the water ran round about the altar; and he filled the trench also with water.

36 And it came to pass at the time of the offering of the evening sacrifice, that Elijah the prophet came near, and said, LORD God of Abraham, Isaac, and of Israel, let it be known this day that thou art God in Israel, and that I am thy servant, and that I have done all these things at thy word.

37 Hear me, O LORD, hear me, that this people may know that thou art the LORD God, and that thou hast turned their heart back again.

38 Then the fire of the LORD fell, and consumed the burnt sacrifice, and the wood, and the stones, and the dust, and licked up the water that was in the trench.

39 And when all the people saw it, they fell on their

NEW REVISED STANDARD VERSION

1 KINGS 18:20 So Ahab sent to all the Israelites, and assembled the prophets at Mount Carmel. 21 Elijah then came near to all the people, and said, "How long will you go limping with two different opinions? If the LORD is God, follow him; but if Baal, then follow him." The people did not answer him a word. . . .

30 Then Elijah said to all the people, "Come closer to me"; and all the people came closer to him. First he repaired the altar of the LORD that had been thrown down; 31 Elijah took twelve stones, according to the number of the tribes of the sons of Jacob, to whom the word of the LORD came, saying, "Israel shall be your name"; 32 with the stones he built an altar in the name of the LORD. Then he made a trench around the altar, large enough to contain two measures of seed. 33 Next he put the wood in order, cut the bull in pieces, and laid it on the wood. He said, "Fill four jars with water and pour it on the burnt offering and on the wood."

34 Then he said, "Do it a second time"; and they did it a second time. Again he said, "Do it a third time"; and they did it a third time, 35 so that the water ran all around the altar, and filled the trench also with water.

36 At the time of the offering of the oblation, the prophet Elijah came near and said, "O LORD, God of Abraham, Isaac, and Israel, let it be known this day that you are God in Israel, that I am your servant, and that I have done all these things at your bidding. 37 Answer me, O LORD, answer me, so that this people may know that you, O LORD, are God, and that you have turned their hearts back." 38 Then the fire of the LORD fell and consumed the burnt offering, the wood, the stones, and the dust, and even licked up the water that was in the trench. 39 When all the people saw it, they fell on their faces and said, "The LORD indeed is God; the LORD indeed is God."

faces: and they said, The LORD, he is the God; the LORD, he is the God.

people did not answer him a word. 1 Kings 18:21.

BACKGROUND

God's brave prophet, Elijah, decided to challenge Ahab's pagan prophets to a showdown. Elijah had seen how Ahab was being manipulated by his powerful wife, Jezebel, into permitting idolatrous and immoral rites everywhere in the northern kingdom of Israel. Perhaps to Elijah's dismay, the royal pair had imported hundreds of foreign pagan prophets. With the backing of the king and queen, these cult leaders were doing everything possible to direct the people of Israel away from worshiping the Lord and obeying His precepts.

Elijah went to Ahab and demanded an opportunity to show that the Lord is supreme. Ahab accepted Elijah's challenge. After assembling at Mount Carmel, the king brought 450 prophets of Baal and 400 prophets of Asherah [uh-SHEER-uh]. Against them stood only Elijah and the Lord of Israel (1 Kings 18:17-19).

The contest was simple. Whichever god ignited the wood on the altar for a sacrifice would be acclaimed as the one who was really divine and all-powerful (18:23-24). Before the contest began, however, Elijah stood before the crowd of Israelites and declared, *"How long will you go limping with two different opinions? If the LORD is God, follow him; but if Baal, then follow him"* (18:21).

The contest began with hundreds of false prophets prancing and shouting for hours in a vain attempt to get their idols to respond. At noontime Elijah began mocking them. Despite their frantic efforts, their idol failed to respond (18:25-29).

The drama intensified when Elijah called the people to draw closer as he rebuilt the altar of the Lord and then drenched the sacrifice and altar with water. The prophet then addressed the Lord, asking for fire to descend on the sacrifice. The fire of the Lord suddenly crashed down, and consumed the sacrifice, the wood, and the altar. The Israelites were awestruck! The Lord had displayed His superiority over every rival, which prompted the people to acknowledge Him as the one true and living God (18:30-39).

NOTES ON THE PRINTED TEXT

In the third year of the severe drought, the Lord told Elijah that He was going to send rain on the earth. Thus, the prophet was to declare this news to King Ahab. In addition, Elijah was to convey God's extreme displeasure with the people's idolatry. In fact, it was time for the nation to make a decision. Israel had to choose between Baal and the Lord. There could be no waffling on the matter (1 Kings 18:1-16).

Elijah offered a challenge to Ahab. By himself, Elijah would take on all 850 prophets of Baal and Asherah. Ahab readily agreed and issued a proclamation summoning all the citizens to Mount Carmel (18:17-20). This was one of the heights on which places of worship to Baal had been built. In choosing this spot for the coming encounter, Elijah moved into Baal's home territory.

When the people had gathered, Elijah challenged them to decide for the Lord. The prophet characterized them as a spiritually lame people who were seeking support from both Yahweh and Baal. However, they could not follow both. Elijah thus called the nation to make a decision. *Elijah then came near to all the people, and said, "How long will you go limping with two different opinions? If the LORD is God, follow him; but if Baal, then follow him"* (18:21).

The people were silent, which undoubtedly disappointed Elijah. He then dictated the terms of the contest. Two altars were to be built, one for the Lord and one for Baal. Firewood and sacrifices were to be placed on each stone platform. Then, representatives of each god would call upon their deity to kindle the wood on the altar. Whichever god answered would be accepted as supreme (18:23-24).

Elijah stepped aside and invited Baal's prophets to go first. They split the logs and hacked apart a bull. Throughout the morning they slowly bobbed and weaved as they prayed and chanted to their idol. But when noontime arrived, Baal had still not responded. Elijah taunted the prophets, asking if Baal was quietly thinking, or asleep, or perhaps relieving himself. This evidently prompted the false prophets to perform a prolonged and frenzied dance. Then swords and lances flashed through the air as the false prophets drew blood in a ritualistic exercise. Still, there was no answer from their idol. It was now late afternoon and the false prophets' time had expired; so they stopped their antics (18:25-29).

Elijah then said to all the people, *"Come closer to me," and all the people came closer to him* (18:30). The prophet next repaired the destroyed altar of the Lord with 12 stones, with each one representing one of Israel's 12 tribes. Elijah also dug a trench around the rebuilt altar. He then placed the logs and the sacrificial bull on the altar. Elijah surprised the crowd by ordering that four large earthenware crocks of water were to be dumped on the altar. This was done two more times until the altar, the wood, and the sacrificial bull were drenched and the trough around the altar was filled with water (18:31-35).

In the sight of all the people, Elijah approached the altar he had made (18:36). This took place at the customary time when the Israelites offered the evening sacrifice; this would have been around 3:00 P.M. Elijah said, *"Oh LORD, God of Abraham, Isaac, and Israel, let it be known this day that you are God in Israel, that I am your servant, and that I have done all these things at your bidding. Answer me, O LORD, answer me, so that this people may know that you, O LORD, are God, and that you have turned their hearts back"* (18:36-37).

Suddenly the fire of the Lord flashed down from heaven, and flames consumed the altar and its contents. It even licked up all the water that was in the ditch (18:38). The astonished people fell to the ground and declared, *"The LORD indeed is God; the LORD indeed is God"* (18:39). For that moment and in that place, the Lord turned the hearts of the people back to Him.

SUGGESTIONS TO TEACHERS

The famous contest between Elijah and the hundreds of false prophets has such drama that you will find plenty of teaching material for this week's lesson. Be sure to point out that God is the central figure in this episode. He alone enabled Elijah to take a courageous stand for Him.

1. TIMIDITY. A minor character in this drama is a palace official of Ahab's named Obadiah (not the same as the writer of the Old Testament book of that name). This man tried to be faithful to the Lord but feared for his own safety if he relayed Elijah's message to the king (1 Kings 18:3-16). This response is typical of how we sometimes feel. We want to be Christians but shrink back when doing certain acts seems too threatening or costly.

2. TROUBLER. When Ahab finally met Elijah, he angrily called the prophet a *"troubler of Israel"* (18:17). By this Ahab implied that Elijah was a threat to the normal functioning of Israelite society, as seen in the severe drought and famine the nation had to endure. Ask your students who was really the nation's *"troubler"*—Ahab or Elijah? Remind the members of the class that those causing the greatest trouble for a nation are people who persist in ignoring God's ways.

3. TEST. Elijah challenged Ahab's false prophets to a contest. Let the account of the episode on Mount Carmel unfold, and allow your students to share their insights and comments. Don't let the lesson get bogged down on the details of the account, and also don't suggest that it's all right to put the Lord to the test anytime we want. The essential point is that God is supreme above all so-called gods (1 Cor. 8:4-6).

4. TESTIMONY. Elijah asked the assembled Israelites, *"How long will you go limping with two different opinions?"* (1 Kings 18:21). From this we see that trying to follow the Lord and also the idols of the world is spiritually crippling. At this point invite your students to list some "idols" that exist in the world today. Then note that nothing must ever displace God as being the Lord of their lives.

5. TAUNTS. If you have time, let some of the humor in the biblical account come to light. For instance, your students will undoubtedly chuckle when they learn about Elijah's mocking of Ahab's false prophets.

6. TRIUMPH. This week's lesson makes it clear that God is all-supreme in His authority and power. Regardless of the challenge, God will always prevail. Perhaps the greatest challenge to God's plans and power came at the Cross. But even there the Lord demonstrated conclusively that nothing—not even death itself—can thwart His loving intentions.

■ **TOPIC:** Remain Committed

■ **QUESTIONS:** 1. Why did Elijah challenge all the false prophets of Baal to a contest? 2. Why did Elijah use 12 stones to repair the altar of the Lord? 3. What effect do you think Elijah's prayer had on the people assembled on Mount Carmel? 4. Why are the false gods of the world a poor substitute for the one true God? 5. Why is it sometimes hard for us to trust the Lord as completely as we should?

■ **ILLUSTRATIONS:**

Remained Committed. On January 23, 1909, three years before the *Titanic* disaster, two ships collided in a dense fog off the coast of Nantucket. One was the luxury liner *Republic*; it was carrying hundreds of American tourists to Europe. The other ship was the *Florida*; it was bringing Italian immigrants who had survived an earthquake to America. Over 1,500 lives were at stake when the two ships crashed into each other and began to sink.

Jack Binns was a 26-year-old wireless operator on board the *Republic*. As his cabin filled with icy water while his ship was sinking, Binns continued to tap out messages for help, hoping that a nearby vessel would pick up his signal. Binns worked his wireless set for 24 hours straight in the dark and freezing cold. Because of his courageous commitment to duty, the *Baltic* picked up his urgent message for help and steamed toward the stricken vessels. Binns stayed at his post and relayed steering instructions to the rescue ship. All but five persons were saved.

Later Binns testified in Congress urging that a federal law be passed requiring that every ship carry a wireless transmitter and have it operating 24 hours a day. His pleas went unheard. Three years later 1,500 lives were lost on the *Titanic*— the same number that Binns had helped save after the collision of the *Republic* and the *Florida*. Binns turned down offers to play the celebrity or hero, and modestly continued his career as a wireless operator, committed to serving and saving others.

Gap in Faithful Living. Americans claim that they are solidly attached to their Bibles. For instance, 93 percent of all homes contain at least one Bible. One of the country's largest religious publishing houses reports selling 8 million copies of the Bible every year. An astonishing 33 percent of American adults say that they read the Bible at least once a week. But surveys show surprising gaps between reading and retention. Over 54 percent cannot name the authors of the four Gospel accounts. Nearly 63 percent don't know what a Gospel is. Fifty-eight percent cannot name five of the Ten Commandments. And one out of ten Americans thinks that Joan of Arc was Noah's wife!

What kind of commitment do these statistics suggest? What would Elijah have to say to religious people in America?

On-going Conflict. What accounts for the growing popularity of wrestling on television? Despite the poor acting, absurd routines, and inane conversations, wrestling remains one of the most widespread forms of entertainment available. Some claim that it is a soap opera constantly built on the battle between good and evil. Others, however, think it's a form of amusement that appeals to humanity's unspiritual nature.

In either case, you as a believer are daily confronted with the on-going conflict between good and evil. You are not a spectator. Like the spiritual, moral, and ethical choices that the Israelites had to make, you will sometimes have to choose between whom you will serve—whether the God of Scripture or the idols of money, power, popularity, and sex (to name a few). Heed Elijah's exhortation and make your choice for God!

■ **Topic:** Make Your Choice

■ **Questions:** 1. Why did Elijah force the people to choose between Baal and the Lord? 2. Why did Elijah thoroughly drench the altar and everything on it and around it with water? 3. What prompted the people to declare the Lord to be God? 4. Why is it important for us to choose to follow the Lord exclusively? 5. How can we prevent the false gods of the world from becoming substitutes for God?

■ **ILLUSTRATIONS:**

Toxic Crusaders. Teenagers Maria, Fabiola, and Anita were attending high school in 1999 in their Los Angeles neighborhood where most of the children are Hispanic or African American. These three girls learned that during construction of a new middle school in their community the soil and the ground water under the building were contaminated with highly toxic chemicals.

As members of a local community-based group of persons concerned about environmental health, Maria, Fabiola, and Anita called governmental agencies, passed out flyers, and went door to door to alert parents. The school authorities insisted that there was no danger and that the new building was safe. And despite attempts by the police to prevent the three from handing out material, the trio of toxic crusaders remained committed.

The teenagers called a community meeting, and invited school district officials, environmental agencies, and the news media. They succeeded in convincing school officials not to enroll children in the new building. Speaking for the three, Anita said, "One day, you're going to have to stand on your own two feet for something you believe in. Why not get an early start?"

False Gods. Many people come to a tragic end because they worship false gods. Some are wicked people, having made a god out of sensual pleasure. Others are upstanding people, yet they too have worshiped false gods. I wonder if this was true of a young farmer who committed suicide when his venture in farming failed. I say this because of a comment made by his wife. She remarked to me, "Farming wasn't just a job with Floyd. It was his identity, his nationality, his religion."

Whenever an occupation or anything temporal takes number one priority in life, it becomes our god. John admonished us not to love the things of the world, for it breeds arrogance and selfish desires (1 John 2:15-16). Let us ensure that we don't love anything more than the true and living God revealed in the Bible. Only He can help us when our plans are shattered, our health fails, or death beckons. Be sure you love and worship only Him.

Faith and Character. Faith and character are needed if we are to take the costly steps to renew our relationship with the Lord. Oswald Chambers, in a book entitled *My Utmost for His Highest*, observed the following about faith and character:

> The final stage in the life of faith is attainment of character. There are many passing transfigurations of character; when we pray we feel the blessing of God enwrapping us and for the time being we are changed, then we get back to the ordinary days and ways and the glory vanishes. The life of faith is not a life of mounting up with wings, but a life of walking and not fainting. It is not a question of sanctification; but of something infinitely further on than sanctification, of faith that has been tried and proved and has stood the test.

MICAIAH: COURAGEOUS PROPHET

BACKGROUND SCRIPTURE: 1 Kings 22:1-40
DEVOTIONAL READING: Proverbs 12:13-22

KEY VERSE: Micaiah said, "As the LORD lives, whatever the LORD says to me, that I will speak." 1 Kings 22:14.

4

KING JAMES VERSION

1 KINGS 22:15 So he came to the king. And the king said unto him, Micaiah, shall we go against Ramoth-gilead to battle, or shall we forbear? And he answered him, Go, and prosper: for the LORD shall deliver it into the hand of the king.

16 And the king said unto him, How many times shall I adjure thee that thou tell me nothing but that which is true in the name of the LORD?

17 And he said, I saw all Israel scattered upon the hills, as sheep that have not a shepherd: and the LORD said, These have no master: let them return every man to his house in peace.

18 And the king of Israel said unto Jehoshaphat, Did I not tell thee that he would prophesy no good concerning me, but evil?

19 And he said, Hear thou therefore the word of the LORD: I saw the LORD sitting on his throne, and all the host of heaven standing by him on his right hand and on his left.

20 And the LORD said, Who shall persuade Ahab, that he may go up and fall at Ramoth-gilead? And one said on this manner, and another said on that manner.

21 And there came forth a spirit, and stood before the LORD, and said, I will persuade him.

22 And the LORD said unto him, Wherewith? And he said, I will go forth, and I will be a lying spirit in the mouth of all his prophets. And he said, Thou shalt persuade him, and prevail also: go forth, and do so.

23 Now therefore, behold, the LORD hath put a lying spirit in the mouth of all these thy prophets, and the LORD hath spoken evil concerning thee. . . .

26 And the king of Israel said, Take Micaiah, and carry him back unto Amon the governor of the city, and to Joash the king's son;

27 And say, Thus saith the king, Put this fellow in the prison, and feed him with bread of affliction and with water of affliction, until I come in peace.

28 And Micaiah said, If thou return at all in peace, the LORD hath not spoken by me. And he said, Hearken, O people, every one of you.

NEW REVISED STANDARD VERSION

1 KINGS 22:15 When he had come to the king, the king said to him, "Micaiah, shall we go to Ramoth-gilead to battle, or shall we refrain?" He answered him, "Go up and triumph; the LORD will give it into the hand of the king." 16 But the king said to him, "How many times must I make you swear to tell me nothing but the truth in the name of the LORD?" 17 Then Micaiah said, "I saw all Israel scattered on the mountains, like sheep that have no shepherd; and the LORD said, 'These have no master; let each one go home in peace.'" 18 The king of Israel said to Jehoshaphat, "Did I not tell you that he would not prophesy anything favorable about me, but only disaster?"

19 Then Micaiah said, "Therefore hear the word of the LORD: I saw the Lord sitting on his throne, with all the host of heaven standing beside him to the right and to the left of him. 20 And the LORD said, 'Who will entice Ahab, so that he may go up and fall at Ramoth-gilead?' Then one said one thing, and another said another, 21 until a spirit came forward and stood before the LORD, saying, 'I will entice him.' 22 'How?' the LORD asked him. He replied, 'I will go out and be a lying spirit in the mouth of all his prophets.' Then the LORD said, 'You are to entice him, and you shall succeed; go out and do it.' 23 So you see, the LORD has put a lying spirit in the mouth of all these your prophets; the LORD has decreed disaster for you." . . .

26 The king of Israel then ordered, "Take Micaiah, and return him to Amon the governor of the city and to Joash the king's son, 27 and say, 'Thus says the king: Put this fellow in prison, and feed him on reduced rations of bread and water until I come in peace.'"

28 Micaiah said, "If you return in peace, the LORD has not spoken by me." And he said, "Hear, you peoples, all of you!"

Monday, June 18	1 Kings 22:1-5	*Israel and Judah Become Allies*
Tuesday, June 19	1 Kings 22:6-12	*The Lying Prophets of Ahab*
Wednesday, June 20	2 Chronicles 18:4-11	*Bad Advice for Jehoshaphat*
Thursday, June 21	1 Kings 22:13-28	*Micaiah Predicts Failure*
Friday, June 22	2 Chronicles 18:12-27	*Micaiah's True Answer*
Saturday, June 23	1 Kings 22:29-40	*Defeat and Death of Ahab*
Sunday, June 24	1 Kings 22:41-53	*Jehoshaphat, Jehoram, and Ahaziah's Reign*

BACKGROUND

Prophets such as Elijah and Elisha convincingly demonstrated that Yahweh was supreme in power and authority. But tragically, this did little to curb the idolatry, immorality, and injustice being encouraged by Ahab and his scandalous wife, Jezebel. (Many think she was actually the dominant figure in promoting wickedness in Israel). God's spokespersons continued to be harassed, and Ahab only minimally acknowledged them.

Micaiah [mih-KAY-uh] was one of those prophets of the Lord who had several unpleasant encounters with Ahab. The historical context for one of these meetings is as follows. Jehoshaphat [jih-HUSH-uh-fat], king of Judah, and Ahab met to consider a joint campaign to liberate the fortified town of Ramoth-Gilead from its Aramean occupiers. Ahab's stable of hired prophets enthusiastically backed the military endeavor. But Jehoshaphat, being suspicious of their glib words, asked if there were a true prophet of the Lord who could be consulted (1 Kings 22:1-7). Ahab reluctantly mentioned Micaiah, grumbling, *"I hate him, for he never prophesies anything favorable about me, but only disaster"* (22:8).

The messenger who went to get Micaiah urged him to go along with the opinion of all the other prophets. But Micaiah stated that he would only declare what the Lord had told him to say. He was then ushered into the impressive presence of the two kings, the 400 paid prophets, and the large crowd of Israelites (22:9-14).

At first, Micaiah sarcastically echoed the opinion of the false prophets, assuring Jehoshaphat and Ahab of sweeping victory (22:15). But when Ahab pressed Micaiah to state what he really thought, the prophet fearlessly declared that the military campaign would end in disaster, and that the Lord had put a lying spirit in the mouths of all the hired prophets (22:16-23).

Ahab's reaction to Micaiah's unfavorable pronouncement was to throw him into prison until the king returned victorious. The prophet told Ahab and all the people that if the king returned successfully, then the Lord had not spoken through Micaiah. The prophet went to a cell, but Ahab went to his death in the battle against the Arameans (22:24-35).

NOTES ON THE PRINTED TEXT

Ancient historical records indicate that Ahab allied himself with Syria and 10 other rulers to fight against the Assyrians at Qarqar, Syria, on the Orontes River in 853 B.C. Ahab alone contributed 10,000 foot soldiers and 2,000 chariots to the coalition effort. The campaign proved to be successful, for the Assyrians did not again venture into the region for about four or five years.

However, once the threat was gone, Israel and Syria contended for Gilead and its fertile fields. Ahab, determined to take Ramoth-Gilead, a key center for control of the area, urged Judah's king to unite with him against the Syrians. Jehoshaphat agreed to the idea, but then asked Ahab to seek the Lord's guidance in the matter (1 Kings 22:1-5).

Ahab followed the custom of the day by summoning a cadre of false prophets. The king wanted to know whether God would bless his coming campaign with success. All the court prophets roared their approval, praised the monarch's wisdom, and announced that God was on Ahab's side. Jehoshaphat was still uncertain and asked whether there might be a second opinion. Reluctantly, Ahab admitted that another prophet, Micaiah, had not been brought in because he never had anything good to say about Ahab's plans. Nevertheless, Jehoshaphat wanted to hear from everyone, and so Ahab dispatched a messenger to fetch Micaiah (22:6-9).

When the messenger found Micaiah, he urged the prophet to go along with the other prophets and speak favorably of Ahab's plans. But Micaiah declared that he would only say what the Lord had revealed to him. When he had come to Ahab, the king bluntly asked, *"Micaiah; shall we go to Ramoth-gilead to battle, or shall we refrain?"* (22:15). In response, Micaiah sarcastically spoke of Ahab experiencing a glorious victory against the enemy. *"Go up and triumph; the LORD will give it into the hand of the king."*

Ahab became suspicious, for the response was unlike any of Micaiah's previous words. And evidently the tone was odd. Thus, Ahab demanded the truth. *"How many times must I make you swear to me nothing but the truth in the name of the LORD?"* (22:16).

Micaiah responded by describing a vision that depicted Israel's defeat. A disaster awaited across the Jordan. Without Ahab, their shepherd, the sheep of Israel would be scattered. *"I saw all Israel scattered on the mountains, like sheep that have no shepherd; and the LORD said, 'These have no master; let each one go home in peace'"* (22:17). Though Ahab would perish in the battle, the Israelite survivors would be allowed to return to their homes (22:36).

Ahab was disgusted with Micaiah's pronouncement of doom and whined about it to Jehoshaphat. *"Did I not tell you that he would not prophesy anything favorable about me, but only disaster?"* (22:18). Then Micaiah declared that a lying spirit was deceiving Ahab's paid prophets (22:19-22). *"So you see, the LORD has put a lying spirit in the mouth of all these your prophets; the LORD has decreed disaster for you"* (22:23).

The other prophets were furious. One named Zedekiah even slapped Micaiah across the face (22:24-25). Ahab then ordered that Micaiah be imprisoned and fed nothing but bread and water. The king declared that when he returned from his military victory, he would deal with Micaiah (22:26-27). But Micaiah declared that if Ahab returned from battle, it would prove that Micaiah was a false prophet. *"If you return in peace, the LORD has not spoken by me"* (22:28).

In the battle, Ahab disguised himself while urging Jehoshaphat to wear the robes of a king. The deception failed. A stray arrow struck Ahab in the chest, mortally wounding him. However, he refused to leave the field of battle. The Bible states that Ahab continued to lead his troops while blood from his wound ran down to the floor of his chariot. He soon bled to death (22:29-35).

SUGGESTIONS TO TEACHERS

While still a senator, John F. Kennedy wrote a best-seller called *Profiles in Courage*. The book offered sketches of persons who took courageous stands, often at great personal sacrifice, for the sake of the United States. In this week's lesson, we take a close look at the profile of a prophet of exceptional courage. As you discuss Micaiah, be sure to stress to your students that Christians are constantly called to take courageous stands for God.

1. PLOT BY TWO KINGS. Introduce the biblical narrative by relating how Ahab of Israel and Jehoshaphat of Judah schemed to embark on a military campaign for their own gain and glory.

2. PERMISSION BY PAID PROPHETS. King Ahab's large retinue of hired prophets readily approved the rulers' plans. How easy it is to assume that God goes along with our schemes! Sometimes we are pressured to give approval in the Lord's name for the sake of organizational unity or for the sake of what is called a noble cause. But we should always be wary that we do not glibly approve of every plan those in power may present to us.

3. PRESUMPTION BY ZEDEKIAH. False prophets often get center stage and lots of approval. Consider Zedekiah. He acted like a big shot when he not only declared victory for Ahab and Jehoshaphat but also reproved Micaiah for predicting defeat (1 Kings 22:11, 24). Invite your students to discuss how one determines whether a person is a spiritual fraud.

4. PRESSURE TO CONFORM. Be sure to bring up the details of how Micaiah was pressured to go along with the majority opinion. For instance, who was he to oppose the collective will of all the other prophets? Also, what threats to his personal well-being did Micaiah face if he refused to voice the party line? Invite your students to share how they felt when others pressured them to say or do things that seemed improper.

5. PROPHECY BY MICAIAH. Despite the possibility of disapproval and abuse, Micaiah courageously declared the truth of the Lord. The prophet realized that he would pay a heavy price for his unpopular pronouncements. Nevertheless,

Micaiah stood firm, and thus proved himself to be a true spokesperson for God. Ask your students when they had to take a stand for the Lord that called for courage.

6. PUNISHMENT FOR A COURAGEOUS CRITIC. Once Micaiah made his declaration of doom, things turned ugly for him. Such is sometimes the "reward" society pays Jesus' followers. He too suffered injustice, agony, and disgrace for declaring the truth. But God honored Him, and the Lord will also honor us for courageously speaking the truth.

FOR ADULTS

■ **TOPIC:** Speak Truth
■ **QUESTIONS:** 1. Why did Micaiah first respond to Ahab's question with a declaration of victory? 2. How do you think Jehoshaphat felt when Ahab whined to him about Micaiah's pronouncement of doom? 3. How was it possible for God to remain holy and allow a lying spirit to deceive Ahab and his hired prophets? 4. Why is it sometimes hard for us to speak the truth? 5. What happens when we shirk our responsibility to speak the truth?

■ **ILLUSTRATIONS:**

Truth-Speaking Martyr. Some refer to Harry T. Moore as America's first civil rights martyr. Moore campaigned for justice and equality for African Americans in obscure towns in Florida before and immediately after World War II. At that time, Florida was third in the nation in lynchings. The Ku Klux Klan had infested the ranks of local politicians, business people, and police officers. Florida State officials were not sympathetic to civil rights complaints. Moore quickly acquired the reputation of being a "troublemaker" during the late 1930s and 40s.

This brave man sued to get equal pay for African American teachers, started voter registration drives, and fired off letters to the governors about the latest atrocity against African Americans. Unlike later civil rights leaders, Moore had no national media to publicize his cause. And he did not have the support of people from the north to finance him. Nevertheless, because Moore believed fervently in equality and democracy, he spoke the truth despite the presence of threats.

Like many other spokespersons of truth, Harry Moore paid with his life. He was killed in a bombing attack on Christmas Day, 1951. His death, however, was not in vain. Because of Moore's courageous efforts, Florida's African American voter registration was years ahead of that in the other southern states.

The Lying Cleric. Sometimes people claiming to speak as religious leaders turn out to be spiritual frauds, as in Micaiah's time. In the sixteenth century, Coronado took 2,000 men into the desert north of Mexico looking for the Seven Cities of Cibola, reputed to consist of magnificent palaces and temples filled with gold and silver. The expedition was guided by a cleric named Marcos, who claimed to have seen Cibola. Eager for the treasure, Marcos and his party of Coronado's soldiers marched over 1,000 miles back into what is now New Mexico. But the promised fabulously wealthy cities turned out to be a humble Zuni Native American settlement built of adobe huts. Marcos quickly left, and hurried back to Spain, where he became known as the Lying Cleric.

God, the Source of Truth. , Thomas á Kempis was a cleric who served in an Augustinian convent near Zwolle, Holland, during the thirteenth century. The following excerpt, which is taken from his work entitled *The Imitation of Christ*, exhorts us to look to God, not the things of the world, for truth.

> He to whom the eternal Word speaks is set free from many opinions. From that one Word are all things and all things speak; and this is the Beginning, which also speaks to us. No man without that understands or judges rightly. O God, who art the truth, make me one with Thee in continual love! I am weary often to read and hear many things. In Thee is all that I desire and long for. Let all teachers hold their peace; let all creatures be silent in Thy sight; speak to me alone.

■ TOPIC: Stand for Truth

■ QUESTIONS: 1. How could Ahab tell that at first Micaiah was speaking sarcastically? 2. What was Micaiah saying when he described the armies of Israel as being like sheep with no shepherd? 3. How do you think Micaiah felt when he learned that he would be imprisoned for declaring the truth? 4. How did God vindicate Micaiah? 5. How can we overcome obstacles we face in speaking the truth?

■ ILLUSTRATIONS:

Promoter. Lakita Garth, former Miss Black America, uses her talents to encourage teenagers to remain chaste. Garth is the founder of Sex Education Character Support, a public school program that encourages abstinence, and she has been featured in numerous publications and on television shows. Having learned the art of self-control from her mother, Garth admits that she was the only child in her family to escape drugs, gangs, and the consequences of unchaste behavior. Today, she courageously encourages young people to stand up for what is right.

It takes courage to advocate curfews and boundaries. It also takes courage to promote self-control and self-discipline. Like Micaiah, Garth speaks the truth, and so should you!

Stand Firm. "Come on. We're all going!" Jake's friends urged him repeatedly to skip school on that hot, humid Friday afternoon and go whitewater rafting with them. As daily temperatures soared into the 90's and as his senior year was just about over, the offer felt enticing. Thankfully, however, Jake said *no*. But his friends continued to pressure him to go along. He heard them say some of the following: "Everyone is going." "Why won't you?" "You'll miss a good time." "Are you trying to impress some teacher?" "Wimp!"

Because Jake knew that it was wrong to skip school, he stood firm in his decision. Later, the other teens privately told Jake that they admired the way he remained true to what he believed. Micaiah also felt the pressures from his peers to go along with the crowd. However, he refused to do so and honored the Lord by standing firm for the truth.

Questioned Board's Authority. Graduation was set for early June, 1999. Scott, like many students, eagerly looked forward to his commencement at the high school he had attended. However, Scott was told that he would not be graduating with his classmates. The school board had decided that he would not even be allowed to participate in commencement exercises.

The reason is that Scott has Downs Syndrome. The law mandates that students such as Scott must receive education through the age of 21. Even though Scott had successfully completed all the requirements for graduation, the district argued that if he graduated, it would no longer have to provide for his education, something that the district felt it had an obligation to do. Therefore, the board acted to bar Scott from graduation.

Scott's parents, other parents, and especially the students of the high school were all outraged. Everyone went to a special board meeting to confront and question the board's action and the board's authority. Students repeatedly spoke on Scott's behalf.

The outcome remained the same. Fairness and common sense were abandoned, and Scott was not allowed to graduate. A state arbitrator upheld the board's decision. Like the students at that high school, Micaiah confronted authority. And sadly, like the school board meeting, reason and truthfulness did not win.

JUDGMENT ON JUDAH AND ISRAEL

BACKGROUND SCRIPTURE: Amos 1—2
DEVOTIONAL READING: Hebrews 10:26-30

KEY VERSE: Thus says the LORD: For three transgressions of Judah, and for four, I will not revoke the punishment; because they have rejected the law of the LORD, and have not kept his statutes. Amos 2:4a.

KING JAMES VERSION

AMOS 2:4 Thus saith the LORD; For three transgressions of Judah, and for four, I will not turn away the punishment thereof; because they have despised the law of the LORD, and have not kept his commandments, and their lies caused them to err, after the which their fathers have walked:

5 But I will send a fire upon Judah, and it shall devour the palaces of Jerusalem.

6 Thus saith the LORD; For three transgressions of Israel, and for four, I will not turn away the punishment thereof; because they sold the righteous for silver, and the poor for a pair of shoes;

7 That pant after the dust of the earth on the head of the poor, and turn aside the way of the meek: and a man and his father will go in unto the same maid, to profane my holy name:

8 And they lay themselves down upon clothes laid to pledge by every altar, and they drink the wine of the condemned in the house of their god.

9 Yet destroyed I the Amorite before them, whose height was like the height of the cedars, and he was strong as the oaks; yet I destroyed his fruit from above, and his roots from beneath.

10 Also I brought you up from the land of Egypt, and led you forty years through the wilderness, to possess the land of the Amorite.

NEW REVISED STANDARD VERSION

AMOS 2:4 Thus says the LORD:
For three transgressions of Judah,
  and for four, I will not revoke the punishment;
because they have rejected the law of the LORD,
  and have not kept his statutes,
but they have been led astray by the same lies
  after which their ancestors walked.
5 So I will send a fire on Judah,
  and it shall devour the strongholds of Jerusalem.
6 Thus says the LORD:
For three transgressions of Israel,
  and for four, I will not revoke the punishment;
because they sell the righteous for silver,
  and the needy for a pair of sandals—
7 they who trample the head of the poor into the dust
    of the earth,
  and push the afflicted out of the way;
father and son go in to the same girl,
  so that my holy name is profaned;
8 they lay themselves down beside every altar
  on garments taken in pledge;
and in the house of their God they drink
  wine bought with fines they imposed.
9 Yet I destroyed the Amorite before them,
  whose height was like the height of cedars,
  and who was as strong as oaks;
I destroyed his fruit above,
  and his roots beneath.
10 Also I brought you up out of the land of Egypt,
  and led you forty years in the wilderness,
  to possess the land of the Amorite.

5

HOME BIBLE READINGS

BACKGROUND

The middle of the eighth century B.C. saw both the northern kingdom of Israel and the southern kingdom of Judah mired in evil ways. Around 760 B.C., God called a man who carried no credentials as a prophet to speak out to those who were violating the Mosaic covenant. That spokesperson, Amos, was a shepherd and farmer, not one formally trained and officially recognized as a prophet. Despite this, his message still reverberates down through the centuries.

Amos directed some of his most scathing denunciations against Bethel, the city where the great pagan shrine of Israel stood. But he didn't leave it there. Amos also blasted the surrounding Gentile nations such as the people of Damascus, Gaza, Tyre, Edom, Ammon, and Moab. All these places were guilty of war atrocities, slave trading, and other cruelties both against God's people and others (Amos 1:1—2:3).

We can imagine that Amos's audience nodded in approval as he condemned their pagan neighbors. Then the prophet turned his attention to his home country of Judah, which was Israel's sister nation. In Amos's eyes, Judah's sins were worse than those of its pagan neighbors. Not only had the Judahites violated the Mosaic covenant, but worse, they had blasphemed against the Lord (2:4-5).

How Amos's listeners must have enjoyed hearing those words! But the prophet had not yet finished. His final target was the northern kingdom of Israel. He pronounced doom on his hearers and the nation for Israel's lack of justice toward the poor and oppressed, for their widespread sexual immorality, and for their idolatrous worship. Amos then reminded the smug Israelites that God could and would destroy them and their nation just as He destroyed the wicked Amorites (2:6-10).

NOTES ON THE PRINTED TEXT

Amos was a shepherd and fig grower, not a prophet by vocation (Amos 1:1; 7:14). Though he may not have had the formal religious training of his professional counterparts, he nevertheless was inspired by the Lord. Amos's audience most likely listened with delight to his prophecies about Israel's neighbors. As God's spokesperson marched around the compass points, each country's indictment began with a stylistic phrase: *Thus says the* LORD: *For three transgressions of . . . and for four, I will not revoke the punishment* (2:4).

But perhaps the delight of the audience turned to shock as Amos saved some of his harshest words for the people of Judah. The prophet declared, *they have rejected the law of the LORD, and have not kept his statutes, but they have been led astray by the same lies after which their ancestors walked.* In other words, the people of the southern kingdom of Judah were steeped in idolatry. For its sin, Judah, as well as Jerusalem, would be annihilated. *So I will send a fire on Judah, and it shall devour the strongholds of Jerusalem* (2:5).

Amos, though, wasn't done yet. In fact, his most blistering words were reserved for the northern kingdom of Israel. Amos's listeners again heard the familiar formula opening the indictment. *Thus says the LORD: For three transgressions of Israel, and for four, I will not revoke the punishment* (2:6).

Next, the prophet listed the specific transgressions: *because they sell the righteous for silver, and the needy for a pair of sandals.* Amos condemned the unjust treatment of the poor by the rich. The wealthy were utilizing the judicial system to exploit the impoverished. People were forced into slavery for small debts, such as the cost of a pair of sandals. Amos reiterated the charge of oppression. The rich were profiting off of the poor, even squashing the neediest of God's people. The wicked were *they who trample the head of the poor into the dust of the earth, and push the afflicted out of the way* (2:7).

Amos also condemned the sexual immorality of Israel. Promiscuity had risen to such a degree that society tolerated a father and his son having intimate relations with the same slave girl. *Father and son go in to the same girl, so that my holy name is profaned.* The marriage covenant between a man and a woman was being ignored and God, the guarantor of that agreement, was being mocked.

Returning to the exploitation of the poor, Amos again blasted the rich for the misuse of the law. *They lay themselves down beside every altar on garments taken in pledge; and in the house of their God they drink wine bought with fines they imposed* (2:8). In the law of Moses, the outer cloak could be used as collateral for a loan. It was the pledge of repayment. The clothing, however, was to be returned at each sundown, for it was the borrower's only means of warmth at night. The rich disregarded the law and slept on these garments, perhaps at the shrines of pagan gods. In addition, the rich were drunk on wine purchased with money extorted from the impoverished. The wicked thus defiled God's house with their drunken debauchery.

Amos next reminded the Israelites of God's saving actions in history. *Yet I destroyed the Amorite before them, whose height was like the height of cedars, and who was as strong as oaks* (2:9). The Amorites were a strong native people of Canaan. But they were no match for God. He enabled the Israelites to defeat them. Moreover, before that the Lord *had brought you up out of the land of Egypt, and led you forty years in the wilderness, to possess the land of the Amorite* (2:10).

Yet, despite all that God had done for Israel, His people remained entrenched in sin. Therefore, judgment was the only option left for God to pursue (2:12-16).

SUGGESTIONS TO TEACHERS

A young successful businesswoman stated, "Most of my friends aren't at all religious, and if they are, they fall into a feel-good spirituality." Her companion nodded in agreement and then added, "People we work and party with frankly don't feel it's anybody's business how we live or what we do. The main thing is to be happy."

With slight variations, these words express the outlook and values not only of the baby boomers and Generation Xers but also of most Americans today. Likewise, these words sum up the attitude of Amos's hearers in Israel in the eighth century B.C. This outspoken prophet's stern warnings were not well received then, and may not be welcomed today. But God's message must be heard!

1. COMMISSIONED AND COMMITTED. Amos was a lay person, not a professional prophet. That didn't matter, however, for the Lord had commissioned him to prophesy (Amos 7:14-15). Thus, despite Amos's humble background, God used him mightily. Here is an opportunity for you to remind your students that committed lay people are just as much key persons in speaking for the Lord as paid clergy.

2. CONDEMNATION. Amos's contemporaries felt God would approve of them, regardless of how much they ignored their basic responsibilities before Him. Such an attitude of disobedience would inevitably cause moral collapse, and eventually personal and national disaster, according to Amos.

3. CALUMNIES LISTED. Amos's list of the Israelites' ways of disobeying the Lord deserves a careful look. Have your students examine and comment on what the prophet said. Some of the iniquities he mentioned are forms of social injustice, such as ignoring the poor. Other transgressions he noted are forms of sexual immorality. All of them led to God's judgment of His people.

4. CONSEQUENCES OF SIN. Amos reminded his listeners about the doom the wicked Amorites experienced. The prophet then warned that the same grim day of reckoning would come for Israel and Judah. From this we see that all human actions have consequences and that God holds us accountable for what we think, say, and do. Be sure to stress that God's will cannot be ignored and that He will not be trifled with.

5. COMING CALAMITY. Amos bluntly told his audience that Israel would suffer calamity as a result of its sins. Unpleasant though it may be, sometimes we have to face up to the sins of our own culture. Is the nation we live in exempt from God's judgment?

FOR ADULTS

■ **TOPIC:** Consequences of Disobedience

■ **QUESTIONS:** 1. Why had the people of Judah rejected the law of the Lord? 2. How did God plan to judge Judah and Jerusalem? 3. Why were the sins of Israel so despicable? 4. What was significant about the way God had judged the Amorites? 5. What benefits do you see in being ethical with others?

■ **ILLUSTRATIONS:**

Costly Consequences. An east coast high school soccer team had an outstanding season in the fall of 1998. With exceptionally talented players, it moved to the state playoffs. The team won their first two tournament games and were poised to move on to the championship. Then two star starting players, a goalie and a half-back, were arrested and charged with having alcohol in their possession and drinking in a car on the Saturday night before the semifinals.

Both players, who had known the rules about not using alcohol, were immediately suspended from the team. Hampered by not having these two key players, the soccer team lost 3-1, despite good performances by substitute players. The team coach voiced the feelings of disappointment that everyone else felt: "Some kids made the team their priority, and some didn't. And it's obvious who the ones are who didn't."

Tuning Fork Truth. An old music teacher once showed his minister a tuning fork hanging on a cord. Striking the tuning fork and listening to the hum for a moment, the teacher said, "That is the good word. That is G, and no matter how the weather may change or what may happen in human affairs, it remains G." Continuing, he pointed out that refusing to listen to the correct note and trying to do the performance in another key would result in discordant music. As a musician, he knew the consequences of not obeying the basic tenets of harmony. The same is true with God's spiritual and moral requirements!

Staggering Statistics. One in four American children under the age of 6 is living in poverty. More than one in four children live in single-parent households, an increase of 118 percent since 1970. Nearly 3 million children were reported abused or neglected in 1999, more than double the figure for 1989. Among African American teens aged 15 to 19, guns are the leading cause of death. The second and third causes of death among American young people are suicide and homicide. What will be the consequences of these figures? What would Amos have to say to us in the light of these staggering statistics?

FOR YOUTH

■ **TOPIC:** Can You Pay the Price?

■ **QUESTIONS:** 1. In what ways had the people of Judah been led astray? 2. Why was God going to punish Judah and Jerusalem? 3. How had the Israelites profaned God's holy name? 4. What had God done for Israel in the past? 5. Why should Christians obey a higher ethical standard than nonbelievers?

Children at Risk. Nationally, 14 percent of American children are at risk, so claimed a 1999 "Kids Count" report issued by Baltimore's Annie E. Casey Foundation. At risk is defined as experiencing four or more of the chronic "risk factors" that make a child susceptible to a lifetime of suffering.

Such factors include growing up in a single-parent home (27 percent of children in the United States live in such a setting). The second factor is poverty (one in four American children lives in poverty). The third factor is unemployment (30 percent of American children live in a home with an unemployed parent or parents). Other factors are dependence on welfare, no health insurance, and hunger.

The report calls for local, state, and federal governments to focus on creating an environment that is more nurturing, secure, and supportive. Amos might sound a similar call as he reviewed the "trampling" of our nation's children!

Reason for Judgment. A survey conducted by the Center for Drug and Alcohol Studies at the University of Southern Illinois showed that in February 1998, 42 percent of college students engaged in binge drinking. (This is defined as consuming four or more drinks in a row.) In addition, the survey showed that 94 percent of students believed their fellow students drank at least once a week. Generally, drinking occurred in younger classes. Senior students acted more responsibly.

Once seen as a rite of passage for youth, now colleges and universities are realizing that the excessive alcoholic consumption must be curbed. Student drinking is a health risk and produces many consequences. Amos also described the consequences of alcoholism in the ancient society of Israel. He declared that God was displeased with such immoral behavior.

More on Judgment. Teens are generally considered the highest sexually active group in society. The consequences for this immorality are enormous. Sadly, for every five promiscuous teens, two have sexually transmitted diseases. Another statistic is that those who engage in premarital sex have a higher divorce rate than those who have abstained. Obviously, pregnancy can be a consequence. Amos thundered God's judgment on Israel's immorality. Clearly, the Lord still thinks that being promiscuous is sinful.

Bad Decision's Consequences. The battle of Midway abruptly changed the course of World War II in the Pacific. Up to that point, the Japanese had experienced nothing but victory. But on the morning of June 3, 1942, the situation dramatically changed. The Americans followed up a Japanese air attack on Midway Island with one of their own from the island and from aircraft carriers.

Admiral Nagumo had four aircraft carriers (the Akagi, Kaga, Soryu, and Hiryu, which were all Pearl Harbor veterans), two battleships, two cruisers, several destroyers, and a few support craft. Nagumo used his fleet to beat back every American plane. The admiral then received word that an additional attack would be necessary to invade Midway. However, Nagumo also received surprising information about the presence of additional American ships, including an aircraft carrier.

This news caught the admiral by surprise and prompted him to hesitate in making a decision. His own airborne planes needed to land and refuel. Others sat ready on the aircraft carrier decks. A colleague named Admiral Yamaguchi advised that an immediate air attack be launched on the American fleet, and other officers agreed with this advice.

But Nagumo ignored the counsel of the other admirals and ordered that the flight decks be cleared of all aircraft. Thus, fully loaded planes, laden with bombs and torpedoes, were moved below in the hanger bay as the returning planes were landed and readied for a second attack.

Meanwhile planes from the American aircraft carrier, Yorktown, flew over the Japanese armada and found the flight decks of the four enemy aircraft carriers crowded with planes that were ready to be launched and loaded with fuel and explosives. The American pilots immediately decided to attack. By day's end, all four of the Japanese carriers and a heavy cruiser lay at the bottom of the Pacific Ocean.

The American victory occurred because a Japanese admiral ignored the wise advice of his subordinates. Similarly, the failure of believers to obey God is sometimes due to their refusal to listen to the wise council of their friends in the faith.

EMPTY OFFERINGS

BACKGROUND SCRIPTURE: Amos 4—5
DEVOTIONAL READING: Malachi 1:6-14

KEY VERSE: Let justice roll down like waters,
and righteousness like an everflowing stream. Amos 5:24.

KING JAMES VERSION

AMOS 4:2 The Lord GOD hath sworn by his holiness, that, lo, the days shall come upon you, that he will take you away with hooks, and your posterity with fish-hooks.

3 And ye shall go out at the breaches, every cow at that which is before her; and ye shall cast them into the palace, saith the LORD.

4 Come to Bethel, and transgress; at Gilgal multiply transgression; and bring your sacrifices every morning, and your tithes after three years:

5 And offer a sacrifice of thanksgiving with leaven, and proclaim and publish the free offerings: for this liketh you, O ye children of Israel, saith the Lord GOD.
. . .

5:20 Shall not the day of the LORD be darkness, and not light? even very dark, and no brightness in it?

21 I hate, I despise your feast days, and I will not smell in your solemn assemblies.

22 Though ye offer me burnt offerings and your meat offerings, I will not accept them: neither will I regard the peace offerings of your fat beasts.

23 Take thou away from me the noise of thy songs; for I will not hear the melody of thy viols.

24 But let judgment run down as waters, and righteousness as a mighty stream.

NEW REVISED STANDARD VERSION

AMOS 4:2 The Lord GOD has sworn by his holiness:
The time is surely coming upon you,
when they shall take you away with hooks,
even the last of you with fishhooks.
3 Through breaches in the wall you shall leave,
each one straight ahead;
and you shall be flung out into Harmon,
says the LORD.
4 Come to Bethel—and transgress;
to Gilgal—and multiply transgression;
bring your sacrifices every morning,
your tithes every three days;
5 bring a thank-offering of leavened bread,
and proclaim freewill offerings, publish them;
for so you love to do, O people of Israel!
says the Lord GOD. . . .
5:20 Is not the day of the LORD darkness, not light,
and gloom with no brightness in it?
21 I hate, I despise your festivals,
and I take no delight in your solemn assemblies.
22 Even though you offer me your burnt offerings
and grain offerings,
I will not accept them;
and the offerings of well-being of your fatted animals
I will not look upon.
23 Take away from me the noise of your songs;
I will not listen to the melody of your harps.
24 But let justice roll down like waters,
and righteousness like an everflowing stream.

BACKGROUND

Though Amos hailed from Tekoa (about 6 miles southeast of Bethlehem and 10 miles south of Jerusalem), the prophet thundered some of his denunciations against Bethel and Gilgal (Amos 4:4). These were places in which the Israelites worshiped idols instead of God (Hos. 4:15-17).

As far as the Lord was concerned, Israel as a nation was as good as dead. God's judgment was about to descend in the form of an invasion by Assyria. Israel had been warned repeatedly of its sins by God's prophets, but had refused to repent. Every segment of life had become corrupt (Amos 4:2-3).

Perhaps most unforgivable was the corruption of worship. Amos scathingly denounced the false religion that infected the life of the nation. These practices included a wide range of idolatry and superstition as well as lewd practices and child sacrifice. Participating in these activities in the name of religion multiplied the sins of the Israelites (4:4-5).

Even those claiming to be loyal to the Lord came under Amos's indictment. Their elaborate rituals and impressive ceremonies (in which they called on the name of the Lord) were particularly offensive to God because the people were guilty of ignoring the hungry and poor. Amos announced that God cared most of all for justice (5:10-15, 21-24).

The prophet also insisted that the coming day of the Lord would not be the occasion for God to elevate Israel and crush the nations (contrary to what the people thought). Rather, it would be a time of reckoning for the Israelites and their nation. The great Assyrian war machine would deport many people to distant provinces and populate their homeland with prisoners whom the enemy had forced to resettle from other captured territories (5:16-20).

NOTES ON THE PRINTED TEXT

Amos understood that the sins and shortcomings of Israel could not be blamed on individuals alone, but also included the leaders of the nation. Evidently Amos delivered his messages at the religious sanctuary of Bethel in the northern kingdom of Israel. There the prophet criticized the whole judicial system, the outwardly religious merchants, and the upper-class women of

Samaria, whom he labeled as *cows of Bashan* (Amos 4:1). In other words, these pampered and pleasure-seeking women selfishly pushed their husbands to oppress the helpless in order to support their lavish lifestyles.

Amos declared that a time would come when the wicked rich would be led away with hooks in their noses. (We know from ancient history that the Assyrians frequently led away captives in single file, with fishhooks being fastened through each of their noses.) Also, through the broken and breached walls of Samaria, the Israelites would be marched off to exile. *The time is surely upon you, when they shall take you away with hooks, even the last of you with fishhooks. Through breaches in the wall you shall leave, each one straight ahead, and you shall be flung out into Harmon, says the LORD* (4:2-3).

Using a bit of irony, Amos summoned the Israelites to wallow some more in their idolatrous ways. *Come to Bethel—and transgress; to Gilgal—and multiply transgression* (4:4). Bethel was located about 12 miles north of Jerusalem. Jeroboam, the first ruler of the northern kingdom of Israel, placed an altar and golden calf there and made the city a rival center of worship to Jerusalem (1 Kings 12:28-33). Gilgal was a city located to the east of Jericho and not far from the fords of the Jordan River. During the eighth century B.C., Gilgal became a center for religious apostasy, pagan worship, and heathen sacrifices (Hos. 9:15; 12:11).

Amos next listed the traditional offerings associated with worship. Some think the prophet used a satirized version of an anti-Jerusalemite saying, perhaps popular at the time in the north. *Bring your sacrifices every morning, your tithes every three days; bring a thank-offering of leavened bread, and proclaim freewill offerings, publish them; for so you love to do, O people of Israel! says the Lord GOD* (Amos 4:4-5).

The sacrifice was an animal offering, part of which was given to God, while the rest of which was eaten by the family as a meal in communion with God. The tithe was a tenth of the land's yield. The thank offering was made to praise God for His blessings. While leavened bread was used at sacred meals, it was not offered to God. The freewill offering was made as an expression of the worshipers' devotion. Amos charged that the offerings were only an outward show of religiosity, not of true commitment to the Lord.

Amos also dashed the people's expectation surrounding the day of the Lord. Far from being a time of deliverance, peace, and prosperity, the day would be one of calamity for them. Judgment, not joy, would characterize that day. *Is not the day of the LORD darkness, not light, and gloom with no brightness in it?* (5:20).

Amos then condemned the impious rituals of the people. *I hate, I despise your festivals, and I take no delight in your solemn assemblies* (5:21). Nothing of Israel's religious life brought pleasure to the Lord. In fact, He would not even accept the nation's sacrifices. *Even though you offer me your burnt offerings and grain offerings, I will not accept them; and the offerings of well-being of your fatted animals I will not look upon* (5:22). The all-powerful Lord was also nauseated by the nation's religious music. *Take away from me the noise of your songs; I will not listen to the melody of your harps* (5:23).

God's requirement was justice and righteousness. Like the waters of a flash flood rolling down a wadi (a dry desert streambed) after the winter's rain, fairness and equality in the judicial systems and concern and compassion for all God's people, especially the poor, were to flow freely. *But let justice roll down like waters, and righteousness like an everflowing stream* (5:24).

SUGGESTIONS TO TEACHERS

When is worship a sham? When is it real? What should we look for when we worship? Is worship mostly well-rehearsed choral music, beautiful liturgies, and eloquent speakers? These are the kinds of questions raised by the material you will cover in this week's lesson.

1. DELUDING HUMAN ATTAINMENTS. Form and rituals without repentance and concern for the hurting count for nothing with God. Amos warned that worship in Israel was spiritually empty because the people failed to back their elaborate words to God with acts that promoted peace and justice. From this we see that social concerns go hand-in-hand with prayer and personal piety.

2. DEFAMING GOD'S GLORY. Take a few moments to consider Amos 5:4-6, where the prophet accused Israel of trifling with their Creator. Sometimes in our worship, we act as if the all-powerful Lord can be manipulated to do our bidding. Amos (as well as the rest of Scripture) emphasizes that people cannot ever control God. We are meant to serve the Lord, not the other way around.

3. DECLARING GOD'S INTENTION. Next, focus the attention of your students on 5:14-15, *Seek good and not evil, that you may live. . . . Hate evil and love good, and establish justice.* Why are these virtues lacking among believers today, and how can the church reemphasize them? Give specifics.

4. DENOUNCING VAIN WORSHIP. Amos dealt sternly with those blithely longing for the day of the Lord because they thought God would rescue them and make everything pleasant. Instead, Amos stated that it would be a time of reckoning for Israel. Have your students consider the implications of 1 Peter 4:17, which says, *For the time has come for judgment to begin with the household of God; if it begins with us, what will be the end for those who do not obey the gospel of God?*

5. DEMANDING JUSTICE AND RIGHTEOUSNESS. End the lesson time by discussing Amos 5:21-24. Be sure to stress that worship without justice and righteousness is empty.

FOR ADULTS

■ **TOPIC:** Empty Offerings

■ **QUESTIONS:** 1. Why did Amos stress that the Lord had sworn by His holiness (Amos 4:2)? 2. Why did Amos exhort his listeners to transgress at Bethel and Gilgal (4:4)? 3. Why did God despise Israel's festivals and solemn assemblies? 4. How could the Israelites reestablish the priority of justice and righteousness in their nation? 5. How can we unclutter our minds of everyday concerns so that we can focus on the concerns of God?

■ **ILLUSTRATIONS:**

Mistaken Religion. Doris, a teacher of second graders in a parochial school, had a bright idea one day as an assignment for the children in her religion class. She told them to take paper and crayons and make a picture to show what they would do if they were to spend a day with Jesus. The kids eagerly went to work, and Doris felt pleased that valuable spiritual lessons were being learned. Then one tyke approached her carrying her nearly-finished drawing and asked, "Teacher, how do you spell Bloomingdales?"

Garbage Problems. In one day, a typical American creates nearly four and a half pounds of garbage. And in 1999, we produced a total of 217 million tons of garbage, up from 88 million tons only 40 years ago. Much of our trash is food waste. The report of our prodigious amount of throwaway stuff at a time when hunger and malnutrition are widespread in certain areas of the world, including the United States, should disturb us. The Old Testament prophets thundered against such a wasteful lifestyle in which some had plenty while others had little or nothing. Our offerings of prayer and worship are empty if we do not show concern for the hungry, poor, and oppressed.

Money as Servant, Not Master. William Jennings Bryant, the well-known political figure early in the twentieth century, was never mistaken for being a social philosopher. Yet he did have a fitting response to those who worshiped the idol of financial gain. "Money is to be the servant of people," he once stated, "and I protest against all theories that enthrone money and debase humankind."

FOR YOUTH

■ **TOPIC:** Phony or For Real?

■ **QUESTIONS:** 1. What was Amos trying to tell the Israelites by declaring that they would be taken away with fishhooks (Amos 4:2)? 2. How did the people's expectations of the day of the Lord differ from what Amos had proclaimed? 3. Why were Israel's burnt offerings unacceptable to God? 4. In what ways is Amos's message still relevant today? 5. How is it possible for people to go through the motions of worshiping God and yet be unjust to others?

■ **ILLUSTRATIONS:**

Only a Show. Melvin Adams, a former Houston Rocket basketball player and now with the Harlem Globetrotters, described his mother waking him each

Sunday to go to church. He went with his mother, but sat in the back of the church in the last pew. Instead of an open Bible on his lap, he held an open copy of *Sports Illustrated,* which he read. Outwardly, Melvin looked religious and committed, but his worship participation was only a show. Not until much later in his life did he finally make a commitment to Christ.

Like Adams, many youth are mechanical in their worship participation. They may sit in church, but their minds are somewhere else. Their worship is phony, for they make empty offerings of praise to God. Amos called his listeners to make their offerings to Lord genuine and wholehearted.

End of Time. A Peanuts cartoon strip pictured an upset Peppermint Patty. She had heard that the end of the world was near. Trembling, she asked her friend, Marcie, "What if the world ends tonight?" Marcie responded, "I promise there'll be a tomorrow, sir. In fact, it is already tomorrow in Australia."

Many youth now, as well in Amos's time, reflect Marcie's belief. They assume that the end will be a wonderful time when God will bless His people. Yes, this is true for believers. But the prophet also said that the end would be a time of judgment for those who have not committed themselves in faith to the Lord. All lives will undergo scrutiny.

More Commitment? One happy and surprising note is that the number of American teenagers attending worship has risen. In 1975, the number on an average weekend was 47 percent. In 1999, the number had risen to 55 percent. Another significant sign is the increase in volunteer service. Perhaps some youth finally are making more than empty offerings to the Lord. They are trying to offer genuine worship and truly work for justice and righteousness in the world.

GOD'S LOVE FOR ISRAEL

BACKGROUND SCRIPTURE: Hosea 1—2
DEVOTIONAL READING: Psalm 100

KEY VERSE: "I will have pity on the house of Judah,
and I will save them by the LORD their God." Hosea 1:7a.

KING JAMES VERSION

HOSEA 1:2 The beginning of the word of the LORD by Hosea. And the LORD said to Hosea, Go, take unto thee a wife of whoredoms and children of whoredoms: for the land hath committed great whoredom, departing from the LORD.

3 So he went and took Gomer the daughter of Diblaim; which conceived, and bare him a son.

4 And the LORD said unto him, Call his name Jezreel; for yet a little while, and I will avenge the blood of Jezreel upon the house of Jehu, and will cause to cease the kingdom of the house of Israel.

5 And it shall come to pass at that day, that I will break the bow of Israel in the valley of Jezreel.

6 And she conceived again, and bare a daughter. And God said unto him, Call her name Lo-ruhamah: for I will no more have mercy upon the house of Israel; but I will utterly take them away.

7 But I will have mercy upon the house of Judah, and will save them by the LORD their God, and will not save them by bow, nor by sword, nor by battle, by horses, nor by horsemen.

8 Now when she had weaned Lo-ruhamah, she conceived, and bare a son.

9 Then said God, Call his name Lo-ammi: for ye are not my people, and I will not be your God. . . .

2:1 Say ye unto your brethren, Ammi; and to your sisters, Ru-hamah.

2 Plead with your mother, plead: for she is not my wife, neither am I her husband: let her therefore put away her whoredoms out of her sight, and her adulteries from between her breasts;

3 Lest I strip her naked, and set her as in the day that she was born, and make her as a wilderness, and set her like a dry land, and slay her with thirst.

4 And I will not have mercy upon her children; for they be the children of whoredoms.

NEW REVISED STANDARD VERSION

HOSEA 1:2 When the LORD first spoke through Hosea, the LORD said to Hosea, "Go, take for yourself a wife of whoredom and have children of whoredom, for the land commits great whoredom by forsaking the LORD." 3 So he went and took Gomer daughter of Diblaim, and she conceived and bore him a son.

4 And the LORD said to him, "Name him Jezreel; for in a little while I will punish the house of Jehu for the blood of Jezreel, and I will put an end to the kingdom of the house of Israel. 5 On that day I will break the bow of Israel in the valley of Jezreel."

6 She conceived again and bore a daughter. Then the LORD said to him, "Name her Lo-ruhamah, for I will no longer have pity on the house of Israel or forgive them. 7 But I will have pity on the house of Judah, and I will save them by the LORD their God; I will not save them by bow, or by sword, or by war, or by horses, or by horsemen."

8 When she had weaned Lo-ruhamah, she conceived and bore a son. 9 Then the LORD said, "Name him Lo-ammi, for you are not my people and I am not your God." . . .

2:1 Say to your brother, Ammi, and to your sister, Ruhamah.

2 Plead with your mother, plead—
for she is not my wife,
and I am not her husband—
that she put away her whoring from her face,
and her adultery from between her breasts,

3 or I will strip her naked
and expose her as in the day she was born,
and make her like a wilderness,
and turn her into a parched land,
and kill her with thirst.

4 Upon her children also I will have no pity,
because they are children of whoredom.

HOME BIBLE READINGS

BACKGROUND

The northern kingdom of Israel continued on a downward spiral of moral and spiritual decline throughout the eighth century B.C. About 750 B.C., another spokesperson for the Lord appeared on the scene; his name was Hosea. Like other prophets of God, Hosea urged the Israelites to repent of their sins and return to the Lord in faith and obedience.

Apparently Hosea experienced the heartbreak of an unfaithful wife. God used the example of Hosea's marriage to illustrate the way He felt about faithless Israel. As Hosea's wife, Gomer, had broken her marriage vows and became a harlot, so too Israel had strayed into adulterous relationships with idols. Hosea felt the indescribable pain of being betrayed by the one he had loved so deeply. This mirrored how the Lord felt over the treachery of His chosen people (Hos. 1:2-3).

The Lord was so intent on bringing Israel back to Himself that He directed Hosea to bestow names on his three children that served as constant public reminders of the nation's calling and failures. Hosea named his eldest son Jezreel as a reminder that God would punish the house of King Jehu and bring about the downfall of the nation for the Israelites' infidelity to the Lord (1:4-5).

The next child was Lo-ruhamah, the Hebrew for "not loved" or "not pitied." This was a way of stating that God would no longer have pity on faithless Israel. The name of the third child was Lo-ammi, the Hebrew for "not [my] people." This was a vivid announcement that God no longer would call the Israelites His chosen ones. Each of these names was a stern warning of God's profound disappointment at Israel's sinful behavior (1:6-8).

In this week's lesson we will learn that just as Hosea and God showed love to those who had treated them unlovingly, so too the Lord continuously reaches out in love to His most rebellious children. Regardless of our sin, everyone can be redeemed and forgiven if we are willing to seek Him. When we turn to God in faith, He will shower us with His love and transform our lives with His grace.

NOTES ON THE PRINTED TEXT

God issued a tough and shocking order to Hosea, a godly Israelite living in the northern kingdom during the ungodly reign of King Jeroboam II (about 793–753 B.C.). *"Go, take for yourself a wife of whoredom and have children of whoredom, for the land commits great whoredom by forsaking the LORD"* (Hos. 1:2).

In other words, God eviently directed Hosea to marry a sexually unfaithful woman and have children by her who would themselves become sexually promiscuous. The reason for the unusual injunction was that Israel had proven spiritually unfaithful by having other lovers besides the Lord. (Or perhaps the children would be considered promiscuous only through association with their mother.)

The prophet obediently married Gomer. So he went and took Gomer, daughter of Diblaim (1:3). (We don't know anything more about Diblaim than this.) For a while Hosea and Gomer seemed to enjoy a fairly stable family life. They remained together several years, at least long enough to have three children.

Gomer gave birth to a son, and the Lord commanded Hosea to *"name him Jezreel"* (1:4). Jezreel referred to the northern hill country plain where many people connected with the house of Ahab had been brutally massacred by Jehu. The Lord, through Hosea, announced that the house of Jehu would be punished for the crime. *"In a little while I will punish the house of Jehu for the blood of Jezreel, and I will put an end to the kingdom of the house of Israel."* Additionally, the military might of the northern kingdom, *"the bow of Israel"* (1:5), would be destroyed on that plain.

Gomer next gave birth to a daughter, and the Lord commanded Hosea to *"name her Lo-ruhamah, for I will no longer have pity on the house of Israel or forgive them"* (1:6). The darkest blot on Israel's past would not be forgotten. The child's name, which can be paraphrased "she is not pitied," reiterated the promise of desolation. God would no longer have any compassion on faithless Israel. He would, however, continue to care for Judah (1:7).

Approximately two or three years later (the average time to wean a child), Gomer gave birth to a second son (1:8). The Lord commanded Hosea to *"name him Lo-ammi, for you are not my people and I am not your God"* (1:9). In announcing that Israel was no longer His people, God in effect was saying that He had divorced them.

In 2:1 we find Hosea relating God's undying love for Israel. Then the Lord again spoke as if Israel was no longer His "wife." He addressed the nation indirectly by calling on her "children," or individual Israelites, to rebuke her. Their testimony would contribute to her conviction. If Israel wanted to escape judgment, she had to abandon her idolatrous and immoral ways. *Plead with your mother, plead—for she is not my wife, and I am not her husband—that she put away her whoring from her face, and her adultery from between her breasts* (2:2).

If Israel failed to repent, then God would punish her. First, He would strip off her clothes. This reflects the ancient practice of shaming an adulterous woman by exposing her nakedness in public. Second, the Lord would make Israel like a desert. The picture is one of barrenness and hardship. *I will strip her naked and expose her as in the day she was born, and make her like a wilderness, and turn her into a parched land, and kill her with thirst* (2:3).

Third, God would not show His love to Israel's children. The idea is that the Lord's relational bond with His people would be severed. *Upon her children also I will have no pity, because they are children of whoredom* (2:4).

What a high price to pay for worshiping idols, engaging in sexual immorality, and permitting injustice to exist! Despite Israel's unfaithfulness, God was still faithful and merciful. He would continue to hold His arms of love out to His people, even to the point of placing obstacles in their wayward path to turn them back to Him.

SUGGESTIONS TO TEACHERS

How would you describe God's love to someone who asked what that compassion is like? Perhaps as a Christian you might talk about the Cross. But could you come up with some other illustration of the sacrificial and undeserved caring of God (which we see in Jesus laying down His life)? Hosea's experience is a superb example of God's love.

1. MARRIAGE SHOWING GOD'S CONCERN. Hosea's heartbreaking experience of having his beloved wife, Gomer, leave him and turn into a harlot provided the scenario for Hosea's messages. This prophet realized that God felt the same hurt and heartache toward His wayward and unfaithful people. Remind your students that the Lord is not aloof or dispassionate. His emotional involvement with us is greater than we realize.

2. MESSAGE STATING THE NATION'S CONDITION. Have your students note the names Hosea gave to his three children and the significance of each of these names. This prophet wanted to make as public a statement as possible about the transgressions of God's people. While we would not saddle our children with such names, we should be willing to go public with our understanding of how God wants His people to live.

3. MISERY SURFACING FROM ISRAEL'S AFFAIR. Hosea compared Israel's unfaithfulness to God to Gomer's infidelity. The hurt and harm of her behavior was deep and destructive. Even more hurtful and harmful was Israel's insistence on her "affairs" with idols.

What are some of the false gods of our time that we are inclined to run off with? Power? Success? Popularity? Violence? Greed? Pleasure? When any of these (or others) become more interesting and absorbing than the Lord, we have become unfaithful to Him. Talk with your students about the importance of maintaining unwavering commitments, especially to the Lord.

4. MEMORY SUMMONING PEOPLE'S RETURN. Allow sufficient lesson time to get across Hosea's message of God's astonishing mercy. Despite broken vows, God refuses to forget us and give us up as His beloved people. In these days when many despair about the church or see no hope for the future, encourage your students to note Hosea's words of promise.

■ **TOPIC:** Broken Vows

FOR ADULTS

■ **QUESTIONS:** 1. Why did God command Hosea to marry a promiscuous woman? 2. Why would God *"break the bow of Israel in the valley of Jezreel"* (Hos. 1:5)? 3. Why did God insist that Israel put away her immoral and idolatrous practices? 4. For both Gomer and Israel, what new behavior needed to be learned before restoration could take place? 5. Why is learning to love unconditionally part of the Christian's spiritual growth process?

■ **ILLUSTRATIONS:**

Broken Promises. A certain minister announced to his congregation one Sunday that he planned to preach on vows the following week. "To help you understand the sermon, I'd like each of you to read the seventeenth chapter of the Gospel of Mark," he said. "Would you promise to read this chapter?" Heads nodded everywhere, and several assured him out loud that they would keep their vow to read that portion of Scripture.

The following Sunday, as the pastor stood to deliver his sermon, he said, "Last Sunday, I announced I would be preaching on making and keeping vows. I asked each of you to vow to read the seventeenth chapter of Mark. Now will all those who have kept their vow to read that chapter please raise their hand."

Every hand went up. The pastor smiled and continued. "Mark has only 16 chapters. I will now proceed with my sermon on making and keeping vows."

Permanent Vows. Gomer, Hosea's wife, was unfaithful to her marriage vows. The heartbreaking experience served as a way for Hosea to tell God's people how they were not keeping their vows to the Lord.

Vows to a marriage partner, like our vows to the Lord, are meant to be kept. With almost half of all marriages in the United States failing and ending, we are called to remember that the commitment to one's spouse is modeled on God's commitment to us through Christ. God has vowed to stay with us, caringly, faithfully, and permanently. In turn, we as husbands and wives give our word to the Lord, to one another, and to the public that we will remain together caringly, faithfully, and permanently.

Tragically, many enter into the marriage relationship along the lines indicated in a cartoon in *The Wall Street Journal* (May 11, 1999). A prospective bride and groom are shown standing before a pastor, with the husband-to-be asking, "Do you have a ceremony less drastic than marriage?"

Prophet-like Poem. A church newsletter carried this poem, which tells of the way we all break our vows to the Lord.

> I think that I shall never see
> A church that's all it ought to be;

A church whose members never stray
Beyond the straight and narrow way.
A church that has no empty pews,
Whose pastor never has the blues,
A church whose deacons always deak
And none is proud and all are meek;
Where gossips never peddle lies,
Or make complaints or criticize.
Where all are always sweet and kind
And to all others' faults are blind.
Such perfect churches there may be,
But none of them are known to me.
But still we'll work and pray and plan
To make our own the best we can.

FOR YOUTH ▉ **TOPIC:** Who Will Be Faithful?
▉ **QUESTIONS:** 1. How did Hosea respond to God's incredible instructions? 2. What did God mean when He declared concerning Israel, *"you are not my people and I am not your God"* (Hos. 1:9)? 3. Why did God plan to judge Israel so severely? 4. What promise does Hosea's account hold for those who fail spiritually or morally? 5. How is loving as God loves different from loving as the world loves?

▉ **ILLUSTRATIONS:**

Key to Happiness. Most people generally assume that being single and living the carefree life of a young swinger is truly happy. There appear to be no responsibilities or duties except to oneself.

Numerous studies, however, have demonstrated that faithfully married people live happier lives than those who are single. Most recently, Wayne State sociologists Steven Stack and J. Ross Eshleman studied 18,000 adults in 17 industrialized countries including Japan, Canada, Australia, and Europe, and they concluded that couples living in faithful marriages were happier than couples who were cohabiting together, and much happier than singles.

Gomer never understood that being committed to her spouse (Hosea) could have led to happiness. Gomer thought that satisfaction came outside the bounds of marriage. This led her to a variety of relationships with other men in the impossible quest to find joy. Ultimately, she never did realize that the key to happiness lay in being loyal to her spouse.

Weakened Institution. If the family is the main institution of American life, what is the shape of our nation? Consider that 30 percent of American children grow up in a single-parent home. The single parent is just as likely to have never married (35%) as divorced (37%). According to the latest U.S. Census Bureau statistics in "Marital Status and Living Arrangements," the number of unmarried couples living together, almost 4 million, is 7 times more than the 1970 figure. Small wonder that some youth fear that the basic institution of society—marriage—is crumbling.

God calls for faithful commitments between a husband and a wife. This was the model that Hosea tried to demonstrate through his relationship with Gomer.

Long-Term Consequences. Voluminous research has documented the effects of marital infidelity and divorce on children. A team of psychologists from Catholic University of Milan, Italy, compared 160 teens from intact homes with solid marriages with a similar number of those young people from homes with broken marriages. Those from the shattered homes had a higher level of distrust of other people, were fearful of a marital commitment, less confident of themselves, more suspicious of others in general, and more likely to engage in premarital and extramarital sexual relationships.

God calls for faithful commitment to Himself and to one's spouse and family. The long-term consequences for those who are in committed relationships with God and their families are a healthier and more emotionally stable world.

GOD'S COMPASSION FOR ISRAEL

BACKGROUND SCRIPTURE: Hosea 11
DEVOTIONAL READING: Psalm 103:8-14

KEY VERSE: I led them with cords of human kindness, with bands of love. I was to them like those who lift infants to their cheeks. I bent down to them and fed them. Hosea 11:4.

KING JAMES VERSION

HOSEA 11:1 When Israel was a child, then I loved him, and called my son out of Egypt.

2 As they called them, so they went from them: they sacrificed unto Baalim, and burned incense to graven images.

3 I taught Ephraim also to go, taking them by their arms; but they knew not that I healed them.

4 I drew them with cords of a man, with bands of love: and I was to them as they that take off the yoke on their jaws, and I laid meat unto them.

5 He shall not return into the land of Egypt, but the Assyrian shall be his king, because they refused to return.

6 And the sword shall abide on his cities, and shall consume his branches, and devour them, because of their own counsels.

7 And my people are bent to backsliding from me: though they called them to the most High, none at all would exalt him.

8 How shall I give thee up, Ephraim? how shall I deliver thee, Israel? how shall I make thee as Admah? how shall I set thee as Zeboim? mine heart is turned within me, my repentings are kindled together.

9 I will not execute the fierceness of mine anger, I will not return to destroy Ephraim: for I am God, and not man; the Holy One in the midst of thee: and I will not enter into the city.

NEW REVISED STANDARD VERSION

HOSEA 11:1 When Israel was a child, I loved him,
  and out of Egypt I called my son.
2 The more I called them,
  the more they went from me;
they kept sacrificing to the Baals,
  and offering incense to idols.
3 Yet it was I who taught Ephraim to walk,
  I took them up in my arms;
  but they did not know that I healed them.
4 I led them with cords of human kindness,
  with bands of love.
I was to them like those
  who lift infants to their cheeks.
  I bent down to them and fed them.
5 They shall return to the land of Egypt,
  and Assyria shall be their king,
  because they have refused to return to me.
6 The sword rages in their cities,
  it consumes their oracle-priests,
  and devours because of their schemes.
7 My people are bent on turning away from me.
  To the Most High they call,
  but he does not raise them up at all.
8 How can I give you up, Ephraim?
  How can I hand you over, O Israel?
How can I make you like Admah?
  How can I treat you like Zeboiim?
My heart recoils within me;
  my compassion grows warm and tender.
9 I will not execute my fierce anger;
  I will not again destroy Ephraim;
for I am God and no mortal,
  the Holy One in your midst,
  and I will not come in wrath.

8

HOME BIBLE READINGS

BACKGROUND

Hosea might have been the only writing prophet from the northern kingdom to actually preach against that nation. Knowing how Israel had wandered into sinful ways perhaps better than any outsider, Hosea compared the behavior of God's people to that of his unfaithful wife, Gomer. Just as Gomer had engaged in sexually promiscuous behavior, so too Israel had prostituted herself to idols (Hos. 1:2).

Hosea laid out in detail the ways in which the Israelites had philandered. They had venerated a pantheon of idols. The people delighted in participating in degrading fertility rituals. And they continually refused to return to God. All these iniquities constituted spiritual adultery, and it broke God's heart (2:5-23).

Evidently after bringing her three children into the world, Gomer returned to her previous immoral ways. Just as Hosea had obeyed God's difficult command to marry an unfaithful woman, so too he obeyed the difficult command to take Gomer back. This reunion was to serve as a powerful reminder of God's love for His wayward people (3:1-5).

Hosea also used other metaphors to illustrate the Lord's compassion for His people. Hosea spoke of God in terms of a caring mother tenderly looking after her beloved child. Here the images are unmistakably feminine. The Lord is portrayed as the gentle and constantly attentive parent taking a little one by the hand to help the child learn to walk, and picking up and cradling in loving arms the crying child who'd fallen and needed comforting (11:1-4). This description of the tender side of God's personality is unsurpassed.

God yearned for the wayward Israelites to remember the nurturing love He had poured out on them down through the centuries. The Lord cried, *How can I give you up, Ephraim? How can I hand you over, O Israel?* (11:8). Despite the nation's outrageous behavior, God still cherished His people.

NOTES ON THE PRINTED TEXT

As the father of three children, Hosea drew on his experience to describe in parental terms God's dealings with Israel. Hosea reminded his listeners that God had chosen Israel. The Lord had established the relationship. He had liberated the helpless young child from Egyptian slavery and led him through the wilderness. *When Israel was a child, I loved him, and out of Egypt I called my son* (Hos. 11:1).

Tragically, however, the child proved to be rebellious and disobedient. Despite the Lord's love, care, and exhortations, the child left home to pursue Baal and other false gods, and to offer pagan sacrifices. *The more I called them, the more they went from me; they kept sacrificing to the Baals, and offering incense to idols* (11:2).

The prophet detailed all that the Lord had done for His people. He had helped them take their first hesitant steps as a nation and had carried them along through many dark and difficult days. God had hugged His people and cared for them when they were sick. *Yet it was I who taught Ephraim to walk, I took them up in my arms; but they did not know that I healed them* (11:3).

Like a caring parent, the Lord nurtured, taught, and fed His people. He lovingly and gently led them down the path of life. The tender compassion of God was like the affectionate hug that a parent would give to a child. *I led them with cords of human kindness, with bands of love. I was to them like those who lift infants to their cheeks. I bent down to them and fed them* (11:4).

In light of God's love, the Israelites' persistence in idolatry, immorality, and injustice was inexcusable. Thus, the Lord would not withhold His judgment on the nation. His people would not return to Egypt, where they once had been slaves; rather, they would be conquered and ruled by the Assryians. *Assyria shall be their king, because they have refused to return to me* (11:5).

Hosea prophesied during the final years of the northern kingdom of Israel's life as a nation. Perhaps fewer than 10 years separated the prediction of a sword devouring the cities and consuming the nation's oracle-priests and its fulfillment in 722 B.C. *The sword rages in their cities, it consumes their oracle-priests, and devours because of their schemes* (11:6).

The commitment of the Israelites to the Baals and other idols inclined them to prefer the sensual worship of paganism to the moral standards of their covenant with the Lord. They backslid from the righteousness of God's law to the immorality of paganism. No matter how many prophets called Israel back to the *Most High* (11:7), the toboggan slide downward continued.

God, however, refused to completely wipe out His people. He was torn between both love and punishment. *How can I give you up, Ephraim? How can I hand you over, O Israel? How can I make you like Admah? How can I treat you like Zeboiim?* (11:8). These two cities, both located along the southern end of the Dead Sea, were destroyed for their wickedness along with Sodom and Gomorrah.

The Lord greatly loved His people. He simply could not annihilate them. While He would severely discipline the Israelites like a stern parent, He would not sever His relationship with His people. *I will not execute my fierce anger; I will not again destroy Ephraim; for I am God and no mortal, the Holy One in your midst, and I will not come in wrath* (11:9).

SUGGESTIONS TO TEACHERS

Hopefully, you have never had someone you love turn away and reject you. But if you've known a parent who has had a youngster run away from home, or a man or woman whose spouse had deserted them, you can get some idea of how God feels when His people are unfaithful to Him.

1. ACHE OF DISAPPOINTMENT. Perhaps as no other in the Old Testament, Hosea portrayed the Lord's sense of hurt and disappointment over being rejected by His people. Point out to your students that we often take God's care for granted, just as some children take their parents' love for granted. Have the members of your class offer examples of gifts and mercies from the Lord that believers sometimes assume are their due.

2. AWARENESS OF DEPENDENCY. In Hosea 11:3 and 4, the prophet described how God nurtured His people. Have your students note the tender, protective aspect of God's character. Often, we speak only about what may seem to be disciplinary aspects of God's character. Here we see an intense desire on God's part to care for His people in the ways that gentle, loving parents would look after their little ones.

3. APPOINTMENT WITH DESTRUCTION. Hosea put the heartbreak of God in vivid terms that people could understand. The more God reached out to Israel, the more the people turned away to idols. Despite Israel's unfaithfulness, God nurtured His people as a loving parent. But Hosea promised that their waywardness inevitably would bring them calamity.

4. ANGER OF THE DIVINE. Hosea knew that God is not impassive. The Lord cares so deeply that He responds with the feelings of intense grief when His people spurn Him. The anger of God is not an outburst of rage; rather, His anger is the deep, hurt-filled disappointment that comes from finding His loved ones unresponsive to His compassion and kindness.

5. AGONY OF DIVINE LOVE. Many in your class have already known the pain of having loving acts rejected. Others have experienced the ache of a relationship broken by someone dear to them. Most have known the tension of refusing to give up on people they love who rebel against their values. God also feels this way! But God still cares. Remind your students that each member is called, as Hosea was, to declare God's love to others, including those outside the church.

FOR ADULTS

■ **TOPIC:** Rejected Love

■ **QUESTIONS:** 1. How had God shown His love for Israel in the past? 2. Why did the Israelites spurn God's love? 3. How would God discipline His wayward people? 4. What tension existed between God's love for His people and the necessity to punish them for their iniquities? 5. What characteristics of a young child should we forsake as spiritually mature children of God?

■ ILLUSTRATIONS:

Rejected Love. Michael Reagan, son of the former President, wrote a book entitled *On the Outside Looking In.* In it Michael poignantly related how he felt his love for his famous father was apparently rejected. On one occasion, young Reagan and two friends won the Outboard World Championship of 1967. Michael Reagan was featured in the newspapers and on television as a winner. Apparently Ronald and Nancy Reagan had never showed Michael much affection or appreciation. Despite this, Michael felt certain that they would hear about his accomplishment and finally welcome him because of his award. Longing for some word of love and appreciation, Michael waited expectantly to hear from his parents. He never heard from them, to his intense disappointment.

Rejected for Centuries. In the sixteenth century, Nicolaus Copernicus discovered that the earth revolved around the sun. Copernicus's book, *De Revolutionibus Orbium Coelestium,* was formally denounced as heresy and placed on the list of forbidden titles for centuries. A few years later, a devout astronomer named Galilei Galileo constructed one of the first good telescopes, and showed that Copernicus's theory was correct.

Though Galileo professed his love for the church, he also maintained his devotion to truth. The leadership, however, demanded he retract his findings and submit to the traditional notion that the sun and all the planets revolved around the earth. Galileo pleaded for truth. But he, his discoveries, and his writings were formally condemned in 1616. Galileo was stigmatized as a heretic and driven from the church. It was not until 1992 that the leadership of the church admitted its error. Finally, nearly four centuries later, it was formally declared that the church had wrongly rejected Galileo, an illustrious son of the faith, and had erred by condemning him.

Rejected Love. Algeria has been the scene of horrific carnage during the past 10 years, especially as the government has battled fanatical religious extremists who are determined to gain power through slaughter and terrorism. On the night of March 26, 1996, seven Christians were abducted from their residence as hostages by the extremists. The Algerian authorities refused to release imprisoned rebels in exchange for the Christians. On May 21, 1996, the bodies of the seven believers were discovered, their throats having been cut. On the desk of one of the deceased a note was found, which read in part:

> If it should happen one day that I become a victim of terrorism . . . I
> should like, when the time comes, to have a moment of lucidity which
> would allow me to beg forgiveness of God and of all my fellow human
> beings, and at the same time to forgive with all my heart the one who
> would strike me down. To you, the friend of my final moment, who would
> not be aware of what you are doing I say this: Thank you . . . in whom I

see the face of God. And may we find each other, happy good thieves, in Paradise, if it pleases God, the Father of us both. Amen.

FOR YOUTH	■ **TOPIC:** Why Does Love Hurt?

■ **QUESTIONS:** 1. Why was it important for the Israelites to know that God had loved them in the past? 2. Why did God continue loving the Israelites even when they spurned His love? 3. Why were the Israelites bent on turning away from God, despite all He had done for them (Hos. 11:7)? 4. Why did God refuse to completely wipe out Israel? 5. Why is it better to fall into the hands of God rather than human hands when it is time for punishment?

■ **ILLUSTRATIONS:**

A Father's Love. Prison chaplains report that when Christian groups distribute cards for Mother's Day, the response is almost 100 percent. Nearly every inmate mails a card to his or her mother. However, when the same groups come into jail and offer cards for Father's Day, there is almost no interest. Seldom are there any takers for cards. Most inmates simply do not feel their dads cared about them. In light of Hosea's image of God as our heavenly Father, what should be the nature of a human father's love for his children?

No Love Experienced. Late in her life actress Marilyn Monroe was asked how often she felt love. She replied that she felt love only once in her life when one of her foster mothers was putting on her make up and stopped and touched her on the top of her nose with her powder puff and gave her a smile. Just for a moment, the screen star said, she felt love. Small wonder that the blonde screen star's life ended tragically. On the other extreme, Hosea described the lavish love, care, and anguish of a committed parent for his child. The prophet said that this is the type of love that God had for His people.

Recognized Contribution. When Green Bay Packer Coach Vince Lombardi lay dying in a Washington hospital, he was visited by one of the National Football League's greatest defensive ends, Willie Davis. When Davis came out of Lombardi's room, he was asked why he had traveled some 3,000 miles from California to see Lombardi. Davis responded, "I had to."

The reporters followed Davis out of the hospital and persisted, asking the athlete why he had traveled so far to see the coach. Davis's response was the same. As he got into a cab, the reporters again asked why he had come. Finally Davis said, "That man made me feel important. Any one who makes you feel important, you will travel halfway around America for." Davis recognized the contributions that Lombardi had made in his life. Contrast Davis's action with that of the Israelites. Despite all that God had done for them, they spurned His unfailing love.

What God Requires

BACKGROUND SCRIPTURE: Micah 3; 6:1-8
DEVOTIONAL READING: Proverbs 21:2-3

KEY VERSE: He has told you, O mortal, what is good; and what does the LORD require of you but to do justice, and to love kindness, and to walk humbly with your God? Micah 6:8.

KING JAMES VERSION

MICAH 3:9 Hear this, I pray you, ye heads of the house of Jacob, and princes of the house of Israel, that abhor judgment, and pervert all equity.

10 They build up Zion with blood, and Jerusalem with iniquity.

11 The heads thereof judge for reward, and the priests thereof teach for hire, and the prophets thereof divine for money: yet will they lean upon the LORD, and say, Is not the LORD among us? none evil can come upon us.

12 Therefore shall Zion for your sake be plowed as a field, and Jerusalem shall become heaps, and the mountain of the house as the high places of the forest. . . .

6:6 Wherewith shall I come before the LORD, and bow myself before the high God? shall I come before him with burnt offerings, with calves of a year old?

7 Will the LORD be pleased with thousands of rams, or with ten thousands of rivers of oil? shall I give my firstborn for my transgression, the fruit of my body for the sin of my soul?

8 He hath shewed thee, O man, what is good; and what doth the LORD require of thee, but to do justly, and to love mercy, and to walk humbly with thy God?

NEW REVISED STANDARD VERSION

MICAH 3:9 Hear this, you rulers of the house of
  Jacob and chiefs of the house of Israel,
who abhor justice
  and pervert all equity,
10 who build Zion with blood
  and Jerusalem with wrong!
11 Its rulers give judgment for a bribe,
  its priests teach for a price,
  its prophets give oracles for money;
yet they lean upon the LORD and say,
  "Surely the LORD is with us!
  No harm shall come upon us."
12 Therefore because of you
  Zion shall be plowed as a field;
Jerusalem shall become a heap of ruins,
  and the mountain of the house a wooded height. . . .
6:6 "With what shall I come before the LORD,
  and bow myself before God on high?
Shall I come before him with burnt offerings,
  with calves a year old?
7 Will the LORD be pleased with thousands of rams,
  with ten thousands of rivers of oil?
Shall I give my firstborn for my transgression,
  the fruit of my body for the sin of my soul?"
8 He has told you, O mortal, what is good;
  and what does the LORD require of you
but to do justice, and to love kindness,
  and to walk humbly with your God?

9

HOME BIBLE READINGS

BACKGROUND

Micah was from the town of Moresheth Gath (Mic. 1:1, 14), which was located in the foothills of Judah about 20 miles southwest of Jerusalem. Though Micah was a resident of the country and removed from the national policies of Judah, God nonetheless called him to proclaim a message of judgment to the rulers and inhabitants of Jerusalem.

Micah's prophetic ministry overlapped the reigns of Jotham (750–735 B.C.), Ahaz (735–715 B.C.), and Hezekiah (715–686 B.C.). The prophet's indictments of social injustices and religious corruption were particularly suited to the reign of Ahaz. The northern kingdom of Israel fell during the ministry of Micah, and this explains why the prophet dated his messages with only the mention of Judean kings. It also explains why he principally directed his comments to the southern kingdom, where he lived.

The economic prosperity and the absence of international crises, which had marked the days of Jeroboam II (793–753 B.C.), were slipping away. It was a time when Syria and Israel invaded Judah and in which Assyria overthrew Syria and Israel (during the reign of Ahaz). When Hezekiah withdrew his allegiance from Assyria, this prompted Sennacherib to besiege Jerusalem, though it proved unsuccessful due to the Lord's gracious intervention.

Instead of growing closer to God out of gratitude for His blessings, Judah and Israel had slipped into moral bankruptcy. Those who became wealthy during this time ruthlessly exploited the poor. Consequently, Micah predicted the fall of both Samaria and Jerusalem, focusing more on the Babylonian captivity of the southern kingdom and the eventual restoration of its people.

NOTES ON THE PRINTED TEXT

Of all people, the spiritual and political leaders of Judah should have understood how important justice was to the social fabric of their nation. These princes and prophets often heard and settled disputes among people. Their decisions were final. The people looked to these leaders for justice, but instead these men were perverting justice for personal gain.

In a blistering summary, the prophet declared, *Hear this, you rulers of the house of Jacob and chiefs of the house of Israel, who abhor justice and pervert all equity, who build Zion with blood and Jerusalem with wrong!* (Mic. 3:9-10). Here we see Micah summoning the officials to listen and charging them with detesting equity. Some think the prophet had in mind the seizure of the poor's property by the rich or the conscription of forced labor gangs to build up Jerusalem.

Micah specified the corrupt leaders' misdeeds. *Its rulers give judgment for a bribe, its priests teach for a price, its prophets give oracles for money; yet they lean upon the LORD and say, "Surely the LORD is with us! No harm shall come upon us."* (3:11). The political and judicial system sold favorable treatment and verdicts. Even the nation's religious leaders gave instructions for a price. Micah was critical of their overriding greed, not necessarily that they were paid for a service. Worst yet, the false prophets gave oracles for money. The prophet was also critical of the leaders' false confidence of God's presence and protection. They believed that God would never let anything bad happen to the nation or to Jerusalem.

Micah didn't go along with the fraudulent leaders. He warned that one day Mount Zion would be plowed like an open field. In fact, all of Jerusalem would be reduced to rubble. Only a field of thorns would remain. This announcement of catastrophe must have shocked the leaders. *Therefore because of you Zion shall be plowed as a field; Jerusalem shall become a heap of ruins, and the mountain of the house a wooded height* (3:12)

In chapters 4 and 5 of Micah we read about God's reign over His perfect kingdom. Then in 6:1-8 we encounter a courtroom scene where God, the judge, tells His people what He requires of them and recites all the ways they have wronged both Him and others.

Using a rhetorical question, Micah asked, *"With what shall I come before the LORD, and bow myself before God on high? Shall I come before him with burnt offerings, with calves a year old?"* (6:6). In other words, would various sacrifices restore Israel's shattered relationship with God? What might the Lord require? Micah escalated the offerings to the height of absurdity. *"Will the LORD be pleased with thousands of rams, with ten thousands of rivers of oil? Shall I give my first-born for my transgression, the fruit of my body for the sin of my soul?"* (6:7). In other words, would a mere imperfect human sacrifice adequately atone for all of the nation's sins?

Micah declared that no religious ritual or sacrifice would suffice. God had different requirements that were to be demonstrated in the lives of His people. *He has told you, O mortal, what is good; and what does the LORD require of you but to do justice, and to love kindness, and to walk humbly with your God?* (6:8).

To do justice means to treat others with honesty, integrity, and equity. To love kindness means to be loyal to God and merciful to others. This is not done impulsively, but rather as a consistent part of our lives. To walk humbly with God means to be circumspect in what we say and modest in our demeanor. We willingly chose to follow the Lord and submit to His will.

SUGGESTIONS TO TEACHERS

Many persons are cynical about their leaders. The scandalous behavior and the unscrupulous practices of certain government and religious officials have caused confusion and disillusionment, especially among the younger generation. Some media personalities' lack of values has also had a corrupting effect. Some of your students may be wondering what is right and what is wrong, and also how God wants them to act. This week's lesson will help address these important issues.

1. CONTENTION WITH CIVIL LEADERS. Micah said that the practices of corrupt rulers and government officials were reprehensible. Their greed and callous disregard for the needs of the underclass was devastating the poor and hungry. The impoverished were like helpless lambs in the midst of cunning and savage beasts. This reminds us that those in government have a responsibility to look after the hurting and forgotten in society.

2. CONDEMNATION OF RELIGIOUS LEADERS. Micah referred to corrupt prophets and priests, and his words remind us who call ourselves "God's people" that we carry a heavy burden of duty to the impoverished living around us. Your congregation is probably already doing noble service through a food pantry and participation in housing programs for the poor. Are there other areas that should be addressed? Also, how do you overcome "compassion fatigue"?

3. CONSEQUENCES OF DISOBEDIENCE. Like all prophets, Micah warned his hearers that their heartless lack of concern for those suffering in society would result in the destruction and end of their comfortable way of life. How do Micah's pronouncements apply to our society?

4. CONTROVERSY WITH THE COVENANTED COMMUNITY. Micah, like Hosea, told how deeply disappointed God was with His faithless nation. The disobedient had deliberately broken the sacred relationship between God and His people, and this in turn immensely grieved the Lord. How do your students think God feels toward the church in general and toward their congregation in particular?

5. CONCENTRATION ON GOD'S REQUIREMENT. Be sure to focus at length on Micah 6:8, especially discussing what it means to *do justice, and to love kindness, and to walk humbly* before God. You might even want to save the largest part of the lesson time to discuss this key verse. Why not encourage your students to commit this verse to memory?

| **FOR ADULTS** | ■ TOPIC: High Expectations
■ QUESTIONS: 1. In what ways had the nation's leaders abhorred justice? 2. Why did the nation's leaders think that no harm would |

come to them? 3. Why were the various sacrifices and offerings mentioned in Micah 6:6-7 unacceptable to the Lord? 4. Why did God stress the importance of justice, kindness, and humility? 5. What moral standards are God's people today expected to follow?

■ ILLUSTRATIONS:

Prophetic Stand. Congressman Tony Hall was concerned about helping the hungry. When the Select Committee on Hunger in Congress was terminated a few years ago, Hall worried that his colleagues would neglect those who lacked enough to eat and adequate diets. His wife suggested that he fast. After praying and seeking the counsel of fellow Christians, he undertook a water fast to call attention to the urgent needs of those lacking sufficient food. "When I did that," Hall reported, "I separated myself from my colleagues. I felt like I was alone."

But Hall continued with the fast. It was difficult and also humbling. After two weeks of fasting, he felt that there was no hope that the Committee would be restored. But at that point, students and community groups heard about his commitment, and were impressed that a politician would fast. Shortly thereafter, the administration and the World Bank made strong suggestions about curbing world hunger. Congressman Hall spoke to the House of Representatives. The majority leader confessed, "I feel ashamed. You have embarrassed us in the right way." Hall's lonely stand illustrates the kind of concern all believers should have for the impoverished.

Rich Are Richer. The number of billionaires has expanded to over 200 in the world, and they pushed their collective net worth to over $1 trillion. But the gap between the wealthiest and the rest is widening. Currently, the richest fifth of the world's population accounts for 86 percent of all private consumption. But in Africa, the average household consumes 20 percent less than it did 25 years ago. Meanwhile natural resources as well as household purchasing power are declining.

The richest fifth of the world's people buy nine times as much meat, have access to nearly 50 times as many telephones, and use more than 80 times as many paper products and motorized vehicles than the poorest fifth. Americans spend more than $8 billion annually on cosmetics, whereas it would cost only $6 billion to provide basic education for the children in developing countries who have no schooling. Europeans spend $11 billion yearly on ice cream; about $9 billion would provide water and basic sanitation to the more than 2 billion people worldwide who lack safe water or hygienic toilets.

Micah's message to the well-off people of the world continues to be a challenge. And the prophet's words about God demanding justice, kindness, and humility are still true!

More than Eating Humble Pie. What is true repentance? The following excerpt from *Mere Christianity* by C. S. Lewis nicely answers this crucial question.

Now what was the sort of "hole" man has got himself into? He had tried to set up on his own, to behave as if he belonged to himself. Fallen man is not simply an imperfect creature who needs improvement: he is a rebel who must lay down his arms. Laying down your arms, surrendering, saying you are sorry, realizing that you have been on the wrong track and getting ready to start life over again from the ground floor—that is the only way out of a "hole." This process of surrender—this movement full speed astern—is what Christians call repentance. Now repentance is no fun at all. It is something much harder than merely eating humble pie. It means unlearning all of the self-conceit and self-will that we have been training ourselves into for thousands of years. It means killing a part of yourself, undergoing a kind of death.

FOR YOUTH

■ **TOPIC:** What Is Required?
■ **QUESTIONS:** 1. What injustices were the priests and prophets of the nation guilty of committing? 2. What calamity did the Lord have planned for Judah and Jerusalem? 3. What does it mean to *do justice, and to love kindness, and to walk humbly with your God* (Mic. 6:8)? 4. How can Micah's prophecy about God's judgment against Judah serve believers today? 5. What are some worldly pursuits that the Spirit has helped you to let go of?

■ **ILLUSTRATIONS:**

Chicago Boy's Response. Alex Kotlowitz of *The Wall Street Journal* did a study of two boys growing up in the "jects" (the public housing projects) in Chicago. He reported that one mother commented on his proposal to write about her children. She said, "There are no children here."

These women (who usually are single and head the household) watch their children caught in the despair and violence of the community. Understandably, these kids know little about a normal childhood. When Kotlowitz asked one 10-year old what he wanted to be when he grew up, the youngster replied, "If I grow up, I'd like to be a bus driver." (Please note, he said "if," not "when.")

Modeling Care. South Bend's Center for the Homeless helps dozens of people each day. What is surprising is that young alumni and students run it from the University of Notre Dame's Center for Social Concerns.

Consider Shannon Cullinan. She developed a landscaping business that employs homeless people for eight months of training and then places them in other landscaping companies, especially as it cares for the properties in the City of South Bend, Memorial Hospital, WNDU Broadcasting, and the University properties. Then there's Drew Buscarieno. He developed a medical clinic, early childhood center, and drug and alcohol treatment center. He also developed educational facilities, job training, and care for the mentally ill.

Praised by the executive director of the National Coalition for the Homeless as a model of collaboration between university students and the local community, the center seeks to find solutions to the problems of the homeless. Here is a group of young people working to implement what God requires in their lives.

Wretched Excess. Realtors state that a four-car garage is a "must" now for many of the 40-something, "gotta have it all" generation. Likewise, bakers report that the cake is the newest status symbol. Each party cake must outdo the previous party's cake. Therefore, it is important how outrageous and garish each decorated cake is made.

It is not unusual for a bakery to spend 3 weeks on an individual cake that will cost thousands of dollars. For instance, one man ordered a 40" by 16" three dimensional cake to replicate his metallic blue-gray sports car. The finished cake cost $2,200, according to the *New York Times*. Ironically, at the same time the homeless and hungry are being herded from the street corners of New York!

In the face of such excesses, what would Micah have said? Might he have accused the populace of unjust and inhuman treatment of others?

ISAIAH'S CALL

BACKGROUND SCRIPTURE: Isaiah 6
DEVOTIONAL READING: Acts 26:12-20

KEY VERSE: I heard the voice of the Lord saying, "Whom shall I send, and who will go for us?" And I said, "Here am I; send me!" Isaiah 6:8.

KING JAMES VERSION

ISAIAH 6:1 In the year that king Uzziah died I saw also the Lord sitting upon a throne, high and lifted up, and his train filled the temple.

2 Above it stood the seraphims: each one had six wings; with twain he covered his face, and with twain he covered his feet, and with twain he did fly.

3 And one cried unto another, and said, Holy, holy, holy, is the LORD of hosts: the whole earth is full of his glory.

4 And the posts of the door moved at the voice of him that cried, and the house was filled with smoke.

5 Then said I, Woe is me! for I am undone; because I am a man of unclean lips, and I dwell in the midst of a people of unclean lips: for mine eyes have seen the King, the LORD of hosts.

6 Then flew one of the seraphims unto me, having a live coal in his hand, which he had taken with the tongs from off the altar:

7 And he laid it upon my mouth, and said, Lo, this hath touched thy lips; and thine iniquity is taken away, and thy sin purged.

8 Also I heard the voice of the Lord, saying, Whom shall I send, and who will go for us? Then said I, Here am I; send me.

9 And he said, Go, and tell this people, Hear ye indeed, but understand not; and see ye indeed, but perceive not.

10 Make the heart of this people fat, and make their ears heavy, and shut their eyes; lest they see with their eyes, and hear with their ears, and understand with their heart, and convert, and be healed.

11 Then said I, Lord, how long? And he answered, Until the cities be wasted without inhabitant, and the houses without man, and the land be utterly desolate,

12 And the LORD have removed men far away, and there be a great forsaking in the midst of the land.

NEW REVISED STANDARD VERSION

ISAIAH 6:1 In the year that King Uzziah died, I saw the Lord sitting on a throne, high and lofty; and the hem of his robe filled the temple. 2 Seraphs were in attendance above him; each had six wings: with two they covered their faces, and with two they covered their feet, and with two they flew. 3 And one called to another and said:

"Holy, holy, holy is the LORD of hosts;
the whole earth is full of his glory."

4 The pivots on the thresholds shook at the voices of those who called, and the house filled with smoke.

5 And I said: "Woe is me! I am lost, for I am a man of unclean lips, and I live among a people of unclean lips; yet my eyes have seen the King, the LORD of hosts!"

6 Then one of the seraphs flew to me, holding a live coal that had been taken from the altar with a pair of tongs. 7 The seraph touched my mouth with it and said: "Now that this has touched your lips, your guilt has departed and your sin is blotted out." 8 Then I heard the voice of the Lord saying, "Whom shall I send, and who will go for us?" And I said, "Here am I; send me!"

9 And he said, "Go and say to this people:

'Keep listening, but do not comprehend;
keep looking, but do not understand.'

10 Make the mind of this people dull,
    and stop their ears,
    and shut their eyes,
so that they may not look with their eyes,
    and listen with their ears,
and comprehend with their minds,
    and turn and be healed."

11 Then I said, "How long, O Lord?" And he said:
"Until cities lie waste
    without inhabitant,
and houses without people,
    and the land is utterly desolate;

12 until the LORD sends everyone far away,
    and vast is the emptiness in the midst of the land."

HOME BIBLE READINGS

BACKGROUND

About the same time that Amos, Hosea, and Micah lived, another prophet named Isaiah came upon the scene in Judah. This bold preacher lived during the tumultuous times when the Assyrians snuffed out the northern kingdom of Israel and threatened the existence of the southern kingdom of Judah.

Scholars place Isaiah's career between 740 and 681 B.C. Throughout his long ministry, he preached about the Lord's righteousness, warned about judgment for sin, and proclaimed God's love and forgiveness. Isaiah also prophesied the glory that awaits those who remain faithful to God.

Isaiah's call to serve the Lord came at a time of crisis in the nation. King Uzziah (or Azariah) had died (Isa. 6:1). This able ruler had provided over five decades of stability and prosperity for Judah (792–740 B.C.). Uzziah's death meant that his successors would be Jotham (750–735 B.C.) and then eventually Ahaz (735–715 B.C.), both known for their morally weak characters. The loss of a beloved national leader such as Uzziah and the unsettled situation it created in the palace undoubtedly affected Isaiah at the start of his ministry.

In this week's lesson we will learn that Isaiah had a vision of the glorious Lord sitting on His lofty throne. Perhaps the idea is that though an earthly king had died, the King of the universe still reigned on high. And though the Lord was in heaven, His robe, symbolizing His majesty, reached to earth.

Scripture tells us that no one has ever seen or can see the Lord (1 Tim. 6:16). Knowing this, how was it possible for Isaiah to have seen God? In response, we should remember that God is spirit, and thus invisible (John 4:24). This means that no one has seen or can see Him in His true essence. However, the Lord has at times chosen to manifest Himself temporarily in one visible form or another. Such a visible manifestation is called a "theophany." This term comes from two Greek words: *theos*, which means "God," and *phaino*, which means "to appear." What Isaiah saw, then, was an appearance of God, not God in His essence.

At first, it may seem odd that Isaiah's commission to prophesy does not come until chapter 6, following five chapters of prophecies. (These chapters deal with such themes as judgment, discipline, exile, restoration, and blessing.) But probably Isaiah placed his commissioning account here to demonstrate he had the credentials to deliver the opening series of oracles against Judah.

NOTES ON THE PRINTED TEXT

The year King Uzziah died was about 740 B.C. He remained leprous until his death because he tried to take over the high priest's duties (2 Chron. 26:18-21). Though Uzziah was generally a good king with a long and prosperous reign, many of his people turned away from the Lord.

Isaiah's lofty view of God gives us a sense of the Lord's greatness, mystery, and power. The Lord used Isaiah's vision to commission him as His messenger to His people. Isaiah was given a difficult assignment. He had to tell people who believed they were blessed by God that the Lord was going to destroy them instead because of their disobedience.

The throne, the attending seraphs or angels, and the threefold "holy" all stressed God's supreme holiness. In a time when moral and spiritual decay was high, it was important for Isaiah to seek God in His moral purity and perfection. *In the year that King Uzziah died, I saw the Lord sitting on a throne, high and lofty; and the hem of his robe filled the temple. Seraphs were in attendance above him; each had six wings; with two they covered their faces, and with two they covered their feet, and with two they flew. And one called to another and said: "Holy, holy, holy is the LORD of hosts; the whole earth is full of his glory"* (Isa. 6:1-3).

The glorious singing shook the temple to its foundations, and the entire sanctuary was filled with smoke. The incident served as a sobering reminder that God is both king and judge over all creation. *The pivots on the thresholds shook at the voices of those who called, and the house was filled with smoke* (6:4).

As Isaiah stood before the Lord, he was overwhelmed by his own impurity, sinfulness, and unworthiness. He realized that before the one who was perfect, no one human can stand and live. *And I said: "Woe is me! I am lost, for I am a man of unclean lips, . . . yet my eyes have seen the King, the LORD of hosts!"* (6:5).

Upon Isaiah's confession of sinfulness, a seraph flew over him with a hot coal that had been taken from the altar. This coal symbolized the redeeming power of God to purge and forgive sins. *Then one of the seraphs flew to me, holding a live coal that had been taken from the altar with a pair of tongs. The seraph touched my mouth with it and said: "Now that this has touched your lips, your guilt has departed and your sin is blotted out"* (6:6-7).

The prophet then heard God's voice as He spoke from His throne. *"Whom shall I send, and who will go for us?"* (6:8). A messenger was needed for the difficult assignment. Without hesitation, Isaiah volunteered. *And I said, "Here am I; send me!"* Though shortly before the prophet had felt unfit to serve God, now he was eager to do so.

God immediately ordered Isaiah to preach. However, his preaching would have little impact and serve to solidify the determination of the nation to live by its own standards, not God's law. *"Go and say to this people: 'Keep listening, but do not comprehend; keep looking but do not understand.' Make the mind of this people dull, and stop their ears, and shut their eyes, so that they may not look with their eyes, and listen with their ears, and comprehend with their minds, and turn and be healed"* (6:9-10).

With such a discouraging commission, Isaiah asked, *"How long, O Lord?"* (6:11). In other words, how long would he have to proclaim judgment, despair, and desolation to people who refused to listen?

God's answer was equally disconcerting. Isaiah was to preach until the widespread devastation had been accomplished and a deportation had removed at least part of the populace. *"Until cities lie waste without inhabitant, and houses without people, and the land is utterly desolate; until the LORD sends everyone far away, and vast is the emptiness in the midst of the land"* (6:11-12).

The news of coming exile must have shaken Isaiah. But God gave him good news with the bad. A remnant of the nation—a *"tenth"* (6:13)—would survive the future exile. This refers to the portion of Jews who returned from Babylon.

SUGGESTIONS TO TEACHERS

Undoubtedly your students have heard of someone being "called" by God. Perhaps some of the members of your class feel a bit uncomfortable with this term. Or perhaps they might have serious questions about what it means to be called by God. Some might even feel slightly resentful since occasionally those who supposedly experienced a divine "call" were considered spiritually superior by others. This week's lesson should help clarify the matter of God's calling a person.

1. AWE BEFORE THE CREATOR. While in the presence of the Lord, Isaiah caught a glimpse of His majesty and power. Such an extraordinary experience called for a reverent response. The talk that we sometimes hear these days of God being some sort of "buddy in the sky" is irreverent. It should not take place among those who genuinely worship the Lord.

2. AWARENESS OF FAILURE. Isaiah immediately realized how undeserving he was of God's favor. Isaiah's sense of personal inadequacy and national failure was overwhelming. A genuine call means an awareness of how great God is and how unmerited we are of His grace.

3. ACCEPTANCE BY GOD. The keynote in a true call of God is knowing His love! Isaiah knew that he had been forgiven. Similarly, divine grace floods the consciousness of those who have experienced God's call.

4. ANSWER TO GOD'S CALL. Those who are called by God have a keen awareness of His nearness and goodness. Such an awareness demands a response. Isaiah's *"Here am I; send me!"* (Isa. 6:8) is at the heart of every genuine call.

5. ACCOUNTABILITY BEFORE GOD. A call from God always entails a task. It also includes the responsibility to fulfill that task. In the case of your students, that means leading a consistently obedient life of service to others. Emphasize that everyone who believes in Christ has been divinely summoned to minister to others in His name.

■ **TOPIC:** Answering God's Call

■ **QUESTIONS:** 1. What was profound about the vision Isaiah had of God? 2. What is the significance of God being called *"holy, holy, holy"* (Isa. 6:3)? 3. Why was it important for Isaiah to realize his sinfulness before God would commission him? 4. Why would God's people be so unresponsive to Isaiah's message? 5. Have there been times when you felt overwhelmed by the presence and power of God? If so, explain why.

■ **ILLUSTRATIONS:**

Friend's Plea. God's call sometimes comes through the request of a friend. Homerun king Mark McGwire learned that. He heard the alarming statistics about child abuse from his friend Ali Dickson. Dickson, who volunteers at Stuart House, a national advocacy center for sexually abused youngsters in Santa Monica, California, introduced McGwire to the kids behind the numbers.

"Until you get in there and really understand, you have no concept," said the baseball star. "I mean, to see a child walking through the door, knowing that child had been sexually abused, knowing the scars that little boy or little girl is going to have to deal with the rest of their lives, how can it not hit home?" McGwire has committed $3 million of his baseball salary to his Foundation for Children. This great athlete was called to serve in this commendable way by the plea of his friend, Ali Dickson.

Cry for Help. Sometimes, God's call comes through the need a person sees around him or her. Likewise, God's call always is a summons to serve. And usually the call to meet a need means not only serving but also sacrificing.

During the early hours of February 3, 1943, the American troopship, the U.S.A.T. *Dorchester* was hit by a torpedo while ferrying 902 troops across the Atlantic. Though the soldiers had been ordered to sleep with their lifejackets on, many deep in the hold had disregarded the order because of the engine's heat or because the lifejackets were uncomfortable.

The stricken ship began to take on water rapidly. In less than 30 minutes, it slipped beneath the Atlantic's icy waters. The explosion had knocked out the power and made radio contact impossible with other ships.

In the darkness on the *Dorchester,* chaos reigned. The explosion had killed scores, and many others were seriously wounded. Frightened soldiers groped about in the smoke and darkness. Through the pandemonium, according to those present, four Army chaplains brought hope and help. Chaplains George Fox, Alexander Goode, John Washington, and Clark Poling quickly and quietly fanned out among the soldiers, calming the frightened, tending the wounded, guiding the disoriented to lifeboats, encouraging the despairing, and praying with the dying.

When some soldiers struggled topside to the deck without lifejackets, the four chaplains broke open a locker and distributed stored life preservers. The supply was soon exhausted. Then the four chaplains removed their own lifejackets and handed them to four frightened young men who had none. The last survivors saw of these four was of them linking arms and praying together. Bracing themselves against the slanting deck, their voices could be heard offering prayers.

Chosen. God's call is a sense that the Lord has claimed our life. Kathleen Norris, who is an author and poet, described what that call means to her friends in communal life.

> These men and women tell me that one question that bites pretty hard in their early years . . . is why anyone would choose to live this way, deprived of the autonomy and abundance of choices that middleclass Americans take for granted. We're taught all our lives to "keep our options open," but a commitment to communal life puts an end to that. It's not a choice but a call."

FOR YOUTH

■ **TOPIC:** Count Me In!

■ **QUESTIONS:** 1. If you were Isaiah, what would strike you the most about the experience he had? Why? 2. Why do you think Isaiah said, *"Woe is me!"* (Isa. 6:5)? 3. What does Isaiah's willing response to God's commission say about him? 4. What calamity did God say was awaiting the people of Judah? 5. How might God use you to share the message of His love and grace to others?

■ **ILLUSTRATIONS:**

Hardened Hearts. Most of you are familiar with cholesterol. This is the glistening white soapy substance that attaches itself to the inside of blood vessels. As it thickens and builds up, it causes heart attacks, hardening of the arteries, or blockages in blood vessels.

God called Isaiah to his prophetic ministry because of the hardened hearts of the people toward the Lord. Tragically, the Israelites' years of indifference toward God had blocked off their awareness of His love. God ordered Isaiah to tell the people how serious their condition was.

The Lord wanted the prophet to know that He would strengthen him and be with him throughout his long and difficult ministry. Knowing this would help Isaiah avoid becoming discouraged or frustrated. Remember Isaiah when you feel frustrated at not being heard by others.

Unsure? An 18-year-old high school senior wrote Abigail Van Buren, or "Dear Abby," in September, 1998, for help in seeking her "calling in life." Stating that grades were not a problem and that going to a university was planned, the student admitted she did not know what studies or career to pursue. She signed the letter,

"Unsure." Isaiah was far from being "unsure" about his calling in life. He knew that God had commissioned him and had a definite course of action for the prophet.

Courage to Stand. In 1521 Martin Luther appeared before the Diet of Worms, presided over by Charles V, Holy Roman Emperor. Luther's life was clearly in danger. He acknowledged that the books considered heretical were his own, but he refused to repudiate them unless convicted that he had strayed from the Scriptures.

One tradition has held that Luther's concluding words in his heroic declaration were "Here I stand. I cannot do otherwise." A solitary person, filled with courage from his fresh reading of Scripture, dared to challenge the might of the church and state in his day. In so doing, he helped to set in motion the Protestant Reformation.

ISAIAH AND AHAZ: A CHALLENGE TO RELY ON GOD

BACKGROUND SCRIPTURE: Isaiah 7; 2 Kings 16; 2 Chronicles 28
DEVOTIONAL READING: Psalm 33:4-12

KEY VERSE: The LORD himself will give you a sign. Look, the young woman is with child and shall bear a son, and shall name him Immanuel. Isaiah 7:14.

KING JAMES VERSION

ISAIAH 7:1 And it came to pass in the days of Ahaz the son of Jotham, the son of Uzziah, king of Judah, that Rezin the king of Syria, and Pekah the son of Remaliah, king of Israel, went up toward Jerusalem to war against it, but could not prevail against it.

2 And it was told the house of David, saying, Syria is confederate with Ephraim. And his heart was moved, and the heart of his people, as the trees of the wood are moved with the wind.

3 Then said the LORD unto Isaiah, Go forth now to meet Ahaz, thou, and Shear-jashub thy son, at the end of the conduit of the upper pool in the highway of the fuller's field;

4 And say unto him, Take heed, and be quiet; fear not, neither be fainthearted for the two tails of these smoking firebrands, for the fierce anger of Rezin with Syria, and of the son of Remaliah.

5 Because Syria, Ephraim, and the son of Remaliah, have taken evil counsel against thee, saying,

6 Let us go up against Judah, and vex it, and let us make a breach therein for us, and set a king in the midst of it, even the son of Tabeal:

10 Moreover the LORD spake again unto Ahaz, saying,

11 Ask thee a sign of the LORD thy God; ask it either in the depth, or in the height above.

12 But Ahaz said, I will not ask, neither will I tempt the LORD.

13 And he said, Hear ye now, O house of David; Is it a small thing for you to weary men, but will ye weary my God also?

14 Therefore the Lord himself shall give you a sign; Behold, a virgin shall conceive, and bear a son, and shall call his name Immanuel.

15 Butter and honey shall he eat, that he may know to refuse the evil, and choose the good.

16 For before the child shall know to refuse the evil, and choose the good, the land that thou abhorrest shall be forsaken of both her kings.

17 The LORD shall bring upon thee, and upon thy people, and upon thy father's house, days that have not come, from the day that Ephraim departed from Judah; even the king of Assyria.

NEW REVISED STANDARD VERSION

ISAIAH 7:1 In the days of Ahaz son of Jotham son of Uzziah, king of Judah, King Rezin of Aram and King Pekah son of Remaliah of Israel went up to attack Jerusalem, but could not mount an attack against it. 2 When the house of David heard that Aram had allied itself with Ephraim, the heart of Ahaz and the heart of his people shook as the trees of the forest shake before the wind.

3 Then the LORD said to Isaiah, Go out to meet Ahaz, you and your son Shear-jashub, at the end of the conduit of the upper pool on the highway to the Fuller's Field, 4 and say to him, Take heed, be quiet, do not fear, and do not let your heart be faint because of these two smoldering stumps of firebrands, because of the fierce anger of Rezin and Aram and the son of Remaliah. 5 Because Aram—with Ephraim and the son of Remaliah—has plotted evil against you, saying,

6 Let us go up against Judah and cut off Jerusalem and conquer it for ourselves and make the son of Tabeel king in it. . . .

7:10 Again the LORD spoke to Ahaz, saying, 11 Ask a sign of the LORD your God; let it be deep as Sheol or high as heaven. 12 But Ahaz said, I will not ask, and I will not put the LORD to the test. 13 Then Isaiah said: "Hear then, O house of David! Is it too little for you to weary mortals, that you weary my God also?
14 Therefore the Lord himself will give you a sign. Look, the young woman is with child and shall bear a son, and shall name him Immanuel. 15 He shall eat curds and honey by the time he knows how to refuse the evil and choose the good. 16 For before the child knows how to refuse the evil and choose the good, the land before whose two kings you are in dread will be deserted. 17 The LORD will bring on you and on your people and on your ancestral house such days as have not come since the day that Ephraim departed from Judah—the king of Assyria."

HOME BIBLE READINGS

BACKGROUND

Isaiah lived at a time when Assyria was the dominant power in the ancient Near East. This mighty nation demanded heavy tribute from the all territories it had subdued, including Israel and Judah. Backed by the strongest and most ruthless war machine of the day, Assyria brought terror for over a century to that part of the world.

As it turns out, the area containing the nations of Israel and Judah lay in the path of Assyrian military campaigns against Egypt, its greatest rival. Any invasion of Egypt meant crossing through Palestine, and Israel and Judah lived in terror of the Assyrian threat. Small countries like Israel and Judah found themselves forced to pay vast sums regularly to stave off having cities burned and populations slaughtered. Israel made the fatal error of attempting a revolt, and suffered the destruction of its capital and the deportation of its people.

Before Israel's fall, however, the kings of Syria and Israel formed a coalition in 735 B.C. against Assyria. King Ahaz of Judah was pressured to join the alliance, but he refused to do so. This prompted the kings of Syria and Israel to attack Judah in the hope of dethroning Ahaz and installing a king who would go along with them (Isa. 7:1-6).

Ahaz, not being a person of strong moral fiber and courage, feared the worst and quavered. Isaiah was perhaps the one person in the king's royal court with faith and discernment during this crisis. At the Lord's direction, Isaiah told Ahaz not to panic before the schemes of his enemies. When the Lord (through Isaiah) told Ahaz to ask for a sign, the king refused. But God gave the king a sign anyway. The Lord said that before a child yet to be born was old enough to know right from wrong, Judah's enemies would be destroyed (7:7-17).

NOTES ON THE PRINTED TEXT

The king of Assyria and his powerful war machine were threatening Palestine. Judah's foreign policy was to offer no opposition to Assyria but rather only to appease the superpower. However, King Pekah [PEE-kah] of Israel had an anti-Assyrian policy. He had allied himself with King Rezin [REE-zin] of Damascus, who had long suffered from the Assyrian overlords.

Pekah sought to form a coalition with Egypt, figuring that such an alliance would force Assyria to look elsewhere for military conquests. Since Judah lay between Israel and Egypt, it was vital that King Ahaz join the group. When he refused, Israel and Syria invaded Judah, intent on overthrowing the government in Jerusalem and replacing it with a puppet ruler (Isa. 7:1). Understandably, Ahaz and the nation of Judah were terrified. *When the house of David heard that Aram had allied itself with Ephraim, the heart of Ahaz and the heart of his people shook as the trees of the forest shake before the wind* (7:2).

The Lord ordered Isaiah to take his son, Shear-jashub [SHE-are-JAH-shubb] (a name meaning "a remnant shall return"), and meet Ahaz. Isaiah was to reassure the monarch that the Lord was his best defense against any enemy threat. At this time Ahaz was inspecting the waterworks (such a water supply was vital during a siege) at Fuller's Field near the Gihon [GEYE-hahn] Spring. Here an ingenious system of shafts had been dug through solid stone to a reservoir (7:3).

Isaiah counseled Ahaz to stand fast, rather than be afraid, and to trust in God. The two threatening, neighboring kings were like smoking embers of a log that could be easily extinguished. *Take heed, be quiet, do not fear, and do not let your heart be faint because of these two smoldering stumps of firebrands* (7:4). Neither Israel nor Damascus would succeed in their wicked schemes, for God would protect Judah (7:5-6).

The threat posed by Damascus and Samaria deeply distressed Ahaz. Realizing this, the Lord spoke again to him through Isaiah the prophet (7:10). *Ask a sign of the LORD your God; let it be deep as Sheol or high as heaven* (7:11). Despite this generous offer, the king refused. Ahaz sounded very spiritual when he declared, *I will not ask, and I will not put the LORD to the test* (7:12). Ahaz did not want a sign from the Lord because he had made up his mind to solicit help from Assyria (2 Kings 16:7-9).

Isaiah summoned Ahaz to listen to what the Lord had to say. *"Hear then, O house of David! Is it too little for you to weary mortals, that you weary my God also?"* (Isa. 7:13). Though the king refused to ask for a sign, the Lord would supply one. *Look, the young woman is with child and shall bear a son, and shall name him Immanuel* (7:14).

Isaiah said that by the time this child, who was yet to be born, was old enough to eat curds and honey, he would know enough to choose what was right and reject what was wrong (7:15). Isaiah also promised that *before the child knows how to refuse the evil and choose the good, the land before whose two kings you are in dread will be deserted* (7:16). The enemies' destruction would happen so quickly that the child's name, Immanuel (or "God with us"), would remind Judah of the Lord's unmistakable intervention.

Ephraim originally departed from Judah in 931 B.C when the once united kingdom was divided in two. That was a time of significant distress, turmoil, and humiliation for the people of God (1 Kings 12:16-24). Isaiah prophesied that God would use the Assyrians to distress and humble Judah even more (Isa. 7:17-18).

The enemy would invade the nation, conquer its cities, overthrow its fortresses, and devastate its vineyards and farmlands (vss. 19-25). Such would be the high price God's people would pay for not trusting in Him.

SUGGESTIONS TO TEACHERS

Have you ever found yourself going through a rough time in life and wondering whether God would help you? "If only God would give me some sign or proof that He's really present and is helping me," sighed one man who had lost his wife, then his job, and then learned he had cancer. All believers sometimes struggle in their faith. Your aim in this week's lesson is to encourage your students to continue trusting in God even in the most difficult situations.

1. RELUCTANCE TO TRUST. Like us, Ahaz found it hard to put his confidence in the Lord rather than human power and wisdom. Invite your students to discuss why it seems so difficult for Christians to lean on God.

2. RESPONSIBILITY TO HEED. Here are some thought-provoking questions to ask your students. What does it mean to trust God? When did trusting in God seem most difficult for you? Why was this so? What is our responsibility in the face of our fears and doubts?

3. REFUSAL TO RELY. God graciously offers His presence, care, and wise guidance to anyone who leans on Him in faith. Ahaz's refusal to rely on God brought about His indignation. The Lord used Isaiah to censure the king for his timidity and whining.

4. REFERENCE TO THE CHILD. Though the king refused to ask for a sign, the Lord would still supply one. The promised birth of Immanuel would remind the people of Judah that God had delivered them from Assyria. We know from the New Testament that the birth of Jesus signifies the unique presence of God among us and the promise of receiving His salvation (Matt. 1:21-23).

FOR ADULTS

■ TOPIC: Trusting God's Care

■ QUESTIONS: 1. Why did the kings of Israel and Syria want to attack Jerusalem? 2. Why did the Lord want Isaiah's son, Shear-jashub, to go with him to meet Ahaz? 3. Why did God invite Ahaz to ask for a sign? 4. Why did God insist on giving Ahaz a sign? 5. Which current national problems do you feel ought to be at the top of your prayer list? Why?

■ **ILLUSTRATIONS:**

Lesson from Trapeze Artists. The Flying Rodleighs, a troupe of South African trapeze performers, and the late Henri Nouwen, the Dutch author, became close friends during the last years of Nouwen's life. Watching the Rodleighs in action gave Nouwen insights into the meaning of trusting God. The daredevil flyer swinging high above the crowd had learned to let go of the trapeze, then simply stretch out his arms and wait for the strong arms of the catcher to pluck him out of the air. As the Rodleighs reminded Nouwen, "The flyer must never catch the catcher; he must wait in absolute trust!"

The same idea applies to our relationship with God. Like the performer letting go of the trapeze and stretching out trusting arms to be grabbed by the catcher, a believer must be willing to let go of the usual human ways of seeking protection and to rely on God. Until a person is willing to allow himself or herself to be caught in the loving hands of the Lord, that person has not understood what it means to rely absolutely on God. This is what Isaiah tried to instill in King Ahaz.

The Risk of Faith. On May 21, 1927, 25-year-old Charles A. Lindbergh took off in a small airplane from a flying field in New York, and flew alone for 25 hours across the Atlantic. Sitting on a wicker chair to save weight and carrying five ham sandwiches, the young flyer took the risk of soloing across the ocean. He dared to attempt what others had hesitated to do.

Sometimes faith in God is like a lonely solo flight into the dark and scary unknown. Faith means the risk of embarking on the untried and uncharted, with no proof of success but with every assurance of victory. We are confident that the Lord will stand by our side throughout the episode.

Prayer. George Gallup, Jr., conducted a poll of Americans in 1997, asking them whether they agreed or disagreed with the following statement: "Prayer is an important part of my daily life." Seventy-six percent agreed either "completely" or "mostly" with this statement. A year later Gallup conducted another survey in which he asked, "Do you ever pray to God?" Eighty-eight percent of the interviewees said they did.

More importantly, what do Americans pray about? In 1999 a poll was done for the Christian Broadcasting Network, which asked that question. The most prevalent subject of prayer was concern for one's own health or the health of family and friends. Nineteen percent asked for personal help or guidance, and six percent prayed for world peace.

What this survey indicates is that not many Americans, on a percentage basis, have prayed about national problems in recent years. Today's figures would probably reflect the same level of concern for national problems. Certainly personal issues should be a vital part of our prayers, but we also need to pray about the affairs of our nation.

FOR YOUTH

■ TOPIC: Bad News/Good News!
■ QUESTIONS: 1. How did Ahaz and the people he ruled feel when they learned that Israel and Syria had formed an alliance against Judah? 2. Why did God (through Isaiah) encourage Ahaz not to fear the enemy

threat? 3. Why did Ahaz refuse to accept God's offer of a sign? 4. What would be significant about Emmanuel? 5. In what tangible ways has God answered your prayers recently?

■ ILLUSTRATIONS:

True Resolve. In March 1850, the following advertisement appeared in a San Francisco newspaper: "Wanted: young, skinny, wiry fellows not over 18. Must be expert riders willing to risk death daily. Orphans preferred. Wages $25 per week. Apply to Central Overland Express."

The Pony Express wanted young persons who would put their jobs ahead of their lives, if necessary. The Pony Express went out of business a long time ago, but God is still looking for people such as you and me who are thoroughly committed to Christ. We must be willing to risk anything and everything for Him—even apparent failure by the world's standards. Often that means waiting until eternity to be rewarded for our devotion.

Weak Foundations. The late Francis Schaeffer, in his book *How Should We Then Live?* illustrated the inevitable consequences of having anything other than God as the basis of our trust.

> A culture or an individual with a weak base can stand only when the pressure on it is not too great. As an illustration, let us think of a Roman bridge. The Romans built little humpbacked bridges over many of the streams of Europe. People and wagons went over these structures safely for centuries, for two millennia. But if people today drove heavily loaded trucks over these bridges, they would break. It is this way with the lives and value systems of individuals and cultures when they have nothing stronger to build on than their own limitedness, their own finiteness. They can stand when pressures are not too great, but when pressures mount, if then they do not have a sufficient base, they crash—just as a Roman bridge would cave in under the weight of a modern six-wheeled truck. Culture and the freedoms of people are fragile. Without a sufficient base, when such pressures come, only time is needed—and often not a great deal of time—before there is a collapse.

PRONOUNCEMENT OF DOOM

BACKGROUND SCRIPTURE: Isaiah 5
DEVOTIONAL READING: Mark 12:1-9

KEY VERSE: Ah, you who call evil good and good evil, who put darkness for light and light for darkness, who put bitter for sweet and sweet for bitter! Isaiah 5:20.

KING JAMES VERSION

ISAIAH 5:1 Now will I sing to my wellbeloved a song of my beloved touching his vineyard. My wellbeloved hath a vineyard in a very fruitful hill:

2 And he fenced it, and gathered out the stones thereof, and planted it with the choicest vine, and built a tower in the midst of it, and also made a winepress therein: and he looked that it should bring forth grapes, and it brought forth wild grapes.

3 And now, O inhabitants of Jerusalem, and men of Judah, judge, I pray you, betwixt me and my vineyard.

4 What could have been done more to my vineyard, that I have not done in it? wherefore, when I looked that it should bring forth grapes, brought it forth wild grapes?

5 And now go to; I will tell you what I will do to my vineyard: I will take away the hedge thereof, and it shall be eaten up; and break down the wall thereof, and it shall be trodden down:

6 And I will lay it waste: it shall not be pruned, nor digged; but there shall come up briers and thorns: I will also command the clouds that they rain no rain upon it.

7 For the vineyard of the LORD of hosts is the house of Israel, and the men of Judah his pleasant plant: and he looked for judgment, but behold oppression; for righteousness, but behold a cry.

NEW REVISED STANDARD VERSION

ISAIAH 5:1 Let me sing for my beloved
    my love-song concerning his vineyard:
My beloved had a vineyard
    on a very fertile hill.
2 He dug it and cleared it of stones,
    and planted it with choice vines;
he built a watchtower in the midst of it,
    and hewed out a wine vat in it;
he expected it to yield grapes,
    but it yielded wild grapes.
3 And now, inhabitants of Jerusalem
    and people of Judah,
judge between me
    and my vineyard.
4 What more was there to do for my vineyard
    that I have not done in it?
When I expected it to yield grapes,
    why did it yield wild grapes?
5 And now I will tell you
    what I will do to my vineyard.
I will remove its hedge,
    and it shall be devoured;
I will break down its wall,
    and it shall be trampled down.
6 I will make it a waste;
    it shall not be pruned or hoed,
    and it shall be overgrown with briers and thorns;
I will also command the clouds
    that they rain no rain upon it.
7 For the vineyard of the LORD of hosts
    is the house of Israel,
and the people of Judah
    are his pleasant planting;
he expected justice,
    but saw bloodshed;
righteousness,
    but heard a cry!

12

HOME BIBLE READINGS

BACKGROUND

Like Jesus centuries later, the Old Testament prophets often used parables to get across their message. Isaiah related one such parable that left his hearers in shock. Choosing the familiar image of a vineyard, Isaiah knew that every person present would understand immediately that he was talking about the nation of God's chosen people (Isa. 5:1-7).

Sadly, God's chosen people had come to regard themselves as privileged. Judah had forgotten that God had chosen His people to live obediently. Instead of a concern for all members of the community, including the poor and marginalized, as stated in the Mosaic law, social injustices were widespread.

The nation had gone through the transition from an agricultural society of small farming landholders to a society where a class of wealthy entrepreneurs grew and who greedily ignored their needy fellow Israelites. The poor became helpless pawns. The rich indulged in luxurious living, while the underclass went hungry. All the leaders, including the temple priesthood, ignored the oppressive conditions of the impoverished.

Isaiah knew that he would be out of step with nearly everyone in power in Judah. Nonetheless, he answered God's call to speak out against these conditions and to warn the nation of impending calamity. Isaiah's parable compared God's beloved people to a carefully tended and cultivated vineyard, but a vineyard that yielded wild, bitter grapes instead of sweet ones.

NOTES ON THE PRINTED TEXT

Some think that Isaiah joined other Judahites during a huge boisterous harvest festival to celebrate another successful growing season. If this is so, then amidst the rejoicing, Isaiah presented a song that described a landowner (namely, God) and the love that He had for His vineyard (namely, His people). *Let me sing for my beloved my love-song concerning his vineyard: My beloved had a vineyard on a very fertile hill* (Isa. 5:1).

The owner lavished great care on the vineyard. It was located on a rich and fertile hill where it could receive plenty of sun and rain on its terraces. The ground was thoroughly hoed to loosen the dirt and clear the weeds and to prevent the ground from cracking or caking in the summer heat. Stones were cleared and used for the terraces. The choicest vines were planted and pruned each year.

In the middle of the vineyard, a tower was constructed to watch against thieves and animals, to store tools, and to offer a shady spot to rest. A stone winepress was also hewn. (At Tell en Nasbeh, north of Jerusalem, one such winepress was found. It was a square measuring 9 feet by 9 feet with a vat 3 feet square and 2 feet deep.)

Everything was done in anticipation of a wonderful harvest. However, the vines bore only wild grapes that were small and bitter! The owner had *dug it and cleared it of stones, and planted it with choice vines; he built a watchtower in the midst of it, and hewed out a wine vat in it; he expected it to yield grapes, but it yielded wild grapes* (5:2).

Given the owner's shattered expectations, Isaiah asked his listeners to give their opinion. The prophet wanted to know who was at fault in this situation. Had the owner somehow been negligent in his care of the vineyard? Is that why it yielded bitter fruit? Was there anything else the owner could have been done? In each case the owner had done all he could to ensure an abundant, succulent harvest. *And now, inhabitants of Jerusalem and people of Judah, judge between me and my vineyard. What more was there to do for my vineyard that I have not done in it? When I expected it to yield grapes, why did it yield wild grapes?* (5:3-4).

Isaiah quickly and without warning passed God's judgment. In fact, the Lord Himself declared the punishment. The vineyard would be totally destroyed and abandoned. The hedge of thorns and briars that prevented cattle and small animals from entering would be torn out. The stone walls would be broken. The whole vineyard would be left untended with only the weeds and scrub vegetation remaining (5:5-6).

Isaiah next explained that the people of Israel and Judah were God's vineyard. The Lord had anticipated faithfulness, justice, and righteousness, but found only corruption, bloodshed, and cries from the oppressed. Divine judgment was the consequence for such iniquities. *For the vineyard of the LORD of hosts is the house of Israel, and the people of Judah are his pleasant planting; he expected justice, but saw bloodshed; righteousness, but heard a cry!* (5:7).

Isaiah's parable was fulfilled in part with the downfall of Israel, the 10 tribes to the north, in 722 B.C. After the Assyrian invasion, the northern kingdom in Palestine looked exactly like the unfruitful vineyard—stripped and barren. Judah and Jerusalem would likewise be sacked and destroyed by the Babylonians in 586 B.C.

SUGGESTIONS TO TEACHERS

The theme of judgment is not a popular one in our society. How many times have you been told not to judge others? We even hear non-Christians quoting Jesus' words in Matthew 7:1. But of course, they take His statements out of context when they use them to argue that there is no hell.

Because some professed Christians have assumed the role of God's messengers to condemn our society without satisfactorily demonstrating God's love and compassion, we tend to recoil from being identified with these people. Thus we hesitate to offend the sensibilities of nonbelievers and Christians who are in sin by speaking of God's judgment. But as we can see in reading about what eventually happened to the Judahites, who rebelled against God, divine judgment will certainly happen. No one can escape God's wrath—none except those who have trusted in Christ for salvation.

1. INTENTION OF THE OWNER. As you examine the parable of the vineyard, be sure to note the great effort of the owner to make it as productive as possible. Also note his expectation that a bountiful yield of sweet grapes would result. The meaning of this parable is that God wanted His people to respond to His care by living uprightly. How is this also true of us, His community, the Church?

2. INTERROGATION OF ISRAEL. Focus for a time on Isaiah 5:3 and 4, where God asked what more could He have done for His people to ensure their fruitfulness. As Christians we know that God has done everything He possibly could to redeem us from sin. Thus, it's not unreasonable for Him to expect abundant spiritual fruit from us. As Jesus said in John 15:8, *"My Father is glorified by this, that you bear much fruit."*

3. INVERSION OF VALUES. Isaiah spelled out the way the culture had twisted God's ways so that evil was regarded as good and vice versa. People became *wise in [their] own eyes* (Isa. 5:21), loving pleasure and luxury while trampling on the poor and forgetting the oppressed. What would Isaiah have to say to us today?

4. INIQUITY'S RESULTS. Isaiah warned that his nation could not continue to survive as long as it rebelled against God. This truth has been proven throughout history. Any society embracing greed and neglecting basic social justice sows the seeds of its own destruction.

5. INVADER'S APPROACH. Isaiah saw more clearly than most what was happening in his world, and he foretold an incursion by a conquering foreign power. This finally happened when the Babylonians crushed Jerusalem in 586 B.C. This tragedy could have been avoided had God's people turned from their evil ways.

FOR ADULTS

■ TOPIC: Accepting God's Judgment

■ QUESTIONS: 1. Why do you think God portrayed Himself as a landowner and His people as a vineyard? 2. Why did God do so much for His people knowing that they would eventually rebel against Him? 3. Why was God innocent of any negligence regarding the way He had treated His people? 4. Why was God upright in permitting Judah and Jerusalem to be sacked and destroyed? 5. What are some ways you can take a stand against the presence of dishonesty and injustice in the world?

■ ILLUSTRATIONS:

Pushing Away. Isaiah and the rest of the Old Testament prophets frequently reminded their hearers that they were rejecting God. The words of God's spokespersons should warn us also not to reject the Lord. But sometimes we view their warnings as being irrelevant.

Perhaps the Dutch can help us in this regard. They use the Dutch word *afstofen* to translate the term "reject." In Dutch, *afstofen* means "to push away," as in pushing away a boat from a pier. The seafaring Dutch understood immediately the meaning of the prophets' warning against "pushing away" from the Lord. The image of refusing to be tied fast in a trusting relationship with God suggested to this nation of mariners that they, like their oceangoing vessels, would be in peril if they pushed away from the pier instead of not being permitted to establish a safe and firm mooring.

Sadie's Loss. A woman named Sadie served as a housemother for many years in a school for missionaries' children in the Philippines. Sadie loved books. She had brought a large collection of beautiful volumes with her when she came from the United States to the Philippines. Though she initially loaned out a few to some favored children, Sadie preferred to hoard her prized library in a footlocker under her bed. She seldom bothered to open the footlocker or to take out any of her treasured volumes. For years, her books remained in the footlocker under her bed.

One night Sadie thought she heard a faint gnawing noise. After searching everywhere in the room, she finally discovered that the sounds were coming from the footlocker under her bed. She opened the locker, and to her dismay, she found nothing but an enormous pile of dust. Termites had devoured all the precious books in her treasured library!

God's judgment is somewhat like that. Just as Sadie had hoarded her expensive books rather than share them (or even use them), so too God's people in the Old Testament had refused to share or show His mercy to others. Such a miserly attitude led to their eternal loss, not gain.

Costly Consequences. During the past decade, more than 110 million land mines have been scattered in 68 countries during various military conflicts. Another 119 million are stockpiled around the world. Sowing these deadly devices brings a terrible harvest. Each month, according to the United Nations Human Development Report, more than 2,000 people—many of them innocent children—are killed or maimed by accidentally coming in contact with these hidden lethal explosive devices.

Some persons with a humanitarian concern for the innocent civilian victims of these land mines have pressed to have them outlawed, or at least destroyed in areas where they remain a constant threat to persons nearby. Would not Isaiah plea for us to do away with such terrible threats to the lives of innocent persons?

■ TOPIC: How Could This Happen?

■ QUESTIONS: 1. What attitude did God convey to His people by calling them His *beloved* (Isa. 5:1)? 2. What had God done to ensure the spiritual fruitfulness of His people? 3. How did God describe the calamity that would eventually fall upon Judah? 4. What did God expect from His people and what did He actually get? 5. Why would God place such a high priority on His people being honest and just? How can you, as a member of His spiritual family, cultivate these virtues in your life?

■ ILLUSTRATIONS:

Disappointment. May was a 46-year-old mother of three children when she was diagnosed with gastric cancer. An operation followed but failed to remove all of the cancer. Chemotherapy next followed with periodic days of hospitalization. Still, the hardest problem was not the nausea or the pain; rather, it was seeing the apparent indifference of her three children.

Two high schoolers and a middle schooler would walk by the dining room where May's bed had been set up and would perhaps say "Hi," and acknowledge her presence, before moving on to their own rooms. She confided in her pastor the hurt and sadness of seeing years of love and devotion to them forgotten so quickly when the illness appeared. They seemed not to notice her feelings of pain and disappointment toward them.

Long before this woman vocalized her feelings, the prophet Isaiah voiced God's disappointment with His people. Rather than shower Him with gratitude and affection, they spurned His love.

Concerns. After the Columbine High School shootings in April 1999 at Littleton, Colorado, students were asked what was the greatest concern in their lives. The potential for violence at school, traditionally a spot of safety, topped the list. Violence and oppression are causes of concern. The prophet Isaiah summoned his people to end these two problems in their society. What can we, as Christians, do about it?

Fatigued? A recent *Time* magazine quoted what observers of humanity have dubbed as "compassion fatigue." This is the inevitable downward spiral in the intensity with which each of us feel the human needs of others. Hunger, illness, refugee problems, civil strife, and wars all blaze across our television screens each day, but fail to stir us to pray or to give. We simply no longer care.

Centuries ago, Isaiah saw the effects of compassion fatigue within his own people. Despite his repeated exhortations, the Judahites remained largely indifferent to the needs of the impoverished and oppressed.

ISRAEL TAKEN INTO CAPTIVITY

BACKGROUND SCRIPTURE: 2 Kings 17:1-23
DEVOTIONAL READING: Exodus 20:1-6

KEY VERSE: The LORD was very angry with Israel and removed them out of his sight; none was left but the tribe of Judah alone. 2 Kings 17:18.

KING JAMES VERSION

2 KINGS 17:6 In the ninth year of Hoshea the king of Assyria took Samaria, and carried Israel away into Assyria, and placed them in Halah and in Habor by the river of Gozan, and in the cities of the Medes.

7 For so it was, that the children of Israel had sinned against the LORD their God, which had brought them up out of the land of Egypt, from under the hand of Pharaoh king of Egypt, and had feared other gods,

8 And walked in the statutes of the heathen, whom the LORD cast out from before the children of Israel, and of the kings of Israel, which they had made.

9 And the children of Israel did secretly those things that were not right against the LORD their God, and they built them high places in all their cities, from the tower of the watchmen to the fenced city.

10 And they set them up images and groves in every high hill, and under every green tree:

11 And there they burnt incense in all the high places, as did the heathen whom the LORD carried away before them; and wrought wicked things to provoke the LORD to anger:

12 For they served idols, whereof the LORD had said unto them, Ye shall not do this thing.

13 Yet the LORD testified against Israel, and against Judah, by all the prophets, and by all the seers, saying, Turn ye from your evil ways, and keep my commandments and my statutes, according to all the law which I commanded your fathers, and which I sent to you by my servants the prophets.

14 Notwithstanding they would not hear, but hardened their necks, like to the neck of their fathers, that did not believe in the LORD their God.

15 And they rejected his statutes, and his covenant that he made with their fathers, and his testimonies which he testified against them; and they followed vanity, and became vain, and went after the heathen that were round about them, concerning whom the LORD had charged them, that they should not do like them.

16 And they left all the commandments of the LORD their God, and made them molten images, even two calves, and made a grove, and worshipped all the host of heaven, and served Baal.

NEW REVISED STANDARD VERSION

2 KINGS 17:6 In the ninth year of Hoshea the king of Assyria captured Samaria; he carried the Israelites away to Assyria. He placed them in Halah, on the Habor, the river of Gozan, and in the cities of the Medes.

7 This occurred because the people of Israel had sinned against the LORD their God, who had brought them up out of the land of Egypt from under the hand of Pharaoh king of Egypt. They had worshiped other gods 8 and walked in the customs of the nations whom the LORD drove out before the people of Israel, and in the customs that the kings of Israel had introduced. 9 The people of Israel secretly did things that were not right against the LORD their God. They built for themselves high places at all their towns, from watchtower to fortified city; 10 they set up for themselves pillars and sacred poles on every high hill and under every green tree; 11 there they made offerings on all the high places, as the nations did whom the LORD carried away before them. They did wicked things, provoking the LORD to anger; 12 they served idols, of which the LORD had said to them, "You shall not do this." 13 Yet the LORD warned Israel and Judah by every prophet and every seer, saying, "Turn from your evil ways and keep my commandments and my statutes, in accordance with all the law that I commanded your ancestors and that I sent to you by my servants the prophets." 14 They would not listen but were stubborn, as their ancestors had been, who did not believe in the LORD their God. 15 They despised his statutes, and his covenant that he made with their ancestors, and the warnings that he gave them. They went after false idols and became false; they followed the nations that were around them, concerning whom the LORD had commanded them that they should not do as they did. 16 They rejected all the commandments of the LORD their God and made for themselves cast images of two calves; they made a sacred pole, worshiped all the host of heaven, and served Baal.

13

Monday, August 20	2 Kings 17:1-6	*Assyria Defeats King Hoshea*
Tuesday, August 21	2 Kings 17:7-13	*Israel Sinned and Disobeyed God*
Wednesday, August 22	2 Kings 17:14-18	*Reasons for Israel's Captivity*
Thursday, August 23	2 Kings 17-19-23	*Summary of Israel's Iniquity*
Friday, August 24	2 Kings 17:24-28	*Assyria Resettles Samaria*
Saturday, August 25	2 Kings 17:29-41	*Pagan Worship Prevails in Samaria*
Sunday, August 26	Exodus 20:1-6	*The One True God*

BACKGROUND

We have studied how both the northern kingdom of Israel and the southern kingdom of Judah persisted in disobeying the Lord. Despite the entreaties of a series of devoted prophets, God's people continued to flaunt His will. The prophets had warned that such betrayal would bring disaster. But the people, often encouraged by wicked leaders, stubbornly thought that God would never allow them to suffer the doom the prophets had foretold. Meanwhile, the spreading moral dry rot meant that the collapse of both nations was inevitable.

Israel, the nation of the 10 northern tribes, was the first to totter and fall. After foolishly entering into a pact with Egypt, King Hoshea revolted against Assyria. Then in 725 B.C., Shalmaneser V of Assyria unleashed his army against Israel. With unimaginable fury, the Assyrian forces pummeled the northern kingdom. Archaeological excavations of Israelite cities have shown how complete the devastation was by the Assyrians (2 Kings 17:3-4).

Samaria, the capital, was powerfully fortified, and managed to hold out for over three terrible years. Though Shalmaneser V died during the siege, his successor, Sargon II, captured the city. His records report that he marched away over 27,000 survivors to distant parts of his empire. He then brought in foreign peoples whom he had deported from their homelands far to the east, and forced them to settle in the territory of Israel (17:5-6).

Judah's turn came well over a century later. In 597 B.C., the new international superpower, Babylon, forced the southern kingdom to pay tribute as a vassal nation. Judah later rashly rebelled, and the Babylonian armies crushed Jerusalem in 586 B.C. (25:1-21).

NOTES ON THE PRINTED TEXT

The prophets of the day had long been proclaiming that Assyria would be the instrument of God's judgment against His wayward people. Their prophecies came true under Hoshea, Israel's last king. In 725 B.C., Hoshea made an attempt to gain independence from Assyria, after withholding tribute on several occasions. Shalmaneser V acted swiftly, moving his Assyrian soldiers and laying waste to Israel. He besieged the heavily fortified capital city of Samaria. The siege dragged on for three suffering-filled years. Finally, in 722 B.C., the city fell to Assyria's new king, Sargon II (2 Kings 17:1-5).

Sargon followed the Assyrian policy of deportation. The peoples of subjugated territories were replaced with others from other conquered areas. Sargon's records, excavated at Khorsabad, indicate that he deported over 27,000 people to distant parts of the Assyrian Empire. *In the ninth year of Hoshea the king of Assyria captured Samaria; he carried the Israelites away to Assyria. He placed them in Halah, on the Habor, the river of Gozan, and in the cities of the Medes* (17:6).

The writer of Kings denounced Israel's sin, detailing that the captivity occurred due to the nation's transgressions against the Lord. *This occurred because the people of Israel had sinned against the LORD their God, who had brought them up out of the land of Egypt from under the hand of Pharaoh king of Egypt* (17:7).

The historian chronicled the charges. They had *worshiped other gods and walked in the customs of the nations whom the LORD drove out before the people of Israel, and in the customs that the kings of Israel had introduced* (17:7-8). The 10 northern tribes had violated the first three commandments by adopting Canaanite worship practices. Even Israel's kings, who were supposed to encourage the spiritual, moral, and religious purity of the nation, had neglected their duty and endorsed idolatrous ways.

The people of Israel secretly did immoral things in violation of God's decrees. They *built for themselves high places at all their towns, from watchtower to fortified city; they set up for themselves pillars and sacred poles on every high hill and under every green tree; there they made offerings on all the high places, as the nations did whom the LORD carried away before them. They did wicked things, provoking the LORD to anger; they served idols, of which the LORD had said to them, "You shall not do this"* (17:9-12).

High places were hilltop pagan shrines with stone altars that the people had dedicated to Baal and other fertility cults. Pillars of mud, stone, or brick were erected at some of these shrines. Often the pillars and sacred poles bore the name of the city and became an object of veneration. Not only did Israel copy the Canaanites but also the people set up and venerated their own shrines and idols, which was a violation of God's commandments. This action provoked the Lord to anger.

The prophets had repeatedly urged the people of Israel and Judah to repent from their evil ways and keep God's laws. *Yet the LORD warned Israel and Judah by every prophet and every seer, saying, "Turn from your evil ways and keep my commandments and my statutes, in accordance with all the law that I commanded your ancestors and that I sent to you by my servants the prophets"* (17:13).

Tragically, God's people remained obstinate and refused to listen. Stubbornly they continued to disobey, and like their ancestors they followed after false gods. *They would not listen but were stubborn, as their ancestors had been, who did not believe in the LORD their God* (17:14).

The writer continued to detail the transgressions of God's people. They not only neglected but also rejected God's laws, which He had specified in the Mosaic covenant. No thought was given to worshiping God, only to venerating idols. *They despised his statutes, and his covenant that he made with their ancestors, and the warnings that he gave them* (17:15).

Growing more specific, the writer condemned the northern kingdom of Israel for setting up the two calves made from metal (which were fertility symbols), for engaging in child sacrifice, and for worshiping the stars. Israel's sins were inexcusable and only showed how far the nation had departed from the Lord. *They rejected all the commandments of the LORD their God* (17:16).

SUGGESTIONS TO TEACHERS

When a reporter asked a popular entertainer about his reputation for adulterous affairs and other immoral acts, the man replied, "Why can't I do as I please? It's my life, and I'm entitled to all the fun I want." This notion, whether referring to immoral behavior or any other deviant practice, seems to be seeping through our society. It also pervaded the northern kingdom of Israel.

Despite all the warnings issued by God through His prophets, the people remained entrenched in their sin. The dire consequences came when Assyria conquered Samaria, the capital of the northern kingdom, and carried the inhabitants into captivity. The point of your lesson this week is that wallowing in sin leads to dire consequences.

1. CONFUSION IN COMMITMENT. The failure to be loyal to the Lord led the people of Israel to engage in evil practices. Look at the way in which the writer of 2 Kings put it: *[They] secretly did things that were not right against the LORD* (17:9); *[they] despised his statutes, and his covenant* (17:15); *[they] rejected all the commandments of the LORD* (17:16); and *they sold themselves to do evil* (17:17).

2. CONSEQUENCES TO CONTRARINESS. The twisted thinking and perverted ways of the leaders and people of Israel eroded their sense of living uprightly before the Lord. In short, they ceased to be aware that they belonged to God. What about us? How conscious are we of living in a virtuous way in God's sight?

3. CONTINUATION OF CONTEMPT. The prophets urged God's people to repent. But whatever efforts the people made to heed God and amend their ways were brief and insincere. Discuss with your students what it means to genuinely repent.

4. CONTENT OF THE COVENANT. Undoubtedly, you have mentioned to your students the covenant that God made with Israel. At this point in the lesson, have the members of your class again reflect on the covenant's meaning. Be sure to stress that God wants His people to live holy lives.

5. CONCERN FOR CONDUCT. "Don't talk to me about love; show me!" The words of the old song apply also to our behavior as Christians. Our commitment to the Lord must be exhibited in the way we live. Faith is what we do, not merely what we believe (Jas. 2:18).

FOR ADULTS	■ **TOPIC:** Experiencing Sin's Consequences ■ **QUESTIONS:** 1. What did the writer of 2 Kings say was the reason why God allowed Assyria to conquer Israel?

son why God allowed Assyria to conquer Israel? 2. In what ways had the Israelites venerated pagan deities? 3. Why was it foolish for the Israelites to copy the practices of the Canaanites? 4. What does God's sending His prophets to the northern kingdom reveal about His feelings for the Israelites? 5. If our lives are inconsistent with our faith, how does that diminish our influence in addressing national problems?

■ **ILLUSTRATIONS:**

Difficult Discovery. A White House correspondent for a television station made a grueling trip to Germany to cover the president's visit there. The reporter came back with a case of laryngitis. But he dismissed his hoarseness, declaring that throat problems were an occupational hazard. The correspondent had dealt with a husky voice and throat maladies many times before, and made light of his laryngitis. But the hoarseness persisted.

Instead of taking it easy, the reporter gave several speeches around the country and tried to maintain his busy broadcasting schedule. But when the throat problem continued, he finally went to a specialist, who discovered two nodes behind his vocal cords. Thankfully, the nodes proved to be benign and not cancerous. The physician said the nodes might disappear on their own if the correspondent would remain silent for five weeks. But the reporter was not enthusiastic about this prescription. "If I don't talk, I don't eat," he groused.

This reporter experienced the results of refusing to obey simple health rules in caring for his voice. Similarly, Judah experienced the consequences of refusing to obey the moral requirements of God. Disobedience always brings disappointment and sometimes disaster.

Lacking Reference Point. Several years ago, the Pennsylvania Department of Transportation set out to replace a bridge. After demolishing the old structure, workers began building a new one, laboring from each side of the river. Everything seemed to be proceeding nicely until it was discovered that the two spans arching out from the opposite banks were not in line with each other. In fact, by the time the two sides came closer, one was wide of the other by 13 feet! Investigators finally discovered that the supervisors of the work crews on the two sides of the river had been using their own reference point.

In life, people and nations alike must rely on an external moral reference point (namely, God and His Word). Israel and its leaders refused to acknowledge this truth and suffered accordingly.

Pet Food and Hunger. Americans and Europeans spend over $17 billion each year to feed their pets. This is $4 billion more than the estimated annual total needed to provide basic health and nutrition for everyone in the world. The prophets would have condemned these kinds of contrasts. The gap between the haves and the have-nots, whether in ancient Israel or in modern western nations, is displeasing to God.

FOR YOUTH

■ TOPIC: Here Come the Consequences!

■ QUESTIONS: 1. What did the king of Assyria do to the people of Israel after conquering them? 2. What were some of the pagan customs that the Israelites adopted from their neighbors? 3. Why do you think the worship of other gods enticed the Israelites? 4. What might have been some of the obstacles the prophets experienced when they publicly addressed Israel's sins? 5. Which do you think is better: to know how to argue for our point of view, or to be able to lead others to our point of view with a biblical lifestyle? Why?

■ ILLUSTRATIONS:

History Comes Alive. His serial number, 431074, is quickly recited. He says he can remember it because the number sticks in his mind. The number was given to him 80 years earlier when he enlisted in the U.S. Army. Andrew York, 102 years old, freely shares his experiences of World War I (the troop ship, uniform, food, trenches, and so forth) with young people in schools. His accounts intrigue them and make history come alive.

Perhaps you find yourself intrigued by the account recorded in Scripture about the downfall of Israel. The writer, though, did not gloss over the reasons for the nation's demise. And neither did the writer hide the fact of God's judgment.

The Professor Was Right. In 1985, Professor Neil Postman wrote a book entitled *Amusing Ourselves to Death*. He warned that the death of our culture would not come from a brutal, outside force but rather from our own quiet acquiescence in the substitution of entertainment for rational public discourse.

Part of our acceptance would be the corruption of education, politicians as actors, cheating in sports, and the public's outrage or indifference when the media took a matter seriously. As a nation's moral foundations crumbled, ethics would be forgotten, and entertainment would be all that was desired. Spiritual decay would set in. Postman's thesis seems to be true. Certainly it can be seen in Israel's downfall.

Admit It! The following quote by actress Katharine Hepburn reminds us how important it is to accept responsibility for our actions (from *Words of Wisdom: More Good Advice*, by William Safire and Leonard Safire).

> You learn in life that the only person you can really correct and change is yourself. You can't do that with anyone else. But you can do it with yourself, if you want to sufficiently. Now we are taught you must blame your father, your sisters, your brothers, the school, the teacher—you can blame anyone, but never blame yourself. It's never your fault. But it's always your fault, because if you wanted to change, you're the one who has got to change. It's as simple as that, isn't it?